The early modern English sonnet

The Manchester Spenser

The Manchester Spenser is a monograph and text series devoted to historical and textual approaches to Edmund Spenser – to his life, times, places, works and contemporaries.

A growing body of work in Spenser and Renaissance studies, fresh with confidence and curiosity and based on solid historical research, is being written in response to a general sense that our ability to interpret texts is becoming limited without the excavation of further knowledge. So the importance of research in nearby disciplines is quickly being recognised, and interest renewed: history, archaeology, religious or theological history, book history, translation, lexicography, commentary and glossary – these require treatment for and by students of Spenser.

The Manchester Spenser, to feed, foster and build on these refreshed attitudes, aims to publish reference tools, critical, historical, biographical and archaeological monographs on or related to Spenser, from several disciplines, and to publish editions of primary sources and classroom texts of a more wide-ranging scope.

The Manchester Spenser consists of work with stamina, high standards of scholarship and research, adroit handling of evidence, rigour of argument, exposition and documentation.

The series will encourage and assist research into, and develop the readership of, one of the richest and most complex writers of the early modern period.

General Editors Joshua Reid, Kathryn Walls and Tamsin Badcoe
Editorial Board Sukanta Chaudhuri, Helen Cooper, Thomas Herron, J. B. Lethbridge, James Nohrnberg and Brian Vickers

Also available
A Concordance to the Rhymes of The Faerie Queene   Richard Danson Brown and J.B. Lethbridge
A Supplement of the Faery Queene: By Ralph Knevet   Christopher Burlinson and Andrew Zurcher (eds)
English literary afterlives: Greene, Sidney, Donne and the evolution of posthumous fame
Elisabeth Chaghafi
A Companion to Pastoral Poetry of the English Renaissance   Sukanta Chaudhuri
Pastoral poetry of the English Renaissance: An anthology   Sukanta Chaudhuri (ed.)
Spenserian allegory and Elizabethan biblical exegesis: A context for The Faerie Queene
Margaret Christian
Comic Spenser: Faith, Folly and The Faerie Queene   Victoria Coldham-Fussell
Monsters and the poetic imagination in The Faerie Queene: 'Most ugly shapes and horrible aspects'
Maik Goth
Celebrating Mutabilitie: Essays on Edmund Spenser's Mutabilitie Cantos   Jane Grogan (ed.)
Spenserian satire: A tradition of indirection   Rachel E. Hile
Castles and Colonists: An archaeology of Elizabethan Ireland   Eric Klingelhofer
Shakespeare and Spenser: Attractive opposites   J.B. Lethbridge (ed.)
Dublin: Renaissance city of literature   Kathleen Miller and Crawford Gribben (eds)
A Fig for Fortune by Anthony Copley: A Catholic response to The Faerie Queene   Susannah Brietz Monta
Spenser and Virgil: The pastoral poems   Syrithe Pugh
The Burley manuscript   Peter Redford (ed.)
Renaissance psychologies: Spenser and Shakespeare   Robert Lanier Reid
Spenser and Donne: Thinking poets   Yulia Ryzhik (ed.)
European erotic romance: Philhellene Protestantism, renaissance translation and English literary politics
Victor Skretkowicz
Rereading Chaucer and Spenser: Dan Geffrey with the New Poete   Rachel Stenner, Tamsin Badcoe and Gareth Griffith (eds)
God's only daughter: Spenser's Una as the invisible Church   Kathryn Walls
William Shakespeare and John Donne: Stages of the soul in early modern English poetry   Angelika Zirker

The early modern English sonnet
Ever in motion

EDITED BY RÉMI VUILLEMIN, LAETITIA
SANSONETTI AND ENRICA ZANIN

Manchester University Press

Copyright © Manchester University Press 2020

While copyright in the volume as a whole is vested in Manchester University Press, copyright in individual chapters belongs to their respective authors, and no chapter may be reproduced wholly or in part without the express permission in writing of both author and publisher.

Published by Manchester University Press
Oxford Road, Manchester M13 9PL

www.manchesteruniversitypress.co.uk

British Library Cataloguing-in-Publication Data
A catalogue record for this book is available from the British Library

ISBN 978 1 5261 4439 3 hardback
ISBN 978 1 5261 6383 7 paperback

First published 2020
Paperback published 2022

The publisher has no responsibility for the persistence or accuracy of URLs for any external or third-party internet websites referred to in this book, and does not guarantee that any content on such websites is, or will remain, accurate or appropriate.

Typeset by
Servis Filmsetting Ltd, Stockport, Cheshire

Contents

Notes on contributors vii
Acknowledgements x

    Introduction 1
    Laetitia Sansonetti, Rémi Vuillemin, Enrica Zanin

I   **Shaping the sonnet, from Italy and France to England** 15

1   English Petrarchism: from commentary on poetry to poetry as commentary 17
    William John Kennedy

2   Early modern theories of the sonnet: accounts of the quatorzain in Italy, France and England in the second half of the sixteenth century 31
    Carlo Alberto Girotto, Jean-Charles Monferran, Rémi Vuillemin

II   **Performing the English sonnet** 59

3   Sonnet-mongers on the early modern English stage 61
    Guillaume Coatalen

4   In and out: Shakespeare's shifting sonnets. From *Love's Labour's Lost* to *The Passionate Pilgrim* 78
    Sophie Chiari

III   **Placing the sonnet: sonnets isolated or sequenced** 93

5   'Small parcelles': unsequenced sonnets in the sixteenth century 95
    Chris Stamatakis

6   'And sweetly nectarize this bitter gall': Gabriel Harvey's sonnet therapy 114
    Elisabeth Chaghafi

| 7 | Barnabe Barnes's sonnet sequences: moral conversion and prodigal authorship
Rémi Vuillemin | 128 |

IV Editing the sonnet 141

| 8 | *The Muses Garland* (1603): fragment of a printed verse miscellany
Hugh Gazzard | 143 |
| 9 | The sonnet sequence as speech sound continuum: how we read *Shake-speares Sonnets*
Andrew Eastman | 185 |

Bibliography 196
Index 223

Notes on contributors

Elisabeth Chaghafi's research mainly focuses on book history and the works of Edmund Spenser and Gabriel Harvey. She has also written on Thomas Speght's use of Spenser in his edition of Chaucer's works, the structure of John Derricke's *Image of Irelande* and the idea of poetic friendship in the biographical works of Izaak Walton and John Aubrey. A monograph on the afterlives of early modern English authors is forthcoming. She teaches at Tübingen University (Germany).

Sophie Chiari is professor of early modern studies at Université Clermont Auvergne, France. She is the author of several monographs including *Shakespeare's Representation of Weather, Climate, and Environment: The Early Modern 'Fated Sky'* (Edinburgh University Press, 2019). She has edited collections of essays such as *The Circulation of Knowledge in Early Modern English Literature* (Ashgate, 2015), *Spectacular Science, Technology and Superstition in the Age of Shakespeare* with Mickaël Popelard (Edinburgh University Press, 2017) and *Freedom and Censorship in Early Modern English Literature* (Routledge, 2019). Her new book, *Performances at Court in the Age of Shakespeare*, edited with John Mucciolo, is forthcoming from Cambridge University Press in 2020.

Guillaume Coatalen is senior lecturer in early modern English literature at Université de Cergy-Pontoise (France) with a strong interest for unedited material in manuscript. His latest publication is *Two Elizabethan Treatises on Rhetoric: Richard Rainold's Foundacion of Rhetoricke (1563) and William Medley's Brief Notes in Manuscript (1575)* (Brill, 2018). He is currently working on Queen Elizabeth I's French correspondence and on a book on the image of poets in early modern English plays.

Andrew Eastman is senior lecturer in the Anglophone Studies Department at Université de Strasbourg (France), and is the author of numerous essays on poetic practices in modern and contemporary United States poetry. Recent work includes 'Me, After Me: Whitman's Rhyme' (*Whitman Feuille à feuille*, Editions Rue d'Ulm, 2018); and 'Hearing Things in the Poems of Elizabeth Bishop' (forthcoming).

Hugh Gazzard has held posts at several colleges in the University of Oxford, and currently teaches there at Harris Manchester College. His recent publications include articles on attributions – to Sir Philip Sidney (in *Sidney Journal*), and to Nicholas Breton (in *Studies in English Literature*) – of poems in or relevant to *The Muses Garland*.

Carlo Alberto Girotto is senior lecturer in Italian Studies at Université Sorbonne Nouvelle – Paris 3. He has published extensively on Ariosto's *Orlando furioso*, Anton Francesco Doni and other authors of the Italian Renaissance. He also works on epistolography and art theory in the Renaissance and the Baroque age, and is a contributor to the 'Malvasia project' at the CASVA – Center for Advanced Study in the Visual Arts at the National Gallery of Art, Washington, D.C.

William John Kennedy is Avalon Foundation Emeritus Professor in the Humanities in the department of Comparative Literature at Cornell University. His publications include three books on European Renaissance poetry: *Authorizing Petrarch* (Cornell University Press, 1994), *The Site of Petrarchism: Early Modern National Sentiment in Italy, France, and England* (Johns Hopkins University Press, 2003), and *Petrarchism at Work: Contextual Economies in the Age of Shakespeare* (Cornell University Press, 2016).

Jean-Charles Monferran is professor of sixteenth-century French literature at Sorbonne Université in Paris. His work is particularly concerned with poetry and poetics. He is the editor of several French early modern poetic treatises, and the author of a monograph on the topic (*L'Ecole des Muses*, Droz, 2011). He has recently co-edited with Nathalie Dauvois and Michel Jourde a collective volume on the reception of Horace (*'Chacun son Horace': Appropriations et adaptations du modèle horatien en Europe XVe–XVIIe siècles*, Champion, 2019).

Laetitia Sansonetti is senior lecturer in English literature and translation studies at Université Paris Nanterre. She has published articles on Shakespeare, Spenser, Marlowe and Chapman. Her recent publications include a co-edited volume entitled *Auteurs-traducteurs* (with Christine Berthin and Emily Eells, Presses de Paris Nanterre, 2018). Her research bears on the reception of the classics and questions of authorship and authority, and she has started a research project on translation and polyglossia in early modern England, funded by a five-year grant from Institut Universitaire de France.

Chris Stamatakis is a lecturer in Renaissance English literature at University College London, and author of *Sir Thomas Wyatt and the Rhetoric of Rewriting: Turning the Word* (Oxford University Press, 2012). Besides a co-edited volume on *Shakespeare, Italy, and Transnational Exchange* (Routledge, 2017), recent publications have addressed Gabriel Harvey's Italian reading and early Tudor literary criticism. Forthcoming works include a chapter on sixteenth-century sonnets for the *Oxford History of Poetry in English* and an edition of Thomas Nashe's *Christs Teares over Jerusalem* (Oxford University Press).

Rémi Vuillemin is senior lecturer in early modern English literature at Université de Strasbourg (France). The author of a monograph on Michael Drayton's sonnet sequences (*Le Recueil pétrarquiste à l'ère du maniérisme: Poétique des sonnets de Michael Drayton, 1594–1619*, Champion, 2014), his work bears on the early modern English sonnet, its reception past and present and early modern poetic theory. He has recently co-edited a collective volume on *Strasbourg and the English Reformation*

(Presses Universitaires de Strasbourg, 2018) and is currently working on a project on the ordering of lyric collections.

Enrica Zanin is senior lecturer in comparative literature at Université de Strasbourg (France). Her work is mainly concerned with the circulation of Renaissance Italian literary models and poetics in early modern Europe. She has published two monographs on early modern drama and dramatic theory and she is now leading a project, founded by a five-year grant from Institut Universitaire de France, on the European circulation of short fiction, from Boccaccio to Cervantes.

Acknowledgements

The research project from which the present volume originates has benefited from the help of our respective institutions. We would like to thank the following research units for their support: SEARCH and Configurations Littéraires (EA 2325 and 1378, Université de Strasbourg), CREA (EA 370, Paris Nanterre) and Pléiade (EA 7338, Université Paris XIII). We also wish to convey our thanks to the colleagues we have solicited for their expert opinion and whose comments and input have been invaluable.

We are grateful to the general editors of *The Manchester Spenser* series, Tamsin Badcoe and Josh Reid, to the editorial team at MUP, to Matthew Frost and Deborah Smith, and to the anonymous readers at MUP for their acute suggestions.

We must acknowledge the debt we owe to Anne-Valérie Dulac, who accompanied us through the stages that led to putting this volume together. We can hardly do justice to the extent of her contribution as a fellow scholar and as a friend.

Finally, we would like to issue heartfelt thanks to Julian B. Lethbridge and Jean-Jacques Chardin, without whose encouragements and continuous support our initial project could not have taken shape and led to the production of the present volume.

Introduction

Laetitia Sansonetti, Rémi Vuillemin, Enrica Zanin

*My Verse is the true image of my Mind,
Euer in motion, still desiring change;
And as thus to Varietie inclin'd,
So in all Humors sportiuely I range:
 My Muse is rightly of the* English *straine
 That cannot long one Fashion intertaine.*[1]

Academic works on the sonnet published since the 1980s have often taken its features for granted. Until recently and the development of 'New Formalism', interest in form has been largely superseded by other concerns, many of them of more significance to the struggles that broke out in British and North American academia at the time.[2] With the 1980s and the advent of New Historicism and cultural studies, much was uncovered about the way poets used sonnets to fashion their selves, express new forms of subjectivity, negotiate their social positions or articulate their desires and/or sexualities.[3] The environment of courtly poetics has been reassessed, and identity has been the subject of much criticism, in terms of gender, nationhood or race.[4] The study of the religious sonnet was expanded and strengthened by the 'religious turn' of the 1990s, and household names of religious sonneteers such as John Donne and George Herbert have been joined by those of Anne Locke, Henry Locke, William Alabaster, Barnabe Barnes, Henry Constable and others.[5]

As a consequence of these evolutions, the scope of studies on the early modern sonnet has considerably widened. While they used to be largely restricted to Shakespeare, Sidney, Spenser and Donne, they have now come to include a much wider range of authors. While Shakespeare's *Sonnets* attract by far the greatest number of commentators, Spenserian and Sidneian criticism has been considerably renewed. Since the 1980s, female authors, including such major sonneteers as Anne Locke (thought to be the author of the very first sonnet sequence in English) and Mary Wroth have been added to the canon.[6] The temporal scope has widened too, with calls to focus efforts on the early Elizabethan period, and a steady production of studies on authors of sonnets who wrote or were published as late as the 1620s and 1630s, the most prominent of whom were Donne and Herbert.[7] The Anglocentric perspective of literary studies on the sonnet has been questioned by a continuing stream of studies on the Scottish sonnet (from the 'casket sonnets' of Mary, Queen of Scots – which, admittedly, might be better categorised as French sonnets – to sonnets by the so-called 'Castalian band', a group of Scottish poets who gathered at the court of James VI in the 1580s and early 1590s, including William Fowler, to studies of Drummond of Hawthornden). The development of studies on Petrarchism and on the relationships between English sonneteers and their continental predecessors and contemporaries, has contributed, in particular, to a reconsideration of the reception of Italian culture in the English context.[8] Finally, the critical vocabulary that has been undergirding sonnet studies for more than a century has begun to be reassessed.[9]

Despite all these evolutions, however, the sonnet (a term which conveys the notion of a very strictly codified formal pattern) has rarely been interrogated as a category.[10] This may be due to the rejection of approaches favouring textual closure often gathered under the label of New Criticism that has been voiced in British and North American academia since the end of the 1970s. The looser concept of 'lyric' has been used more consistently and more often. It was better suited to interrogating such themes as identity (or self-fashioning), gender and desire – not least because it allowed critics to include analyses of poems of more than fourteen lines in their works. With its implicit connections with the Romantic and post-Romantic conception of poetry as expressing the depths of the self's interiority (a definition which would have been largely, but perhaps not completely, anachronistic in the sixteenth century), the lyric could easily be representative of the modernity contained in the phrase 'early modern'. If the sixteenth, seventeenth and eighteenth centuries are seen as a prefiguration of modernity (a possible implication of the label 'early modern'), then the term 'lyric' can encompass a variety of definitions, and can therefore be used in widely different approaches. Sometimes the category of 'lyric' has been a convenient way of not dwelling on formal issues that were of limited interest for critics concerned with other questions.

The term has also been the subject of heated debates over the last decades, especially in American academia, focusing on issues of definition, but also on the very historicity of the term – sometimes going as far as to imply that the lyric of the sixteenth century could unproblematically be tackled in the same way as a nineteenth-century poem, or, on the contrary, that it was an invention of twentieth- and twenty-first-century American criticism.[11] While we understand the necessity to envisage the lyric from a transhistorical perspective, and to uncover continuities in the history of poetry, we also deem it crucial to bear in mind that early modern theorists did not define the term as we do. One of the central ways the Italian sixteenth century redefined the lyric was by including Petrarch in its canon. As Guido Mazzoni explains, the lyric developed as an all-inclusive genre to reconcile classical *auctoritates* and Petrarch, the most eminent modern *auctoritas* at the time, canonised by Bembo early in the century, also grouping together such diverse classical forms as the elegy, the ode, the epigram, the hymn and others.[12] Petrarch's *Canzoniere* itself exemplified the diversity of lyric forms. The sonnet, which is probably seen today as the lyric form *par excellence*, was not generally accepted as such by sixteenth-century French theorists; in England, there was a connection between the lyric and the sonnet, but it was not as straightforward as is often believed (see Chapter 2). When Sidney asserts in his *Defence of Poesie* that 'the lyric is larded with passionate sonnets',[13] for instance, he acknowledges the lyric as collected poetry, and problematises the tension between inclusive and exclusive definitions of it: he might mean that the sonnet was a type of lyric, but he might equally imply that 'passionate sonnets' are not lyrics but find themselves associated with more narrowly defined lyric poems (odes, for instance) in volumes of collected poetry.

The sonnet itself poses problems of definition. In the strictest sense, the sonnet corresponds to Gascoigne's definition[14] or to the Petrarchan form as exploited by Milton; in a more general sense, the sonnet is a little song and/or poem about love sung by a lover. Only a few scholars have felt the need to challenge the strict definition of the English sonnet as a fourteen-line poem in iambic pentameter following a defined rhyming pattern, which many studies take for granted.[15] Let us mention two of those groundbreaking and extremely stimulating efforts: Cathy Shrank has claimed that sonnet studies should take into account authors usually considered (at best) to have paved the way for the 1590s (such as Barnabe Googe, George Turberville or George Gascoigne) and study them in their own right, even if they have not produced sonnets in the strictest sense of the term.[16] Amanda Holton, on the other hand, has recently argued that the sonnet (as a poem made up of fourteen lines of verse) was not as new as it was claimed to be in England in the second half of the sixteenth century.[17] According to her, several features of the sonnet often considered to be defining characteristics thereof were already present in Middle English poetry. In that view, the novelty of the form in sixteenth-century England might have been a claim, but not a fact.

The sonnet as a strictly defined poetic form does not seem to have reached the same significance in England as in Italy and France, perhaps because English was felt to be in need of prosodic codification. To a large extent, the polishing of English seems to have made more sense to English theorists than the Englishing of the sonnet (see Chapter 2). Although the sonnet undeniably participated in the attempts to improve the English language, it was never explicitly theorised as having specific relevance in achieving such a goal.

The question of the form of sonnet sequences has also been a vexed issue. The tension between lyric mode and narrative has been a structuring dichotomy in the field: while such a prominent critic of the sonnet as Heather Dubrow seems to have grown increasingly suspicious of the notion of narrativity, many studies still consider it a central aspect of sonnet collections.[18] Several attempts have been made to characterise the structure of sonnet sequences, from numerological readings to the hypothesis of the 'Delian structure'.[19] The notion of sonnet sequence (a phrase coined by Dante Gabriel Rossetti in 1881 that has no exact equivalent in the French or Italian critical traditions, for instance) remains a core aspect of the way early modern English sonnets are considered – with the effect of maintaining the 1590s as the centre of sonnet studies, with overtones of strong formal autonomy and narrative continuity that recent studies in book history tend to undermine rather than confirm.[20] As the present volume shows, this centrality has somewhat obscured other (and perhaps more significant) aspects of English sonneteering. Despite frequent calls to accept a looser definition of the terms 'sequence' and 'sonnets', a number of poetic collections including sonnets or similar forms have been neglected, and making them more widely available would encourage further studies. Other forms of continuity, such as that allowed by *mise-en-page*, deserve to be studied as much as modes of extracting and repurposing poems. Poems were collected and assembled in many different ways. Several projects on verse collection and verse miscellanies, in particular, have bloomed over the last decade, and their conclusions qualify the notion of sequence as well as what we know about modes of poetic collection in the context of a renewed interest in book history in literary studies since the 1990s and the material turn of the 1990s and 2000s.[21]

Although the canon has been expanded to good effect, many minor sonneteers are still largely ignored by academic criticism, and even very significant sonneteers such as Samuel Daniel or Michael Drayton have received comparatively little attention. Despite the fact that the borders of studies on the early modern sonnet in English have been redefined, the relationships between the English sonnet and its Continental sources still tend to be downplayed, or simplified. Gordon Braden has criticised in particular what he calls the 'parody theory', which reduces the Petrarchan tradition to something to be lampooned by English sonneteers:

> that is the voice of a modern sensibility that has, for its own reasons, never been under the spell of Petrarchan sonneteering ... Major bodies of Renaissance poetry are unintelligible without at least some responsiveness to such a spell, and a compelling account of Shakespeare's place in this tradition cannot merely make him (like us) superior to it. Something more complicated is called for.[22]

Not many comparative analyses of the significance of the early modern sonnet in England and in other European countries have been produced.[23] More generally, questions concerning the perception and reception of the sonnet have not yet been addressed extensively and are only emerging as a topic of interest to scholars. Studies of Shakespeare's plays and their often (though not always) ludicrous Petrarchan lovers suggest that the sonnet was mostly the target of mockery. But it has less often been put forward that stages crowded with puling lovers also testify to the success of the sonnet. The study of early modern discourses on the sonnet has to our knowledge rarely, if ever, been attempted in any systematic way. The development of studies on Petrarchism has given rise to extremely useful and thought-provoking studies, and has contributed to the advent of studies on the religious sonnet. But in certain cases, the very idea that the sonnet is primarily a poem on love and desire (secular or sacred) has tended to erase its conditions of publication and/or utterance. However, sonneteers (especially minor ones) are still regularly accused of naivety. Studies that insist on desire and self-fashioning sometimes misapprehend the relationship between speakers and authors – understandably so, since it is a notoriously difficult question that is still open to debate. The notion of exemplarity, for instance, which is central to Thomas P. Roche Jr's *Petrarch and the English Sonnet Sequences* (1989), would deserve to be taken into account more systematically. Writing about love is not necessarily writing about oneself, and the performance of a poetic alter ego can also be an author's strategy whose aim does not primarily have to do with the constitution of an identity, but rather partakes of a social strategy of self-promotion.

One book is of course not enough to provide in-depth treatment of all those issues. The aims of this volume are primarily to give more prominence to emerging research directions, to suggest new perspectives in sonnet criticism, and therefore open up further exchanges. It relies on two currently blooming strands of criticism. Book history has brought fruitful contributions to literary criticism; in the field of sonnet studies, it has produced seminal works such as Wendy Wall's *The Imprint of Gender: Authorship and Publication in the English Renaissance* (1993) and Arthur Marotti's *Manuscript, Print, and the English Renaissance Lyric* (1995). Their conclusions have perhaps not been fully exploited yet. Similarly, the perspective adopted by the authors in this volume echoes the recent renewal of interest in textual studies sometimes called 'New Formalism'.[24] The chapters are grounded in close reading, philology, textual editing, translation studies, the study of textual revisions or of reception; they all pay careful attention to the texts in their linguistic and material forms. This is not tantamount to a rejection of historical readings; rather, each chapter of the present volume, 'while (re)turning to matters of form, seeks not to set aside but to capitalise upon the theoretical and methodological gains of New Historicism, and in doing so to fulfil the promise of a historical formalism', to borrow Stephen Cohen's terms.[25] As far as the time scope of the volume is concerned, we have opted for an enlarged vision of the sonnet, going roughly from Wyatt and Surrey to the end of the seventeenth century. It seems necessary, however, to keep a focus on the last decades of the sixteenth century and the early decades of the seventeenth century: although it is no longer possible to argue that the sonnet suddenly bloomed again in the 1580s after decades of oblivion, the period remains a significant one in the history of the English sonnet. What is more, the very fact that previous approaches might have overstated the cultural centrality of the period makes its reassessment all the more necessary.

The nine chapters of this book, which tackle canonical (Shakespeare, Sidney, Spenser) but also far less prominent (Harvey, Barnes) sonneteers, taken together, depict the English sonnet as a widely practised form with strong cultural significance, despite the coexistence of two contradictory trends: on the one hand, the repeated belittling of the sonnet as mere trifle, on the other, its ubiquity and the visible wish to monumentalise it. The elusive nature of the early modern English sonnet also has to do with a lack of interest in its formal codification until the end of the sixteenth century, and what implicit principles of composition there were seem to have been more closely stated and followed from the 1580s onwards; for a short period of time, a strict codification of the sonnet seems to have held sway. In that regard, the two decades from the early 1580s to the early 1600s remain a key moment. As the sonnet appeared more and more often in print, especially in collections including mostly, if not only, sonnets, and as the sonnet became more systematically associated with love, poetic treatises attempted to codify it, complaints arose about its constraints, and sonnets and sonneteers began to be much more frequently satirised. Ridiculous melancholy lovers began to crowd the stages. More generally, the sonnet was more systematically connected with the passions and the attempt to temper them at the end of the sixteenth century. It follows logically that sonnets were a primary means of expressing the tension between balance and unbalance, self-mastery and excess, morals and sexuality. Perhaps as a consequence, the sonnet and the Petrarchan language of love were often caricatured, especially through variations on the most obvious device of Petrarchan love poetry: the blazon.

Belying such limited vision of the form, the contributors to this volume show as much the self-enclosure of the English sonnet as the diversity of its contexts. There is undoubtedly some continuity between the sonnet's function as a piece of epideictic rhetoric and as a poetic form, and between its social uses and its status as a work of art. Sonnet collections were of strong cultural significance in England, as they were in Italy and France. As Monferran puts it in Chapter 2, 'each country seems to have produced its own sonnet form', and it also appears that not all countries devoted the same attention and care to the codification and prescription of that form. The sonnet, even after being Englished, tended to display its relationship to its foreign origin, using a 'vocabulary of nativisation' (Stamatakis's phrase, see Chapter 5). This tension is one of the reasons for the constant dynamism of sonnet writing, which in many instances amounts to a dialogue with the sonnet tradition in general, and with French and Italian literature in particular, through translation, imitation or commentary.[26]

This also means that there is a form of collective dimension to sonnet writing which can be both intercultural and social (see especially Chapters 1 and 3 to 8). The sonnet can also make sense in different contexts through a different mode of interaction: extraction and repurposing, processes that reveal the continuity between the literary and the social through which sonnets might escape the control of their creators, and partake in the performance of highly strategic social acts both within the economy of print and within the economy of patronage. The recasting of the sonnet in new moulds (from manuscript to print, but also from print to the stage) ensured its wider circulation, changed its meaning and subverted both its purposes and its initial social status as a courtly text.

Modes of sonnet publication were formally and socially diverse, from dedicatory sonnets to sequences, from stand-alone poems to miscellanies. The miscellanies were the means through which the sonnet gained a wide readership, but could also be part of a socially elitist trend in the late sixteenth century (Chapter 8). The writing of linked sonnets testifies to the tendency to group sonnets together, either to accompany other writings (Chapter 6) or to constitute full sequences – which could also respond to or comment on each other (Chapter 7). The uses of the sonnet here exemplified show that there is a continuum between the stand-alone sonnet and the sequence. Reflecting on sequentiality from different perspectives, both Chapter 5 and 9 offer approaches that open the historical perspective of the volume to the question of what conditions our reading of Shakespeare's *Sonnets* today. The uses of the sonnet in devotional poetry, as well as its affinities with the epigram, hence with satire (whether the sonnet is the target, the means of sweetening the satire or the satirical form itself), point to the generic and thematic plasticity of the form (see in particular Chapters 2, 5, 6 and 7).[27] Perhaps more surprisingly, several chapters note the association of the sonnet with the ballad, or even the drinking song (see Chapters 2, 3 and to a lesser extent 8), throughout the sixteenth and seventeenth centuries.

The chapters in this book provide examples of the role of the poems and of their material features in their social environment. Gazzard's edition (Chapter 8) gives us information about the printer Thomas Archer's entourage and the possibly collective gathering of fragments for *The Muses Garland*,[28] and insists on the miscellany's 'extraordinarily bold' and 'unambiguous projection, at its very beginning, of the plaintive and courtly voice of Essex'. Chaghafi (Chapter 6) and Vuillemin (Chapter 7) deal with works related to the Nashe–Harvey quarrel; Chiari (Chapter 4) focuses on Jaggard's strategies. The business connections of the printers, the relationships between authors, printers, compilers and their connections are put forward. Authors are shown to adopt strategies of self-promotion and self-representation rather than self-fashioning – a way of considering specific contexts rather than stating generalities, of reconsidering the individual sense of the sonnet and of avoiding the most slippery connotations of the term 'lyric'.

The first section, 'Shaping the sonnet, from Italy and France to England', adopts an approach that is both historical and intercultural, analysing the production and theoretical codification of the sonnet in Italy, France and England.

In Chapter 1, William J. Kennedy insists on the role of the commentary both as format and as poetic practice: Petrarch was received in England not just through editions and translations but also through commented editions. Kennedy shows that the rewriting of Petrarch's poems by English sonneteers is very likely to have been informed by the Italian commentaries on the *Canzoniere* produced in the course of the sixteenth century. He proposes to consider poetic practice itself as a form of commentary, and thereby opens new perspectives in sonnet criticism.

Carlo Alberto Girotto, Jean-Charles Monferran and Rémi Vuillemin's comparative study in Chapter 2 of accounts of the sonnet in Italian, French and English poetic treatises of the second half of the sixteenth century considers them in their prescriptive dimension, but also, and perhaps more significantly, as indications of the evolving status of the sonnet in each of the three countries. While the codification of the sonnet had been previously established in Italy, where the main preoccupation seems to have been to grant a large degree of liberty to its practitioners, its definition in France was formalised in the 1550s, as it was appropriated by the *Pléiade* and rewritten as a native form. In England, by contrast, despite Surrey's early creation of a specifically English model, the main concern seems to have been the definition of the poetic features of the English language rather than the inner mechanisms of the sonnet. The variety of sonneteering practices in England might therefore be related to the loose codification of the form, at least until the last decades of the century. Poetic treatises published in the late sixteenth century and early seventeenth century seem to indicate that it was the moment when the sonnet achieved a much more clear-cut and prescriptive form, now described by the English in much the same way as mid-century French theorists such as Sébillet had done.

The second section, 'Performing the English sonnet', is about representations and performances of the sonnet. While desperate (and often incompetent) lovers performed sonnets on stage, thereby providing dramatic representations of manuscript culture, the translation of sonnets from stage to page could be tantamount to the performance of a social act whose relevance relied on the prestige of the author. The two chapters in this section thus document both the reception and the (re)uses of the sonnet in the early modern period.

In Chapter 3, Guillaume Coatalen studies the figure of the sonneteer in early modern drama after the sonnet craze of the 1590s. He shows that the ubiquity of the sonnet in the theatre of the period testifies to its enduring popularity as a form, but also as a label more generally pointing to short poems about love, as 'sonnets' continued to be referred to long after the waning of the poetic form up until (at least) the early eighteenth century. The sonneteer was consistently mocked as 'effeminate and decadent' over the period. The mere mention of the sonnet, it seems, was an extremely powerful tool of characterisation, which also foregrounded the social and economic uses of poetry, and the appropriation of the form both by nobles and by poets from non-aristocratic backgrounds.

Chapter 4 exemplifies varied uses of the same sonnets through a detailed analysis of the decontextualisation and repurposing of the sonnets by Shakespeare that first appeared in *Love's Labour's Lost* which were then published in William Jaggard's *The Passionate Pilgrim* – in other words, it looks into the shift from dramatic representations of manuscript culture to the resetting of the poems in the context of print culture. Sophie Chiari shows how such recontextualisation changes their meaning and their social significance. She argues that the publication of the poems in Jaggard's collection was a strategic move eerily anticipated in *Love's Labour's Lost* and later exploited by Heywood as well, emphasising the prestige of Shakespeare's name in social and commercial terms.

The third section, 'Placing the sonnet: Sonnets isolated or sequenced', further investigates the meaning of the location, arrangement and environment of early modern sonnets. It focuses on poems that have rarely been studied for various reasons: their isolation, their inclusion in series of poems that tend to evade the better-known label of 'sequence', or simply the fact that their author is not regarded as a canonical sonneteer. The three chapters in this section raise the issue of the role of the sonnet or of sonnet-groupings in their context, from the level of the individual sonnet to the interaction between sequences.

Chris Stamatakis (Chapter 5) argues that, contrary to the beliefs of a critical tradition that has mostly studied early modern sonnets as poetic elements in sequences, the sonnet is 'a form that flourishes in *un*sequenced contexts', and more particularly when the self-referentiality of the sonnet celebrates native eloquence and expresses the tensions inherent in an Englished foreign form. The stand-alone sonnet, Stamatakis argues, often advertises itself as self-enclosed, whether a dedicatory or commendatory poem, or part of prefatory material or a gift.

Chapter 6 explores the function of collected sonnets whose status is not absolutely clear either. 'Greene's Memorial', a series of sonnets appended to Gabriel Harvey's *Foure Letters* (1592) that was instrumental in the quarrel between Thomas Nashe and the Harvey brothers, could be construed as an intermediary between commendatory or occasional sonnets and the longer sonnet sequences of the 1590s. Elisabeth Chaghafi insists that, regardless of their literary value, or lack thereof, Harvey's sonnets deserve to be studied in their own right. Their function, she argues, is for Harvey to show his ability to temper his passions and compensate for the aggressive tone of the *Foure Letters*, a strategic move to present himself as reasonable.

The final chapter of the section focuses on Barnabe Barnes's two sonnet sequences, *Parthenophil and Parthenophe* (1593) and *A Divine Centurie of Spirituall Sonnets* (1595), which are also (even if more remotely) related to the Harvey–Nashe controversy. Like Chaghafi, Vuillemin sees the conjunction between sonnet writing and print publication as a strategic move. If Barnes flaunts his poetic and rhetorical abilities in the first sequence, he then uses his second sequence to stage his moral conversion and his recantation of his past sins. The two separate sequences work as a sort of diptych within a specific authorial strategy, which suggests that the logic of rearrangement, commentary and 'retrospective patterning'[29] is relevant to the study of interactions between separate sonnet sequences.

The last section, 'Editing the sonnet', both illustrates the issues debated in the rest of the book and opens them to the consideration of modern editing practices. It provides both practice and theory: the first modern edition of an early seventeenth-century printed poetic miscellany and a critique of current editing practices. It includes a new document and a discussion of the editing of the most canonical early modern sonnets, those of Shakespeare.

Hugh Gazzard offers an exceptional document: the first modern edition of *The Muses Garland* (?1603), a short printed poetic miscellany comprising five sonnets – including versions of sonnets by Spenser and two previously unknown poems attributed to 'S.P.S.', presumably Sir Philip Sidney, an attribution that Gazzard deems 'credible'. His full diplomatic edition is accompanied by a detailed introduction which offers precious insight into the practice of miscellany-gathering, providing evidence of the specific poetic and political issues it raises via a thorough analysis of both the contributors and the contents of the recently discovered fragment. By doing so, it also reopens many of the themes that the previous sections of the volume put forward: poetic arrangement, the connections between poems in one volume, and their social and cultural backgrounds.

In the last chapter, Andrew Eastman's very precise close readings show how contemporary editing practices tend to disrupt the poetics of Shakespeare's *Sonnets* as a sequence. His examples mostly focus on the punctuation and on the syntax of the sonnets. Eastman does not locate the continuity of the *Sonnets* in narrativity, but rather in the rhythm, or 'sound continuum', of the sequence. His approach, based on Henri Meschonnic's theory of rhythm, powerfully reviews the vexed issue of the unity of Shakespeare's *Sonnets* from a perspective that is both historicised and innovative, and encourages us to reconsider both literary and editorial approaches to the 1609 Quarto. As he concludes, 'the beauties of punctuation in the Quarto are inseparable from the sound continuum of the sequence, and from its epistemology of English, the way it leads us to reflect on what lies hidden in the words we breathe'.

Notes

1 Michael Drayton, *Idea*, 'To the reader', lines 9–14 in *Poems: by Michael Drayton, Esquire* (London: John Smethwicke, 1619).
2 On New Formalism, see for instance M. Levinson, 'What Is New Formalism?', *PMLA*, 122:2 (March 2007), 558–69, and C. Levine, *Forms: Whole, Rhythm, Hierarchy, Network* (Princeton, Oxford: Princeton University Press, 2015). For applications of New Formalism to early modern literature, see in particular M.D. Rasmussen (ed.), *Renaissance Literature and Its Formal Engagements* (Basingstoke: Palgrave, 2002), B. Burton and E. Scott-Baumann (eds), *The Work of Form: Poetics and Materiality in Early Modern Culture* (Oxford: Oxford University Press, 2014). Some interest in the form of the sonnet can be found in anthologies of the sonnet such as E. Hirsch and E. Boland (eds), *The Making of a Sonnet: A Norton Anthology* (New York, London: Norton & Company, 2008), and P. Levin (ed.),

The Penguin Book of the Sonnet: 500 Years of a Classic Tradition in English (London: Penguin Books, 2001), or in editions of or commentaries on Shakespeare's *Sonnets* published well after the age of structuralist criticism, such as H. Vendler's *The Art of Shakespeare's Sonnets* (Cambridge, MA: Belknap Press, 1997), K. Duncan-Jones's Arden Shakespeare edition (London: Thomas Nelson & Sons Ltd, 1997), C. Burrow's edition of *The Complete Sonnets and Poems* (Oxford: Oxford University Press, 2002), or C. Shrank and R. Lyne's edition of *The Complete Poems of Shakespeare* (London, New York: Routledge, 2018), whose conclusions on the form of the sonnets are echoed in the present volume.

3 See S. Greenblatt, *Renaissance Self-Fashioning from More to Shakespeare* (Chicago, London: University of Chicago Press, 1980) pp. 115–56, esp. 145–50; J. Fineman, *Shakespeare's Perjured Eye: The Invention of Poetic Subjectivity in the Sonnets* (Berkeley: University of California Press, 1986); A.F. Marotti's seminal article, '"Love is not love": Elizabethan Sonnet Sequences and the Social Order', *English Literary History*, 49 (1982), 396–428, and P. Innes, *Shakespeare and the English Renaissance Sonnet: Verses of Feigning Love* (London: Macmillan Press, 1997); H. Dubrow, *Echoes of Desire: English Petrarchism and its Counterdiscourses* (Ithaca, London: Cornell University Press, 1995). On homosexuality in the sonnets, see for instance J. Pequigney, *Such Is My Love: A Study of Shakespeare's Sonnets* (Chicago: University of Chicago Press, 1985); B. Smith, *Homosexual Desire in Shakespeare's England: A Cultural Poetics* (Chicago: University of Chicago Press, 1991); J. Goldberg, *Sodometries: Renaissance Texts, Modern Sexualities* (Stanford: Stanford University Press, 1992).

4 See S. May, *The Elizabethan Courtier Poets: The Poems and Their Contexts* (Columbia, London: University of Missouri Press, 1991); C. Bates, *The Rhetoric of Courtship in Elizabethan Language and Literature* (Cambridge: Cambridge University Press, 1992). Those works are part of a renewal of interest in court culture in the 1980s and the 1990s anticipated by the founding of the International Courtly Literature Society in 1973, fuelled by New Historicism in the late 1970s and in the 1980s, and exemplified in the creation of the Society for Court Studies in 1995. On gender, see for instance N. Vickers, 'Diana Described: Scattered Women and Scattered Rhyme', in E. Abel (ed.), *Writing and Sexual Difference* (Chicago, London: University of Chicago Press, 1982), pp. 95–109; B.L. Estrin, *Laura: Uncovering Gender and Genre in Wyatt, Donne and Marvell* (Durham, NC, London: Duke University Press, 1994); I. Maasen, 'Canonized by Love? Religious Rhetoric and Gender-Fashioning in the Sonnet', in S. Rupp and T. Düring (eds), *Performances of the Sacred in Late Medieval and Early Modern England* (Amsterdam, New York: Rodopi, 2005), pp. 169–88. On nationhood, the landmark study is W.J. Kennedy, *The Site of Petrarchism: Early Modern National Sentiment in Italy, France, and England* (Baltimore, London: Johns Hopkins University Press, 2003). On race, see for instance K. Hall, *Things of Darkness: Economies of Race and Gender in Early Modern England* (Ithaca: Cornell University Press, 1995), and M. Hunt, 'Be dark but not too dark. Shakespeare's Dark Lady as a Sign of Color', in J. Schiffer (ed.), *Shakespeare's Sonnets: Critical Essays* (New York, London: Garland Publishing, 2000), pp. 368–89.

5 See the foundational work of B. Lewalski, *Protestant Poetics and the Seventeenth-Century Religious Lyric* (Princeton: Princeton University Press, 1979), and, more specifically on the sonnet sequences, T.P. Roche Jr's seminal *Petrarch and the English Sonnet Sequences* (New York: AMS Press Inc., 1989). For the notion of a 'religious turn', see K. Jackson and A.F. Marotti, 'The Turn to Religion in Early Modern English Studies', *Criticism*, 46:1 (winter 2004), 167–90.

6 The sheer number of articles and books written on those two writers makes it impossible to give a complete account of the criticism produced on them in the last thirty years. A very useful account of the criticism written on Anne Locke can be found in R.C. Evan and J. Moody, 'The Religious Sonnets of Anne Vaughan Lock: An Overview of Scholarship, 1989-1999', *Ben Jonson Journal: Literary Contexts in the Age of Elizabeth, James and Charles*, 22:2 (November 2015), 269–81. See also K.A. Coles, *Religion, Reform, and Women's Writing in Early Modern England* (Cambridge, New York, Melbourne: Cambridge University Press, 2008), and M. White (ed.), *Ashgate Critical Essays on Women Writers in England, vol.3: Anne Locke, Isabella Whitney, Aemilia Lanyer* (Farnham, Burlington: Ashgate, 2009). On Mary Wroth, see C. Kinney (ed.), *Ashgate Critical Essays on Women Writers in England, 1550-1700, vol.4: Mary Wroth* (Farnham, Burlington: Ashgate, 2009). See also M.N. Paulissen, *The Love Sonnet of Lady Mary Wroth: A Critical Introduction* (Salzburg: Institut für Anglistik und Amerikanistik Universität Salzburg, 1982), G.F. Waller, *The Sidney Family Romance: Mary Wroth, William Herbert, and the Early Modern Construction of Gender* (Detroit: Wayne State University Press, 1993), N.J. Miller, *Changing the Subject: Mary Wroth and Figurations of Gender in Early Modern England* (Lexington: University Press of Kentucky, 1996). See also R. Smith, *Sonnets and the English Woman Writer, 1560-1621: The Politics of Absence* (Basingstoke: Palgrave Macmillan, 2005), and M.B. Moore, *Desiring Voices: Women Sonneteers and Petrarchism* (Carbondale: Southern Illinois University Press, 2011).

7 For a call to study texts of the mid-century or of the early Elizabethan era, see in particular C. Shrank's '"Matters of love as of discourse": The English Sonnet, 1560–1580', *Studies in Philology*, 105:1 (winter 2008), 30–49, and Stephen Hamrick's introduction to S. Hamrick (ed.), *Tottel's Songs and Sonettes in Context* (Farnham: Ashgate, 2013). There has also been a strong renewal of interest in *Tottel's Miscellany*, with the publication of P. Marquis's edition in 2007, a Penguin edition by A. Holton and T. MacFaul in 2011, and the *Verse Miscellanies Online* project led by M. O'Callaghan. See http://verse miscellaniesonline.bodleian.ox.ac.uk (date accessed: 20 April 2019). The MLA online database records a total of about 35 articles on the sonnets or Donne and Herbert for the period 2000–17. That is half as much as all the other sonneteers combined (70), excluding Shakespeare (160). This is the result of a search conducted in August 2017.

8 On the Scottish sonneteers, see for example P. Bawcutt, 'James VI's Castalian Band: A Modern Myth', *Scottish Historical Review*, 80 (2001), 251–9; N. Royan and S. Mapstone (eds), *Langage Cleir Illumynate: Scottish Poetry from Barbour to Drummond, 1375–1630* (Amsterdam: Rodopi, 2007); S. Verweij, 'The Manuscripts of William Fowler: A Revaluation of The Tarantula of Love, A Sonnet Sequence, and Of Death', *Scottish Studies Review*, 8:2 (autumn 2007), 9–23; R.D.S. Jack, 'Petrarch and the Scottish Renaissance Sonnet', *Proceedings of the British Academy*, 146 (2007), 259–73. It must be said, however, that numerous seminal works on the Scottish sonnet were produced in the 1960s and 70s. On Mary Stuart's sonnets, see for instance M.E. Burke, 'Queen, Lover, Poet: A Question of Balance in the Sonnets of Mary, Queen of Scots', in M.E. Burke, J. Donawerth, L.L. Dove and K. Nelson (eds), *Women, Writing, and the Reproduction of Culture in Tudor and Stuart Britain* (Syracuse: Syracuse University Press, 2000), pp. 101–18; P. Herman, '"Mes subjectz, mon ame assubjectie": The Problematic (of) Subjectivity in Mary Stuart's Sonnets', in P.C. Herman (ed.), *Reading Monarchs Writing: The Poetry of Henry VIII, Mary Stuart, Elizabeth I, and James VI/I* (Tempe: Arizona Center for Medieval and Renaissance Studies, 2002), pp. 51–78; F. Rigolot, 'When Petrarchan Errors Become Political Crimes: Mary Stuart's French Sonnets to Bothwell', in E. Vinestock, D. Foster and N. Kenny (eds), *Writers in Conflict in Sixteenth-Century France* (Durham: University of Durham, 2008), pp. 37–50; R. Smith, '"Plaintes Full of Dissimulation": The Casket Sonnets, Female Complaint and True Crime', in P. Salzman (ed.), *Expanding the Canon of Early Modern Women's Writing* (Newcastle-upon-Tyne: Cambridge Scholars, 2010), pp. 125–42. On the English poets and their Continental predecessors, see for instance A.L. Prescott, *French Poets and the English Renaissance* (New Haven, London: Yale University Press, 1978); S. Minta, *Petrarch and Petrarchism: The English and French Traditions* (Manchester: Manchester University Press, 1980), R. Greene, *Post-Petrarchism: Origins and Innovations of the Western Lyric Sequence* (Princeton: Princeton University Press, 1991), W.J. Kennedy, *Authorizing Petrarch* (Ithaca, London: Cornell University Press, 1994), *The Site of Petrarchism*, and *Petrarchism at Work: Contextual Economies in the Age of Shakespeare* (Ithaca, London: Cornell University Press, 2016), A. Fox, *The English Renaissance: Identity and Representation in Elizabethan England* (Oxford: Blackwell, 1997).

9 See in particular C. Warley, *Sonnet Sequences and Social Distinction in Renaissance England* (Cambridge: Cambridge University Press, 2005), chapters 1 and 2, respectively pp. 1–18 and 19–44.

10 See note 2 and the collection edited by M.C. Schoenfeldt, *A Companion to Shakespeare's Sonnets* (Oxford: Blackwell, 2007).

11 See V. Jackson and Y. Prins (eds), *The Lyric Theory Reader: A Critical Anthology* (Baltimore: Johns Hopkins, 2014).

12 G. Mazzoni, *Sulla poesia moderna* (Bologna: Il Mulino, 2005), pp. 56–65.

13 See G. Alexander (ed.), *Sidney's 'The Defence of Poesy' and Selected Renaissance Literary Criticism* (London: Penguin Books, 2004), p. 35.

14 'Then have you sonnets. Some think that all poems (being short) may be called sonnets, as indeed it is a diminutive word derived of "suonare", but yet I can best bestow to call those sonnets which are of fourteen lines, every line containing ten syllables. The first twelve do rhyme in staves of four lines by cross metre, and the last two, rhyming together, do conclude the whole. There are dizains and sixains, which are of ten lines and of six lines, commonly used by the French, which some English writers do also term by the name of sonnets,' *Certayne Notes of Instruction* ... in Alexander (ed.), *Sidney's 'The Defence of Poesy' and Selected Renaissance Literary Criticism*, p. 245.

15 For two general but useful studies of the sonnet, see M.G. Spiller, *The Development of the Sonnet: An Introduction* (London, New York: Routledge, 1992), and A.D. Cousins and P. Howarth (eds), *The Cambridge Companion to the Sonnet* (Cambridge: Cambridge University Press, 2011).

16 In '"Matters of love as of discourse"…'.

17 A. Holton, 'An Obscured Tradition: The Sonnet and Its Fourteen-Line Predecessors', *Review of English Studies*, 62:255 (June 2011), 373–92. For another study insisting on connections between early

modern sonnets and medieval literature, see D. Sokolov, *Renaissance Texts, Medieval Subjectivities: Rethinking Petrarchan Desire from Wyatt to Shakespeare* (Pittsburgh, PA: Duquesne University Press, 2017).

18 See H. Dubrow, '"Incertainties now crown themselves assur'd": The Politics of Plotting Shakespeare's Sonnets', *Shakespeare Quarterly*, 47 (1996), 291–305; 'Neither Here Nor There: Deixis and the Sixteenth-Century Sonnet', in M. Thain and J. Culler (eds), *The Lyric Poem: Formations and Transformations* (Cambridge: Cambridge University Press, 2013), pp. 30–50. For studies that insist on the narrativity of the sequences, see for instance D. Kambaskovic-Sawers, '"Never was I the golden cloud": Ovidian Myth, Ambiguous Speaker and the Narrative in the Sonnet Sequences by Petrarch, Sidney and Spenser', *Renaissance Studies*, 21:5 (November 2007), 637–61; E. Heale, 'Songs, Sonnets and Autobiography: Self-Representation in Sixteenth-Century Verse Miscellanies', in H. Dragstra, S. Ottway, and H. Wilcox (eds), *Betraying Our Selves: Forms of Self-Representation in Early Modern English Texts* (Basingstoke: Macmillan-St Martin's, 2000), pp. 59–75.

19 For numerological readings of sonnet sequences, see A. Fowler, *Triumphal Forms: Structural Patterns in Elizabethan Poetry* (Cambridge: Cambridge University Press, 1970), Roche, *Petrarch and the English Sonnet Sequences*, T.W.N. Parker, *Proportional Form in the Sonnets of the Sidney Circle: Loving in Truth* (Oxford: Oxford University Press, 1998). On the hypothesis of the 'Delian structure', see J. Kerrigan (ed.), *William Shakespeare, The Sonnets and A Lover's Complaint* (Harmondsworth: Penguin, 1986), pp. 13–18, Duncan-Jones's edition of Shakespeare's Sonnets, pp. 88–95, and Roche's *Petrarch and the English Sonnet Sequences*, pp. 343–4 and 440-61. The hypothesis is questioned by H. Dubrow in '"Dressing old words new"? Re-evaluating the "Delian Structure"', in M.C. Schoenfeldt (ed.), *A Companion to Shakespeare's Sonnets* (Oxford: Blackwell, 2007), pp. 90–103.

20 George Gascoigne mentioned 'sonnets in sequence', but not 'sonnet sequences' in *The Adventures of Master F.J.*. See W.T. Going, 'Gascoigne and the Term "Sonnet-Sequence"', *Notes & Queries*, 1 (May 1954), 189–90. Rossetti coined the phrase 'sonnet sequence' to refer to his poetic collection *The House of Life* in its 1881 edition. The term was first applied to Victorian sonnet sequences. Some of the first uses (if not the first) of the term to point to Elizabethan sonnet collections can be found in M.F. Crow's edition of Lodge's *Phillis* and Fletcher's *Licia, Elizabethan Sonnet Cycles – Phillis by Thomas Lodge, Licia by Giles Fletcher* (Chicago: A.C. McClurg and Co,. 1896) and in S. Lee's *Elizabethan Sonnets. Newly Arranged and Indexed*, vol. 1 (London: Archibald and Co., 1904). Lee does not employ the term consistently throughout his work. On early modern writing as a process of compilation rather than narrativisation, see for instance J.T. Knight's *Bound to Read: Compilations, Collections and the Making of Renaissance Literature* (Philadelphia: University of Pennsylvania Press, 2013).

21 On verse collections, see *Early Modern Manuscript Poetry: Recovering Our Scribal Heritage* (Sheffield) and *Verse Miscellanies Online* (Oxford and Reading). Recent works include J. Eckhardt's *Manuscript Verse Collectors and the Politics of Anti-Courtly Love Poetry* (Oxford: Oxford University Press, 2009), and J. Eckhardt and D. Starza Smith (eds), *Manuscript Miscellanies in Early Modern England* (Farnham, Burlington: Ashgate, 2014). The seminal studies of the sonnet and lyric poetry from the perspective of book history are A.F. Marotti's *Manuscript, Print, and the English Renaissance Lyric* (Ithaca, London: Cornell University Press, 1995), and W. Wall's *The Imprint of Gender: Authorship and Publication in the English Renaissance* (Ithaca, London: Cornell University Press, 1993). Literary studies focusing on materiality include for instance P. Fumerton, *Cultural Aesthetics. Renaissance Literature and the Practice of Social Ornament* (Chicago: University of Chicago Press, 1991) and R. Kalas, *Frame, Glass, Verse: The Technology of Poetic Invention in the English Renaissance* (Ithaca, London: Cornell University Press, 2007).

22 See G. Braden's 'Shakespeare's Petrarchism', in J. Schiffer (ed.), *Shakespeare's Sonnets: Critical Essays* (New York: Garland Publishing, 1999), pp. 163–83, esp. 165.

23 W.J. Kennedy's three books listed at the beginning of this introduction are significant exceptions.

24 See M. Levinson, 'What Is New Formalism?', and B. Burton and E. Scott-Baumann, *The Work of Form*.

25 See S. Cohen, 'Introduction', in S. Cohen (ed.), *Shakespeare and Historical Formalism* (Aldershot: Ashgate, 2007), pp. 1–27, esp. 2–3.

26 R. McCabe has also recently noted 'the intertextual nature of dedicatory rhetoric'. See *Ungainfull Arte: Poetry, Patronage, & Print in the Early Modern Era* (Oxford: Oxford University Press, 2016), p. 9. On commentary, imitation and translation, see T.M. Greene's seminal study, *The Light in Troy: Imitation and Discovery in Renaissance Poetry* (New Haven: Yale University Press, 1982); J. Lawrence, '*Who the Devill Taught Thee So Much Italian?*' *Italian Language Learning and Literary Imitation in Early Modern England* (Manchester: Manchester University Press, 2005); and A.E.B. Coldiron, *Printers Without Borders: Translation and Textuality in the Renaissance* (Cambridge: Cambridge University Press, 2015).

27 The association between the sonnet and the epigram was already noted by R.L. Colie in *Shakespeare's Living Art* (Princeton: Princeton University Press, 1974), pp. 68–135.
28 In that sense, Gazzard's perspective is very much in keeping with J. Powell's recent hypothesis of a circle of poets behind the composition of *Tottel's Miscellany*. See J. Powell, 'The Network behind *Tottel's Miscellany*', *English Literary Renaissance*, 46:2 (Spring 2016), 193–224.
29 See B. Herrnstein Smith, *Poetic Closure: A Study of How Poems End* (Chicago: Chicago University Press, 1968), p. 119. See also N. Fraistat, 'Introduction', in N. Fraistat (ed.), *Poems in Their Place: The Intertextuality and Order of Poetic Collections* (Chapel Hill, London: University of North Carolina Press, 1986), p. 8.

I

Shaping the sonnet, from Italy and France to England

1

English Petrarchism: from commentary on poetry to poetry as commentary

William John Kennedy

A profusion of literary commentary in the European Renaissance defines the period as an age of exegesis. In addition to building upon ancient and medieval modes of textual gloss and interpretive commentary, humanist scholars introduced new modes of philological, historical, rhetorical and intertextual commentary. In Italy their push to excavate authorial meanings from ancient texts came to include modern vernacular texts by Dante, Petrarch and Boccaccio. The development of print technology in the fifteenth century spread printed editions of these authors with accompanying commentaries throughout Europe. Through these channels sixteenth-century English poets received Petrarch's *Rime sparse* in richly annotated editions that explicated, commented upon and shaped their models for lyric poetry.[1] In what follows, I am going to argue that these authors in turn produced a body of English Petrarchism imitated by poets who shaped their own poems as critical commentaries upon the work of forerunners. The poets to whom I will refer include Wyatt and Surrey in the first generation of Italian reception, Sidney and Spenser in the next generation of English imitation, and Drayton and Shakespeare in the final generation of English Petrarchism.

Commentators and commentaries

With respect to Petrarch and his Italian commentators, the earliest editions of his vernacular poems include anti-papal, pro-imperial glosses composed by the peripatetic humanist scholar Francesco Filelfo at the despotic Visconti court in Milan during the 1440s (published unfinished in 1476); by the Ghibelline lawyer Antonio da Tempo in Padua (1477); and by the entrepreneurial Veronese publisher Hieronimo Squarzafico who completed Filelfo's commentary in 1484. At Venice in 1501, Aldus Manutius issued a carefully prepared edition of Petrarch's *Rime*, for which he recruited the skills of the humanist scholar Pietro Bembo. The latter subsequently wrote a full-length dialogue in defence of Petrarch in *Prose della volgar lingua* (Writing in the Vernacular, 1525), authorising the poet's archaic Tuscan style as the supreme model for Italian lyric.

That same year, in what would become the most widely reprinted edition of Petrarch's vernacular poems, the Venetian editor Alessandro Vellutello rearranged the accepted sequence of poems to narrate a dramatically coherent account of the poet's life and his love for Laura. Later editors such as Giovanni Andrea Gesualdo in

Venice (1533), Sylvano da Venafro also in Naples (1533) and Bernardino Daniello in Padua (1536, expanded in 1549) would emphasise Petrarch's rhetorical skills in deploying classical myth, literary allusion and poetic figuration. Other editors hospitable to Reformation theology such as Fausto da Longiano in Modena (1532), Antonio Brucioli in Ferrara (1548) and Ludovico Castelvetro in Modena (1582) would foreground Petrarch's scriptural and doctrinal references and his criticism of the Avignon papacy. Taken together, these approaches to the *Rime sparse* mediated Petrarch's reception in England, offering multiple versions of Petrarch as a public figure, poet, lover, scholar and Christian moralist.

Of the 143 editions of Petrarch's *Rime sparse* that appeared between 1470 and 1600 and are catalogued in Cornell University's Fiske Petrarch Collection, three-quarters (108 editions) offer some form of commentary on the poetry. They variously include a biography of the poet, attributions of his classical and medieval sources and analogues, identifications of historical allusions, lexical glosses and concordances of key words, tabulations of rhyme patterns, and other helpful materials.[2] Except for Aldus Manutius's 1501 edition (which includes an important afterword on editorial procedures, but no textual annotation), the ten commentaries to which I have called special attention are the most detailed, systematic and complete ones, offering poem-by-poem interpretative analysis, whether in the form of headnotes, footnotes or marginal commentary.

The question of which editions reached England is an open one. Catalogues of school, university and private libraries, inventories of books owned by particular individuals and speculation about the circulation of Italian-language books among immigrant populations in London offer some clues. Cambridge University lists an edition of Petrarch's *Le cose volgari* (inventoried between 1550 and 1593, possibly as one of Aldus Manutius's imprints published with that title) and three unidentified editions of Petrarch's *Rime* (inventoried between 1589 and 1593).[3] The 1605 catalogue of Oxford's Bodleian Library lists three reprints of the *Rime* with commentaries by Antonio da Tempo and Filelfo (1515), Vellutello (1545) and Gesualdo (1553).[4] A 1665 inventory of some 4,500 items in the Sidney family library in Kent lists two quarto volumes simply as *Petrarcha 4° bis* with no identification of publisher, editor or commentator, and no date of acquisition. It also lists a second edition of Petrarch's *opera*, comprising four volumes in one folio without commentary, from the press of Sebastian Henricpetrus at Basel in 1581.[5] Surprisingly there is no mention of Petrarch in Gabriel Harvey's personal library (192 volumes), nor in inventories of over eleven thousand volumes distributed among 137 estates.[6] Still, we know that the *Rime sparse* were enthusiastically read and quoted in Italian, were selectively translated into English and were widely imitated by major English authors.

Access to reading commentaries on Petrarch in Italian depended upon opportunities for learning to read Italian. Vernacular languages were not part of school or university curricula, but grammar-school training in Latin provided a gateway for foreign language study through self-instruction or private tutorials. Upper-class poets such as Wyatt and Sidney sharpened their skills in Italian and French upon the whetstone of ambassadorial missions. Middle-class merchants and military adventurers could gain language experience through travel abroad. London had long attracted foreign-born merchants and artisans, and polyglot language-learning manuals emphasised the acquisition of their languages for practical purposes. While the anonymous *A Plain Pathway to the French Tongue* (c. 1575) advertised itself as *Very profitable for Marchants*, William Thomas's *Principal Rules of the Italian Grammar* (1550) presented itself *For the Better Understanding of Boccace, Petrarke, and Dante*.[7] The latter proved to be the first of twelve Italian handbooks and four Italian dictionaries published in England during the Tudor–Stuart period. John Florio's *The Second Frutes ... of Diuers but Delightsome Tastes to the Tongues of Italians and Englishmen* (1580) augmented the author's earlier pedagogical effort, *First Fruites* (1578), with serious attention to literary expression.[8] Florio quotes from Petrarch's *Trionfi* and paraphrases passages from Boccaccio, Aretino, Ariosto and Tasso. The same author's *Queen Anna's New World of Words* (1611) provides a list of editions from which its entries are derived. They include the 1533 edition of Petrarch's *Rime* with Gesualdo's commentary *sopra il Petrarcha*.[9]

We can identify specific copies of Petrarch's work owned or used by some sixteenth-century poets. George Gascoigne (though without evidence that he used it much) possessed Gesualdo's edition of *Il Petrarcha*, which offers the century's most extensive rhetorical commentary on the *Rime*.[10] In *Hekatompathia* (1582), Thomas Watson translates four of Petrarch's sonnets, quoting from their Italian originals with number references that correspond to their placement in the reordered sequence of Vellutello's *Il Petrarcha*.[11] Ben Jonson, despite his resistance to Petrarchan poetry, possessed a mutilated 1581 Basel reprint of Petrarch's *opera*.[12] Other examples might inform or disappoint us. As will appear below, various poems by Wyatt and Surrey imply a general knowledge of commentaries by Vellutello and Gesualdo respectively, while a couple of poems by Sidney and Spenser refer in specific terms to commentaries by Gesualdo and Fausto da Longiano respectively.

Equally important are the ways in which these English poets comment on the Petrarchism of their predecessors in England. The influence of commentaries on a reader's, writer's or translator's understanding of canonical texts is by no means a one-way street. Readers of commentaries engage in dialogue with writers of them, endorsing some of their insights, questioning others and perhaps as often as not rejecting their interpretations in favour of alternative ones. When such readers are themselves writers, they may create new texts by imitating, borrowing from and rewriting earlier texts from perspectives opposed to those of earlier authors. And so on. Such writers are again in dialogue with earlier authors and commentators, to whom they respond with creative initiative. They have moved from reading poems with commentaries on them to writing their own poems as a form of commentary upon what preceded them.

Sir Thomas Wyatt and Henry Howard, Earl of Surrey

The starting point of English Petrarchism during the reign of Henry VIII is Thomas Wyatt, followed by his younger, more deeply pedigreed friend, the Earl of Surrey. Both of them would run afoul of Henry VIII, who briefly imprisoned the former on possible grounds of flirting with Anne Boleyn and ordered the latter to be beheaded for quartering the royal arms. And both of them – Wyatt, whose diplomatic missions to France and Italy in 1526–27 facilitated his approach to the *Rime sparse*; and Surrey, whose interest in Petrarch's verse dates from the mid-1530s – experimented with translating, adapting and imitating a few dozen of Petrarch's sonnets. Their respective versions of Petrarch's sonnet 140, 'Amor, che nel penser mio vive et regna' ('Love, who lives and reigns in my thought'), illustrate competing approaches to the poem augured by its Italian commentators.

These commentators differ among themselves as to whether Petrarch acts as an aggressive lover who threatens Laura's honour, or as a passive lover who suffers from her rejection. Vellutello, echoing Antonio da Tempo, explains that Petrarch's 'Amor' personifies love as Cupid, and that, because the lover approaches Laura with cupidinous desire, he deserves 'the rebuke that she displayed against his unbridled will' ('il repugnar che M.L. contra il suo sfrenato uoler faceua') (fol. 41r). Wyatt's version of the poem emphasises the lover's brashness, inscribing his action in jagged trochaic rhythms, abrupt turns of phrase and provincial Kentish verb endings in *-eth* that convey his lack of shame or embarrassment: 'The long love, that in my thought I harber / And in my hart doth kepe his residence'.[13] The prick of Cupid's arrow goads the speaker 'with bold pretence' until the beloved 'with his hardinesse takes displeasure'. Unstrung by love, he comports himself poorly.

Surrey's version, by contrast, offers a more sympathetic view of the lover as a victim of Laura's disdain. This view resonates with the opinion of Gesualdo and later commentators for whom the scornful beloved 'has made him bear in patience his pangs of love' ('portar li facea patientemente l'amoroso affanno') (fol. CXCVIIIr). Accordingly Surrey's poem comments upon Wyatt's precedent by reinstating Petrarch's decorum. It begins with a dignified personification of 'Love, that liveth, and raigneth in my thought', and ends wittily with the same word 'love', now stripped of personification: 'Swete is his death, that takes his end by love'. Unlike Wyatt's rough-hewn Cupid, Surrey's deity is stately, aristocratic and in full control, elegantly clad in chivalric 'armes' and accustomed to 'raigne' in the speaker's thought (with a triple pun on 'reign', 'rein in' and 'rain'). And unlike Wyatt's bold lover, Surrey's has learned to cover his 'hot desire / With shamefast cloke'. From the start, the speaker retains his composure in regular iambics until the poem's smoothly resolved final line, 'Swete is his death'.

As courtly amateurs for whom poetry was an avocation rather than a profession, neither Wyatt nor Surrey published his work. Their posthumous publication came in an anthology of 271 early Tudor poems assembled at the beginning of Elizabeth's reign by Richard Tottel, *Songs and Sonnets Written by the Right Honorable Lord Henry Howard Late Earl of Surrey and Others* (1557, with eight augmented and revised editions to 1587). This collection includes ninety-seven poems by Wyatt, forty by Surrey and the remainder by Nicholas Grimald, Lord Vaux, John Heywood, Thomas Churchyard and others. Primarily a publisher of books on English common law and property law, Tottel directed his miscellany to students and young attorneys at the Inns of Court, 'for profit of the studious of Englishe eloquence'.[14] The volume makes a distinct intervention in three ways. First, it brought into print aristocratic poets from Henry VIII's era who wrote for an intimate court circle with little or no expectation of reaching a wider readership. Second, Tottel likely solicited the volume's many 'anonymous' poems from Inns of Court students as responses to and commentaries upon Wyatt, Surrey and their noble confrères. Third, the proliferation of its editions into the later Elizabethan era left a legacy for succeeding poets to imitate, exploit and comment upon well into the next century. Its beneficiaries included members of the aristocratic elite (such as Philip Sidney), of the urban merchant and broadly professional population (such as Edmund Spenser) and of a rising class of professional writers, poets and dramatists (such as Michael Drayton and William Shakespeare).

Philip Sidney and Edmund Spenser

Sidney's *Defence of Poesy* (c. 1580) seems to embrace Tottel's estimate of Wyatt and Surrey, but with critical reservations and incisive commentary.[15] For example, it includes Surrey's lyrics (but not Wyatt's) in his pantheon of English poetry, crediting the former with 'many things tasting of a noble birth and worthy of a noble mind'.[16] His own *Astrophil and Stella* (c. 1581–82), however, reverses this judgement by echoing Wyatt's raw energy and wit with an occasional jab at Surrey's high-toned grace and polish. If Petrarchan swagger and panache had led to a bad end for both of them, then why not moralise the risks of their poetic endeavours? From Wyatt Sidney derives the comic self-disparagement of his literary alter ego, the love-stricken Astrophil. Like Petrarch's Laura, Sidney's Stella refers to a real woman, but in ways that are both more direct and less obvious. She was a daughter of the Earl of Essex, Penelope Devereux, to whom the poet had been engaged in 1576 when he was twenty-two years old and she was thirteen. Sidney reneged upon the marriage deal, probably to hold out for a yet more prestigious match but, as the Essex family's fortunes later rose, he came to regret his decision.[17] Sonnet 33 intimates as much as Astrophil complains: 'I might, unhappie word, o me, I might, / And then would not, or could not see my blisse: … / But to my selfe my selfe did give the blow'.[18] The consequences of the speaker's rash decision colour his persona.

Many, perhaps even most, of the 108 sonnets and ten songs in *Astrophil and Stella* may have originated in various stages of composition but, upon the engagement and marriage of his former fiancée to Lord Rich in 1581, Sidney reflected upon the cost of squandering his once-advantageous betrothal and he designed a narrative scheme to accommodate the older poems to his present misfortune. Like Wyatt and Surrey, he composed his sonnets not for printed publication or broad dissemination but for a coterie readership of family, friends, associates and acquaintances who knew him and his personal tribulations – a coterie whose reactions might well have been forgotten by the 1590s. This readership could laugh with him, not at him, as he recounts in his narrative sequence the missteps and reversals on his road to maturity, and the wiser among them could admire his capacity for witty self-criticism and his potential for growth.

A good example in *Astrophil and Stella* is sonnet 47, 'What, have I thus betrayed my libertie', a poem that clearly echoes Petrarch's sonnet 97, 'Ahi bella libertà, come tu m'ài, / Partendoti da me' ('Ah sweet liberty, how by departing from me'). Petrarch's Italian commentators had focused upon the lover's moral life in this poem, evoking St Paul's 2 Corinthians 3:17, 'Where is the spirit of God, there is liberty'.[19] Gesualdo imparts a Neoplatonic turn to his discussion in which Laura's 'heavenly beauty' ('beltà celeste') ought to raise those who behold her 'to the status of a Platonic and true lover' ('al Platonico & al vero amante', fol. CXXIXr), while Castelvetro adds that, like the mythic Actaeon, mere mortals 'do not behold a divine being without being harmed' ('non vegga cosa diuina senza danno') (184). Astrophil, however, lacks the emotional discipline and maturity to prevent liberty from collapsing into licence, and the outcome is actually funny as his anxieties leach out in plain view. Defiantly questioning his class-based privileges, he raises self-doubt about his rank and status: 'Can those black beames such burning markes engrave / In my free side? Or am I borne a slave, / Whose necke becomes such yoke of tyranny?' Summoning virtue in the sestet, 'Vertue, awake!', Astrophil rouses himself to reject Stella's seductive allure. At that very moment, his recalcitrant beloved appears before him. On the verge of renouncing her, he suddenly halts. In a comic reversal, one glimpse of her eyes paralyses him: 'Let her go. Soft, but here she comes. Go to, / Unkind, I love you not: O me, that eye / Doth make my heart give to my tongue the lie.' In this unconscious, involuntary moment of weakness, Astrophil ends up acting foolishly.

A striking example of Sidney's contrastive use of Petrarch is sonnet 71, 'Who will in fairest booke of Nature know', with its direct echo from Petrarch's sonnet 248, 'Chi vuol veder quantunque pò Natura' ('Whoever wishes to see how much Nature'). Italian commentators such as Vellutello had responded to Petrarch's sonnet as a self-reflective commentary upon the writer's art and craft. For Vellutello, readers 'would judge his rhymes about her to be deaf and dumb by comparison with her excellence' ('giudicherranno le rime fatte nelle sue lodi da lui, rispetto alla eccellentia di lei, esser mute e sorde', fol. 112v). Astrophil describes his readers as those cognisant of 'How Vertue may best lodg'd in beautie be', and he sets out to improve their understanding of 'those faire lines which true goodnesse show'. He nonetheless fails this critical test as he seriously misreads Petrarch. In the sestet Stella 'does strive all minds to move', but her impact on Astrophil disproves these claims: 'So while thy beauty draws the heart to love, / As fast thy virtue bends the heart to good: / But ah, Desire still cries, give me some food.' As the verse limps with the off-rhymes of *move/love* and *good/food*, the poem's formal effects undermine the speaker's ideal when he abandons it to his own desire.

Understood from this perspective, Sidney's poem evokes a strain of criticism pursued by commentaries on the *Rime sparse*. In discussing Petrarch's sonnet 248, Gesualdo points to the moral flaws of Petrarch's all too frail, all too human lover. In the poem's penultimate line, 'my wit [is] overcome by the excess of light' ('L'ingegno offeso dal soverchio lume'), the commentator compares Petrarch to 'nightbirds whose eyesight is assaulted by the bright splendour of the sun' ('augelli notturni, la cui vista é tanto offesa dal chiaro splendore del sole', fol. CCXCIIIIr). Astrophil veers in this direction when he figures reason as an 'inward' sun 'from whose light those nightbirds flie'. The avian trope, absent from Petrarch but echoing from Gesualdo's gloss, suggests that Sidney has read Gesualdo and appropriated this embellishment to expose Astrophil's purblind folly.

The unauthorised publication of *Astrophil and Stella* in 1591 prompted other poets to respond by disseminating their own sonnet collections, precipitating a sonnet craze. Samuel Daniel, tutor to Mary Sidney's children, might have assisted in pirating her brother's work (possibly in a misguided effort to please her) since twenty-eight of his own sonnets appeared in the volume. A year later he augmented these poems with twenty-seven others and published them as *Delia, … with the Complaint of Rosemond*. In a more complicated way, Edmund Spenser followed suit. His juvenile translations of Petrarch's canzone 323 and Du Bellay's *Songe* along with his apprenticeship translation of *The Ruines of Rome: by Bellay* reveal his early attraction to Petrarchism and the sonnet form. Upon the success of books 1 to 3 of *The Faerie Queene* in 1590, he published many of these early poems in a volume named *Complaints* in 1591, possibly to sustain his authorial visibility until issuing the second instalment of his allegorical romance epic five years later. In the mid-1580s he had evidently tried his hand at writing love sonnets, but he withheld them from print at that time.[20] In 1595 he published a cycle of love sonnets with the title *Amoretti* with perhaps some of them deploying his earlier efforts at sonnet writing. To them he added his marriage poem *Epithalamion* as a counter to and commentary upon English Petrarchism.

Spenser's *Amoretti* aims at an emergent and diverse readership, a new and upwardly-mobile book-buying public drawn from the mercantile and professional population of an urban middle class.[21] To all intents marketed for highly literate and sophisticated Londoners, as well as for gentry elites who gathered there, it aimed well beyond the landholding aristocracy. *Amoretti* designs a radically new narrative in which a formerly incautious lover in the Sidneian mode accedes to a reciprocal and now companionate marriage with his beloved.[22] As a commentary upon earlier amatory poetry, the first part of the sequence registers all the preferences of an old-style Petrarchan lover bent upon sexual gratification. The beloved's virtue soon tempers his egotism, even as his ardour arouses her interest without compromising her integrity. Whereas Sidney invited a coterie readership to laugh with him and not at him in depicting his alter-ego Astrophil, Spenser pays his more diverse but no less sophisticated readership the compliment of being able to recognise the difference between what he says and what he leaves unsaid in an evolving relationship with his beloved.

The speaker of the *Amoretti*'s early sonnets regards love as a recreational sport. Sonnet 13, 'In that proud port, which her so goodly graceth', endows her with a conjunction of virtues that controls his impulses and solicits moderation: 'Whiles her faire face she reares up to the skie: / and to the ground her eie lids low embaseth, / most goodly temperature ye may descry, / Myld humblesse mixt with awfull majesty.'[23] The poem's model is Petrarch's sonnet 215, 'In nobil sangue vita humile et queta' ('In noble blood a humble and quiet life'), which attributes to Laura a harmonious conjunction of opposing qualities, a 'tempering' of physical beauty with moral virtue. Petrarch's commentator Fausto da Longiano forecasts Spenser's 'goodly temperature' when he concludes that Laura is a miracle of nature: '[Petrarch] terms it a miracle of nature that two opposing qualities are joined in one body with such marvelous tempering' ('Chiama miracolo di natura, due nimiche esser giunte in vn corpo con si mirabil tempre', fol. 80v). Likewise with Spenser's beloved, flesh unites with spirit to compound perfection and motivates the speaker to mend his worldly ways.

Sonnet 58, 'Weake is th'assurance that weake flesh reposeth', announces a decisive turning point. As though to signal a disruption, a cryptic headnote prefaces the text as a commentary upon not only the poem but also the course of English Petrarchism: 'By her that is most assured to her selfe'. If we add to the phrase a participle such as 'spoken' or 'argued', it would seem that this poem records the beloved's voice as she rebukes her lover for his misguided importuning. The following poem, sonnet 59, 'Thrise happie she, that is so well assured', ends with the lover's affirmation: 'But he most happy who such one loves best'. It appears, then, that the two poems constitute a dialogue in which first the beloved speaks and then the lover replies. This intrusion of the beloved's voice two-thirds of the way through the *Amoretti* adverts to Petrarch's sonnet 250 at nearly the same point in the *Rime sparse* when Laura speaks to her lover: 'Do not hope ever to see me on earth' ('Non sperar di vedermi in terra mai', sonnet 250). In Petrarch's poem, the beloved's words foreshadow her death. In Spenser's, they foreshadow the lover's moral conversion. She would speak to admonish him against valuing her for a physical beauty that 'devouring time' and 'changeful chance' will ravage. With her concluding question, 'Why then doe ye proud fayre, misdeeme so farre', she avows her love for the frustrated and as yet unrequited lover, to whom she protests that he is 'most assured' of her fidelity.

Throughout the sequence, Spenser's approach to the speaker's redemption is oblique. The substantial reprinting of sonnet 35, 'My hungry eyes, through greedy covetize', as sonnet 83 in the 1595 edition of *Amoretti* provides an example. Aside from some altered punctuation, the only difference between the two texts is the revision of 'having' in line 6 to 'seeing' in sonnet 83. Whether accidental or deliberate, the reprinting prompts a multivalent reading as the poem's meaning shifts in each context. We could view the revision – if deliberate – as Spenser's self-commentary upon the original poem, upon its position in the sequence, and even upon the status of English Petrarchism. In sonnet 35, the speaker seems to emphasise his restless emotion; in sonnet 83 he shifts to a high-minded concern with the beloved's transcendent beauty.

> My hungry eyes, through greedy covetize
>   Still to behold the object of theyr payne:
>   With no contentment can themselves suffize, ...
> For lacking it, they cannot lyfe sustayne,
>   And seeing it [sonnet 35: having it], they gaze on it the more.

In sonnet 83, the substitution of 'seeing' for 'having' cancels some of the speaker's 'hungry', even 'greedy', self-regard. In reference to sensory perception, the active participle 'seeing' directs the action toward the object that the speaker sees, the beloved herself, beyond his own egotistical 'gratification'. *Mutatis mutandis*, in the earlier poem his eyes turn resolutely inward, as the ensuing comparison between his own eyes and those of Narcissus implies: 'In their amazement like Narcissus vaine / whose eyes him starv'd: so plenty makes me poore'.

An analogue to this poem is Petrarch's sonnet 45, 'Il mio adversario in cui veder solete / gli occhi vostri ch'Amore e 'l ciel honora' ('My adversary in whom you are wont to see your eyes, which Love and Heaven honour'). The 'adversary' is Laura's mirror, which displaces her gaze from the speaker to herself. Bernardino Daniello reads the figure as an emblem of self-regard associated with female narcissism: 'For women take counsel with the mirror' ('Che le donne si consigliano con lo specchio', fol. 35r). A contrasting commentary by Gesualdo identifies Laura's reflected image with the beginning of her self-awareness. She comes to understand that physical beauty is only a shadow of ideal beauty, and this understanding enables her to grow in virtue: 'Whereas self-knowledge is the beginning of knowledge and virtue, so loving oneself is a cause of eternal salvation' ('Onde come il conoscer se stesso è il principio di savere e di virtute, così l'amare se stesso è cagione d'eterna salute', fol. LXIIv). These readings stand at issue when Spenser's sonnet 35 is repeated as his sonnet 83. It is as though the second version of the poem were commenting on and competing with its first version as well as with earlier examples of English Petrarchism just as Petrarch's commentators had done by offering different interpretations of his poems in competition with one another.

Michael Drayton and William Shakespeare

One year before Spenser published his *Amoretti*, Michael Drayton published his first sonnet collection, *Ideas Mirrour* (1594). A year earlier he had published *Idea, the Shepheards Garland*, a collection of eclogues in homage to and commentary upon the poetry of Sidney's *Arcadia* and Spenser's *Shepheardes Calender*. Drayton's sonnets pay homage to Sidney's *Astrophil and Stella* and Samuel Daniel's *Delia*. His prefatory sonnet, for example, proclaims its debt to Sidney by lifting from the latter's sonnet 71 'I am no Pickpurse of anothers wit'.[24] Drayton's later references to Sidney and Daniel prove more subtle and nuanced. Sonnet 28 of *Ideas Mirrour*, for example, weaves together an echo ('Some wits there be, which lyke my method well') from sonnet 15 of *Astrophil and Stella*, where Sidney mocks 'dictionary's method' of alliteration, with a contrasting echo ('And say my verse runnes in a lofty vayne') from sonnet 4 of *Delia*, where Daniel resorts to 'humble accent'. Commenting upon both predecessors' espousals of authenticity, Drayton boasts 'Who writes my Mistres praise, can never write amisse' and steps up his claim by expanding the line to hexameter. In a late revision for his collected *Poems* (1619, as sonnet 42), he reverts to a modest pentameter, 'Writing her prayse, I cannot write amisse', and removes any hint of wilful bluster.

Drayton proved to be an inveterate reviser of his own work, issuing and reissuing his poems with additions, deletions and emendations in five subsequent editions (1599, 1600, 1602, 1605, 1619). His broadening field of reference came to include Spenser's *Amoretti* in his 1599 edition, where sonnet 44, 'Whilst thus my Pen strives to eternize thee', recaptures Spenser's eternising motif from his sonnet 75, 'My verse your vertues rare shall eternize'. Drayton's 1619 edition also includes Shakespeare among its models, notably (though speculatively) in its most celebrated poem, sonnet 61 'Since there's no helpe, Come let us kisse and part, / Nay, I have done: You get no more of Me', which can be seen as a rejoinder to Shakespeare's 'slave' sonnets 57–8 and as a commentary upon Shakespeare's renunciation sonnet 87. Commentary here renders its judgement both ways *in utramque partem* as a reversal of servitude and an appropriation of initiative.

In 1609, ten years before Drayton's final version of *Idea*, Shakespeare's *Sonnets* emerged in print after a long gestation in manuscript.[25] Its earliest poems are sonnets 127–54 which concern the speaker's adulterous relationship with a Dark Lady, and seem to have been composed in a spirit of parody at the height of the sonnet craze during the early 1590s. Sonnets 104–26 reflect social currents around the turn of the century with some topical references to events in 1603–4. Sonnets 1–103 largely concern the speaker's association with a self-centred Young Man, and they likely belong to a period between 1594 and 1596 with subsequent revisions in the first sixty or so poems.[26]

An example from the Dark Lady group is sonnet 128 ('How oft, when thou my music music play'st').[27] The poem depicts the belover's performance on a spinet-like keyboard, 'that blessed wood whose motion sounds / With thy sweet fingers', which the speaker regards with a mixture of annoyance and jealousy. An Elizabethan precedent is sonnet 54 of Daniel's *Delia* (1592), 'Like as the Lute that ioyes or els dislikes'.[28] Daniel's poem depicts the profound effect of the beloved's lute-playing upon an attentive speaker: 'O happie ground that makes the musique such, / And blessed hand that giues so sweete a tuch'. Its Italian analogue is Petrarch's sonnet 167, 'Quando Amor i belli occhi a terra inclina' ('When Love bends her lovely eyes to the ground'). Here Cupid acts as a maestro who directs a musical performance by Laura which ravishes the speaker: 'I feel my heart sweetly stolen away' ('Sento far del mio cor dolce rapina'). For Gesualdo, the music 'restrains his great desire' ('affrena il gran desir', fol. CCXVIIIr). For Bernardino Daniello, Laura's music echoes the harmony of the cosmos in which, according to Plato's myth of Er in book 10 of his *Republic*, each note contributes to 'a song in praise of the deities' (un canto in lode de gli Dei, fol. 98v).

Shakespeare's sonnet comments upon Daniel's poem by bringing the beloved's music back down to earth. Addressing the Dark Lady as 'my music', the speaker portrays her as a creator of dissonant and discordant notes, inducing the speaker's discomfort with 'The wiry concord that mine ear confounds'. He hyperbolises the proximity of the Lady's fingers to the wooden keyboard – 'How oft ... / Do I envy those jacks that nimble leap / To kiss the tender inward of thy hand' – and as he jumps from one verse to the next, the enjambment of 'leap / To kiss' mimics his distracted humour. Measured against Daniel's poem and commentaries on Petrarch's analogue, the Dark Lady's digital promiscuity disturbs him 'Whilst my poor lips, which should that harvest reap, / At the wood's boldness by thee blushing stand'. The contact of her fingers with the keyboard arouses the speaker's jealousy and frustrates his sexual desire.

The tonalities of sonnets 1–126 prove more varied and complex. Petrarchan echoes there revert not to the *Rime sparse* nor to Italian commentaries on it but rather to precedents in English poetry and specifically to the poetry of Sidney and Spenser. Sonnet 17, 'Who will believe my verse in time to come', negotiates echoes from both poets in a complex form of commentary upon Elizabethan Petrarchism. The poem's opening lines and prevailing argument evoke Sidney's sonnet 71, examined above as Sidney's rewriting of Petrarch's sonnet 248. Astrophil's assessment of Stella's virtue through the act of 'reading [poetic] lines' generates in Shakespeare's poem the speaker's effort to 'write the beauty' of the Young Man's excellence 'in fresh [poetic] numbers'. So Shakespeare's sonnet argues that any reader might be pardoned for doubting his claim that 'Such heav'nly touches ne'er touched earthly faces'. The argument overturns Astrophil's diffidence about the effect of Stella's virtue upon him, which itself inverts Petrarch's argument that Laura brings forth virtue in everyone who encounters her. In this circuitous way Shakespeare registers Sidney's imitation of Petrarch's sonnet as a betrayal of it while presenting his own sonnet as a simulacrum of Petrarch's original, though with no guarantee that he had ever even read it.

In the same poem we find important echoes from Spenser. Sonnet 5 of Spenser's *Ruines of Rome* indirectly evokes Petrarch's sonnet 248 by translating Du Bellay's imitation of it in sonnet 5 of his *Les Antiquitez de Rome*: 'Who lists to see what ever nature, arte, / And heaven could doo, O *Rome*, thee let him see'.[29] Here the poet compares modern Rome to its ancient counterpart 'like a corpse drawne forth out of the tombe'. The line reverberates in Shakespeare's sonnet with the poet's comparison of his verse to the Young Man's qualities: 'It is but as a tomb / which hides your life'. Spenser's sonnet 32 in *Ruines* later turns to Rome's artefacts that endure 'not in paper writ'. The phrase reverberates in Shakespeare's sonnet with the speaker's reflection upon 'my papers, yellowed with their age'. The final injunction of Spenser's sonnet 32 in *Ruines* to 'Cease not to sounde these olde antiquities' emerges in Shakespeare's sonnet 17 with its derogation of the 'stretchèd meter of an ántique song', dismissively associated with 'a poet's rage'. We may perhaps find here a distant reference to Spenser's sonnet 69 in *Amoretti* whose speaker abandons poetic *furor* in favor of a carefully honed craftsmanship and skill, 'Gotten at last with labour and long toyle'.

Other examples of Shakespeare's debts to Spenser occur in the 'eternising' topos of sonnets 55, 60, 63–5 and 81. The first of these poems, 'Not marble, nor the gilded monument / Of princes shall outlive this pow'rful rhyme' (sonnet 55), announces this topic by expressing the speaker's confidence in his 'pow'rful rhyme' to guarantee the Young Man's immortality. The poem interweaves two classical antecedents, first from Horace's ode 3.30 ('I have made a monument more durable than bronze' ('Exegi monumentum aere perennius')), and the second from the conclusion of Ovid's *Metamorphoses* (15.871–9), directly echoing Arthur Golding's 1567 translation of these lines.[30] Another Ovidian echo marks the end of its second quatrain, 'Nor Mars his sword, nor war's quick fire shall burn / The living record of your memory'. While 'sword' and 'fire' call up Golding's translation of Ovid in which 'Nor sword, nor fyre … / Are able too abolish quyght' (15.985–6), the phrasing 'Mars his sword' evokes Spenser's archaising syntax. The 'living record of your memory' likewise summons the eternising power of verse from sonnet 32 of Spenser's *Ruines of Rome*: 'Hope ye my verses that posteritie / Of age ensuing shall you ever read'.

I will close by returning to Philip Sidney as Shakespeare himself returned to Sidney across the arc of his poetic career. The group of sonnets 78–89 about the speaker's literary rivals situates the poet in a literary milieu that he interrogates. In relation to English Petrarchism, sonnet 76 prefaces that group with a reflection of the speaker's regard for Sidney. The second half of its first quatrain, 'Why with the time do I not glance aside / To new-found methods and to compounds strange', recalls Astrophil's indictment of 'dainty wits' and 'Pindar's apes' who 'with strange similes enrich each line' (*Astrophil and Stella*, sonnet 3). Astrophil's criticism aims at the style of Ronsard, master of extravagant neologisms and compound word-formations, a feature that Shakespeare's speaker imitates in his own compound-formation of 'new-found methods', which glances at Astrophil's criticism of 'new-found tropes' (sonnet 3). Astrophil denounces *Pléiade*-style Petrarchism only to adopt his own version of it without quite acknowledging the model that it refers to.

Similar evasions haunt Shakespeare's second quatrain, which begins 'Why write I still all one, ever the same, / And keep invention in a noted weed'. Short of repeating the same formulaic diction, it might seem impossible for any poet to write 'all one, ever the same' as Astrophil professes to do at the end of his sonnet 90, 'Since all my words thy beauty doth endite'. Yet Shakespeare's phrase 'noted weed' limits the possibility of endless iteration. As a distinctive ('noted') garment and a 'knotted weed', it refers to a crabbed style that the speaker has cultivated. Even the curious 'That every word doth almost fell my name' in the 1609 Quarto (whose ending most editors emend to 'tell my name') comments on this style. In relation to the garden metaphor implied by 'weed', the speaker's literary reputation ('my name') might seem a tender growth that his excrescent words 'fell' or strangle. The eccentricity of his verse can only 'tell' or reveal the author's identity in every turn of phrase, 'Showing their birth, and where they did proceed'. The protean, radically changeful style of *Sonnets* challenges the claim that it is 'all one, ever the same', by promoting multiple shifts of meaning within the poem.

It turns out, then, that as commentaries on the sonnets of Sidney and Spenser, the sonnets of Shakespeare and, to a lesser extent, Drayton re-enact the kinds of critical commentaries on Petrarchan sonnets that illustrious predecessors had attempted. Sidney had approached Petrarchism as a courtly phenomenon spurred by the earlier achievements of Wyatt and Surrey, and he designed the narrative frame of *Astrophil and Stella* as an exemplary tale about the lover's fecklessness and narcissism. Spenser approached Petrarchism from an urban, mercantile, gentry and middle-class perspective by designing his narrative frame for *Amoretti* with an ageing widower's discovery of companionate marriage as an antidote to courtly excesses. In their contrastive ways both Sidney and Spenser reflect upon the courtly and anti-courtly attitudes articulated by Wyatt and Surrey in their translations of Petrarch. The latter in turn had confronted Petrarch in dialogue with at least some Italian commentaries on the *Rime sparse*. Coming at the end of a literary cycle obsessed with Petrarchism, Drayton and Shakespeare engaged their skills as poets to reflect upon the English development and variation of this poetic mode. In their hands poetry and poetic commentary became one.

Notes

1 Italian editions with commentaries to which I will refer and quote from are A. Vellutello, *Le volgare opera del Petrarcha con la espositione di Alessandro Vellutello da Lucca* (Venice: Giovanni Antonio Nicolini da Sabbio e Fratelli, 1525); S. Fausto da Longiano, *Il Petrarcha col commento di M. Sebastiano Fausto da Longiano* (Venice: Francesco di Alessandro Bindoni e Mapheo Pasini, 1532); G.A. Gesualdo, *Il Petrarcha colla spositione di Misser Giovanni Andrea Gesualdo* (Venice: Giovanni Antonio Nicolini e Fratelli da Sabbio, 1533); B. Daniello, *Sonetti canzoni e triomphi di M. Francesco Petrarca, con la*

spositione di Bernardino Daniello da Lucca (Venice: Pietro e Gianmaria Nicolini da Sabbio e Fratelli, 1549); and L. Castelvetro, *Le rime del Petrarca brevemente sposte per Lodouico Castelvetro* (Basel: Pietro de Sedabonis, 1582), p. 184. For an account of these major commentaries, see W.J. Kennedy, *Authorizing Petrarch* (Ithaca, London: Cornell University Press, 1994), pp. 25–113. Subsequent quotations from Petrarch refer to *Canzoniere*, ed. M. Santagata (Milan: Mondadori, 3rd edn, 2008), with translations from R.M. Durling, *Petrarch's Lyric Poems* (Cambridge, MA: Harvard University Press, 1976).

2 *Cornell University Library Catalogue of the Petrarch Collection Bequeathed by Willard Fiske*, compiled by Mary Fowler (London: Oxford University Press, 1916), pp. 71–111.

3 E.S. Leedham-Greene (ed.), *Books in Cambridge Inventories: Book Lists from the Vice-Chancellor's Court Probate Inventories in the Tudor and Stuart Periods*, 2 vols (Cambridge: Cambridge University Press, 1986), vol. 1, pp. 100 and 120.

4 J. Thomas, *The First Printed Catalogue of the Bodleian Library, 1605: A Facsimile* (Oxford: Clarendon Press, 1986), p. 368.

5 J.L. Black, W.R. Bowen and G. Warkentin, *The Library of the Sidneys of Penshurst Place, circa 1665* (Toronto: University of Toronto Press, 2013), p. 280.

6 V. Stern, *Gabriel Harvey: His Life, Marginalia, and Library* (Oxford: Clarendon Press; New York: Oxford University Press, 1979), pp. 193–225; and R.J. Fehrenbach and E.S. Leedham-Green, eds, *Private Libraries in Renaissance England: A Collection and Catalogue of Tudor and Early Stuart Book Lists*, 5 vols (Tempe: Medieval and Early Renaissance Texts and Studies, 1992–98).

7 See the facsimile reprint of *Plain Pathway* by R.C. Alston (Menston: Scolar Press, 1968) and of *Principal Rules* by R.C. Alston (Menston: Scolar Press, 1968). For a survey of such foreign language manuals, see my '"Les langues des hommes sont pleines de tromperies": Shakespeare, French Poetry, and Alien Tongues', in Z. Lesser and B.S. Robinson (eds), *Textual Conversations in the Renaissance* (Aldershot: Ashgate Press, 2006), pp. 91–111.

8 See the facsimile reprint of *Second Frutes*, with an introduction by R.C. Simonini Jr (Gainesville: Scholars' Facsimiles and Reprints, 1953). For Florio's contribution to linguistic study, see M. Wyatt, *The Italian Encounter with Tudor England: A Cultural Politics of Translation* (Cambridge: Cambridge University Press, 2005), pp. 157–204.

9 See the facsimile reprint of *New World*, with an introduction by R.C. Alston (Menston: Scolar Press, 1968), sigs ¶5v–¶6v.

10 Gascoigne's autographed title page of a 1553 reprint appears as the frontispiece of C.T. Prouty, *George Gascoigne: Elizabethan Courtier, Soldier, and Poet* (New York: Columbia University Press, 1942). G.W. Pigman III (ed.), *A Hundred Sundrie Flowres* (Oxford: Clarendon Press, 2000), reports that the volume, now in the library of Loyola University, Chicago, shows no sign of active use (see note p. 465).

11 T. Watson, *The Hekatompathia*, with an introduction by S.K. Heninger (Gainesville: Scholars' Facsimiles and Reprints, 1964).

12 Now in the Folger Library; see C. Martin, 'Retrieving Jonson's Petrarch', *Shakespeare Quarterly*, 45 (1994), 89–92. As mentioned above, this reprint presents no commentary on the Italian poetry; my inspection of the Folger copy revealed that it lacks many folio leaves and offers no definite evidence of Jonson's personal annotation.

13 Quotations from Wyatt and Surrey refer to their first publication in *Tottel's Miscellany*, ed. A. Holton and T. MacFaul (London: Penguin Books, 2011) as poems 42 and 6 respectively.

14 See the incisive study of its contributors and readership by J.C. Warner, *The Making and Marketing of Tottel's Miscellany, 1557* (Burlington: Ashgate, 2011).

15 For a de-idealising view of Sidney's poetics, see C. Bates, *On Not Defending Poetry: Defence and Indefensibility in Sidney's 'Defence of Poesy'* (Oxford: Oxford University Press, 2017). The following paragraphs are adapted from the chapter on Sidney in my *The Site of Petrarchism: Early Modern National Sentiment in Italy, France, and England* (Baltimore, London: Johns Hopkins University Press, 2003), pp. 163–249.

16 Quotation from *The Miscellaneous Prose of Sir Philip Sidney*, ed. J. van Dorsten and K. Duncan-Jones (Oxford: Clarendon Press, 1973), p. 112.

17 See K. Duncan-Jones, *Sir Philip Sidney: Courtier Poet* (New Haven: Yale University Press, 1991), pp. 230–41.

18 Quotations refer to *The Poems of Sir Philip Sidney*, ed. W.A. Ringler (Oxford: Clarendon Press, 1962).

19 Quotation from *The Geneva Bible: A Facsimile of the 1560 Edition*, ed. L.E. Berry (Madison: University of Wisconsin Press, 1969).

20 See A. Hadfield, *Edmund Spenser: A Life* (Oxford: Oxford University Press, 2012), pp. 240–2 and 313–20.

21 M. Murrin, *Trade and Romance* (Chicago: University of Chicago Press, 2014), pp. 207–25.
22 The following paragraphs are adapted from my chapter on Spenser in *Authorizing Petrarch*, pp. 195–280.
23 Quotations from *Amoretti* refer to *The Yale Edition of the Shorter Poems of Edmund Spenser*, ed. W. Oram, A. Dunlop *et al.* (New Haven: Yale University Press, 1989).
24 Quotations from Drayton refer to *Works*, ed. J.W. Hebbel, K. Tillotson and B. Newdigate, 5 vols (Oxford: Clarendon Press, 1931–41).
25 For dating, see A.K. Hieatt, C.W. Hieatt and A.L. Prescott, 'When Did Shakespeare Write *Sonnets* 1609?', *Studies in Philology*, 88 (1991), 69–109, and the succinct account in W. Shakespeare, *Complete Sonnets and Poems*, ed. C. Burrow, The Oxford Shakespeare (Oxford: Oxford University Press, 2002), pp. 103–11. For dramatic modes of poetry represented in them, see R. Lyne, *Shakespeare, Rhetoric, and Cognition* (Cambridge: Cambridge University Press, 2011), pp. 207–20, and B. Boyd, *Why Lyrics Last: Evolution, Cognition, and Shakespeare's Sonnets* (Cambridge, MA: Harvard University Press, 2012); for dramatic situations framing their narrative, see N. Rudenstine, *Ideas of Order: A Close Reading of Shakespeare's Sonnets* (New York: Farrar, Straus and Giroux, 2014).
26 The following paragraphs are adapted from the chapter on Shakespeare in my *Petrarchism at Work: Contextual Economies in the Age of Shakespeare* (Ithaca, London: Cornell University Press, 2016), pp. 219–312. For the attraction of Shakespeare's sonnets to elite literary coteries, see C.S. Clegg, *Shakespeare's Reading Audiences* (Cambridge: Cambridge University Press, 2017), pp. 22–50.
27 Quotations from *Sonnets* refer to *Shakespeare's Sonnets*, edited with analytic commentary by S. Booth (New Haven: Yale University Press, 1977).
28 Daniel lightly revised the poem for his *Works* in 1601, where it retains the same number from its previous printing; quoted from Daniel, *Poems*, ed. A.C. Sprague (Cambridge, MA: Harvard University Press, 1930), where it appears as number 47.
29 For the influence of *Ruines* on Shakespeare, see A.L. Prescott, 'Du Bellay and Shakespeare's Sonnets', in *The Oxford Handbook of Shakespeare's Poetry*, ed. J.F.S. Post (Oxford: Oxford University Press, 2013), pp. 134–50.
30 See S. Booth's endnote on the poem's sources, *Shakespeare's Sonnets*, pp. 227–30.

2

Early modern theories of the sonnet: accounts of the quatorzain in Italy, France and England in the second half of the sixteenth century

Carlo Alberto Girotto, Jean-Charles Monferran, Rémi Vuillemin

Introduction

According to Stephen Clucas, the last decades of the sixteenth century in England witnessed 'a compressed reception of the Petrarchan tradition':[1] poets, including sonneteers, were inspired by Petrarch, by his Italian and French imitators and, to a large extent, by the imitators of those imitators. This sense of temporal compression also conveys a sense of temporal succession: the sonnet, an Italian form, moved north in the course of the sixteenth century, first to France, then to England.[2] Such a perspective on the history of the sonnet is undoubtedly accurate, but it might also be misleading. Works on cultural transfers and exchanges have shown that the movements of texts and literary forms, and the translations between languages and cultures in the sixteenth century were intense but also selective, and submitted to complex cultural and political tensions.[3] The sonnet did travel north, but through a number of appropriations and transformations. The fact that it came from Italy meant that it had to be adapted to new backgrounds, in which its Italian identity could be put forward, exploited, downplayed or erased.

This makes particular sense in a period that saw the development of a vision of vernacular languages as poetically worthy, and of subsequent attempts to determine a national canon, as attested by such major texts as Bembo's *Prose della volgar lingua* (1525), Du Bellay's *La Deffence et illustration de la langue françoyse* (1549) in France and the preface to *Songes and Sonettes, written by the right honourable Lorde Henry Haward late Earle of Surrey, and others* (a volume also known, and which will be here referred to, as *Tottel's Miscellany*) in England.[4] Local languages were shaped and redefined by literary models; those models often were the writings of classical authors, but they could also be the works of prestigious foreign poets like Petrarch, Ariosto or Sannazaro. To a large extent, the sonnet was part and parcel of that movement, and, despite inevitable temporal discrepancies, was in full bloom in the second half of the century in the three countries. The peak of the sonnet seems to have been short-lived in England, where it thrived in the 1580s and 1590s and declined in the seventeenth century, especially after the 1630s.[5] It was longer in France, starting in the 1540s and 1550s and retaining some cultural significance partly thanks to the neo-Petrarchan revival in the last decades of the century, before waning after

1630, when Ronsard was no longer seen as a worthy poetic model. In Italy, by contrast, the sonnet maintained to a large extent its cultural centrality by undergoing a renewal at the turn of the century under the aegis of Marino. The second half of the sixteenth century was therefore a period when the sonnet triumphed in the three cultures.

Interestingly, it was also an age of intense theoretical reflection on poetry. Theory is an effort to codify and define the boundaries of poetry and of poetic forms, but it is also an indication of the reception of certain poetic forms, especially in the comparative perspective this chapter adopts. It can give insight into the reception of the sonnet, the context in which it gained cultural significance and what issues were raised by the translation, imitation and appropriation of the quatorzain. That is why it will be relevant here to focus on each national theoretical appropriation of the sonnet one after the other. As far as we have been able to trace, no work on the theory of the sonnet in the three countries has been written; though the question is rather well-documented for Italy and France, it is not for England – and for very good reasons, as we will see. Although the main focus of the following pages will be poetic theory, some reminders will be given about the sonnet, its history and its reception in each country. We hope this will contribute to uncovering the specificities of the English sonnet and its reception, and that it will allow us better to situate it within European literature as a whole.

Theories and practice of the Italian Renaissance sonnet – Carlo Alberto Girotto[6]

According to a long tradition, the sonnet is closely related to the origins of Italian literature, as it was allegedly 'invented' by Giacomo da Lentini in the second part of the twelfth century. Thanks to its regular structure – fourteen hendecasyllables organised into two stanzas of four lines (*quartina*) and two of three lines (*terzina*), with some fixed patterns of rhymes – it quickly became one of the most esteemed forms in Italian literature, also becoming with the *canzone* the most frequent one in the Italian lyric.[7] If one excludes the creation of the 'tailed sonnet' (*sonetto caudato*) – a sonnet followed by one or more stanzas of two or three lines, the first of which is normally a *settenario*, with strong comic undertones – only occasional innovations affected this form along the centuries.[8] Its structural regularity and its adaptability to a variety of themes probably contributed to its large diffusion.

Curiously enough, only a few texts give a prescriptive model of what a sonnet is, or in which way(s) it should be built and employed, and the most relevant ones – those of Francesco da Barberino and Antonio da Tempo – date back to the medieval period. Such a lack is mostly evident during the Renaissance period, which is one of the most flourishing ones for the sonnet: few treatises deal exclusively with this form, since a large part of the prescriptive texts consider, more generally, the different poetical forms of the Italian literary tradition. Actually, as I shall show, the theoretical debate seems to be closely related to contemporary practice: in this sense, in order to understand the issues related to the sonnet, it may be worth considering the Italian sixteenth-century milieu and the different voices that steered the evolutions of the form.

The sonnet within the Italian tradition: Bembo and Trissino

As some scholars have proposed, Petrarch's *Canzoniere* is probably the most sophisticated heir of a large tradition of textual groupings, in which the sonnet, the simplest and most compact unit, could be repeated *ad libitum* in a coherent series.[9] For sure, Petrarch and his *Canzoniere*, whose literary importance spread quickly in Italy and later in Europe, gave the sonnet undeniable prominence during the late medieval period and the Renaissance. During the Italian Quattrocento it enjoyed great success both in the productions of courtiers, such as in Matteo Maria Boiardo's *Amorum libri tres*, largely composed of sonnets, and in more tentative experiments, such as the nonsense sonnets of Burchiello, where the 'tailed' sonnet is the most frequent form.[10]

It is nevertheless assumed that the potential of the sonnet form was adequately expressed by poets (and discussed by theorists) only from the very end of the fifteenth century onwards and was carried on in the following decades.[11] In this period of cultural magnificence, the Italian poetic tradition was reread and reinterpreted, often underlining the role of three major authors – Dante, Petrarch and Boccaccio – and the genres they carried out. Among other things, the critical debate considered how to construct a lyric collection and how to confront the literary tradition. Pietro Bembo's *Prose della volgar lingua*, a treatise first published in 1525, is a paradigmatic text of this period, usually regarded as the first prescriptive text of Italian literature. A poet and a cardinal, Bembo created in this dialogue a literary canon that would stand for several centuries: Petrarch and Boccaccio are designed as linguistic and stylistic models in poetry and in prose.[12] In the second book of the *Prose*, in a part devoted to the metrical forms accepted in the Italian tradition, Bembo also devotes some remarks to the sonnet, recalling that 'the number of lines in the sonnets is fixed, as well as part of the rhymes'. If only a few modifications can be made in the structure of the sonnet nevertheless a certain freedom is given to those who want to write a sonnet: according to Bembo, 'in determining the order of the rhymes and, for part of them, their number, the only certain rule is pleasure, according to what those few verses can contain'.[13] Pleasure means here variety, elegance, but also the respect of the general movement of the collection in which each poem is inscribed, following in this sense Petrarch's *Canzoniere*.

Bembo's *Prose* may be considered as the basis for high Renaissance Petrarchism: already widespread in a large part of the intellectual class, who used the cultural model of Petrarch – images, poetic vocabulary, recurrent schemes and situations – to convey the expressions of intimacy and soul, Petrarchism found in Bembo a crucial turning point, which invited scholars and poets to think on the different poetical genres and to systematise them. The sonnet was perceived as an essential element to this cultural phenomenon and, after Bembo, it found its place in the prescriptive treatises devoted to style and poetics.[14] Shortly after the *Prose*, Giovan Giorgio Trissino's *Poetica*, first published in 1529, gives in its fourth book a survey of the most important Italian poetic genres, starting from 'the most used one', the sonnet. Far more detailed than Bembo's presentation and somewhat pedantic, Trissino's work proposes a detailed analysis of the sonnet from a formal point of view: following the Provençal tradition, he remembers the division in *base* and *volta* for the two parts of the sonnet, and he recalls the metrical schemes of rhymes, reducing them to a few combinations. For Trissino, the shape of a good sonnet is closely related to literary canon and to the example of 'good authors' (i buoni autori) that gave a major contribution to the form – essentially Petrarch, Dante and Cino da Pistoia. After a few words about the *sonetti caudati*, which he calls *tornelli*, he adds: 'I shall not discuss things that were neglected by good authors, so I will leave them'.[15] Around 1530, in the early High Renaissance, the Italian sonnet was therefore perceived as an enclosed world, the meaning of which could be understood only by referring to the literary tradition.

Theory and practice: authors' collections and anthologies

The decade in which Bembo and Trissino wrote their treatises coincided with a flourishing season of poetic volumes. Normally, these collections do not give explicit clues on theoretical questions, but they show in practice how the poetic trends evolved along the years, and indicate a possible discrepancy between the Petrarchan model and the Cinquecento debate on poetry. Especially from 1530 on, the will to create a *canzoniere* that may surpass the Petrarchan one emerged among poets: new themes were proposed, and new structures were experimented with, in order to build complex yet deeply coherent collections. In this sense, as a brick of a bigger edifice, the sonnet was perceived as a fundamental element of the renewal of the book of poems (*libro di poesia*) of the High Renaissance.[16]

The compiling of printed editions played an important role in the affirmation of the sonnet form. Especially in the editions of lyric poetry published in the first years of the century, the most recurrent title was *Sonetti e canzoni*: if these terms underline the importance of the two forms within the Italian tradition, one may argue that the order of the two words stresses a sort of priority of the sonnet over the *canzone*. It also suggests the actual proportion between the two forms in each volume: among published and unpublished poem collections of the first Cinquecento, the ratio of sonnets is always higher than the ratio of *canzoni*. For the poets who lived in the period from the end of the fifteenth century to the middle of the sixteenth century, this preference for the sonnet seems to be a sort of evidence, as may be seen in published books (for instance Bernardo Tasso's *Libri degli amori*, 1531–37, or Luigi Alamanni's *Opere toscane*, 1532), in unpublished projects (Ludovico Ariosto's collection of poems, printed only after the death of the author and probably never completed) or in collections often updated by their authors, such as in Pietro Bembo's *Rime*, whose shape was reworked by the Prelate until his death in 1547.[17] But even when themes and patterns of the *Canzoniere* are found in those collections, the autonomy from the Petrarchan paradigm is suggested by the introduction of metrical variations, themes that were rather modern at the time, and a personal *dispositio* of the texts, often tied by internal cross-references.

Around 1540, the number of editions made up only of sonnets increased considerably, sometimes with exceptional results, as in Alessandro Piccolomini's *Cento sonetti* (1549), a poetic collection made up of one hundred sonnets.[18] Only a few words are used to explain this choice in the foreword: Piccolomini actually prefers to engage in a dialogue with Petrarch and the Italian poetic tradition by offering rhyming patterns seldom used in the *Canzoniere* and by broadening the themes of each text, thus reducing the space devoted to the love sonnet, and looking to Horace and the moral Latin tradition.[19]

A similar predilection for the sonnet form appeared in the same period in another production of the Italian Renaissance, the poetic anthologies of various authors ('di diversi autori'). Putting aside some 'archaeological' collections, such as the so-called *Giuntina delle rime antiche* (1527),[20] the first anthology of modern authors was published by Gabriel Giolito de' Ferrari in 1545 with the collaboration of Lodovico Domenichi.[21] As its long title suggests – *Rime diverse di molti eccellentissimi autori* – the most renowned poets of that period appeared in this volume: Vittoria Colonna, Giovanni Della Casa, Giovanni Guidiccioni, Benedetto Varchi, as well as some lesser-known authors.[22] This plural collection was immediately a huge success, and many similar volumes were published until the end of the century. In all these editions, the sonnet is predominant: the 1545 edition, for instance, contains 486 sonnets out of 539 poetical texts (i.e. 90.1 per cent), while the other important form of the Italian tradition, the *canzone*, counts only 3.1 per cent.[23] The Petrarchan model is often respected in the use of themes and metric patterns; but in many cases the use of the sonnet implies, again, a discussion and an attempt to follow alternative ways, finding in more recent authors – Giusto de' Conti, or Pietro Bembo, who incidentally opens the 1545 edition with seventeen sonnets – a reference for the modern form of the sonnet.[24] Even if they are not explicitly justified, the innovations proposed in mid-Cinquecento poetic practice looked for a way to affirm the potential of the sonnet form and to free it from the sometimes oppressive examples of the literary tradition.

The sonnet and modernity

Bembo's and Trissino's treatises, and the several poetic anthologies published in the central years of the century, may be considered as the poetic background to Antonio Minturno's *Arte poetica*, first published in 1563.[25] In the conventional shape of a dialogue, Minturno proposes his *summa* on the different types of poetic forms of Italian literature. The sonnet is discussed in book III, within a fictive dialogue between the poet Bernardino Rota and Minturno himself. The definition given through Rota's questions and Minturno's answers is clear: a sonnet is 'a grave and elegant composition made of words, with a harmonious pattern of rhymes, and a measure of syllables interlaced following a certain number of lines, defined by a certain order'. A sonnet shall not be confused with the epigram:

> the epigram is a part of epic poetry, and the sonnet a part of melic poetry, as is shown by the name itself. As from the sound [*suono*] we have the sonnet [*sonetto*], from the act of singing [*canto*] we have the odes [*canzone*]: actually the sound and the act of singing are the same thing. The one who invented this name just wanted to indicate a short and harmonious song. Even if the term is a diminutive, it does not denote a humble style – on the contrary, it implies harmony and prettiness, without which especially this composition is worth nothing. [...] In the epigram, one does not search for prettiness or harmony, but a sharp repartee or a sentence; in the sonnet, using selected words, elegantly and harmoniously interlaced and ordered, the reader seeks sometimes a grave

feeling, sometimes a sharp one, sometimes a pleasant one. In the epigram, the number of lines is not predetermined, even if, when you have more than two or four verses, one should speak about elegy. In the sonnet the confines are predetermined, and they must not be crossed; moreover, even if the subject of it can be reduced in few lines, it is not similar to the subject of the stanzas of an ode.[26]

According to Minturno, a sonnet is distinguished from an epigram by many elements: the different origins of the two texts (epic poetry versus melic poetry), their different purposes (sharpness versus 'harmony and prettiness'), their different forms (short text of two or more verses versus fixed form of fourteen verses). The nobleness of the sonnet is also underlined by the usual comparison with the ode (*canzone*): as Minturno remarks, even if the measure is necessarily different, the sonnet can deal with subjects treated in longer compositions. This is not fortuitous, since these two major forms of the lyric tradition share a common basis: 'as in an ode we narrate, we pray, we encourage, we admonish, we praise, we blame, we awake the affections of our soul, in a sonnet we do the same'.[27] Following Trisino, Minturno also recalls that the sonnet knew some evolutions from its origins: ancient and now old-fashioned shapes of the sonnet 'were abandoned by Petrarch and by other poets that after him were held in esteem: they lacked that harmony and that prettiness that a sonnet requires' – and that, we may add, the 'modern poets' sought.[28]

Minturno seems to have accepted the dichotomy between the example of 'good authors' and the exigence of a modern poetry; he also seems to have recognised the excellent results of some poets of his time. As a sort of take on the mid-century discussion, this also appears in other treatises published after the fine experience of the anthologies 'di vari autori'. A great part of Girolamo Ruscelli's treatise on the way of composing poetic texts, published in 1558–59, insisted for instance on some stylistic devices of the sonnet form, such as the practice of 'cutting the verse' (*spezzare il verso*), that is to say the creation of a complex syntax that surpasses the metrical limits of the verses, or those of the quatrains and the tercets. Considered by Ruscelli 'the most prominent nobleness of the style', this device is seen as typically modern, since it was introduced in the sonnet by Bembo and Giovanni Della Casa as a feature of the so-called *gravitas*.[29]

That the debate on the sonnet could also be a debate on the modern sonnet in the mature phase of Italian Renaissance seems to be proved by Torquato Tasso's dialogue *La cavaletta*, composed in 1585 and published in 1587.[30] Answering the questions of Orsina and Ercole Cavaletto, a couple after whom the dialogue was named, the *Forestiero Napoletano* – alias Tasso himself – declares that the sonnet does not require 'a low or humble style', contrary to what is still believed by some. Even if the 'tailed sonnets' clearly belong to the comic register, Tasso states that 'the sonnet, in all its shapes, is not meant to receive baseness and modesty'. On the contrary, even if the dimensions do not seem to allow it, the potential of a sonnet can compare to those of a *canzone*.[31] The topical comparison between the two forms is somehow different from what Minturno proposed some years earlier: Tasso is speaking here also as one of the most prolific authors of sonnets of the century. Deeply aware of the rich possibilities of the form, he also remembers those craftsmen of modern sonnets – Bembo, Della Casa, Bernardo Tasso – who used the sonnet to describe noble and even sublime situations. As happens to certain weeds 'that, thanks to farming, grow and pass to the nature of plants', the sixteenth-century sonnet has grown in importance and become more honourable thanks to the innovations proposed by poets, becoming something larger than a small poem.[32]

A noble and distinguished form, at the end of the Cinquecento the sonnet had an illustrious position in the Italian lyric tradition. But this 'Procrustean bed', as this form was often called, was also considered as one of the most difficult forms. According to Stefano Guazzo, the reasons for that were its small dimensions, the fixed number of verses, the pattern of rhymes, the obligation to introduce a good rhythm 'without adding useless words, [or] reducing the ideas in a manner that the sonnet could be weak or obscure': actually the 'excellence and magnificence' of the sonnet does not admit imperfect or worthless parts.[33] After Tasso's *Rime*, theorists also stress the necessity, which was already present in practice, to introduce in each sonnet a *concetto*, an idea that gives at the same time internal coherence and syntactic movement to the text.[34]

The elements we have traced here allowed the sonnet to maintain its predominance in the greatest part of the *canzonieri* published in the seventeenth century. Giovan Battista Marino's *Rime* (1602), the first great poetic collection of the Seicento, gave a peerless contribution to the success of the sonnet, considered as the real testing ground for each poet.[35] Decades later, this preeminence was to be remembered by Federigo Meninni, a poet closely related to Marino's experience, who stated in his *Ritratto del sonetto e della canzone* (1678) that the sonnet was still 'the most harmonious among all forms', that may guarantee a suitable form for 'heroic and noble subjects'.[36] Such a declaration may be considered as the natural privilege the sonnet also enjoyed for the following centuries in Italian literature.

The poetics of the sonnet in the French Renaissance: defining and classifying the sonnet[37] – Jean-Charles Monferran

In France, the sonnet acquired its canonical form immediately, or nearly so: a fourteen-line poem (never more) of two quatrains with identical rhyme schemes (usually enclosed rhymes) and one sestet with its own rhyme scheme; the sonnet was also isometrical and mostly composed of ten- or twelve-syllable lines.[38] As early as the 1550s, a number of discourses were produced by poets or by poetic theorists (often the same people) which laid the foundations for reflection on the poetic form, defined it and raised issues that would still be central in the late sixteenth century. The authors of poetic treatises written in the 1550s first defined the sonnet by insisting on its Italian origin, on its theme, on its rhyme scheme, on its relationship with music and on its internal organisation. Those features, which can be found in most of the French theoretical accounts of the sonnet, will be the main focus of the following pages – whose purpose is mostly to understand what was at stake in defining the sonnet in sixteenth-century France.

The politics of the sonnet: an Italianate early modernity

'Sonne moi ces beaux Sonnets, non moins docte, que plaisante Invention Italienne' (Du Bellay, 1549).[39] Like Du Bellay, French Renaissance theorists made a point of underlining the Italian ascendancy of the sonnet. Such insistence was not fortuitous: it allowed the new generation of poets to break from the French tradition and from poetic forms such as the *dizain* and the *rondeau* – despite their similarities with the sonnet.[40] The sonnet, as the incarnation of (Italian) poetic modernity, displayed the will to produce a new type of poetry opposed to the former local tradition – as French sonneteers often asserted emphatically.

The sonnet did not reach France in 1549, with Ronsard, Du Bellay and their circle, but more than ten years earlier, in 1536. For a few years, however, the sonnet remained largely unexplored. The translation of Petrarch's poems, of course, was an important feature of the first half of the French sixteenth century, but was not integrated within the French poetic tradition. Clément Marot, who is believed, along with Saint-Gelais, to have imported the sonnet into France, did not write more than ten of them, six being translations of poems from Petrarch's *Canzoniere*. The sonnet never became a prominent form in Marot's love poetry – he wrote epigrams, elegies and even *rondeaux* instead. It was Du Bellay who first wrote an original French *canzoniere* made up of sonnets, as the title of the collection indicates: *Cinquante sonnets à la louange de l'Olive* (1549).[41]

In sixteenth-century France, to write a sonnet was to be an explicit or implicit follower of Petrarch, the 'Prince of Poets' ('prince des Poètes Italiens, duquel l'archétype des Sonnets a été tiré', Sébillet, 1548).[42] The sonnet first rose to prominence through the practice of translation: after Marot, Jacques Peletier du Mans translated twelve sonnets by Petrarch (*Œuvres poétiques*, 1547), and Vasquin Philieul translated a large portion of Petrarch's collection (*La Laure d'Avignon*, 1548). Only then could Petrarch's sonnets start to be imitated rather than translated. As poetic theorists explain, to write a sonnet is to rewrite Petrarch (or his Italian imitators). With this theoretical and historical background in mind, it seems clear that Du Bellay's statement ('Your model for the sonnet therefore is Petrarch and several of the modern Italians') implies a hypertextual definition of the sonnet.[43]

For the poets and the poetic theorists of the new generation, each poetic form was defined according to formal and hypertextual criteria. The ode, for instance, was described as a stanzaic composition (a formal definition) and as a rewriting of classical lyric models such as Pindar and Horace (a hypertextual definition). Similarly, the sonnet was defined by a number of metrical and prosodic features as well as by the fact that it consisted in rewriting Petrarch's verses (or those of his Italian imitators) in French – appropriating the prestige of the model, and valorising both the model and the imitation thereof. Originally, therefore, the French sonnet had a threefold function: it announced a break from the native tradition, conjured up the figure of Petrarch and referred to its hypertexts.

The domination of the Petrarchan model was replicated in the structure of French *Canzonieri*, which were composed either of sonnets only (the quintessential form of Petrarchan and Petrarchist[44] poetry) or of a mixture of sonnets, *cansos*, sestinas, ballads and madrigals (a more Petrarchan structure, historically speaking). Such domination led rather quickly to parodies of Petrarchism, but also to the connection between the sonnet and *gravitas*,[45] and, almost immediately, between the sonnet and love. In 1555, Jacques Peletier, witnessing the blooming of sonnet collections devoted to praising ladies since the publishing of *L'Olive*, asserted that love was a defining feature of the sonnet:

> As far as I know, one can find, in our oldest memories of the sonnet, no more ancient origin than with the Italian poets: with whom it has always been frequent: and the most excellent of whom was Francis Petrarch: who composed a great number in honour of his lady Laura. We have all admired and imitated him, and not without good reasons: the great sweetness of the style, *the great aptitude for variation on one single Topic, and the vivid expression of love passions* that are found in his Works.[46]

Using a past tense ('nous l'avons tous admiré'), Peletier suggests that the future of the sonnet might lie not in Petrarchism[47] but rather in new directions.[48] As the sonnet's connection to Petrarchism became looser, its themes and sources grew wider, as testified by Pierre Laudun d'Aigaliers at the end of the century: 'The matter of the sonnet should be elevated, but today it is used for all kinds of subjects' (La matière du Sonnet devrait être grande, mais pour le jourd'huy on s'en sert en toutes choses).[49] The sonnet was not only used as a dedicatory or laudatory poem, or as part of love collections: it also became a tool of Christian and spiritual meditation, an instrument used to describe reality or a satirical poetic form. It seems, however, that love and Petrarchism remained prominent features of the sonnet.[50] Du Bellay's *Regrets* (1557), for instance, although it depicts Du Bellay's sojourn in Rome and satirises life in that city, can be understood as a parody of the *Canzoniere*: love in Rome is impossible – and each sonnet underlines in its own way such a reversal of perspective.

The poetics of the sonnet: the French appropriation

Surprisingly, when the sonnet crossed the Alps and reached France, it immediately received a widely shared distinct new form. As early as 1548, Sébillet, describing very minutely the rhyme scheme of the sonnet, declared that the sestet should ideally open with couplet rhymes. After describing the structure of the quatrains (abba abba), he moves on to the sestet: 'the last six lines can be diversely proportioned: but most often, the first two lines of the six are tuned in couplet rhymes'.[51] Despite admitting the principle of variation for the sestet, Sébillet thereby puts forward Marot's choice of a structure for the sonnet (abba abba cc deed).[52] Such a structure was never used by Italian poets, who privileged two distinct rhymes for the first two lines of the sestet (cdecde or cdedce or cdcdcd). Another rhyming structure, often attributed to Jacques Peletier du Mans (who used it repeatedly in his 1555 *L'Amour des Amours*), also emerged: it also started with couplet rhymes, which were followed by alternate rhymes (abba abba cc dede). The French sonnet was overwhelmingly based on those two rhyme schemes which were alien to Italian poetics.[53]

Of course, the above remarks are necessarily generalisations. They leave aside the first years of the French sonnet, in which poets experimented with new forms (including the Italian ones) before affirming a French specificity.[54] They also downplay Ronsard's role in shaping this formal history of poetry. It is his 1552 *Amours*, however, that imposed the restriction of rhyme schemes to only two possibilities in the French context, with the obvious domination of Marot's rhyme scheme (the first version of the collection included only twenty-one sonnets with ccdede sestets, and 183 with the ccdeed rhyme scheme). Ronsard's model then served as a technical norm. It is only after Ronsard's death and the waning of his influence that Peletier's rhyming scheme became used more regularly: while it was found in fewer than 10 per cent of poems before 1585, it grew in importance in the first decades of the seventeenth century, and became the prevalent form after 1630.[55] More generally, this history of the French sonnet shows that each national appropriation of the poetics of the sonnet left its mark on it, producing a new model. One might think, of course, of the English sonnet with its final couplet rhyme (abab cdcd efef gg),[56] a formal arrangement that neither the French nor the Italian traditions could accept:[57] each country seems to have produced its own sonnet form.

The restriction of the number of possible rhyming patterns was undoubtedly related (at least for Ronsard) to the wish to set the poems to music and to offer musicians more regularity. For that reason,[58] and for the first time in 1552 (*Amours*), Ronsard introduced the alternation between masculine and feminine rhymes in the sonnet, which in turn became a specifically French feature of the sonnet. This technical change had repercussions that were not merely technical: it did not only show a national specificity, but also underlined the sonnet's proximity with music and thereby addressed the issue of classification by including the sonnet in the lyric genre, a controversial and debated choice at the time. Beyond the question of alternate rhymes (which Peletier stands against, probably because for him the sonnet does not necessarily have to be sung),[59] it is the origin and the lyric quality of the sonnet that are discussed. Du Bellay seems to be on the same line as Ronsard when he asserts the proximity of the sonnet to the ode only.[60] Thomas Sébillet chooses another option, likening the sonnet to the epigram.[61] In his typology of poetic genres, chapter I, which focuses on the epigram, is logically followed by a second chapter on the sonnet, and neither of them is connected in any way to the lyric (chapter VI: 'Cantique, chant lyrique ou Ode ou chanson' (Hymn, lyric or ode or song)).[62] Peletier follows Sébillet and emphasises the proximity of the sonnet to the epigram. He first deals with the latter, then focuses on the former, but then moves on to the ode. The position of the sonnet in the taxonomy of genres is an indication of the hesitations of French Renaissance poetic theorists, who might see the sonnets as closer to the epigram than to the ode, as more visual than musical, or as more likely to be materialised in an inscription than to be sung.

The dialectics of the sonnet: a thinking and diversifying machine
The recurring analogy with the epigram in the treatises also has to do with a reflection on the inner workings of the sonnet and on the dynamics of the form. Defining the sonnet as a 'perfect epigram' (parfait épigramme), Sébillet implicitly envisages it as a pointed form organised by a logical tension – a feature of the epigram ('Give the epigram as much fluidity as you can and make sure the last two lines are pointed in conclusion: since in those is the value of the epigram').[63] The sonnet is indeed a pointed form that favours a discursive or linear progression, breaking from more

rounded French forms like the roundelay, the ballad or the *chant royal*, based on the return of the refrain. Peletier goes even further:

> Like the epigram, the sonnet must appear illustrious in its conclusion. But it must also be constructed, unfold progressively and consistently, resound with gravity in all its verses, and be nearly philosophical in its concepts. In other words, it must be as if made of two or three conclusions. For the poet will be acclaimed, who, in the middle of his poem, will satisfy the reader so that it seems to reach its ends: and will then start again, and crown his work with a successful conclusion that is worthy of the beauties of the middle.[64]

Starting from the idea that the sonnet is built on the success and ingenuity of its last lines, he perceives the sonnet as a dialectical form, or, to use Aragon's famous phrase, 'a thinking machine' (une machine à penser):[65] the sonnet must offer not just one but several 'conclusions' as it unfolds.[66] More than other theorists, Peletier insists on the balance to be found between the slow elaboration of successive steps and the final '*pointe*', and on a thought process that construes the sonnet as the research for a continuous '*pointe*'. This surprising reflection, as much that of a poet as that of a mathematician, somehow foreshadows those of other sonnet enthusiasts such as Baudelaire or Bonnefoy, who were also to see the sonnet and its constraints as instruments of thought-production.[67]

Other French Renaissance poetic treatises do not teach us more about the structure of the sonnet. The multiplicity of its forms means that any attempt at establishing a typology was doomed to fail, as the practice of variation prevented any form of classification. The dynamic process brought to the fore by Peletier can be found in extremely varied formal configurations, with stanzaic, syntactic, semantic and rhetoric structures (or even modes of enunciation) that are often superimposed one upon the other or, on the contrary, do not match: sonnets with one, two, three or fourteen sentences, pointed sonnets (with 13–1 or 12–2 structures), sonnets with a turn between the quatrains and the tercets, balanced sonnets, sonnets built on anaphora … The sonnet is as much a diversifying as a thinking machine.[68]

Of course, poetic treatises do not say everything about the interrogations of the practitioners of the sonnet, a radically new form to them. Two issues, in particular, are never tackled. Although most theorists signal the prominent role of the pointed structure of the sonnet – and therefore of its last lines – they remain silent on the care with which poets write their first lines. In the age of the *Pléiade*, it is always the first line (the 'sésame identificatoire', as Cécile Alduy terms it)[69] that gives a reminder that the poem is indeed the reprise of an Italian sonnet, a work of rewriting and imitation. A privileged *locus* for the identification of the hypertext, the *incipit* was soon used to compile tables and indexes at the end of poetic collections, which highlights its role not only in the construction of the sonnet but also in its reception. Finally, the other blind spot in the poetic treatises is related to the arrangement of the sonnets. The poets focused much on their ordering, whether they preferred variation or unity, scattered fragments or sequences.

English theories of the sonnet in the second half of the sixteenth century – Rémi Vuillemin

In England as well, the sonnet was an imported tradition. As far as we know, the sonnet seems to have been adopted by English writers as early as it was by French poets, in the 1530s – and quite logically so, since the two prominent early exponents of the sonnet in English were Sir Henry Howard, Earl of Surrey, who spent a year at the court of Francis I (1532–33), and Sir Thomas Wyatt, who travelled in France and Italy in the late 1520s.[70] Strictly speaking, the chronology that literary history has retained (with the sonnet moving from Italy to France, and then from France to England) has therefore as much to do with the way the sonnet became a significant and widespread literary form as with the moment it was first practised. As discussed above, the sonnet, a predominantly Italian form, became French only through the will to impose a new generation of poets, and to defend and illustrate the French language, from 1549 onwards. Not so in England. The sonnet largely remained a manuscript and a stand-alone form for much of the sixteenth century.[71] Although the 1557 publication of *Tottel's Miscellany* was certainly a landmark in the history of the sonnet, it is only more than three decades later, after 1591 and the (presumably unauthorised) publication of Sir Philip Sidney's *Astrophil and Stella*, that the sonnet is generally considered to have bloomed.

Even the practice of the sonnet took a long time to settle and to become more or less clearly standardised. Although Surrey produced the form now somewhat erroneously known as the Shakespearean sonnet, with its final couplet and characteristic rhyme scheme (abab cdcd efef gg), there were always a number of possible variations (including the well-known Spenserian scheme – abab bcbc cdcd ee), and the term 'sonnet' (also spelled 'sonet') kept its original meaning of 'little song' during and after the century. We have early examples of quatorzains in the miscellanies, and in a number of printed volumes such as Anne Locke's *Meditations of a Penitent Sinner* (1560), Spenser's translations from Petrarch and Du Bellay in Jan van der Noot's *A Theatre for Worldlings* (1569), and Gascoigne's *A Hundreth Sundrie Flowers* (1573), but to a large extent they remain exceptions. Cathy Shrank has shown that what has been considered as the eclipse of the sonnet in the 1560s and 1570s actually corresponds to a period in which poems called 'sonnets' or 'sonets' were generally not fourteen-line poems, although they greatly contributed to the spreading of Petrarchism in England.[72] The standardisation of the sonnet seems to have occurred in the 1580s and appears to have been mostly completed in the 1590s. Even during and after the 'sonnet craze', however, the term 'sonnet' was not always used for quatorzains, and the normalisation of the sonnet according to the native pattern invented by Surrey was never achieved in the way it was in France: the most significant late sonnets of the early modern period, those written by Milton, simply ignore the so-called Shakespearean rhyme-scheme.[73] There were sonnets, including quatorzains, well into the seventeenth century, but after the 1630s, the term was used, at least in print, mostly for commendatory poems, for collections of lyrics of varying lengths or even for broadside ballads.[74] If there was a standardisation of the form, it was therefore a limited and a short-lived one.

The sonnet, a rarely theorised poetic form

Reading works on poetic theory written in England in the second half of the century does not suggest that the sonnet had much of a triumph. There are, of course, obvious reasons to factor in, the first one being the scarcity of critical works dealing specifically with poetry in England until late in the sixteenth century. Though rhetoric was debated and codified in treatises in English published as early as the early 1530s, no fully fledged reflection on poetry seems to have been developed until the 1570s. The first printed works attempting to codify poetry in England, such as John Rainolds's *Oratio in laudem artis poeticae* (according to William Ringler, a speech given at Oxford c. 1572)[75] and Richard Wills's *De Re Poetica* (1573), did not show interest in poetry written in the vernacular. Gascoigne's *Certayne Notes of Instruction Concerning the Making of Verse or Rhyme in English*, published in his *The Posies of George Gascoigne Esquire* (1575), on the contrary, focused on English poetry. This short but significant work paved the way for later developments. It is only in the late 1570s that major works of poetic theory (such as George Puttenham's *The Arte of English Poesie* or Sidney's *Defence of Poesy*) began to be written, and they were not published until the late 1580s and the 1590s. Even so, these works do not linger much on the sonnet, which tends to suggest that the form never reached the cultural centrality it had in Italy, or even in France.

The sonnet received its only thorough formal codification in sixteenth-century England in Gascoigne's 1575 *Certayne Notes of Instruction*, a short treatise that is presented as a practical handbook for poetic composition rather than as an attempt at setting some rules for poetry in English. A number of verse forms are accounted for: rhyme royal, ballads, roundelays, sonnets, 'dizains and sixains', virelays, quatrains, poulter's measure and 'riding rhyme'. Gascoigne integrates medieval and early Renaissance verse forms previously rejected by the *Pléiade*, such as roundelays and virelays, and also Chaucer's 'riding rhyme'. He does not seem to have any desire to define or claim a new poetic tradition, but rather desires to provide advice to gentlemen and court members willing to compose verse. On the sonnet, he asserts the following:

> Then have you sonnets. Some think that all poems (being short) may be called sonnets, as indeed it is a diminutive word derived of 'suonare,' but yet I can best bestow to call those sonnets which are of fourteen lines, every line containing ten syllables. The first twelve do rhyme in staves of four lines by cross metre, and the last two, rhyming together, do conclude the whole. There are dizains and sixains, which are of ten lines and of six lines, commonly used by the French, which some English writers do also term by the name of sonnets.[76]

Gascoigne provides a very precise definition of the English sonnet, but also registers the variety of the forms his fellow Englishmen call sonnets: short poems in general, 'dizains' and 'sixains' in particular. The final remarks of Gascoigne's short treatise indicate the context of use of each form. To him, 'sonnets serve well in matters of love as of discourse'.[77] The sonnet is associated with love, but not restricted to it. It is difficult to see what exactly the term 'discourse' refers to here. The possible meanings can be narrowed down to 'reasoning' or 'argument' (pointing to the potential of the sonnet as a 'thinking machine' and its closeness to, and affinities with, the epigram), narrative (as Gascoigne included himself sonnets in the narrative of the *Adventures of Master F.J.*, which was included in the *Posies* along with *Certayne Notes of Instruction* ...) or possibly 'conversation' (here the courtly practice of performing and/or exchanging manuscript poetry, and especially answer-poems).

Only one other in-depth technical discussion of the sonnet was formulated in an English poetic treatise in the sixteenth century, nearly twenty-five years later.[78] William Scott, in his recently rediscovered *The Model of Poesy* (1599), defines the sonnet as 'a proportion of fourteen verses and suits very well to any such uniform conceit as this is, that is contrived with a continual dependency of sense till it receive the life and completeness in the last verses'.[79] Most of the sonnets that had been published in the 1590s were quatorzains; it seems therefore logical that such standardisation should appear in a treatise written at the very end of the decade. More interestingly, Scott is the only theorist who comments upon the inner logic of the sonnet, which to him is directed towards its completion in the very last verse. He sees the sonnet as a very unified form that belongs to 'pointed poetics' (a phrase I adapt from the French term 'pointe' used and analysed in particular by Mercedes Blanco):[80] based on a 'conceit',[81] it strives towards a completeness, or 'life', that is achieved only in the last verse. By insisting on the movement of the poem towards its end, Scott conveys the idea that the final lines, presumably the couplet, bring a witty conclusion that both enlivens and gives meaning to the whole. This is consistent on two accounts. First, the architecture of the English sonnet, with its final couplet (possibly inherited from Italian *strambotti* in the time of Wyatt), favours an epigrammatic ending. Such structure made sense at the end of the sixteenth century, with the revival of the epigram as an essential genre.[82] Second, Scott probably drew his inspiration from the French treatises of Sébillet and Peletier, who likened the sonnet to the epigram (see above). Scott classifies the sonnet in the category of satire, and more especially the 'satirical epigram', which again makes sense in the context of the revival of satire in the 1590s and of the activity of certain late Elizabethan and early Jacobean sonneteers.[83] The category on which Scott focuses after satire is the lyric, and he includes in it the 'lyrical epigram', which shows that the notion of epigram transcends categories and indirectly suggests that certain sonnets might be lyrics too. It might also have to do with Greek amatory epigrams such as those found in the Planudean anthology, and the categorisation of Catullus's poems as *epigrammata amatoria* in sixteenth-century Italian poetic theory.[84] Scott's phrasing also somehow seems to anticipate David S. Wilson-Okamura's adjustment of Alastair Fowler's theory of poetic modes, according to which the lyric mode was dominant in the sixteenth century, soon to be replaced by the epigrammatic mode in the next century – although Italian and French precedents indicate that the difficulty of distinguishing between sonnet and epigram was nothing new.[85] The notion of 'lyrical epigram' is also mentioned earlier in the treatise, just after a reference to Ovid's *Heroides* (which Scott calls *Heroical Epistles*, perhaps after Drayton's *Englands Heroicall Epistles*, first published in 1597). It is part of a discussion of '*elegiac*, or plaintive' verse, which according to Scott includes both psalms and love sonnets.[86] Scott's words are reminiscent of the etymology the sonnet shares with the psalm as a short song, and the common history of the two forms (which were often practised by the same poets – poets like Marot, Wyatt or Sidney, to name but a few). But by categorising the sonnet as an elegiac poem for the first time in an English poetic treatise, Scott also registers the extremely frequent association of the quatorzain with love in the preceding decades, and, perhaps even more importantly, paves the way for later appreciations of the sonnet as a predominantly expressive poem.[87]

Gascoigne's and Scott's works were exceptions, however. Technical discussions of the sonnet did not abound in the poetic treatises of the period. When one appeared just after the turn of the century, it was rather as a sort of footnote to the quarrel between Campion and Daniel on metrics and rhyme – although it is to us a rare confirmation that the form of the sonnet (at least the fourteen lines) had reached some stability then. Campion indeed complains of the excessive formal rigidity of the sonnet:

> But there is yet another fault in Rime altogether intolerable, which is, that it inforceth a man oftentimes to abjure his matter and extend a short conceit beyond all bounds of arte: for in Quatorzens, methinks, the poet handles his subject as tyrannically as *Procrustes* the thiefe his prisoners, whom, when he had taken, he used to cast upon a bed, which if they were too short to fill, he would stretch them longer, if too long, he would cut them shorter. Bring before me now any the most self-lov'd Rimer, and let me see if without blushing he be able to read his lame halting rime. Is there not a curse of Nature laid upon such rude Poesie, when the Writer is himself asham'd of it, and the hearers in contempt call it Riming and Ballating?[88]

Campion's remarks tend to show that the formal constraints imposed by the sonnet were well-known at this point, and could be seen as an impediment to good poetry, leading its practitioners to artificial shortening or lengthening. His mention of Procrustes is reminiscent of the use of the phrase 'Procrustean bed' to refer to the sonnet in Italian treatises (see the first part of the present chapter). Daniel's reply (his *A Defence of Rhyme* published in 1603) unsurprisingly displays some awareness of the difficulties of the form:

> And indeed I have wished that there were not that multiplicitie of Rymes as is used by many in Sonets, which yet we see in some so happily to succeed, and hath beene so farre from hindering their inventions, as it hath begot conceit beyond expectation, and comparable to the best inventions in the world: for sure is an eminent spirit, whome Nature hath fitted for that mysterie, Ryme is no impediment to his conceit, but rather gives him wings to mount, and carries him, not out of his course, but as it were beyond his power to a farre happier flight [...] Not is this certaine limit observed in Sonnets, any tyrannical bounding of the conceit, but rather reducing it in *girum* and a just forme, neither too long for the shortest project, nor too short for the longest, being but onely employed for a present passion.[89]

Daniel offers to see two major formal constraints of the sonnet (the number of rhymes and the length of the poem) as possibilities for an excellent poet ('an eminent spirit') to reach unprecedented poetic heights – as long as the sonnet is given its proper subject, 'a present passion'. Implicitly, he suggests that one should blame bad poets rather than poetry, an idea that at this time had become a topos of poetic treatises and quarrels.

In most other English treatises on poetry, the technical features of the sonnet are not discussed at all. William Webbe's 1586 *A Discourse of English Poesie* and George Puttenham's 1589 *The Arte of English Poesie*, in particular, are concerned with the technical features available to poets writing in English, but do not really make a point of associating them with specific poetic forms or genres. They seek to provide poets with the tools that would lead to the improvement and good use of the English language, not to give technical definitions of genres and kinds. The scarcity of references to the formal features of the sonnet in the aforementioned texts means not that the English were unaware of them but rather that they had no specific relevance to the project of English poetic theorists. For much of the second half of the sixteenth century, the main issue was to define the tools available to poets in English and to value the vernacular. Technical questions related to the specificities of the English tongue took precedence: what was of prime importance was, for instance, to define the sonorous qualities of English verse, in terms of metrics and of rhyme, or to establish a more general theory of poetry in defence of attacks against it.[90]

It is striking that, for most of the period, English theorists who refer to sonnets generally point to them as part of poetic miscellanies, especially *Tottel's Miscellany*. Sidney writes of 'that lyrical kind of songs and sonnets', quite obviously alluding to Tottel and to the tradition of printed miscellanies that followed its publication, and Puttenham, in one of the few mentions of the term 'sonnet' in his treatise, does as much:[91]

> And because love is of all the other humane affections the most puissant and passionate, and most generall to all sortes and ages of men and women, so at whether it be of the young or old or wise or holy, or high estate or low, none ever could truly bragge of any exemption in that case: it requireth a forme of Poesie variable, inconstant, affected, curious and most witty of any others, whereof the joyes were to be uttered in one sort, the sorrowes in an other, and by the many formes of Poesie, the many moodes and pangs of lovers, throughly to be discovered: the poore soules sometimes praying, beseeching, sometime honouring, avancing, praising: an other while railing, reviling, and cursing: then sorrowing, weeping, lamenting: in the end laughing, with a thousand delicate devises, odes, songs, elegies, ballads, sonnets and other ditties, mooving one way and another to great compassion.[92]

Here the sonnet is just one of many poetic forms devoted to the expression of love – a thematic association that *The Arte of English Poesie* is the first published poetic treatise to put forward so explicitly. Love sonnets (or poems that were not quatorzains but were called sonnets regardless) were also to be found in collections of verse by individual authors such as Googe, Turberville or Gascoigne. Puttenham, like many others before him and after him, praises Wyatt and Surrey as the reformers of the English tongue,[93] and the sonnet is part and parcel of their work. The association of the sonnet with other types of poem is not always flattering: William Webbe refers to 'the uncountable rabble of ryming Ballet makers and compylers of sencelesse sonets' and seems to associate sonneteers with composers of drinking songs, as does Thomas

Nashe in his *Anatomie of Absurditie*.[94] This had become a commonplace of rants against poetry: those who accuse poetry of being sinful, Sidney writes, 'say the lyric is larded with passionate sonnets'.[95] The association of the sonnet with the ballad (or even sometimes with the drinking song) testifies to its identification as a poem to be sung, i.e. as a lyric poem, but in a derogatory perspective. The inclusion of the sonnet within the lyric genre had more and more to do with the theme of love as the end of the sixteenth century drew nearer. This progression is mirrored in the evolution of the reception of Petrarch in the course of the century.

An ambivalent reception of the Italian model

Petrarch was of course regarded as an authority – he had been one since the time of Chaucer. But it seems that he was first mostly known for his Latin works (especially *De Remediis Utriusque Fortunae*) and for his poems that criticised the papacy and Rome.[96] His love poems were much more frequently mentioned and imitated in sources published after the 1550s (which saw the publication of *Tottel's Miscellany*, but also of the first published translation of the *Trionfi* by Henry Parker, Baron Morley). However, direct translations from the *Canzoniere* remained rather rare until the end of the century, especially in comparison to what had happened in France.[97] The most significant moment in this history was undoubtedly the publication of Thomas Watson's *Hekatompathia, or Passionate Centurie of Love* (1582), the first fully Petrarchan poetic sequence published in England. Watson comments on each of his poems, giving its sources and often quoting the original in Italian; this mere fact shows that the poet was willing to flaunt his knowledge of Petrarch's language. The collection also ushered in a period in which Petrarch's name was more systematically associated with love and his relationship with Laura was much more often mentioned. The fashion for Italian and for the Petrarchan model was particularly prominent in the last two decades of the century, including in the practice of sonneteers well-versed in the Italian language such as Samuel Daniel. Comparing the English poets' achievements to Petrarch's remained a common practice, and Sidney even started to complain about poets who 'steal' from Petrarch (*Astrophil and Stella*, sonnet 15).[98] Even so, Anthony Mortimer explains, 'it must be admitted that the English interest in Petrarch rarely goes beyond a few stock favourites which keep turning up throughout the century'.[99] This might be an exaggeration (partly related to the fact that much work still needs to be done on Petrarch's influence in Elizabethan England), but it seems undeniable that the extent to which Petrarch was imitated in England never reached what it had been in France.[100] In the treatises, Petrarch is rarely mentioned as a unique model, but is associated with other authors.[101] His role in improving the Italian language is underlined, and it is as such that English authors (Chaucer, Wyatt and Surrey, or Spenser for instance) are compared to him.[102] Only Puttenham refers to him repeatedly as a technical model in a precise and detailed way.[103] The most vibrant printed praises of Petrarch were formulated by Harvey, who sought to elevate the status of Spenser and to reply to Nashe, Daniel, whose sonnets were perhaps more frequently than those of other poets direct translations or imitations of the Petrarchan text, and who wrote his *A Defence of Poetry* after a decade of intense English sonneteering, and Meres, who calls Petrarch 'the prince of Italian poets'.[104] As a whole, it seems that despite the prestige of the Tuscan poet and the admiration the English professed for his work, Petrarch's direct influence on love poetry was not as foundational as it had been in Italy and France. Petrarch was an ambivalent authority for the English, as he was alternatively seen as a champion of the Protestant cause and the author who had fallen victim to the temptations of earthly love (or was complicit to them).[105]

The love sonnet combined two qualities that could make it morally suspicious: it was about love, and it was an Italian poetic form. Love poetry might corrupt the youth, and was to be avoided.[106] This had become a commonplace that was still frequently articulated at the turn of the seventeenth century.[107] Sidney himself advises to favour spiritual or religious poetry over love poetry, although this seems mostly on account of the fact that love poems are ridiculous and unconvincing.[108] Defenders of poetry such as Sidney also reveal that poetry was accused of being 'the mother of lies'.[109] This must have affected writers of love poetry, since some justification against such an accusation can be found in prefatory material to collections of love poems: Thomas Watson, in his 1582 *Hekatompathia, or Passionate Centurie of Love*, writes that his passions are 'supposed' passions;[110] Fletcher, in a prefatory epistle to *Licia* dated 4 September 1593, claims that 'a man may write of love, and not bee in love'.[111] Love poetry, and especially the love sonnet (usually written in the first person), was the victim of a double bind: it might escape accusations of immorality if the passions it expressed were 'supposed', or represented (i.e., the poetic 'I' was not the poet), but, in that case, it could be accused of lying. Such strain was perhaps made stronger by theories (with a Neoplatonic background) in which love became a paradigm for poetic inspiration and composition.[112]

The accusations against love poetry were made stronger by its association with Italy, a country suspected of being the cradle of popery and debauchery. In Roger Ascham's *Scholemaster* (1560), the Italianised Englishman is famously called a devil incarnate ('*Englese italianato, e un diabolo incarnato*' [sic]).[113] Such criticism was repeatedly voiced in the last decades of the century, and cannot be dissociated from the success of Italian literature in England:[114] it is largely a reaction against a fashion for Italian cultural production that became more widespread from the 1570s to the end of the century. Poets such as Ariosto could corrupt 'chaste ears' with their sinful tales.[115] The accusations of lies and impiety were often directed at poetry in general, rather than just Italian poetry, but Italian poetry was all the more pernicious because it was thought to be witty, and, as a consequence, empty, akin to sophistry and potentially manipulative. In a letter to his brother Robert, Sir Philip Sidney wrote: 'although indeed some [Italians] be excellently learned, yet they are all given so to counterfeit learning, as a man shall learn among them more false ground of things than in any place else that I know. For from a tapster upward they are all discoursers.'[116] The prefatory material to Fletcher's sonnet sequence *Licia* documents some English reactions to poetic (and Italianate) entertainment such as sonnet writing: 'But two reasons hath made [poetry] a thing foolishly odious in this age: the one, that so many base companions are the greatest writers: the other, that our English *Genevian* puritie hath quite debarred us of honest recreation'.[117] The situation must therefore have been made particularly tense by the roughly simultaneous rise of Italianism (i.e., the reception and interpretation of the cultural productions of Italy) and puritanism (understood here as a set of moral and cultural attitudes triggered, among other things, by Calvinism) from the 1560s onwards. Fletcher suggests that poetry was subjected to very strong cultural pressures; but his words might also corroborate Alistair Fox's idea that Italianism provided relief from them: 'one can discern a situation in which a very large body of English men and women were rejecting the world-renouncing strictures of puritanism in favour of the very different discursive configurations to be found in Italian fiction'.[118]

It seems therefore that the sonnet never was a defining element of a developed theory of a specifically English type of poetry, at least in the way it was in Italy or in France. Poetic controversies including the sonnet were focused on wider issues such as the encounter between the liberating influence of Italian poetry and moralistic and puritan tendencies that were increasingly becoming a defining element of English culture, and perhaps also of English national identity. The boom of the sonnet in the 1590s can perhaps partly be explained by the apex of religious and intercultural tensions, as anti-Catholic policies were gaining ground at the same time as Elizabeth's propagandists relied on a largely Catholic imagery to exacerbate her image as their post-Armada triumphant Virgin Queen. Despite the Englishing of the sonnet from the 1530s until the end of the century, one cannot help but wonder if the quatorzain was ever seen in sixteenth- and early seventeenth-century England as something else than a Continental poetic form – a form whose very Englishness consisted in reconstructing and questioning its French or Italian features, either through play or through moralisation. We have evidence that the image of Italian poetry as the mother of vice could be exploited by the English: in Sir John Harington's translation of Ariosto's *Orlando Furioso*, three scenes of copulation were added in the background of the Italian plate illustrating canto 28.[119] This allowed Harington to play deliberately with cultural representations of Italy and to absolve himself from any culpability in the process. The sonnet, as an Italianate poetic form, had to negotiate a perilous course between didacticism, seduction and provocation.[120]

Reconsidering the significance of the English sonnet

It seems that the scarcity of English codifications of the sonnet left a great degree of freedom to its practitioners in terms of formal constraints. In that sense, the English had the same perspective as the Italians in the second half of the century: they were relatively free to conduct poetic experiments. But the two situations were actually quite different, as the norm of the quatorzain in decasyllabic verse was established only at the very end of the century in England and was largely abandoned after 1630. The poetic treatises and debates mirror this progressive codification, and, by the end of the 1590s, their conception of the sonnet shared some common ground with that formulated in France by Sébillet and Peletier several decades before, especially as far as the proximity between the sonnet and the epigram is concerned. Gascoigne's definition, however, was available to at least certain poets much earlier. We know that the term 'sonnet' was used in widely varying senses. Was there really confusion? What seems more likely is that the constraints of the form were not seen as fruitful or particularly relevant for a long time, probably because the English theorists had more pressing issues to address, such as the definition of the prosodic features of their language and of the metrical features of their poetry. The sonnet seems to have had a more permanent significance as an element of a larger ensemble: the poetic miscellany, a type of collection constructed and given cultural centrality by Tottel.

In theoretical terms as well as in poetic practice, the English 'sonnet craze' did not last long. It seems to have corresponded to a moment of tension between Italianism and Puritanism, or at least a moralistic strand consistent with the rise of Puritanism, which makes the sonnet sequences of the 1590s particularly interesting to study. Such a background should certainly lead one to qualify simplistic visions of the love sonnet, and to take some distance from what is often perceived as a set of full-blown attacks against tired conventions: if love sonnets were seen as foreign forms, the attacks against them imply more than the boredom readers might have felt when reading the same conceits over and over again. These attacks might need to be studied in a more systematic way than they have been so far; they might reveal more about the conception of the sonnet in England than theoretical texts – that is, if one is prepared to try to uncover what underlies them. We hope that this chapter can serve as a basis for further explorations of the conceptions of the English sonnet in the period, during, before and after the time of its triumph in the 1590s.

Notes

1 S.S. Clucas, 'Thomas Watson's *Hekatompathia* and European Petrarchism', in M. McLaughlin, L. Panizza and P. Hainsworth (eds), *Petrarch in Britain: Interpreters, Imitators, Translators over 700 years* (Oxford: Oxford University Press, 2007), pp. 217–27, esp. 217.
2 On how the sonnet spread from Italy to France and to England, see Michael G. Spiller's excellent synthesis in *The Development of the Sonnet: An Introduction* (New York: Routledge, 1992).
3 See for instance A.L. Prescott, *French Poets and the English Renaissance: Studies in Fame and Transformation* (New Haven, London: Yale University Press, 1978); A. Fox, *The English Renaissance: Identity and Representation in Elizabethan England* (Oxford: Blackwell, 1997); J. Lawrence, '*Who the Devil Taught Thee So Much Italian?' Italian Language and Literary Imitation in Early Modern England* (Manchester: Manchester University Press, 2005); M. Wyatt, *The Italian Encounter with Tudor England: A Cultural Politics of Translation* (Cambridge: Cambridge University Press, 2005); A.E.B. Coldiron, *Printers Without Borders: Translation and Textuality in the Renaissance* (Cambridge: Cambridge University Press, 2015).
4 Tottel's text is not as developed and elaborate as Bembo's and Du Bellay's. It was not the first text to argue for the value of the vernacular either: rhetoricians started to claim the eloquence of the English language in the 1530s. But it was probably the first text doing so by offering poetic models not presented as translations. On the rise of the English vernacular, see R.F. Jones's classic study, *The Triumph of the English Language: A Survey of Opinions Concerning the Vernacular from the Introduction of Printing to the Restoration* (Stanford: Stanford University Press, 1953).
5 The last major sonnet writer of the period was Milton, whose sonnets seem to have been written from the 1630s to the late 1650s, though they appeared in publications later in the century. The fact that several poetic collections published in the seventeenth century are given a title comprising the word 'sonnet' is misleading: in most of those cases, the term 'sonnet' must be understood as 'little song' or as 'short lyric poem'. On the sonnet between Milton and the late eighteenth century, see R.S. White, 'Survival and Change: The Sonnet from Milton to the Romantics', in A.D. Cousins and P. Howarth (eds), *The Cambridge Companion to the Sonnet* (Cambridge University Press, 2011), pp. 166–84. White contends that the sonnet was neglected and unfashionable rather than extinct in that period.
6 I would like to thank R. Vuillemin and P. Marini. The translations of the Italian texts are mine.
7 See R. Antonelli, 'L'invenzione del sonetto', in *Miscellanea di studi in onore di Aurelio Roncaglia a cinquant'anni dalla sua laurea*, 4 vols (Modena: Mucchi, 1989), vol. 1, pp. 35–75, and A. Roncaglia,

'Note d'aggiornamento critico sui testi del Notaro e invenzione del sonetto', in G. Ruffino (ed.), *In ricordo di Giuseppe Cusimano* (Palermo: Centro di Studi filologici e linguistici, 1992), pp. 9–25.

8   On the *sonetto caudato*, whose origins date back to the end of the fourteenth century, see P. Beltrami, *La metrica italiana* (Bologna: Il Mulino, 1991), pp. 245–6. One may also quote the presence, in some humanistic circles of the north of Italy during the first decades of the Renaissance, of the Latin or 'mediolatin' sonnet: see E.M. Duso, *Il sonetto latino e semilatino in Italia nel Medioevo e nel Rinascimento* (Rome, Padua: Antenore, 2004). I do not consider in this survey the poetical exchanges of letters made of sonnets, a macro-structural constant whose origin may be traced to the thirteenth century, also continuing during the Renaissance.

9   M. Santagata, *Dal sonetto al canzoniere: ricerche sulla preistoria e la costruzione di un genere* (Padua: Liviana, 1989), pp. 131–5.

10 On Boiardo and his close relationship to Petrarch's *Canzoniere* see G. Baldassarri, 'Declinazioni del sonetto a Ferrara nel secondo Quattrocento: gli "Amorum libri" e il Canzoniere Costabili', in L. Facini and A. Soldani (eds), *Otto studi sul sonetto* (Limena: Libreriauniversitaria.it, 2017), pp. 99–128, esp. 99–100; on Burchiello and its poetical collection, significantly conveyed by manuscripts and ancient editions by the title of 'Sonetti del Burchiello', see Burchiello (Domenico di Giovanni), ed. Michelangelo Zaccarello, I sonetti del Burchiello (Turin: Einaudi, 2004). See also F. Magro and A. Soldani, *Il sonetto italiano. Dalle origini a oggi* (Rome: Carocci, 2017).

11 G. Forni, 'Il canone del sonetto nel XVI secolo', *Schede umanistiche*, 2 (1997), 113–22, esp. 113.

12 For the *Prose* see P. Bembo, *Prose e rime*, ed. C. Dionisotti (Turin: UTET, 1992), pp. 71–309.

13 'A' sonetti il numero de' versi è dato, e di parte delle rime; nell'ordine delle rime poi, e in parte di loro nel numero, non s'usa più certa regola che il piacere, in quanto capevoli ne sono quei pochi versi' (Bembo, *Prose e rime*, pp. 152–3). It must be said, as Marco Praloran suggests, that Bembo generally shows more interest in the construction of the verses (*endecasillabo, settenario* etc.) than in the form which contains them. See M. Praloran, 'Metrica e tecnica del verso', in S. Morgagna, M. Piotti and M. Prada (eds), *'Prose della volgar lingua' di Pietro Bembo. Atti del convegno di Gargnano sul Garda (4–7 ottobre 2000)* (Milan: Cisalpino, 2000), pp. 409–21, esp. 413.

14 Among the constitutive elements of Italian Petrarchism, Guglielmo Gorni reminds us of the 'solid metrical form' of the sonnet. See G. Gorni, 'Le forme primarie del testo poetico', in A. Asor Rosa (ed.), *Letteratura italiana*, vol. III (Turin: Einaudi, 1984), pp. 439–518, esp. 475 and 483–4.

15 G.G. Trissino, *La pωetica*, s.n.t. [1529] (colophon: 'Stampata in Vicenza per Tωlωmeω Ianiculω | Nel M D X X I X. | Di Aprile.'), fos XXXVIr–XLIr (quotation from fol. XLIr: 'Ma iω non voljω trattare de le cose che sωnω state da i buoni autωri schifate, però lascierò').

16 On these points, see G. Gorni, 'Il libro di poesia cinquecentesco: principio e fine', in M. Santaga and A. Quondam (eds), *Il libro di poesia dal copista al tipografo (Ferrara, 29–31 maggio 1987)* (Modena: Panini, 1989), pp. 35–41; S. Albonico, *Ordine e numero: studi sul libro di poesia e le raccolte poetiche del Cinquecento* (Alessandria: Edizioni dell'Orso, 2006), pp. 28–9; F. Tomasi, *Studi sulla lirica rinascimentale (1540–1570)* (Rome, Padua: Antenore, 2012), pp. 3–24.

17 For Tasso's *Amori* and its evolution see G. Ferroni, 'Come leggere "I tre libri degli Amori" di Bernardo Tasso (1534–1537)', *Quaderno di italianistica [della Sezione di Italiano dell'Università di Losanna]* (2011), 99–144. For Ariosto's *canzoniere* and its different steps see R. Fedi, *La memoria della poesia: canzonieri, lirici e libri di rime nel Rinascimento* (Rome: Salerno editrice, 1990), pp. 83–115. For Bembo's *Rime* see Albonico, *Ordine e numero*, pp. 1–27, and A. Juri, 'Sintassi e imitazione nei sonetti di Pietro Bembo', in L. Facini and A. Soldani (eds), *Otto studi sul sonetto* (Limena: Libreriauniversitaria.it, 2017), pp. 129–56. Juri discusses the close relationship between syntax and metre; even if some formal evolutions create a distance from his *Prose* and the poetical practice, Bembo's lyrical project is a 'real triumph of the sonnet'. See C. Dionisotti, 'Fortuna del Petrarca nel Quattrocento', *Italia medioevale e umanistica*, XVII (1974), 61–113, esp. 109, and the critical edition of the *Rime*: P. Bembo, *Le rime*, ed. A. Donnini, 2 vols (Rome: Salerno editrice, 2008).

18 A. Vassalli, 'Editoria del petrarchismo cinquecentesco: alcune cifre', in *Il libro di poesia dal copista al tipografo*, ed. M. Santagata, A. Quondam (Ferrara: Panini, 1989), pp. 91–102, esp. 96–8.

19 On these points see F. Tomasi's 'Introduzione', in A. Piccolomini, *I cento sonetti*, ed. F. Tomasi (Geneva: Droz, 2015), pp. 7–30, esp. 13–18.

20 Published in 1527 under the title *Sonetti e canzoni di diversi antichi autori toscani*, the *Giuntina di rime antiche* focuses its attention on the authors 'who gave birth to the Tuscan poetry' and who preceded Petrarch (Dante, Cino da Pistoia, Guido Cavalcanti): see *Sonetti e canzoni di diversi antichi autori toscani*, ed. D. De Robertis, 2 vols (Florence: Le Lettere, 1977).

21 Many contributions have been published in this field in the last two decades: see M. Bianco and E. Strada (eds), *'I più vaghi e i più soavi fiori'. Studi sulle antologie di lirica del Cinquecento* (Alessandria:

Edizioni dell'Orso, 2001); G. Forni, *Forme brevi della poesia: tra Umanesimo e Rinascimento* (Pisa: Pacini editore, 2001), pp. 137–91; Tomasi, *Studi sulla lirica rinascimentale*, pp. 25–94. See also the project 'Lyra', directed by S. Albonico (www.lyra.unil.ch, date accessed: 20 April 2019).

22 See the critical edition of the 1545 collection: F. Tomasi and P. Zaja (eds), *Rime diverse di molti eccellentissimi autori. Libro primo* (Turin: RES, 2001).

23 B. Bartolomeo, 'Notizie su sonetto e canzone nelle "Rime diverse di molti eccellentissimi auttori nuovamente raccolte", libro primo (Venezia, Gabriel Giolito de' Ferrari, 1545)', in M. Bianco and E. Strada (eds), *'I più vaghi e i più soavi fiori'* (Alessandria: Edizioni dell' Orso, 2001), pp. 43–76, esp. 45–6.

24 Fedi, *La memoria della poesia*, pp. 253–63.

25 For Minturno see G. Tallini, '"Voluptas" e "docere" nel pensiero critico di Antonio Minturno', *Esperienze letterarie*, 33:3 (2008), 73–100.

26 '[Il sonetto è] compositione grave e leggiadra di parole con harmonia di rime, e con misura di syllabe tessute sotto certo numero di versi e sotto certo ordine limitata [...]; l'epigramma è particella dell'epica poesia, il sonetto della melica, sì come per lo nome istesso vi si dà a conoscere, conciociacosa che così dal suono il soneto, come dal canto la canzone si dica né altro sia il suono che canto. Onde, chi tal nome gli diede, null'altro volle che breve e leggiadretto canto significare; né, perché la voce sia diminutiva, bassezza alcuna di stile se ne dinota, ma si ben leggiadria e vaghezza, senza la quale questa compositione spetialmente è nulla o poco vale. [...] Oltre a ciò, nell'epigramma né vaghezza né leggiadria di compositione si richiede, ma agutezza di motteggio o di sentenza. Nel sonetto, con le parole elette e vagamente e leggiadramente ordite e composte, hor grave, hor aguto, hor dolce sentimento. Nell'epigramma non si prescrive certo numero di versi, quantunque s'egli n'ha più di duo o di quattro elegia più tosto si debba chiamare. Nel sonetto è determinato il fine, il quale non si può trapassare; né, perciochè la materia che in lui si tratta si può ristringere in pochi versi, non è simile al soggetto delle canzoni divise in stanze.' A. Minturno, *L'arte poetica, nella quale si contengono i precetti heroici, tragici, comici, satyrici e d'ogni altra poesia. Con la dottrina de' sonetti, canzoni et ogni sorte di rime thoscane, dove s'insegna il modo che tenne il Petrarca nelle sue rime* [...] ([Venice]: G.A. Valvassori, 1563), pp. 240–1.

27 'come nelle canzoni narriamo, preghiamo, confortiamo, spaventiamo, lodiamo, biasimiamo, gli affetti dell'animo destiamo, così ne' sonetti anchora.' Minturno, *L'arte poetica*, p. 241.

28 'Io parlo di questa maniera di sonetti la qual è in uso, percioché quella che m'allegate e l'altre anchora [...] nondimeno si sono poi fatte antiche, e dal Petrarca e dagli altri poeti che dopo di lui sono state in pregio si lasciarono, come quelle a cui manca quella vaghezza e leggiadria ch'al sonetto si richiede [...]'. Minturno, *L'arte poetica*, pp. 242–3.

29 G. Ruscelli, *Del modo di comporre in versi nella lingua italiana* (Venice: Giovanni Battista et Melchior Sessa, [1559]) CXLIII–CLVIII: CXLV ('lo spezzar così il verso [...] è la principale grandezza dello stile'). On the concept of *gravitas* within the sonnet, see A. Afribo, *Teoria e prassi della 'gravitas' nel Cinquecento* (Florence: Cesati, 2001), pp. 61–200.

30 C. Gigante, *Tasso* (Rome: Salerno editrice, 2007) pp. 248–9.

31 '[il sonetto] in ciascuna forma è poco acconcio a ricever la bassezza e l'umiltà'. See T. Tasso, *Opere. V. Dialoghi. Apologia in difesa della 'Gerusalemme liberata'. Lettere*, ed. B. Maier (Milan: Rizzoli, 1965), pp. 110–11. On Tasso as an author of sonnets see Gigante, *Tasso*, pp. 309–33.

32 Afribo, *Teoria e prassi della 'gravitas' nel Cinquecento*, pp. 120–32.

33 See Guazzo's *Del paragone della poesia latina et della thoscana*, in S. Guazzo, *Dialoghi piacevoli* [...] (Venice: Gio. Antonio Bertano, 1586) fos 64v–71v: 68v. The definition of the sonnet as a 'Procrustean bed' is ascribed to the poet Claudio Tolomei.

34 On this point see the academic lesson *Del sonetto* by Cesare Crispolti (1563–1608): stressing the importance of this noble and excellent form of the Tuscan tradition ('poema sovra ogn'altra poesia toscana nobile et eccellente'), Crispolti underlines the necessity of the good use of the *concetto*, also considering the small dimensions of the sonnet. See B. Weinberg (ed.), *Trattati di poetica e retorica del Cinquecento*, 4 vols (Bari: Laterza, 1970–74), vol. IV, pp. 193–205.

35 On this point, and on the new form of the *canzoniere* in the seventeenth century see A. Martini, 'Le nuove forme del canzoniere', in *I capricci di Proteo: percorsi e linguaggi del Barocco. Atti del Convegno di Lecce, 23–26 ottobre 2000* (Rome: Salerno, 2002), pp. 199–226.

36 '[Il sonetto] vien giudicato il più armonioso componimento di tutti gli altri. [...] E veramente può dirsi componimento assai grave, essendo formato di ottava e di terza rima, o vogliam dire catena, con le quali si spiegano materie eroiche e grandi'. F. Meninni, *Il ritratto del sonetto e della canzone*, ed. C. Carminati, 2 vols (Lecce: Argo, 2002), vol. I, p. 8.

37 On the history of the French Renaissance sonnet, see A. Gendre's note in *Dictionnaire des lettres françaises: le XVIe siècle*, ed. M. Simonin, revised edition (Paris: Fayard, 2001). Let us only remind

the reader that the sonnet was a prominent poetic form in France for a long while, from Marot to Malherbe, from the late 1540s to the 1630s. At that date, it did not disappear, but its use was restricted to salons. But the sonnet's share in the poetic production declined spectacularly after 1630 to finally come close to disappearing in the eighteenth century. See J. Roubaud, 'La Forme du sonnet français de Marot à Malherbe, Recherche de seconde rhétorique' (PhD dissertation, Université Paris IV Sorbonne, 1989), pp. 275-6. It is only with Romanticism (and especially Nerval and Baudelaire) that the sonnet flourished again, following the rediscovery of *Pléiade* poets after two centuries of neglect.

38 Such canonical form has never prevented the sonnet from allowing an infinite number of variations or from being, right from the start, a privileged form for experimentation: unrhymed sonnets, sonnets in quantitative metrics, *carmen correlativum*, heterometrical sonnets, *bouts-rimés*, 4- or 5-syllable sonnets, prose sonnets ...

39 J. Du Bellay, *La Deffence et illustration de la langue françoyse*, ed. J.-C. Monferran (Geneva: Droz, 2009 [2001]), II, 4, 136. 'Sing me these beautiful sonnets which are a no less learned than pleasing Italian invention'. Translation from *Poetry and Language in 16th-Century France, Du Bellay, Ronsard, Sébillet*, trans., intro. and notes by L. Willett (Toronto: Centre for Reformation and Renaissance Studies, 2003), pp. 71-2.

40 See F. Goyet, 'Le sonnet français, vrai et faux héritier de la Grande Rhétorique', in Y. Bellenger (ed.), *Le Sonnet à la Renaissance, Actes du colloque de Reims* (Paris: Aux Amateurs de Livres, 1988), pp. 31-41. See also T. Sébillet, *Art poétique français*, II, 2, in F. Goyet (ed.), *Traités de poétique et de rhétorique de la Renaissance* (Paris: Livre de Poche, 1990), p. 107.

41 Maurice Scève's *Délie* (1544) was the first French *canzoniere* (1544), but it is entirely made up of *dizains*.

42 Sébillet, *Art poétique français*, II, 2, p. 108. On the centrality of Petrarch in the development of the French sonnet, see J. Balsamo, 'Marot et les origines du pétrarquisme français', in G. Defaux and M. Simonin (eds), *Clément Marot, 'prince des poëtes françois', 1496-1996* (Paris: Champion, 1997), pp. 323-37.

43 Du Bellay, *Deffence*, II, 4, p. 136: 'Pour le sonnet donc tu as Pétrarque et quelques modernes Italiens'. The translation is from *Poetry and Language in 16th-Century France*, p. 72.

44 Here the term 'Petrarchan' refers to poetry written by Petrarch, while the term 'Petrarchist' alludes to the tradition of imitation of Petrarch's poetry.

45 Sébillet, *Art poétique français*, II, 2, p. 108: 'La matière facétieuse est répugnante à la gravité du sonnet, qui reçoit plus proprement affections et passions graves'.

46 Translation and emphasis mine. 'Nous ne trouvons point, au moins que je sache, de plus ancienne mémoire du Sonnet, ni n'avons point plus lointaine origine à lui donner, que les Italiens: Auxquels il a été fort fréquent de tout temps: Et desquels le plus excellent a été François Pétrarque: qui en a composé un bon nombre à l'honneur de sa Dame Laure. Nous l'avons tous admiré, et imité: non sans cause: vu la grand' douceur du style, *la grand' variété sur un seul Sujet*: et *la vive expression des passions amoureuses* qu'on voit en son Œuvre' (emphasis mine). See J. Peletier, *Art poétique*, II, 4, in *Traités de poétique et de rhétorique de la Renaissance*, p. 293, and also *Art poétique* I, 9, p. 277: 'Les Antithèses ou Contrepositions aussi auront bonne grâce: Comme la douce amertume, l'accordante discorde: laquelle est fréquente à nos Poètes, et à moi peut-être trop en mes Sonnets. Mais ce sont Amours.' Amours and sonnets are equated; they originate in the same rhetoric of contraries. This equation had been suggested by Ronsard as early as 1552, as he chose a title in the plural (*Les Amours*), which therefore referred to the sonnets in the collection, and not to the beloved, Cassandre.

47 See J. Balsamo, '"Nous l'avons tous admiré, et imité, non sans cause". Pétrarque en France à la Renaissance: un livre, un modèle, un mythe', in J. Balsamo (ed.) *Les Poètes français de la Renaissance et Pétrarque* (Geneva: Droz, 2004), pp. 13-34.

48 In his chapter on the ode, Peletier writes that both the ode and the sonnet are 'two elegant and agreeable kinds of work *that can be used for all kinds of argument*' ('deux genres d'ouvrages élégants, agréables, *et susceptibles de tous beaux arguments*'). See *Art poétique*, II, 6, p. 296 (emphasis mine).

49 See P. Laudun d'Aigaliers, *Art poëtique françois*, ed. J.-C. Monferran (Paris: STFM, 2000), II, 2, p. 57.

50 See the historical development of Vauquelin de La Fresnaye, *Art poetique françois* (1605), ed. G. Pellissier (Paris: Garnier, 1885), I, lines 559ff. Vauquelin de La Fresnaye mostly quotes French sonnets from the love collections, and sees the publication of *Regrets* as a key moment in the history of the sonnet: 'Et Du Bellay quitant cette amoureuse flame, / Premier fist le Sonnet sentir son Epigrame: / Capable le rendant, comme on voit, de pouvoir / Tout plaisant argument en ses vers recevoir' (lines 587-90).

51 Translation mine. See Sébillet, *Art poétique français*, II, 2, p. 108: 'les six derniers [vers] sont sujets à diverse assiette: mais plus souvent les deux premiers de ces six fraternisent en rime plate'.

52 'Six derniers vers se varient en toutes les sortes que permettent analogie et raison', ibid.
53 In order not to be too restrictive and leave a considerable degree of liberty to the poet, poetic treatises generally remain vague on the rhyme schemes of the sestet. See C. de Boissière, *Art poeticque reduict et abrégé* (Paris: Annet Briere, 1554), pp. 9–10. De Boissière refers only to Marot's scheme, but adds that the sestet should be composed at one's leisure ('à plaisir'). See also Peletier, *Art poétique*, II, 4, p. 294, and Laudun d'Aigaliers, *Art poëtique françois*, II, 2, pp. 57–9.
54 See J.-C. Monferran, 'Le sonnet français: "poème stationnaire" ou "machine à penser"? Étude de l'agencement rimique du sizain autour de 1550', *L'Information Grammaticale*, special issue on the French language in the sixteenth century, 75 (October 1997), pp. 29–32.
55 Roubaud, *La Forme du sonnet français de Marot à Malherbe*, pp. 132 and 275.
56 Not forgetting the rhyme scheme introduced by Spenser, which relies on an adaptation of the principle of *terza rima*: abab bcbc cdcd ee.
57 Roubaud, *La Forme du sonnet français de Marot à Malherbe*, p. 262.
58 On the contrary, only one sonnet in the 1549 *L'Olive* is based on alternate rhymes (only 12 out of 115 in the augmented version of 1550). The alternation between masculine and feminine rhymes, we are told, makes it easier to set the poem to music. In French, feminine rhymes end with an *e* that was still pronounced in the sixteenth century, and therefore include one extra syllable. A feminine decasyllabic line is therefore transcribed as eleven musical notes, while a masculine decasyllabic line is transcribed as ten notes. As a consequence, freely distributing masculine and feminine rhymes means that a musical score can apply only to one poem. On the contrary, when the distribution of masculine and feminine rhymes is done according to a precise and repeatedly used scheme, a musical score can be used for different poems. See J. Vignes, 'Poésie en musique: des *Amours* de Ronsard au "supplément musical"', *Fabula / Les colloques, Relire* Les Amours *de Ronsard*, www.fabula.org/colloques/document3035.php (date accessed: 29 April 2018).
59 Peletier, *Art poétique*, II, 4, p. 294: 'On le [le sonnet] fait maintenant de vers masculins et féminins: chose de curiosité, non de necessité. [...] Ce n'est pas la loi du Sonnet qui les appelle à telle observation.' For more details on that question, see the note on Peletier's *Art poétique* in the first volume of *Œuvres complètes de J. Peletier du Mans*, ed. I. Pantin (Paris: Champion, 2011), pp. 356–7, and Laudun d'Aigaliers, *Art poëtique françois*, II, 2, p. 58. At the end of the century, Laudun d'Aigaliers considers alternation as a rule of the sonnet.
60 See Du Bellay, *Deffence*, II, 4, p. 136: 'Sonne moi ces beaux Sonnets [...] conforme de nom à l'Ode, et different d'elle seulement, pource que le Sonnet a certains Vers reiglez et limitez: et l'Ode peut courir par toutes manieres de Vers librement'. / 'sing me these beautiful sonnets [...], synonymous with the ode but differing only in that the sonnet is more restricted in its length and rhyme scheme. The ode can run on freely in any meter', translation from *Poetry and Language in 16th-Century France*, p. 71. 'Sonnet', like 'ode', originally means 'song'. See F. Rigolot, 'Qu'est-ce qu'un sonnet? Perspectives sur les origines d'une forme poétique', *Revue d'Histoire Littéraire de la France*, 84 (1984), 3–18, and J. Vauquelin de La Fresnaye, *Art poetique françois* (1605) I, line 553 ('Du Son se fist Sonnet, du Chant se fist Chanson').
61 See Sébillet, *Art poétique français*, II, 2, p. 107: 'Le Sonnet suit l'épigramme de bien près, et de matière, et de mesure. Et quand tout est dit, Sonnet n'est autre chose que le parfait épigramme de l'Italien.'
62 Following Sébillet, Laudun d'Aigaliers deals with the sonnet just after the epigram in book II and the ode in book III.
63 Translation mine. See Sébillet, *Art poétique français*, II, 1, p. 107: 'Sois en l'épigramme le plus fluide que tu pourras et étudie à ce que les deux derniers vers soient aigus en conclusion: car en ces deux consiste la louange de l'épigramme'.
64 Translation mine. '[Le Sonnet] a de commun avec l'Epigramme qu'il doit se faire apparaître illustre en sa conclusion. Mais il a de plus qu'il doit être élaboré, doit sentir sa longue reconnaissance, doit résonner en tous ses vers sérieusement: et quasi tout philosophique en conceptions. Bref, il doit être fait comme de deux ou de trois conclusions. Car celui-là emportera le prix, qui au milieu de son écrit, contentera le Lecteur de telle sorte, qu'il semble que ce soit un achèvement: puis rechargera, et couronnera son ouvrage d'une fin heureuse, et digne des beautés du milieu.' Peletier, *Art poétique*, II, 4, p. 294. This passage was still elaborated upon by Guillaume Colletet in his much later *Traitté du sonnet* (1658).
65 L. Aragon, 'Du Sonnet', *Les Lettres Françaises*, 506 (4 March 1954).
66 J. Lecointe has shown that the term 'concepts' that is used here ('conceptions') means both 'thought' and 'pointe'. See '*In cauda venenum*: Montaigne et la formation du conceptisme français', *Montaigne Studies*, 18 (2006), 137–52.
67 Among other examples, see Baudelaire's well-known letter to Armand Fraisse (18 February 1860), Y. Bonnefoy's preface to *Raturer outre* (Paris: Éditions Galilée, 2011), p. 9.

68 See A. Gendre's works, especially *Évolution du sonnet français* (Paris: Puf, 1996).
69 See C. Alduy, *Politique des 'Amours': Poétique et genèse d'un genre français nouveau (1544-1560)* (Geneva: Droz, 2007), p. 362.
70 On the lives of Wyatt and Surrey, see K. Muir, *Life and Letters of Sir Thomas Wyatt* (Liverpool: Liverpool University Press, 1963); P. Thomson, *Sir Thomas Wyatt and His Background* (London: Routledge and Kegan Paul, 1964); E. Heale, *Wyatt, Surrey, and Early Tudor Poetry* (London, New York: Longman, 1998); W.A. Sessions, *Henry Howard, the Poet Earl of Surrey* (Oxford: Oxford University Press, 1999); and S. Brigden, *Thomas Wyatt, the Heart's Forest* (London: Faber & Faber, 2012).
71 On the sonnet as a stand-alone form in sixteenth-century England, see Stamatakis, Chapter 5 below.
72 '"Matters of love as of discourse": The English Sonnet, 1560-1580', *Studies in Philology*, 105:1 (2008), 30-49. Shrank's extremely welcome call to study poets of the 1560s and 1570s raises issues of literary definition and periodisation. If we see the 'sonnets' of that period as deserving the name of sonnet as much as the quatorzains that were published later in the century, what are we to make of the poems that continued to be called 'sonnets' or 'sonets' all through the seventeenth century, but were not quatorzains?
73 Milton's sonnets were based on the Petrarchan model, and were written between the late 1620s and 1658. See B.K. Lewalski and E. Haan (eds), *The Complete Works of John Milton*, vol. III (Oxford: Oxford University Press, 2012), p. xlviii.
74 The term 'sonnet' (like the term 'song') is consistently used as an indicator of the miscellaneity of poetic collections throughout the sixteenth and seventeenth centuries, quite possibly in reference to Tottel's compilation. The association of the term 'sonnet' with love often remained, even in broadside ballads. See for instance H. Crouch, *An Excellent Sonnet of the Unfortunate Loves, of Hero and Leander Tune of, Gerards Mistris.* ([London]: printed for F. Coles, T. Vere and J. Wright, [c. 1674]).
75 See J. Rainolds, *Oratio in laudem artis poeticae*, ed. William J. Ringler, trans. Walter Allen (Princeton: Princeton University Press, 1940).
76 *Certayne Notes of Instruction* ... in Alexander (ed.), *Sidney's 'The Defence of Poesy' and Selected Renaissance Literary Criticism* (London: Penguin Books, 2004), p. 245.
77 Ibid., p. 246.
78 It must be noted, however, that the sonnet was discussed at some length by James VI of Scotland (who would soon succeed Queen Elizabeth I as James I) in his 1584 *Ane Schort Treatise Conteining Some Reuils and Cautelis to be Obseruit and Eschewitt in Scottis Poesie*: 'For compendious praysing of any bukes, or the authoris thairof, or ony argumentis of vther historeis, quhair sindrie sentences and change of purposis are reqyrit, vse *Sonet* verse, of fourtene lynis, and tene fete in euery lyne'. See G.G. Smith (ed.), *Elizabethan Critical Essays*, vol. 1 (Oxford: Clarendon Press, 1904), pp. 208-24. Though this text is out of the scope of the present study, it deserves to be mentioned in so far as we have indications that James's text was read in England: we know, for instance, that Gabriel Harvey owned a copy of the book in which it had been published. See V. Stern, *Gabriel Harvey: His Life, Marginalia and Library* (Oxford: Clarendon Press; New York: Oxford University Press, 1979), esp. p. 223.
79 W. Scott, *The Model of Poesy*, ed. G. Alexander (Cambridge: Cambridge University Press, 2013), p. 81.
80 See M. Blanco, *Les Rhétoriques de la pointe: Baltasar Gracián et le conceptisme en Europe* (Paris: Champion, 1992). Blanco analyses the common ground shared by the early modern poetic concepts of *pointe*, *concetto*, concepto, conceit, *wit*, *agudeza*, etc and sees *pointe* as one of the defining features of seventeenth-century poetry across Western Europe. The term 'pointed' is also used by Spiller, see *The Development of the Sonnet: An Introduction*, p. 11. See also Stamatakis, Chapter 5 below.
81 Scott might have had in mind Tasso's *Discorsi del poema eroico* (1594), according to which *concetti* are to the lyric poem what the fable (*mythos*) is to the epic poem, i.e. structuring devices. See Blanco, *Les Rhétoriques de la pointe*, p. 209.
82 See Blanco, *Les Rhétoriques de la pointe*, and H.H. Hudson, *The Epigram in the English Renaissance* (New York: Octagon Books Inc., 1966).
83 See for example how John Davies parodies and satirises the sonnet in his *Gullinge Sonnets* (which were probably written in 1594), or how Michael Drayton integrated the satiric tradition in *Idea*, in L.H. Westling, *The Evolution of Michael Drayton's Idea* (Salzburg: Institut für Englische Sprache und Literatur, Universität Salzburg, 1974), and R. Vuillemin, *Le Recueil pétrarquiste à l'ère du maniérisme: Poétique des sonnets de Michael Drayton, 1594-1619* (Paris: Champion, 2014), pp. 247-54 and 331-8.
84 See R.L. Colie, *Shakespeare's Living Art* (Princeton: Princeton University Press, 1974), pp. 68-134.
85 See A. Fowler, *Kinds of Literature: An Introduction to the Theory of Genres and Modes* (Oxford: Clarendon Press, 1982), and D.S. Wilson-Okamura, *Spenser's International Style* (Cambridge: Cambridge University Press, 2013), pp. 70-139.

86 *The Model of Poesy*, pp. 27-9.
87 One last remark can be made here: at the end of his treatise, immediately after the lyric, Scott lingers on one last category, which includes the emblem and the *impresa*. It may only be tentatively suggested that the sonnet, especially commendatory sonnets, had affinities with the *impresa* as a device of presentation and self-presentation.
88 T. Campion, *Observations in the Art of English Poesie* [1602], pp. 331-2 in G.G. Smith (ed.), *Elizabethan Critical Essays*, vol. 2 (Oxford: Oxford University Press, 1904), pp. 327-55.
89 S. Daniel, *A Defence of Ryme* [1603], in *Elizabethan Critical Essays*, vol. 2, pp. 356-84. Using the Latin term 'girum', Daniel implicitly compares the sonnet to a circle, the figure of perfection, an 'Orbe of order and forme' as he puts it in the next sentence.
90 Especially in Webbe, Sidney and Scott.
91 See Sidney, *The Defence of Poesy*, pp. 48-9 in Alexander (ed.), *Sidney's 'Defence of Poesy' and Selected Renaissance Literary Criticism*, pp. 3-54. Puttenham's other mentions of the term 'sonnet' correspond to translations from Petrarch by Wyatt. On the Elizabethan miscellanies, see E. Pomeroy's classic study, *The Elizabethan Miscellanies: Their Development and Conventions* (Berkeley, Los Angeles, London: University of California Press, 1973).
92 G. Puttenham, *The Arte of English Poesie. Contrived into Three Bookes: The First of Poets and Poesie, the Second of Proportion, the Third of Ornament* (London: Richard Field, 1589), p. 36.
93 Ibid., pp. 48-50.
94 W. Webbe, *A Discourse of English Poesie* (1586), p. 246, in G.G. Smith (ed.), *Elizabethan Critical Essays*, vol. 1, pp. 226-302. Thomas Nashe, *The Anatomie of Absurditie* (1589), pp. 326-7 in *Elizabethan Critical Essays*, vol. 1, pp. 321-37: 'Hence come our babbling Ballets, and our new found Songs & Sonets, which every rednose Fidler hath at his fingers end, and every ignorant Ale Knight will breath foorth over the potte, as soone as is braine waxeth hote. Be it a truth which they would tune, they enterlace it with a lye or two to make meeter, not regarding veritie so they may make uppe the verse'.
95 Sidney, *The Defence of Poesy*, p. 35.
96 These remarks and those that follow rely on J.C. Boswell and G.M. Braden, *Petrarch's English Laurels, 1475-1700: A Compendium of Printed References and Allusions* (Farnham: Ashgate, 2012). On Petrarch as a 'proto-Protestant' (by far the most commonly expressed vision of Petrarch in sixteenth-century English printed sources) see the introduction to *Petrarch's English Laurels*, p. 4, and Petrarch's *Canzoniere* (also known as *Rime sparse* or *Rerum Vulgarium Fragmenta*), poems 105, 114 and 136-8.
97 A. Mortimer, *Petrarch's Canzoniere in the English Renaissance* (Bergamo: Minerva italica, 1975), p. 20.
98 See for instance *Petrarch's English Laurels*, pp. 78, 127 and 130, in which Surrey, Spenser and Sidney are respectively compared to Petrarch.
99 *Petrarch's Canzoniere in the English Renaissance*, p. 19.
100 See Gordon Braden's insistence that Petrarch's influence on Shakespeare's *Sonnets* has not been sufficiently studied in 'Shakespeare's Petrarchism', pp. 163-83. The argument that much emulation of Petrarch was mediated by the writings of other Petrarchan poets has been questioned (especially as far as Samuel Daniel is concerned), but not disproved as a whole.
101 See Puttenham, *The Arte of English Poesie*, p. 48 (Dante, Ariosto and Petrarch) or Nashe in *Elizabethan Critical Essays* vol. 1, p. 318 (Petrarch, Tasso, Celiano).
102 See Puttenham, *The Arte of English Poesie*, p. 48; Sidney, *The Defence of Poesy*, p. 5.
103 See Puttenham, *The Arte of English Poesie*, pp. 71-3 and 105.
104 See *Elizabethan Critical Essays* respectively vol. 1, pp. 114-15; vol. 2, pp. 259 and 283; vol. 2, pp. 368-9, and vol. 2, p. 314. Daniel sees Petrarch as a multi-faceted and versatile author, equally at ease in Latin and in Italian. On Daniel's direct imitations of Petrarch, see Lawrence, 'Who the Devil Taught Thee So Much Italian?'
105 See for instance *Petrarch's English Laurels*, pp. 81, 94, 103.
106 As early as 1549, for instance, William Baldwin, editor of the *Mirror for Magistrates*, 'expresses his hope that his English version of the biblical Song of Solomon might replace the songs of secular love which were popular at court'. See *The Canticles or Balades of Salomon, phraselyke declared in Englysh metres* (London: William Baldwin, 1549), sig. A3r, and R.W. Maslen (ed.), *An Apology for Poetry (or The Defence of Poesy)* (Manchester, New York: Manchester University Press, third edition, 2002), p. 19, esp. note 39.
107 See for instance W. Vaughan in *The Golden Grove* (1600), book iii, chap. 42, p. 325, in *Elizabethan Critical Essays*, vol. 2, pp. 325-6: 'I conclude that many of our English rimers and ballet-makers deserve for their baudy sonnets and amorous allurements to bee banished, or severely punished'.
108 'But truly, many of such writings as come under the banner of irresistible love, if I were a mistress, would never persuade me they were in love, so coldly they apply their fiery speeches, as men that had

rather read lovers' writings, and so caught up certain swelling phrases [...] than that in truth they feel those passions'. See Sidney, *The Defence of Poesy*, pp. 48–9.
109 Sidney, *The Defence of Poesy*, p. 33. According to Maslen, Sidney's *Defence of Poesy* was mostly written as a refutation of Plato. See *An Apology for Poetry (or The Defence of Poesy)*, p. 10.
110 T. Watson, *Hekatompathia or Passionate Centurie of Love* (London: John Wolfe for Gabriell Cawood, 1582), 'To the frendly Reader'.
111 G. Fletcher, *Licia, or Poemes of Love, in Honour of the Admirable and Singular Vertues of his Lady, to the Imitation of the Best Latin Poets, and Others* (Cambridge: John Legat, 1593), sig. A3r.
112 Sidney insists that, in his psalms, David 'showeth himself a passionate *lover* of that unspeakable and everlasting beauty, to be seen by the eyes of the mind, only cleared by faith'. Further down (p. 29), Sidney allegorises virtue as a beautiful woman, drawing inspiration from *Phaedrus* 250d. See *The Defence of Poesy*, pp. 7, 29 and 339, note 146. See also W. Scott's *Model of Poesy*, pp. 15–16 and pp. 70–1, where he articulates the different kinds of love.
113 R. Ascham, *The Scholemaster* (London: John Daye, 1570), sig. Iiir.
114 Even Petrarch was affected. See for instance how George Whetstone criticised Petrarch (together with Ovid) in his *An Heptameron of Civill Discourses* (London: Richard Jones, 1582), sig. I3v: 'All these were men learned, wise, and in their other actions (for their gravitie) were admyred, and onely for their lightnesse in love, live to this day defamed'. Quoted in *Petrarch's English Laurels*, p. 94.
115 Scott, *The Model of Poesy*, p. 71.
116 Letter quoted in *An Apology for Poetry (or The Defence of Poesy)* p. 120, note 4. Chapman, as late as 1598, denounces 'quidditical Italianistes'. See *Achilles Shield, Translated as the Other Seven Bookes of Homer Out of his Eighteenth Booke of Illiades*, p. 306 in *Elizabethan Critical Essays*, vol. 2, pp. 297–307. It could be added that Lyly's *Euphues, or the Anatomy of Wit* (1578) is also about the conversion of language from an empty (and potentially immoral) wit to verbal skills that promote morality and divinity.
117 Fletcher, *Licia*, sig. A2v.
118 Fox, *The English Renaissance*, pp. 32–3. Of course, such struggle should not be seen as an opposition between the advocates of poetry on the one hand, and Calvinists or Puritans on the other hand. Some of the most vocal defenders of poetry, such as Sidney or Scott, were Calvinists themselves.
119 See J. Scott-Warren, *Sir John Harington and the Book as Gift* (Oxford: Oxford University Press, 2001), p. 30.
120 See Roche, *Petrarch and the English Sonnet Sequences*.

II

Performing the English sonnet

3

Sonnet-mongers on the early modern English stage

Guillaume Coatalen

The phrase 'Sonnet-mongers'[1] is taken from John Marston's play *Parasitaster or the Fawn*, Act 4, in which suitors are described as 'fauour wearers, sonnet mongers, health drinkers, & neat in riches of barbers, & perfumers, & to conclude al that can wy hee or wag the taile'.[2] The term 'monger' – defined by the *Oxford English Dictionary* as 'a merchant, trader, dealer, or trafficker (freq. of a specified commodity); (from the sixteenth cent.) a person engaged in a petty or disreputable trade or traffic'[3] – is blatantly derogatory, as in 'whoremonger', for which 'monger' is the shorter form attested in 1604.[4] Sonnets in Shakespeare's plays have been rather well studied but the presence of the figure of the sonneteer (or sonnetist) on the English stage in the early modern period has not.[5] Patrick Cheney, for instance, is mostly concerned with Shakespeare's engagement with authorship and creation of his own myth as the national poet-playwright, while David Schalkwyk focuses on the performative power of sonnets in Shakespeare's plays.[6] The most useful contribution on poets in Shakespeare's plays is B.J. Sokol's recent synthetical chapter in a guide exploring Shakespeare's artists.[7] To my knowledge, no critical analysis has been written previously on dramatic excerpts discussing the sonnet, apart from those in Shakespeare's plays. Contrary to the embedded sonnets in *Romeo and Juliet* or *As You Like It*, the vast majority of dramatic passages I have chosen here contain not sonnets proper recited by characters alone or otherwise but rather discussions on sonneteering or simply allusions to the sonnet as a poetic genre. The sheer number of comments on sonnets in early modern plays proves that playwrights used plays to stage poets and the art of sonnet making. From the period only a few scattered remarks on the sonnet in critical texts survive and I would like to suggest that substantial untapped material may be found in dramatic texts.[8]

The material this study is based on contains extracts from both major – with a few brief references to Shakespeare – and minor playwrights in which the sonnet, or rather the predominant Petrarchan love sonnet, is discussed both as a poetic form and a tool for social advancement. More specifically, such sonnets played a decisive part in wooing strategies. The following exchange excerpted from *Delectable Demaundes, and Pleasaunt Questions, with their Seuerall Aunswers, in Matters of Loue, Naturall Causes, with Morall and Politique Deuises* (1566) stresses how potent verse is to praise a lover: 'Why do Louers write one to another amorouse sonnets in ryme rather then in prose? Poetrie is the frend of Loue. And all the praise belonging to loue was alwaies more swetely songe and celebrated by Poetes then by Orators.'[9] In sonnet studies, non-Shakespearean plays have been underexploited as crucial sources for poetic and social criticism. Perhaps because sonnets are formal objects obeying strict constraints, literary critics have tended to neglect such material. Yet, sonnets become dynamic objects which play a part in the dramatic action. This offers precious insights into how the form was considered by playwrights and their audiences.

The dramatic sources show how deeply rooted the practice of composing sonnets was in English society well beyond the court. Typically, such plays, which are predominantly comedies, stage amateur sonnetists belonging to the country gentry. The sonneteer's presence in drama is indeed pervasive till the end of the Restoration. Critics tend to focus on the second half of the sixteenth century and more precisely the sonnet craze in the 1590s, but writing sonnets still played a crucial part in the Restoration and later, even though these were not necessarily quatorzains but more often short lyric poems. By the 1640s, attitudes towards sonneteering had changed, the practice itself was frequently satirised in plays, not just Petrarchan sonnets of low quality. This does not mean sonnets were no longer written, but the influence of the smooth style which characterised the verse of poets like Edmund Waller suggests that Petrarchan sonnets were considered too quaint to be taken seriously. The significant number of plays printed in the 1640s and the Interregnum discussing the sonnet proves that the form played a crucial part in defining the newer more classical aesthetics. In William Burnaby's *Reformed Wife* (1700),[10] a character promises to besiege a woman with songs and sonnets, 'that she shall surrender for her own quiet'.

In James Shirley's *Example* (1637),[11] the playwright mentions the hundreds of sonnets written per year:

> You come to turne and winde this Ladies fancie
> With your wit now, but your devices fadge not,
> It is three minutes since shee was dispos'd of,
> And though my stocke of braine will not reach, to
> Make a large joynture of so many hundred
> Sonnets *per annum*, and rare Elegies,
> Some fresh, and some that ha laine 7. yeeres pickled,
> In other languages: yet sheele be content
> With a lesse witty fortune, my estate sir.

The hyperbole is meant to be humorous but it indicates that sonnets (or, at least, poems regarded as sonnets) were still extremely common in the Caroline age. More cynical Ovidian elegies in the manner of John Donne's had not entirely replaced them, even though they were growing more and more fashionable. The metaphor of food is noteworthy, 'Some fresh, and some that ha laine 7. yeeres pickled'. The terms 'fresh' and 'pickled' may point to fish, perhaps pickled herring. The line suggests sonnets were consumed like food, were perishable goods, not the eternal monuments praised by Shakespeare in his own sonnets. Besides 'some that ha laine [have lain] 7. yeeres pickled' indicates that some were kept for long and translated from other languages. Translation and the use of older material are condemned as cheap tricks for fake poets, those incapable of true inspiration.

As a professional playwright writing for the expensive indoor theatres, Shirley sought to distance himself from mere poetasters and to flatter his audience's refined tastes. For Brome, entire trunks of verse, including sonnets, could be filled by gallants: 'what personall Estate / Ist like hee'l leave you, but his Powder glasse, / His Combe and Beard-brush, and perhaps a Trunkfull / Of Elegies, Raptures, Madrigalls and Sonnets?'[12] A trunkful of verse belongs to the gallant's attributes just as much as his 'Powder glasse', 'Comb and Beard-brush', three obvious symbols of vanity. The image is that of a fool wasting his time preening himself before a mirror, and, by adding the bundles of verse in manuscript to the textual vanity, Brome despises the genres of love poetry for encouraging sin. The gallant's lack of personal estate links poverty to this type of verse, which is criticised for being a distraction from more profitable pursuits. Sonnets along with other poetic toys, such as elegies, raptures and madrigals, are not just the fruit of vanity and idleness, they fuel them.

I wish to investigate the paradoxical representation of sonneteering as a consistently demeaned yet inescapable poetic practice, and explore the formal influence of the Petrarchan love sonnet in plays after the waning of the 'sonnet craze'. While the quatorzain became somewhat rarer after the 1630s, the influence of Petrarchan *loci* remained irrefutable in the short lyric poems which replaced the stricter form. Though the historical context and poetics changed radically in the course of a century or so, the playwrights' treatment of the sonnet seems to have remained constant. The sonnet, or rather the Petrarchan sonnet, is invariably considered a hackneyed form; it seems, however, impossible to dismiss it altogether, even when it has long gone out of fashion at court and in literary coteries. I will follow two threads to assess the sonnet's reputation in plays: sonneteering as a mercantile activity practised by incompetent sonneteers, and staging sonneteering to reflect on evolving poetic language.

Sonnets commodified by incompetent poets

Sonnets were often associated with songs. The common label 'songs and sonnets',[13] used for the title of John Donne's posthumous 1633 collection of secular verse, points to the musical nature of the genre, which is faithful to the etymology of the Italian term 'sonetto', the diminutive of 'sound' or 'melody' in Old Provençal. In dramatic material sonnets are almost always discussed in groups of related poetic forms, more rarely alone. This is crucial since modern critics tend to isolate the sonnet from neighbouring forms. A distinction was made between them as in this passage taken from Thomas Tomkis's *Albumazar*, a play performed before the King in Cambridge in 1614, where sonnets seem to require more inspiration: 'Hee that saith I am not in loue, hee lies *De cap à pe*; For I am idle, choicely neate in my cloathes, valiant, and extreme witty: My meditations are loded with metaphors, and my songs sonnets'.[14] Not all songs are sonnets and writing longer and less strict forms was deemed to be easier. The accumulation of metaphors distinguishes Elizabethan sonnets from Jacobean songs, with the notable exception of John Donne's. Extant songs of a longer sort produced by academic circles around 1614 tend to display fewer conceits as opposed to, for instance, Shakespeare's sonnets, and this is simply due to an evolution in poetic style in the first decades of the seventeenth century. The student in

Albumazar, however, stresses the similarity between the songs produced by a lover and sonnets, a point which may sound odd at first. By doing so, he may be mocking the success of Donne's conceits at Cambridge which encouraged students and others to imitate them in their songs.

In plays, sonnets are more often than not condemned as being a waste of time and, worse, a sign of vanity. Composing sonnets distracts gentlemen from more serious pursuits as in Robert Greene's *Gwydonius*, a debate between Love and Folly published in 1584.[15] The work belongs to the subgenre of the debate with its own specificities and was itself translated from the French. In this instance at least, however, what applied to France appears to be relevant in England as well, for the translation encourages the English reader to transpose the contents to his land. In it, sonnets are associated with a series of vices, as seen when Apollo pleads on behalf of Venus who demands justice against Folly, whom she accuses of having abused her son Cupid:

> And I greatly feare that wheras Loue hath inuented so many laudable sciences, and brought foorth so many commodities, that now he will bring great idlenesse accompanied with ignoraunce, that he will cause young Gentlemen to leaue feates of armes, to forsake the seruice of their Prince, to reiect honourable studyes, and to applye them selues to vaine songs and sonnets, to chambring and wantonnesse, to banketting and gluttonie, bringing infinite diseases to their bodies, and sundrie daungers and perills to their persons, for there is no more daungerous companie than of Folly. (fol. 75v)

The passage clearly opposes the courtier's manly virtues, proving his mettle at war, serving his prince and engaged in honourable studies – presumably political philosophy, law, possibly science – and composing 'vaine songs and sonnets'.

The great counter-model to such a disjunction between virility and the practice of poetry is to be found in the martial figure of Philip Sidney, who died fighting for his country after having produced the most acclaimed verse in the vernacular. Given the cultural and social prestige of sonnets at court in the 1580s and 1590s,[16] the passage quoted above may sound odd. One explanation might be that, since Robert Greene never wrote sonnets and was more of a popular prose writer, the translation allowed him to condemn his social betters. A more suitable explanation may be found in the passage's irony. Robert Greene may be mocking widespread condemnation of sonneteering among the professional classes and the more puritanical clergymen. Composing sonnets did compete with legal studies, the 'honourable studies' *par excellence*. The Inns of Court were well-known centres of sonneteering, as is made clear in the following extract taken from the opening lines of Ben Jonson's *Poetaster*, when the servant Luscus warns Ovid that his father is about to enter the room: 'Young master, Master *Ouid*, doe you heare? Gods a me! away with your *songs*, and *sonnets*; and on with your gowne and Cappe, quickly.'[17] The historical Ovid was destined to become a lawyer and Jonson uses this fact to develop his satire of literary circles of which he did not approve and whose members competed directly with him.

For all the rejection voiced repeatedly by poets themselves, sonnets were a commodity in the early modern period. The sonnet's price, however, underlines the part the form played in economic exchanges. Furthermore, the composition of sonnets is reduced to a vulgar mercantile exchange which sheds a practical and cynical light on the idealisation of the mistress. Wooing becomes little more than selling and buying poetic skills. Commendatory sonnets could be written for particular poets but, more significantly still, all those who could afford to do so hired poets for special occasions. As an example from *Northward Hoe* shows, typically a lady would call for a poet 'about a sonnet or an epitaph for her child that died at nurse, or for some deuice about a maske or so'.[18] A sonnet was useful to woo by proxy, as it were, and the lady may have needed a commendatory sonnet to gain favours, or perhaps even a love sonnet written by a male professional poet to send to a lover. In the same play, the Captain confesses his 'desires are to haue some amiable and amorous sonnet or madrigall composed by' the poet's 'Fury' (sig. E2v). Here again, the sonnet is closely linked to another musical form, the madrigal, which set numerous love sonnets, starting with Petrarch's.

Lovers who cannot resist writing abominable sonnets belong to a larger category of incompetent sonneteers in plays. In fact, competent sonneteers do not seem to exist on the stage. Melancholy was fashionable in the Jacobean period, and thought to grant inspiration, which is Ben Jonson's ironical point in *Euery Man in his Humour* (1601) in this conversation between a country gull (Master Stephen) and a town gull (Master Mathew):

> Master Stephen. I truely sir, I am mightily giuen to melancholy.
> Master Mathew. Oh Lord sir, it's your only best humor sir, your true melancholy, breedes your perfect fine wit sir: I am melancholie my selfe diuers times sir, and then do I no more but take your pen and paper presently, and write you your halfe score or your dozen of sonnets at a sitting.[19]

Here, melancholy as the sonneteer's source of inspiration may owe something to Armado in *Love's Labour's Lost* 'turn[ing] sonnet' (1.2.184).[20] The ability to write several sonnets at once is praised as a sign of profound inspiration. Writing a single sonnet was not enough, it seems. Whether they were supposed to form a proper sequence is left undecided but inevitably writing sonnets one after the other would create numerous meaningful echoes between them through repetitions. The irony is of course that quite a few fine poets, including John Donne and Ben Jonson himself, were prone to melancholy for various reasons, ill-health and dire straits being the main ones. The attack on the melancholic humour is sometimes more bitter as in Richard Zouch's *The Sophister* (1639), 'This black stuffe is the excrement of Melancholy: / This sometimes makes him 'mongst the groves and rivers, / Pen Sonnets to the Nymphs and Goddesses',[21] which constitutes scathing criticism of pastoral or mythological sonnets reduced to excrement – the 'black stuffe' refers to black bile but possibly to ink as well, apart from the blatant scatological joke. When the clown mocks lovers in Heywood's *Loves Maistresse* (1636), he names a few rhyming types of love poems and the 'Phillis'es and 'Amorillis'es of pastorals: 'But listen to them and they will fill your heads with a thousand fooleries; observe one thing, there's none of you all sooner in love, but he is troubled with their itch, for hee will bee in his Amorets, and his Canzonets, his Pastoralls, and his Madrigalls, to his Phillis, and his Amorillis.'[22] The terms 'Amorets' and 'Canzonets' may refer to sonnets, 'Canzonets', or little short songs, being strongly reminiscent of Petrarch's *Canzoniere*, in keeping with the definition of the term 'Canzonet' in Edward Phillips's 1658 dictionary, 'a song or sonnet'.[23] Later on, the clown, who plays the part of the lover, adds to the list: 'I have bin so troubled with a Poeticall itch, that I can scratch you out Rimes, and Ballats, Songs, and Sonnetts, Oades, and Madrigalls, till they bleed againe'.[24]

Poetic incompetence and plagiarism go hand in hand. In Thomas Randolph's *Hey for Honesty* (1651), Mercurius, the God of Theft, declares:

> Then let me be your Poet: I'le make you Shewes and Masques, Comedies and Tragedies, Pastorals, Piscatorial Sonnets, Canto's, Madrigals and Ballads, till you are so tickled with laughter, that you cannot stand.[25]

The 'Piscatorial Sonnets' sound grotesque but may refer to Giovan Battista Marino's *Rime Marittime* (Venice, 1602) and Jacopo Sannazaro's earlier *Eclogae Piscatoriae* (1526) which were fashionable in European academic circles.[26] Stealing from other sonnets characterises the ridiculous lover hunting for 'fustian phrases' and foreign words:

> God blesse my eie-sight,
> A Sonnet tis in verse, now on my life
> He hath perusde all the impressions
> Of Sonnets since the fall of Lucifer,
> And made some scuruy quaint collection
> Of fustian phrases, and vplandish worde[27]

The catalogue of types of poems a fool pretends he can write seems to be a trope in comedies, as in George Chapman's *All Fools* (1605). Pedants liked to display their pseudo-knowledge of poetic forms and genres, notably Italian ones, like *rima sdruciola*, a poem whose rhymes are words stressed on their antepenult syllables and rhyming on all three final syllables. The sonnets are either made of twelve – in dozens, or fourteen lines – 'quatorzains' wrongly printed 'Quatorzanies', perhaps to make the word sound Italian:

> I could haue written as good Prose and Verse,
> As the most beggerlie Poet of am all,
> Either accrostique, *Exordion*,
> *Epithalamious, Satyres, Epigrams,*
> *Sonnets in Doozens, or your Quatorzanies,*
> *In any Rime Masculine, Feminine,*
> *Or Sdruciolla, or cooplets,* Blancke Verse[.][28]

The sonnet seems to be the poet's attribute when Lord Tales asks Sir Giles Goosecap: 'Haue you no sonnet of your penne about ye?'[29] In many plays, ridiculous poets write sonnets, or rather 'thinne' sonnets, which suggests they are empty trifles of little worth.[30]

Beyond targeting incompetent would-be poets, playwrights, even when they write sonnets themselves, underline how grotesque the form is. Thus, some plays present monstrous variants of sonnets, like the Cambridge student play *The Returne from Parnassus* which contains a scatological attack on sonneteers: 'And you Maister Amoretto, that art the chiefe Carpenter of Sonets, a priuileged Vicar for the lawlesse

> To loue a Lady, is with heart entire
> To make her Mistresse of his whole desire:
> To sigh for her, and for her loue to weepe;
> As his owne heart her precious fauours keepe:
> Neuer be from her, in her bosome dwell;
> To make her presence heauen, her absence hell.
> Write Sonnets in her praise, admire her beauty:
> Attend her, serue her, count his seruice duty.
> Make her the sole commandresse of his powers,
> And in the search of loue, loose all his howers.

The lines are entirely made of clichés on the lover's conduct. They are also based on a series of figures of style which feature prominently in love sonnets, among them the double hyperbole 'entire … whole'; synonymia doubled with the inversion dictated by the lame couplet, 'To sigh for her, and for her loue to weep'; the double antithesis 'presence heauen … absence hell'; the enumeration 'Attend her, serue her, count his seruice duty'. If 'writ[ing] sonnets in her praise' is part of a larger amorous strategy, it is quite obvious in this self-reflexive passage that sonnets encapsulate best the play-acting involved in making love. Like Shakespeare, Heywood is acutely aware of the intrinsic theatrical nature of the sonnet as a miniature play whose rhetoric embodies and enacts the lover's passions most convincingly.[44]

In Thomas Dekker's *Patient Grissil* (1603), a gull even pretends he can read by pulling out a bundle of sonnets and reading them to the ladies. It is hard to decide whether reading sonnets to ladies was thought to be more effective than sending them. He probably learnt them by heart and recited them: 'Rice. … the gull can neither write nor reade. / Urcenze. Ha ha, not write and reade? why I haue séene him pul out a bundle of sonnets writen, & read them to Ladies.'[45] Sonnets, as vehicles for gossip, induce the fear of humiliation. In Marston's *The Insatiate Countess* (1613), Signior Rogero confesses his (non-existent) role in the attempt against Mendoza Foscari's life (an attempt that did not actually take place), the Duke of Amago's kinsman, so he does not have to admit he has been cuckolded: 'Nay more, my Lord, we feared that your kinsman for a messe of Sonnets, would haue giuen the plot of vs and our wiues, to some needy Poet, and for sport and profit brought vs in some Venician Comedy vpon the Stage'.[46] The 'Venician Comedy' is probably a reference to Marston's own *What You Will* (1601), the only extant Elizabethan comedy set in Venice and, ironically, a play which focuses on the relationship between two rival poets (unless one sees *The Merchant of Venice* as a comedy, as the compiler of the First Folio did).

Though men were expected to send love sonnets to woo, the type of poem is often seen as weak and effeminate in plays. Robert Mead's *Combat of Love and Friendship* (1654) contains a fierce misogynistic attack on poetry according to which women who demand sonnets to be courted turn men into detestable rimers: 'A Ballad-singer and a vext Constable I should take e'm for; but that I know the one to be a boysterously valiant Captain, and t'other a Gentleman abus'd into a Poet by his Mistresse: who, having for a long time courted her with verses only and Sonnets, is now injoyn'd by Her to speak nothing but Rime'.[47] 'Abus'd into a Poet' suggests the Mistress turns him into a poet against his will and the death of prose describes a serious perversion of language. The date of publication, 1654, is interesting in itself since very few love sonnets survive from the Interregnum, which suggests not that few were composed but simply that they did not survive because they were thought to be worthless.

In Francis Beaumont and John Fletcher's *Woman-Hater* (1607), Gondarino declares that all love poetry is fake and addressed to ugly women:

> for how familiar a thing is it with the Poets of our age, to extoll their whores, which they call Mistresses, with heavenly praises? but I thank their furies, and their craz'd brains, beyond belief: nay, how many that would fain seem serious, have dedicated grave Works to Ladies, toothless, hollow-ey'd, their hair shedding, purple fac'd, their nails apparently coming off; and the bridges of their noses broken down, and have call'd them the choice handy works of nature, the patterns of perfection, and the wonderment of Women.[48]

Even though Beaumont and Fletcher do not mention sonnets explicitly, the term 'Mistresses' and the anti-blazon itemising the woman's horrific attributes – 'toothless, hollow-ey'd, their hair shedding, purple fac'd, their nails apparently coming off; and the bridges of their noses broken down' – are typical of burlesque love sonnets. The blazon and anti-blazon were two sides of a rhetorical coin.[49] The original model for the anti-blazon in Beaumont and Fletcher's play may have been Berni's influential creation of an anti-Laura which was part of his anti-Petrarchism.[50] More significantly, the idealised vision of the mistress at the heart of sonneteering is under attack – although one must bear in mind that the author of the attack, Gondarino, is himself ridiculed and punished for his misogyny in the play. Shakespeare used it famously to further his mistress's praise in Sonnet 130 'My mistress' eyes are nothing like the sun'.

Plays contain both general reflections on the sonnet as a literary genre and precise discussions on the technique of sonneteering. These dramatic moments mirror debates at court, among gallants and other readers of verse, and also offer fascinating glimpses into the playwrights' poetics. In John Lyly's *Midas* (1592), Pan defends rustic pastoral poetry against more refined sonnets practised by Apollo on the lute, 'Beleeue me Apollo, our groues are pleasanter than your heauens, our Milk-maides than your Goddesses, our rude ditties to a pipe than your sonnets to a lute'.[51] The lute is the emblematic musical instrument of the court. In Anthony Munday's *Death of Robert* (1601), the king makes an ironical allusion to a precise type of sonnet, the blazon on the female body, when he mocks a character who has addressed verse to the queen:

> King. But he hath had in you, as it should seeme,
> Els would he not make sonnets of your browe,
> Your eye, your lip, your hand, your thigh,
> A plague vpon him: how came he so nigh?
> Nay, now you haue the curst queanes counterfet:
> Through rage you shake, because you cannot raue.
> But answere me; Why should the Bedlam slaue
> Entitle a whole Poem to your kisse,
> Calling it chery, ruby, this and this?
> I tell you, I am iealous of your loue,
> Which makes me breake into this passion.[52]

Immediately after these lines follows a second joke on the sonnets offered to seek patronage in which 'well writ poemes' are carefully distinguished from 'balla[d]izing rimes', or poems as crude as broadsheet ballads. Quite clearly, sonnets are deemed to be vastly superior to ballads and enjoy a special status in the poetic canon. The lines are significant for the strong hierarchy they establish between poetic genres which reflects the social hierarchy. The implication is that refined sonnets are the preserve of the nobility whereas commoners, notably in the country, are incapable of producing more subtle verse than ballads:

> Hubert. Why my good Lord, was neuer Poetry,
> Offred vnto a Ladies patronage?
> Salsbury. Yes, but not taken.
> Hu. Yes, and taken too.
> Though muddy slaues, whose ballatizing rimes,
> With words vnpolisht, shewe their brutish thoughts,
> Naming their Maukins in each lustfull line:
> Let no celestiall beautie looke awry,
> When well writ poemes, couching her rich praise,
> Are offerd to her vnstain'd vertues eye.
> For Poetries high sprighted sonnes will raise,
> True beautie to all wisht eternitie:
> Therefore my Lord, your age is much to blame,
> To thinke a taken Poeme Ladies shame.⁵³

'Maukins' or rather 'Malkins' is quite a derogatory word since it is a typical name for 'a lower-class, untidy, or sluttish woman, especially a servant or country girl' (*OED*, 'malkin, n.') with a possible bawdy joke on 'malkin' as female genitalia. The word contrasts sharply with the lofty diction, choice epithets ('celestial beautie', 'couching her rich praise' 'high sprighted sonnes') and conceit ('offerd to her vnstain'd vertues eye'), the hallmarks of Petrarchan love sonnets.

Practical definitions of poetry may be gleaned from scenes involving poets reading or reciting poetry. Such passages are particularly helpful on poetic composition when they include comments on verse, whether positive or negative. *The Honest Lawyer* (1616) by one S.S. contains one such moment in which the beginning of a grotesque sonnet is recited by Nice, a superstitious but harmless fool, who invites Thirsty to get drunk with poetry. The context of the piece is a brief exchange on poetry dismissed by Thirsty as a trade which 'will scarce make a man drink'. Nice believes too much liquor makes a poet 'threadbare' and recites the lines to illustrate superior poetry:

> Sirrah, I ha' made a Sonnet here to my Mistresse; she n'ere wrought such a one on her Samplar. Lay thine eare close to my musicall tongue, I shall rauish her.
>
> Open thine eares, like an Oyster a sunning
> Euen as the bird, which we Camelion call,
>   doth liue on aire for aye:
> So my kinde heart, euer like a stocke-Doue shall
>   feede on thy loue all day.⁵⁴

The unusual bestiary – the chameleon clashes with the notion of constant love, associated with the relentless comparisons – debunks sonneteers' efforts to find ever surprising images. In his *White Devil* (1612), John Webster mocks the conceits endlessly repeated in Petrarchan sonnets through Flamineo, the secretary to the Duke of Bracciano, a position traditionally held by writers. The character is certainly the playwright's spokesperson: 'what an ignorant asse or flattering knaue might he be counted, that should write sonnets to her eyes, or call her brow the snow of Ida, or Iuorie of Corinth, or compare her haire to the blacke birds bill, when tis liker the blacke birds feather.'[55] By 1612, when Webster's play was printed, the influence of Petrarchan conceits was waning among leading writers and had been replaced by yet more daring conceits such as John Donne's, and a somewhat cynical and down-to-earth treatment of the mistress's idealisation in both Shakespeare's sonnets and Donne's erotic verse. Michael Drayton – whose *Ideas Mirror*, which was first published in 1594, first revised as *Idea* in 1599, and went through eight editions to 1619, clearly belongs to the Petrarchan tradition – distanced himself from the Petrarchan model under James I, when he turned to satire, elegies and his *Poly-Olbion*, a long historical poem celebrating England whose first part appeared in 1613.[56] Generally, more measured Horatian poetics were gaining ground from around 1600 through Ben Jonson and his circle.[57] The composition of both Shakespeare's and Donne's verse began some time during the sonnet craze in the 1590s, which is when the reversal of Petrarchan topoi became common.[58] Another clear rejection of the Petrarchan mode of love poetry appears in Thomas Tomkis's *Lingua* (1607), where Phantastes exclaims:

> Oh heauens, how haue I beene troubled these latter times with Women, Fooles, Babes, Taylers, Poets, Swaggerers, Guls, Balladmakers, they haue almost disrobed me of all the toyes and trifles I can deuise, were it not that I pitty the poore multitude of Printers, these Sonnet-mungers should starue for conceits, for all *Phantastes*. But these puling Louers, I cannot but laugh at them and their Encomions of their Mistresses. They make forsooth her hayre of Gold, her eyes of Diamond, her cheekes of Roses, her lippes of Rubies, her teeth of Pearle, and her whole body of Iuory: and when they haue thus Idol' her like *Pigmalion,* they fall downe and worship her. *Psyche,* thou hast laid a hard taske vpon my shoulders, to inuent at euery ones aske, were it not that I refresh my dulnesse once a day with my most Angelicall presence, 'twere vnpossible for me to vndergo it.[59]

Elsewhere, in Gervase Markham's *Dumbe Knight* (1608), mythological allusions are made fun of: 'sonnets made of *Cupids* burning dart. / Of *Venus* lip, and *Iunoes* maiestie'.[60] A suitor may even be rejected for their accumulation, as in John Fletcher's *Elder Brother* (1637):

> Angellina.
> Troth (if he be nothing else)
> As of the Courtier; all his Songs, and Sonnets,
> His Anagrams, Acrosticks, Epigrammes,
> His deepe and Philosophicall discourse
> Of natures hidden secrets, makes not up
> A perfect husband; He can hardly borrow
> The Starres of the Celestiall crowne to make me
> A tire for my head; nor *Charles* Waine for a Coach,

Nor *Ganimede* for a Page, nor a rich gowne
From *Juno's* Wardrobe, nor would I lye in
(For I despaire not once to be a mother)
Under heavens spangled Canopy, or banquet
My guests and Gossips with imagin'd Nectar,
Pure *Orleans* would doe better; no, no, father,
Though I could be well pleas'd to have my husband
A Courtier, and a Scholar, young, and valiant,
These are but gawdy nothings, If there be not
Something to make a substance.[61]

A gentleman flatly refuses to play the game in Shirley's *Humorous Courtier* (1640):

I make no Sonnets of your anticke dressings,
Cry up your colour of your face, and sweare
Y'are divine peeces, for I know you are not:
I will not draw heavens curse upon me, for
Flattering into pride; say that the Lillies,
Are pale, for envy of your white, and the Roses
Blush, to see better in your cheekes, your haire
Beames, rather drawne up to a net, might catch
Iove when he plaid the Eagle; that your brests
Raise up themselves like two faire Mountainers
Ith' pleasant vale of temptation, I hate this[.][62]

At times, a scene may contain a technical analysis on a poetic device, as in the following passage from Thomas Corneille's *Extravagant Shepherd*, in Thomas Rawlins's 1654 translation, where a shepherd and a nymph discuss whether a lover may address his mistress's eye singular instead of her eyes plural:

Angelica. Such language, Sheepherd, does affront your Mistris,
The brightnesse of her eyes, you see's not common,
They both can charme, and yet you praise but one.
What Rapsodie of love doth make you talk so?

Lysis. Why I assume the language of the Poets.
This style to them was ever held peculiar,
I purposely, like them, spoke but of one,
But yet with no designe t'offend my fairest;
For either of those Suns afford me light,
And when I sweare her faire ey's skill'd to charme,
I speake no more o'th' left than of the right.[63]

The synecdoche alluded to is the *pars pro toto* type common in love poetry, and Petrarchan sonnets in particular, to describe parts of the mistress's body occasionally in a blazon. The single eye often compared to the sun occurs in Shakespeare's sonnet 49, line 6, 'And scarcely greet me with that sun, thine eye'.[64] Lysis may refer jokingly to the first tercet of Petrarch's *Rime* 233, 'For from my lady's right eye – rather her right sun – to my right eye cam the illness that delights me and does not pain me' ('che dal dextr'occhio, anzi dal dextro sole, / de la mia donna al mio dextr'occhio venne / il mal che mi diletta, et non mi dole'), where the mistress's right eye, or rather right sun, is responsible for the lover's delightful illness.[65]

Overall, sonneteers are presented in quite a negative way in plays: they appear to be little more than incompetent parasites. According to the evidence contained in such material, Petrarchan love sonnets are the prerogative of clumsy amateurs and written off as effeminate and decadent.[66] From an early stage, playwrights seem to express their rejection of a poetic mode distinctly *passé*. What is striking is how continuously the excessive language of sonnets is mocked over more than a century. This suggests that the Petrarchan tropes which were particularly successful in English love sonnets in the second half of the sixteenth century endured through time among amateur poets. When received poets in the canon, dramatic or not, had moved on to anti-Petrarchan poetics, or poetics which had little to do with the Petrarchan model, more ordinary rhymers kept on imitating the *Canzoniere*. The comparison between earlier and later plays in which the sonnet and sonneteering are discussed seems to point to the changing social and political status of this predominant poetic form. Indeed, the relative democratisation of the sonnet led to its confinement to the private sphere far from the court where it no longer wielded any sort of influence.

Notes

1 I am grateful to the readers for their fine work. This is the only occurrence in the *Oxford English Dictionary* (Oxford: Oxford University Press), online edition (date accessed: 23 June 2017).
2 J. Marston, *Parasitaster or the Fawn* (London: Printed by T[homas] P[urfoot] for VV. C[otton], 1606), sig. G1v.
3 *OED*.
4 The *OED* records a use of the word in that sense in Thynne's *Emblems & Epigrams* (1604, 1600 according to other entries of the *OED* and to nineteenth-century editor Furnivall): 'What monger maiest thow bee … vnknowne as yett to all this companie? Fforthwith the mann, as pertest of them all, sayed hee a whoremonger was knowne to bee.' See F.J. Furnivall's edition in the Early English Text Society series (London, 1876), p. 68. The *OED* (presumably erroneously) indicates 1871 as the publication date of Furnivall's edition.
5 See G. Whittier, 'The Sonnet's Body and the Body Sonnetized in "Romeo and Juliet"', *Shakespeare Quarterly*, 40:1 (1989), 27–41; H. Vendler, 'Shakespeare's Other Sonnets', in T. Moisan and D. Bruster (eds), *In the Company of Shakespeare: Essays on English Renaissance Literature in Honor of G. Blakemore Evans* (Madison, NJ; London: Fairleigh Dickinson University Press; Associated University Press, 2002), pp. 161–76; P. Cheney, 'Poetry in Shakespeare's Plays', in P. Cheney (ed.), *The Cambridge Companion to Shakespeare's Poetry* (Cambridge: Cambridge University Press, 2007), pp. 221–40; P. Cheney, 'Halting Sonnets: Poetry and Theater in *Much Ado about Nothing*', in M.C. Schoenfeldt (ed.), *A Companion to Shakespeare's Sonnets* (Oxford: Blackwell, 2007), pp. 363–82.
6 D. Schalkwyk, *Speech and Performance in Shakespeare's Sonnets and Plays* (Cambridge: Cambridge University Press, 2002).
7 B.J. Sokol, 'Poets in Shakespeare's Plays', in *Shakespeare's Artists: The Painters, Sculptors, Poets and Musicians in His Plays and Poems* (London: Bloomsbury Arden Shakespeare, 2018), pp. 93–116.
8 Sir John Harington's *Apology for Ariosto* (B. Vickers, *English Renaissance Literary Criticism* (Oxford: Oxford University Press, 1999), p. 312), Sir Philip Sidney's *Defence of Poetry* (Vickers, *English Renaissance Literary Criticism*, pp. 385 and 391), Thomas Campion's *Observations in the Art of English Poesie* (Vickers, *English Renaissance Literary Criticism*, p. 432), and a slightly longer treatment of the constraints of the form in Samuel Daniel's *Defence of Ryme* (Vickers, *English Renaissance Literary Criticism*, pp. 446–7). The only dramatic extract which occurs in Vickers, *English Renaissance Literary Criticism* is the one taken from *Edward III*. Interestingly, it is not listed under sonnet in the 'Index of Topics' perhaps because the term 'sonnet' does not occur but the text is replete with Petrarchan conceits.

9 *Delectable Demaundes, and Pleasaunt Questions, with their Seuerall Aunswers, in Matters of Loue, Naturall Causes, with Morall and Politique Deuises* (London: In Paules Churchyarde by Iohn Cawood for Nicholas Englande, [1566]).
10 W. Burnaby, *Reformed Wife* (London: Printed for Thomas Bennet, 1700), p. 6.
11 J. Shirley, *The Example* (London: Printed by Iohn Norton, for Andrew Crooke, and William Cooke, 1637), sig. I2r.
12 R. Brome, *The Court Begger* (London: Printed for Richard Marriot and Tho. Dring, 1653), sig. N5v.
13 Sir Philip Sidney writes 'lyrical kind of songs and sonnets' in the 1595 edition of his *Defence of Poetry*; see Vickers, *English Renaissance Literary Criticism*, p. 385.
14 T. Tomkis, *Albumazar* (London: printed by Nicholas Okes for Walter Burre, 1615), 2.1.1–2.
15 The Petrarchan sonnet's success just like its rejection was a European phenomenon. In particular, sonnets were dismissed as negligible toys on the Continent at various stages, depending on the spread of Petrarchism. In Italy for instance, Francesco Berni (1497/98 – 26 May 1535) parodied Petrarchan imitators and invented a genre of burlesque verse, 'poesie bernesche'. The most explicit attack on the fake expression of love in Petrarchan sonnets was provided by Du Bellay's long poem 'Contre les Pétrarquistes', published in 1558 in his *Divers Jeux Rustiques* (see J.-Y. Vialleton, 'Le Pétrarque des antipétrarquistes français des années 1550', *Cahiers D'Études Italiennes*, 4 (2006), 99–115). In Spain, in the first quarter of the seventeenth century, Quevedo wrote parodic and burlesque anti-Petrarchan verses, among them the sonnet beginning 'Mientras que, tinto en mugre, sorbí brodio', in which all women are called prostitutes (see I. Navarrete, *Orphans of Petrarch: Poetry and Theory in the Spanish Renaissance* (Berkeley, Los Angeles, Oxford: University of California Press, 1994), pp. 190–233).
16 See S.W. May, *The Elizabethan Courtier Poets: The Poems and Their Contexts* (Columbia, London: University of Missouri Press, 1991).
17 B. Jonson, *Poetaster* (London: Printed [by R. Bradock] for M. L[ownes], 1602), 1.1.4–5. For an example of Petrarchan sonnets written in an Inn of Court, see Guillaume Coatalen, 'Unpublished Elizabethan Sonnets in a Legal Manuscript from the Cambridge University Library', *Review of English Studies*, 54 (2003), 553–65.
18 T. Dekker and J. Webster, *Northward Hoe* (London: by G. Eld, 1607), sig. D4r.
19 B. Jonson, *Euery Man in his Humour* (London: [by S. Stafford] for Walter Burre, 1601), sig. E3v.
20 W. Shakespeare, *Love's Labour's Lost*, ed. G.R. Hibbard (Oxford: Oxford University Press, 2008).
21 R. Zouch, *The Sophister* (London: Printed by J[ohn] O[kes] for Humphrey Mosley, 1639), 5.1, sig. H3r.
22 T. Heywood, *Loves Maistresse* (London: Printed by Robert Raworth, for Iohn Crowch, 1636), sig. E2.
23 E. Phillips, *The new world of English words, or, A general dictionary containing the interpretations of such hard words as are derived from other languages* (1658). Edward Blount has a vaguer definition for the same word, 'a song or ditty', in his *Glossographia* (1661) whilst Elisha Coles agrees with Phillips in the 1677 *English Dictionary* (London: Printed for Peter Parker).
24 Heywood, *Loves Maistresse*, 4.1, sig. I3r.
25 T. Randolph, *Hey for Honesty, Augmented and Published by F.J.* (London: [s.n.], 1651), p. 43.
26 See N. Smith, 'The Genre and Critical Reception of Jacopo Sannazaro's "Eclogae Piscatoriae" (Naples, 1526)', *Humanistica Lovaniensia*, 50 (2001), 213. I am grateful to Carlo Alberto Girotto for drawing my attention to the source.
27 T. Heywood, *The Fayre Mayde of the Exchange* (London: Printed [by Valentine Simmes] for Henry Rockit, 1607), sig. E4r.
28 G. Chapman, *All Fools* (London: Printed [by George Eld] for Thomas Thorpe, 1605), sig. D3.
29 G. Chapman, *Sir Gyles Goosecappe* (London: Printed by Iohn Windet for Edward Blount, 1606), 5.1, sig. K.
30 J. Mayne, *The Citye Match* (Oxford: Printed by Leonard Lichfield, printer to the University, 1639), 1.3, p. 29.
31 *The Returne from Pernassus* (London: Printed by G. Eld for Iohn Wright, 1606), 4.2, sig. G2.
32 B. Holyday, *Technogamia or the Marriages of the Arts* ([London:] Printed by William Stansby for Iohn Parker, 1618), 3.1, sig. F3v.
33 J. Donne, *The Variorum Edition of the Poetry of John Donne Vol. 2 The Elegies*, ed. G.A. Stringer (Bloomington: Indiana University Press, 2000), p. 61, records the word 'comparison' in the headings of MS Folger V.a.125, Bodleian, MS Eng. poet. e. 14, fos 60v–1r, Bodleian, MS Rawl. poet. 142, fol. 18v, Robert S. Pirie, New York, [Frendraught MS], pp. 7–9, recently (but no longer) owned by Pirie. I am grateful to Joshua Eckhardt for this point.
34 This is briefly touched upon, if not explicitly analysed, in K. Ettenhuber, '"Comparisons are Odious"? Revisiting the Metaphysical Conceit in Donne', *Review of English Studies*, 62:255 (2011), 393–413.

35 Love sonnets exemplified a larger rhetoric of courtship at work in a large variety of texts in verse and prose; see Catherine Bates, *The Rhetoric of Courtship in Elizabethan Language and Literature* (Cambridge: Cambridge University Press, 1992).
36 Petrarchan sonnets could be direct translations from Petrarch (see K. Duncan-Jones, 'Bess Carey's Petrarch: Newly Discovered Elizabethan Sonnets', *Review of English Studies*, 50 (1999), 304–19) or English love sonnets exploiting Petrarch's imagery. On the sonnet craze, which was triggered off by the publication of Philip Sidney's *Astrophel and Stella* in 1591, see C. Bates, 'Desire, Discontent, Parody: The Love Sonnet in Early Modern England', in A.D. Cousins and P. Howarth (eds), *The Cambridge Companion to the Sonnet* (Cambridge: Cambridge University Press, 2011), pp. 105–24. Because it includes complete sonnet sequences, the most useful anthology of Elizabethan Petrarchan love sonnets remains M. Evans's *Elizabethan Sonnets* (London: Dent, 1977).
37 See, for instance, Sir John Davies's burlesque *Gullinge sonnets* (1594) and D. Jones, 'An Example of Anti-Petrarchan Satire in Nashe's "The Unfortunate Traveller"', *The Yearbook of English Studies*, 1 (1971), 48–54.
38 Ogmius, the Celtic God of eloquence.
39 J. Shirley, *Changes* (London: Printed by G[eorge] P[urslowe] for William Cooke, 1632), 1.1, 8. On Shirley, see B. Ravelhofer (ed.), *James Shirley and Early Modern Theatre: New Critical Perspectives* (London: Routledge, 2016).
40 Vickers, *English Renaissance Literary Criticism*, pp. 327–8. As explained by the editor (p. 325), the text is '[f]rom *The Raigne of King Edward the third* (1596), as edited by Edward Capell in *Prolusions; or, Select Pieces of Antient Poetry, II. Edward the Third, a Play, Thought to be Writ by Shakespeare* (London, 1760), checked against the edition by George Melchiori in the New Cambridge Shakespeare (1998)'. The passage is discussed in P. Cheney's *Shakespeare's Literary Authorship* (Cambridge: Cambridge University Press, 2012), p. 99.
41 Sir P. Sidney, *Astrophil and Stella*, sonnet 1, 14, *The Major Works*, ed. K. Duncan-Jones (Oxford: Oxford University Press, 1989).
42 W. Shakespeare, *As You Like It*, ed. A. Brissenden (Oxford: Oxford University Press, 1993).
43 T. Dekker and T. Middleton, *The Honest Whore* (London: Printed by Elizabeth Allde, for Nathaniel Butter, 1630), sig. Er.
44 See P. Cheney, '"O, Let My Books Be … Dumb Presagers": Poetry and Theater in Shakespeare's Sonnets', *Shakespeare Quarterly*, 52:2 (summer 2001), 222–54.
45 T. Dekker, H. Chettle and W. Haughton, *Patient Grissil* (London: Imprinted [by E. Allde] for Henry Rocket, 1603), sig. Cr.
46 J. Marston, *The Insatiate Countesse* (London: Printed by T[homas] S[nodham] for Thomas Archer, 1613), sig. F4r.
47 R. Mead, *Combat of Love and Friendship* (London: Printed for M[ercy] M[eighen] G. Bedell and T. Collins, 1654), 2.1, 13.
48 *The Woman-Hater. As it hath beene lately Acted by the Children of Paules* (London: John Hodgets, 1607), 4.1, sig. F4r.
49 A genre launched in France by Marot's 'Blason du Beau Tétin' and further illustrated, amongst a host of other poets, by Maurice Scève in *Blasons Anatomiques du Corps Féminin* first published in 1536 and printed with Charles de La Hueterie's counter-blazons in 1543. See too D. Uman and S. Morrison (eds), *Staging the Blazon in Early Modern English Theatre* (Studies in Performance and Early Modern Drama, Farnham: Ashgate, 2013), and Grant Williams, 'Disarticulating Fantasies: Figures of Speech, Vices, and the Blazon in Renaissance English Rhetoric', *Rhetoric Society Quarterly*, 29:3 (1999), 43–54.
50 See P. Betella, *The Ugly Woman: Transgressive Aesthetic Models in Italian Poetry from the Middle Ages to the Baroque* (Toronto: University of Toronto Press, 2005), 114–17. Beaumont may have known Francesco Berni's most famous poem, *Rime* 31 'Chiome d'argento fine, irte ed attorte', first printed in Florence in 1548 (A.F. Grazzini, ed., *Il primo Libro dell'opere burlesch. Di M. Francesco Berni, di M. Gio. della Casa, del Varchi, del Mauro, di M. Bino, del Molza, del Dolce, & del Firenzuola, ricorretto, & con diligenza ristampato* (Florence: [s.n.], 1548)), which is a parody of a Petrarchan sonnet by Bembo. John Florio includes Berni's burlesque works in his list of sources for his dictionary *A Worlde of Wordes* (London: by Arnold Hatfield for Edw. Blount, 1598).
51 J. Lyly, *Midas* (London: Printed by Thomas Scarlet for I[ohn] B[roome], 1592), sig. D4v.
52 A. Munday, *Death of Robert* (London: [by R. Bradock] for William Leake, 1601), 1.5, sigs Ev–E2r.
53 Ibid., sig. C2r.
54 S.S., *The Honest Lawyer* (London: Printed by George Purslowe for Richard Woodroffe, 1616), sig. E4v.
55 J. Webster, *The White Devil* (London: Printed by N[icholas] O[kes] for Thomas Archer, 1612), sig. B3v.

56 On Drayton and the Petrarchan tradition, see R. Vuillemin, *Le Recueil pétrarquiste à l'ère du maniérisme: Poétique des sonnets de Michael Drayton, 1594–1619* (Paris: Champion, 2014), pp. 115–64.
57 See V. Moul, *Jonson, Horace and the Classical Tradition* (Cambridge: Cambridge University Press, 2006).
58 For an epistolary discussion on changes in poetic taste in the decade, see G. Coatalen, 'Dudley Carleton and "The Libertie of Old Fashioned Poetrie"' on 8 November 1596', *Notes & Queries*, 56:4 (2009), 563–6.
59 T. Tomkis, *Lingua* (London: Printed by G. Eld, for Simon Waterson, 1607), sigs D2v–D3r. See too 'Write sonnets on the ivorie tooth' in James Shirley's *Constant Maid* (London: Printed by I. Raworth, for R. Whitaker, 1640), sig. B4v.
60 G. Markham, *The Dumbe Knight* (London: Printed by Nicholas Okes, for Iohn Bache, 1608), 2.1, sig. D3r.
61 J. Fletcher and P. Massinger, *The Elder Brother* (London: Imprinted by F[elix] K[ingston] for I. W[aterson] and I. B[enson], 1637), 1.1, sig. B2v.
62 J. Shirley, *The Humorous Courtier* (London: Printed by T[homas] C[otes] for William Cooke, 1640), sig. F1v.
63 T. Corneille, *The Extravagant Shepherd*, trans. T. Rawlins (London: Printed by J.G. for Tho. Heath, 1654), sig. D2r.
64 W. Shakespeare, *Complete Sonnets and Poems*, ed. C. Burrow (Oxford: Oxford University Press, 2002).
65 *Petrarch's Lyric Poems*, trans. Durling, the Italian text is taken from F. Petrarca, *Canzoniere Rerum Vulgarium Fragmenta*, vol. II, ed. R. Bettarini (Turin: Einaudi, 2005).
66 On the notions of 'amateur', 'professional' or 'laureate' poet, see R. Helgerson, *Self-Crowned Laureates: Spenser, Johnson, Milton and the Literary System* (Berkeley: University of California Press, 1983).

4

In and out: Shakespeare's shifting sonnets. From *Love's Labour's Lost* to *The Passionate Pilgrim*

Sophie Chiari

Whilst Shakespeare's *Sonnets* did not appear in print before 1609, some of his sonnets were actually published before that date, which seems to suggest that, for an author like Shakespeare, there was hardly such thing as a strictly 'private' circulation of poems in early modern England.[1] In a miscellany of twenty sonnets and lyrics entitled *The Passionate Pilgrim* (1598–99) and printed by William Jaggard, one can find three poems from *Love's Labour's Lost*, a play whose earliest extant quarto edition dates back to 1598.[2] Jaggard's collection, which also contained poems by Richard Barnfield, Bartholomew Griffin (the author of a 1596 sonnet sequence entitled *Fidessa, More Chaste than Kinde*), Christopher Marlowe and, possibly, Sir Walter Raleigh, sold extremely well and was reprinted in 1612 with additional poems by Thomas Heywood. Central to my argument in this chapter is the fact that, in such a collection, Shakespeare's poems are no longer supposed to be spoken on stage but are presented as written poetic language. Now, as a preamble to my subsequent analysis, I would like to make three immediate observations:

First, because the poems in *Love's Labour's Lost* were primarily aimed at spectators, they immediately bypassed the traditional class distinctions generated both by manuscript sonnets (generally first intended for private circles) and by printed ones (aimed at educated readers).

Second, whilst the aristocratic craze for sonnets meant that they were almost immediately circulated to the detriment of their preservation, Berowne's, Longaville's and Dumaine's 'sugared' sonnets to the French ladies (4.2 and 4.3) also circulate for the worst in the realm of Navarre, their contents being badly distorted by their fair recipients.

Third, these sonnets were highly ironical in their original context, but, once decontextualised, they became part of an anthology in which they are deprived of their satirical flavour. Against all odds, they were just as successful in Jaggard's collection (which cashed in on the fashionable practice of textual collecting) as in Shakespeare's innovative comedy.[3]

In this chapter, I will therefore focus on the transgeneric circulation of these three love sonnets in order to look at the nature of poetic transaction in sixteenth-century England. This will eventually lead me to reassess the nature of the relationship between William Jaggard, the printer still often accused of having 'stolen'

Shakespeare's poems for his *Passionate Pilgrim*, and Shakespeare himself, who certainly shared with Jaggard an acute sense of commercial strategy. Were these two men, who belonged to the same world, enemies or shrewd collaborators? Without claiming to make any definitive conclusion on the subject, I intend to shed some light on what remains a vexed issue in Shakespeare studies.

Manuscript sonnets in *Love's Labour's Lost*

Love's Labour's Lost is a play primarily devoted to the interaction between the spoken and the written word. Witty conversations abound, and love poems circulate in manuscript, just like the vast majority of early modern sonnets during Shakespeare's time. By the end of the sixteenth century, there must have been a special excitement in the reading of titillating verse in manuscript, or sonnets devoted to the dangerous topic of succession (dealt with in Shakespeare's sonnet 7, for instance), which greatly preoccupied and strongly displeased the Queen of England.[4]

In *Love's Labour's Lost*, the young men, too, are preoccupied with issues of succession, as we can guess that, if Ferdinand intends to marry, it is primarily to get an heir, anxious as he is to secure his posterity. Yet, the lords' sonnets, unlike Shakespeare's sonnets (when not mediated by any dramatic character other than Will), conceal this fundamental political issue under the varnish of the conventional love-at-first-sight motif. No matter how anxious these immature young men may be about their destiny and their masculinity, they have to put up a bold front and decide to focus on amorous games. Engaged in a 'civil war of wits' (2.1.222), the lords fight *with* and *against* words, and, in this battle, the pen stands for the penis. In fact, *Love's Labour's Lost* sheds fresh light on the traditional representation of women as blank pages waiting to be filled by the male pen/penis.[5] For one soon realises that the ladies are impenetrable, and that the lords' pens are improper. In fact, they do not lead to pleasure but to *pen*ance and re*pen*tence. Each sonnet in the play, then, turns out to be a mortification of sorts, or an unwitty self-punishment paving the way for the final penances imposed on the four lords.

Be that as it may, the young men, at the beginning of the comedy at least, try hard to make the French maids experience a special *frisson* brought about by their deeply idiosyncratic style of letter-writing. Manuscript culture making their otherwise poor poems unique pieces, they hope to flatter (and conquer) the French ladies by giving them the impression that they are the recipients of unique poems, which is, and is not, the case. This is the case because each poem is handwritten and is not multiplied by any printing press (incidentally, this absence of reproduction indirectly reflects the absence of royal progeny in the play). And this is not the case because the poems are so fraught with clichés that, instead of giving the ladies the impression of uniqueness, they create an impression of *déjà vu* which turns out to be totally counterproductive. Being educated and clever, the French Princess and her ladies-in-waiting disapprove of such conventional poetry devoid of creative imitation.[6] Their feeling is exactly that of the spiteful Phantastes in Act 2, scene 2, of a 1607 play by the Cambridge-educated playwright Thomas Tomkis and aptly entitled *Lingua: or The Combat of the Tongue, and the Fiue Senses for Superiority*. Indeed, in a passage analysed by Guillaume Coatalen in Chapter 3 above, Phantastes blames the 'sonnet-mongers' for their artificial language and idealised descriptions:

> Oh heauens, how haue I beene troubled these latter times with Women, Fooles, Babes, Taylers, Poets, Swaggerers, Guls, Balladmakers, they haue almost disrobed me of all the toyes and trifles I can deuise, were it not that I pitty the poore multitude of Printers, these Sonnet-mungers should starue for conceits, for all *Phantastes*. But these puling Louers, I cannot but laugh at them and their Encomions of their Mistresses. They make forsooth her hayre of Gold, her eyes of Diamond, her cheekes of Roses, her lippes of Rubies, her teeth of Pearle, and her whole body of Iuory: and when they haue thus Idold' her like *Pigmalion,* they fall downe and worship her. *Psyche,* thou hast laid a hard taske vpon my shoulders, to inuent at euery ones aske, were it not that I refresh my dulnesse once a day with my most Angelicall presence, 'twere vnpossible for me to vndergo it.[7]

There is no denying the fact that the lords of Navarre feed on 'taffeta phrases' (5.2.406) and idolise their mistresses, just like the poor poets ostracised by Tomkis in his Jacobean comedy – a comedy, it must be said, written when the craze for sonnets was already on the wane. Yet, the young men are not the only ones to blame. In Shakespeare's England, the circulation of love poems typically involved a certain kind of reciprocity between poets and their addressees. In other words, more often than not, 'the transcribed versions of the poems would include the recipient's own revisions, so that the poem became even more definitively the owner's, not the author's; and often as not the author's name would be indicated only by initials, or not at all.'[8] The ladies, here, fail to appropriate their lovers' poems. As a consequence, they never inscribe their comments in the margins – it must be noted, though, that the Princess is not even given this possibility as Berowne has written 'o'both sides the leaf, margin and all' (5.2.8) – and do not respect the implicit rules of courtly correspondence. Actually, they are so obsessed with the material objects offered by their wooers (Shakespeare makes it clear that the Princess receives a jewel from the King, Rosaline a picture of her from Berowne, Katherine a pair of gloves from Dumaine, and Maria some pearls from Longaville) that they forget that the main gifts are the poems themselves, not the objects accompanying them. All in all, if the lords are naive, the maids are presented as cynical consumers. They clearly belong to a culture of commodification that seems at odds with the idea of manuscript culture so dear to the young lords of Navarre. The lords and their hypothetical mistresses therefore represent the early modern tensions at work between manuscript and print culture: both existed side by side, but they put very different qualities to the fore. Otherwise stated, whereas a manuscript sonnet could freely emphasise its own extravagance, printed verse had to comply with tacit rules and codes in order to attract a wider readership. And, in *Love's Labour's Lost,* the fact is that extravagance definitely appears as a specific male quality.[9]

De/recontextualisation: from the stage to the printed page

As Richard Dutton observes in *Shakespeare, Court Dramatist,* '[a]t 2,651 lines, although unexceptional by the standard of Shakespeare's own histories and tragedies, the play is the longest of the 1590s romantic comedies'.[10] In effect, the title page of the 1598 quarto reads: 'Newly corrected and *augmented* By W. Shakespere' (my emphasis) and there are reasons to believe that indeed, the printed play as we have it in Q1 reflects an augmented version of a shorter text aimed at public performance. If we are to believe its 1598 advertisement, the script we actually possess represents the text '[a]s it was presented before her Highness this last Christmas', which suggests, as Dutton convincingly argues, that the available quarto text, which includes obvious revisions and second thoughts resulting in a number of textual muddles, is in fact a text revised by Shakespeare for a performance at the court of Elizabeth I.[11] His reworkings notably consist in expanded passages, and what interests me here is that the lords' sonnets are *not* part of these expansions. They were here right from the beginning, constituting the text's essence, so to speak. While they must have been successful among the young Elizabethan courtiers who could (or could not) recognise themselves in the figures of the four ambitious poets of Navarre, Shakespeare knew that their comic potential could also work quite well in public performances, where they probably generated fewer jaundiced smiles than at court, and more frequent fits of laughter.

Importantly, the lords' poems functioned on several levels depending on the place where the play was being staged. In a court performance, they mainly worked as metadramatic tools,[12] commenting on the spectators' poetic pretensions. In a public performance, they were used as both props and discourse. Indeed, Shakespeare does not simply show us a variety of awkward *billets doux*, he also allows us to hear them being read aloud. He therefore inserts a number of monologues characterised by the insistent use of the first-person pronoun – the young heroes turn out to be particularly narcissistic lovers – and by a mock confessional tone. Navarre and his friends are speaking poetry, but a poetry full of Petrarchan clichés which turns out to be both an obvious parody of Shakespeare's own art and, more subtly perhaps, a way of articulating the otherwise inexpressible difficulties of love.

The budding poets, moreover, reproduce the same errors as those frequently made by Shakespeare's own rival poets, caught in a sometimes sterile rivalry and constrained by the demands of rich patrons whose tastes, whether good or bad, had to be taken into account. In the play, each young lover vies with his friends in order to distinguish himself from their productions and to acquire fame; and each piles up hyperboles, paradoxes and Petrarchan tropes related to sight, tears and despair. Interestingly, the young ladies are both the patrons and the addressees of the love poems, which deeply complicates the task of the lords of Navarre.

As a matter of fact, the lines produced by Ferdinand and his friends sound particularly hollow as they rely on all the clichés of the genre, including meteorological metaphors (the heavens, the thunder, the clouds, the air, the sun) aligning climate with emotions. Berowne's love poem is no exception. It is introduced not as a sonnet but as a 'stanza' (4.2.92) – a relatively new word at the time, since the first recorded use of the term in the *Oxford English Dictionary* dates back to 1596.[13] It is thus up to the listener to construe Berowne's fourteen lines as a sonnet:

Nathaniel. *[Reads]* 'If love make me forsworn, how shall I swear to love?
Ah, never faith could hold, if not to beauty vowed!

> Though to myself forsworn, to thee I'll faithful prove;
> Those thoughts to me were oaks, to thee like osiers bowed.
> Study his bias leaves and makes his book thine eyes,
> Where all those pleasures live that art would comprehend.
> If knowledge be the mark, to know thee shall suffice.
> Well learned is that tongue that well can thee commend,
> All ignorant that soul that sees thee without wonder;
> Which is to me some praise, that I thy parts admire.
> Thy eye Jove's lightning bears, thy voice his dreadful thunder,
> Which, not to anger bent, is music and sweet fire.
> Celestial as thou art, O, Pardon love this wrong,
> That sings heaven's praise with such an earthly tongue'.
>
> (4.2.93–106)

Uttered by a placid curate to whom they were not destined, Berowne's lines will never be interpreted as a sonnet by the incompetent onstage audience embodied by the schoolmaster Holofernes. This should come as no surprise in a play featuring male characters systematically 'ill at reckoning' (1.2.34). Yet, Berowne's love letter actually constitutes a recantation sonnet, in which the cumulative and antithetical effects of 'forsworn', 'swear', 'faith' and 'faithful' convey the paradoxical state of the speaker, imprisoned in his own game: whilst he had promised to vow himself to a life of chastity to meditate and study, he is now bound to love a woman and make her his principal source of knowledge. Now, as Shakespeare mocks the excesses of this sonnet craze, he also tries to reassess the conditions of reception of love poetry in general. Here, Nathaniel's ventriloquism probably distorts the noble intentions of Berowne, who writes to his dark lady without ever mentioning the colour of her skin.

These fourteen lines were reprinted in William Jaggard's *The Passionate Pilgrim* (1599). Regarding the title of this anthology, Berowne's poem perfectly fits the collection. The young man, in his sonnet, blends amorous and religious overtones, and this mixture is put to the fore in the very title of Jaggard's miscellany.[14] Whilst for twenty-first-century readers piety and passion seem poles apart, this was not the case in early modern England. As noted by Joseph Sterrett, the period was marked by the 'fairly easy ability to read the language of erotic love from within a perspective of spiritual devotion and to read spiritual devotion in terms of erotic love'.[15] Shakespeare aligned his sonnets with such abilities, and Jaggard cultivated this appealing association in order to sell his anthology to a wide readership.

At the same time, spiritual devotion and erotic love correspond to the two-part structure characterising the plot of *Love's Labour's Lost*, as the lords of Navarre are first seen as spiritual devotees before showing their true colours and revealing their frustrated sexual appetite. No wonder then if, in *Love's Labour's Lost*, the four male characters keep writing missives to cruel and mocking French ladies. They are thus continually shown in the very act of creating sonnets. Yet, their respective creations prove particularly sterile.

Berowne's sonnet is the first one introduced to the audience, and it is the only one not to appear in the famous eavesdropping scene of 4.3, also known as the play's sonneteering scene and containing the mock purple patches of poetry uttered by the King, Longaville and Dumaine. The King's sonnet, conveying the speaker's egotism and misogyny, has never been detached from the play, contrary to the other two. It is difficult to say why, but that may have something to do with the fact that the King's poem does not really deal with the persona's feelings for an unreachable mistress. Indeed, Ferdinand's verse is devoted to *self*-love, which actually negates man's capacity for genuine love. In sixteen (rather than the traditional fourteen) lines, the King thus complacently imagines that the Princess's eyes send 'beams' on to the tears flowing down his cheeks to create an image of her there.

Longaville, as a willing votary of the King of Navarre, accepts the argument of women's eyes as evidence of their heavenly or goddess-like status. He soliloquises – or he thinks he soliloquises – as follows:

> Longaville. This same shall go.
> (*He reads the sonnet*)
> 'Did not the heavenly rhetoric of thine eye,
> 'Gainst whom the world cannot hold argument,
> Persuade my heart to this false perjury?
> Vows for thee broke deserve not punishment.
> A woman I forswore, but I will prove,
>   Thou being a goddess, I forswore not thee.
> My vow was earthly, thou a heavenly love;
>   Thy grace being gained cures all disgrace in me.
> Vows are but breath, and breath a vapour is.
>   Then thou, fair sun, which on my earth dost shine,
> Exhal'st this vapour-vow; in thee it is.
>   If broken then, it is no fault of mine.
> If by me broke, what fool is not so wise
> To lose an oath to win a paradise?'
>
> (4.3.51–65)

This fourteen-line poem actually follows up on Berowne's own poem by dealing with perjury. It is, like Berowne's verse, submitted to public shaming as it is heard by the wrong recipients in a hilarious eavesdropping scene. This, if anything, shows the interchangeability of the young men in the comedy. Here, Longaville reproduces the sonnet pattern, but his sonnet is strikingly devoid of complex images and ambiguous meanings. This absence is easily understood in the context of the play, as the lords who dream of their 'little academe' are never seen studying a single book. Shakespeare thus conveys Longaville's inexperience as much as his lack of literary practice. Yet, the sonnet was decontextualised and reprinted in *The Passionate Pilgrim* (1599), which means that, against all odds, the poem was directly attributed to Shakespeare and not to Longaville, the character who composes it and reads it out loud (and is mocked for it by his fellow poets in love) in *Love's Labour's Lost*, thus downplaying the distance and the ironic representation of love-poetry writing that is so crucial to the play.[16] The same thing happened with Dumaine's embedded poem, endowed with a similarly transparent meaning, and whose function of parody also entirely disappeared in Jaggard's miscellany.

In his own poem, Dumaine conventionally envies the intimacy of natural elements – here, air or the wind – with the maid (namely Katherine) he would like to seduce:

> Dumaine. (*Dumaine reads his sonnet*)
> 'On a day – alack the day! –
> Love, whose month is ever May,
> Spied a blossom passing faire
> Playing in the wanton air.
> Through the velvet leaves the wind,
> All unseen, can passage find;
> That the lover, sick to death,
> Wished himself the heaven's breath.
> "Air," quoth he, "thy cheeks may blow;
> Air, would I might triumph so!
> But, alack, my hand is sworn
> Ne'er to pluck thee from thy thorn.
> Bow, alack, for youth unmet,
> Youth so apt to pluck a sweet.
> Do not call it sin in me,
> That I am forsworn for thee –
> Thou for whom Jove would swear
> Juno but an Ethiop were,
> And deny himself for Jove,
> Turning mortal for thy love."'
>
> (4.3.93–112)

Like Romeo who, as he falls in love, feels suddenly compelled to write 'numbers' (i.e. verse) ('Now is he for the numbers that Petrarch flowed in,' Mercutio observes in *Romeo and Juliet*, 2.4.38–9), the young lords of Navarre, once enamoured, irrepressibly turn to the poetic clichés of the time. To make things worse, Dumaine does not stick to the standard iambic pentameter but offers instead a series of odd trochaic tetrameter couplets, thereby illustrating the loss alluded to in the play's title. Indeed, his four-foot lines look like maimed pentameters whose harmony and grace they obviously lack and, with their falling rhythm, they celebrate love without conviction. Moreover, the poet's attempt at self-reflexivity turns here into sheer flattery.

To this excessive sentimentalism, some early modern poets opposed an anti-sentimental approach. In 1599, Michael Drayton bluntly asserted in the prefatory material to his *Idea*:

> No farre-fetch'd Sigh shall ever wound my Brest,
> Love from mine Eye a Teare shall never wring,
> Nor in Ah-mees my whining Sonnets drest
>
> (lines 5–7)[17]

Where Drayton dismisses old-fashioned models (which, however, he goes on to follow in his next sonnets), Shakespeare's mock-poem constitutes a basic defence of all the commonplaces of the genre. Yet, for all its deficiencies, Dumaine's sonnet is of great interest precisely because the context, and only the context, still allows us to understand that it is actually multilayered: underneath its naivety, the poem hints at fashionable discourses and at Renaissance self-fashioning.

Dumaine's twenty-line poem is too long to be what we would call today a 'proper' sonnet. But strict definitions of the sonnet were still rare at the time. Broadly defined, sonnets were often perceived as little songs, no matter how many lines they comprised.[18] So, musicality was probably one of the main features of the Elizabethan sonnet, which functioned as part of courtship ritual.[19]

It should then come as no surprise that Dumaine's verse was published both in *The Passionate Pilgrim* and in *England's Helicon* (1600), edited by Nicholas Ling. I will not, here, particularly focus on Ling's version, for the simple reason that it was obviously based on Jaggard's. Indeed, in both cases (i.e in Jaggard's collection and in Ling's book), lines 106 and 107, two lines of self-rebuke, disappear ('Do not call it sin in me, / That I am forsworn for thee'). Be that as it may, by being reinserted in *England's Helicon*, Dumaine's sonnet acquired a new meaning. Its very irrelevance was turned into absolute relevance and its distancing effect into a unifying principle. The marred Arcadia of *Love's Labour's Lost* was, in other words, transformed into a real pastoral, as Ling was keen to situate 'the Muses' spring on native soil as the locus of a shepherd nation of poets, living and dead, featuring such notables as Sidney, Spenser, Marlowe, Raleigh, Drayton, Lodge and Greene'.[20]

The Passionate Pilgrim: 'piracy' and/or literary business?

Let us now briefly return to the example of *The Passionate Pilgrim*. The collection was published in a small octavo edition after September 1598, and a second edition was published in 1599. The work was never entered in the Stationers' Register – which does not necessarily mean that it was a surreptitious publication.[21]

Its compiler, William Jaggard, boldly advertised *The Passionate Pilgrim* 'By W. Shakespeare' notwithstanding the fact that it contained only five pieces by the poet-playwright. It is worth noting that it also included an intriguing text entitled 'Willobie His Avisa' by Henry Willobie. In this strange poem, Shakespeare is a haunting presence, as 'Willobie seeks to recruit Shakespeare's persona to strengthen the praise he offers his own idealised mistress, "Avisa" or "A"'.[22] As noted by James P. Bednarz, the speaker 'consequently uses Shakespeare's triangle as the basis for his own fantasia'.[23] Apart from that odd piece, and apart from the three poems or 'songs' extracted from *Love's Labour's Lost*, which had already been published as part of the printed text of the play and which, if one is to believe the pedant Holofernes, were 'neither savouring of poetry, wit, nor invention' (4.2.139–40), Jaggard's unauthorised volume included transcriptions of manuscript copies of sonnets 138 ('When my love swears that she is made of truth / I do believe her though I know she lies') and 144 ('Two loves I have, of comfort and despair, / Which like two spirits do suggest me still').[24] The two sonnets are not exactly similar to those printed in 1609. Paul Edmondson and Stanley Wells observe that, '[o]nce regarded as debased texts, they are now more commonly thought of as early versions of the poems that Shakespeare later revised'.[25] In all likelihood, Jaggard acquired these two sonnets from 'one of the "private friends" to whom they had been entrusted'.[26]

Amusingly, a very clear-sighted Shakespeare seems to have guessed what would happen to his sonnets. For, in *Love's Labour's Lost*, Berowne's poem is similarly 'pirated' by Costard, who is the mock 'private friend' having a privileged access to Berowne's sonnet – a privilege which is all the more ironic as Costard is probably unable to read fluently, given his low social origins.[27] Costard, out of malice or absent-mindedness, exchanges the sonnet with Armado's letter and gives Berowne's poem to the wrong lady, the illiterate Jaquenetta. She, in turn, becomes the unwitty pirate of Berowne's lines since, exactly like Jaggard a few years later, she circulates them without the permission of their author. The reader's reaction is then embodied by Nathaniel who, reading the poem aloud, distorts it so much so that Holofernes immediately despises it: 'Here are only numbers ratified, but for the elegancy, facility, and golden cadence of poesy, *caret*' (4.2.108–10). Shakespeare thus perfectly understood that, once divulgated, a sonnet could simply lose its substance. Of course, in *Love's Labour's Lost*, he mainly evokes a manuscript culture. The sonnet read aloud by Nathaniel will never be printed in the Arcadian, machine-free world of the lords of Navarre. Yet, the playwright emphasises the possible discrepancy between the conception and the reception of love poetry when readers do not coincide with the addressee and, ironically, he also shows, later in the play, that love poems reaching their addressee can fail as badly as those literally missing their target.

Jaggard, as to him, was too pragmatic to miss his. Even though the whole enterprise has often been seen as fraud (a vision inherited from nineteenth-century criticism),[28] it was apparently perfectly legal, and it was probably triggered (partly at least) by Francis Meres's famous comments on Shakespeare's 'sugared sonnets' in his *Palladis Tamia* (1598). Because Meres's praise created a demand for new sonnets, Jaggard calculated that he had enough prospective buyers to run the risk of publishing a dubious volume. These buyers were not part of the elite, but certainly dreamt of being invited in the restricted circles of the nobility to discover what court poetry was about. Jaggard's ploy, therefore, was to recreate the conditions of coterie poetry reading and to give his readership a seemingly privileged access to Shakespeare the learned poet, as opposed to the popular playwright whom most Londoners were already acquainted with. To increase his prospects, he must have been anxious that his miscellany should be perceived as authentically Shakespearean. So, he logically included poems which, albeit not all written by Shakespeare, were devoted to 'a theme popularly associated with him: hence the inclusion of several sonnets on the love of Venus for Adonis (Shakespeare's erotic narrative currently seeing its fifth printing in six years)'.[29] This hypothesis seems confirmed by the fact that, in order to cash in on the playwright's success, Jaggard 'had [the collection] distributed by William Leake at the sign of the Greyhound in St Paul's Churchyard, the same bookseller who offered *Venus and Adonis*'.[30] The poems are printed only on one side of the page, so that, as critics tend to think, careless buyers may have thought that it contained more poems than it could boast of. I would add another tentative explanation here: many cheap and popular books like almanacs, for instance, included blank pages so as to allow their readers to write their own comments on them. Jaggard did the same with his collection. He, in fact, tried to reproduce the scribal possibilities proposed by manuscript texts in his printed collection – a collection related to the traditional practice of commonplacing.

Interestingly, Jaggard's wish to create an ambivalently titled short anthology which could seem to be from Shakespeare 'encouraged him or his agents to select verse from the period which looked Shakespearean' and, as a result, 'his book gives us some insight into the qualities in Shakespeare's poetry which were valued at the time':[31] witty eroticism, Ovidian style, story-telling capacities. Perhaps Jaggard was a cheat (albeit a well-informed one not trespassing legal bounds), but he was also clearly appreciative of Shakespeare's poetic qualities, so much so that he came to occupy an important position in the printing of the poet-playwright with the publication of the 1623 Folio. So, he can be seen as much as a corrupter (who could 'also be reviled for being one of the tainted sources for John Benson's degraded anthology of Shakespeare's *Poems* in 1640')[32] as the celebrated publisher of the First Folio.

It is difficult to know for sure what Shakespeare thought when *The Pilgrim* first appeared, but, according to Thomas Heywood, the playwright would have disapproved of *The Passionate Pilgrim*'s lengthened third edition (1612). In an often-quoted letter to Nicholas Okes included in his *Apology for Actors*,[33] Heywood declares:

> Here, likewise, I must necessarily insert a manifest injury done me in that worke, by taking the two epistles of Paris and Helen, and Helen to Paris, and printing them in a lesse volume under the name of another, which may put the world in opinion I might steale them from him, and hee, to doe himself right, hath since them published in his own name: but, as I must acknowledge my lines not worthy his patronage under whom he hath publisht them, so the author, I know, much offended with M. Jaggard that (altogether unkowne to him) presumed to make so bold with his name.[34]

It must be said that Heywood himself had been pilfered by Jaggard, who had reproduced nine poems from *Troia Britannica* (1609) in the third edition of his *Passionate Pilgrim* (1612), without any authorisation. All the same, many have taken for granted Heywood's grievance all the more so as he overtly mentions Shakespeare's presumed dissatisfaction with Jaggard's methods to plead his own case. Until quite recently, critics, in particular, have insisted on the unexpected impact of Heywood's accusation, since, after his venomous statement, the original title page of Jaggard's miscellany was soon to be replaced by a new title page which did not mention Shakespeare's name any more.[35]

This correction proves rather intriguing if one considers that Shakespeare had apparently never thought of asking Jaggard to correct the misleading title of his anthology before, whereas he had had plenty of time to do so. The compiler, after all, had presented him as an author[36] – that was surely nothing to complain about – and had increased the publicity surrounding his name. My view, here, is that Heywood's complaint was more a literary posture – something close to a common trope of anger – than a real expression of indignation. Shakespeare may (or, more probably, may not, but we will never know) have voiced his resentment to Heywood, but that point is not central to my argument. What I want to suggest here is that the clever Jaggard probably fully understood Heywood's literary game, the young writer being in quest of a 'literary respectability' that Shakespeare, his elder, had already acquired several years before.³⁷ The printer entered it willingly and subsequently changed the title page of this third edition, thereby creating more buzz around his already well-known anthology, with the silent (and amused?) approval of Shakespeare and Heywood³⁸ (the latter having managed to recall attention to his own works through a rather simple device). Doing so, he killed two birds (or three, actually) with the same stone: by reacting so promptly to Heywood's comment, he served him as well as he continued to serve Shakespeare (being now elevated to a striking absence on *The Passionate Pilgrim*'s title page) and to make his own compilation prosper.

The fact is that, in 1609, Shakespeare presumably authorised the publication of his sonnets because he was aware of the increasing financial possibilities offered by the print market, particularly in the plague year of 1609, rather than because he meant to protect his literary creations from 'pirates'. That the poet-playwright did not bear any particular grudge against the printer is reinforced by what we know of Jaggard's career. Indeed, the latter did not become a renegade after the publication of *The Passionate Pilgrim*. On 17 December 1610, he 'became official printer to the City of London'.³⁹ In spite of his working methods, the very actors of Shakespeare's troupe eventually entrusted him with the production of nothing less than the First Folio. The supreme irony, at least for those critics still condemning Jaggard as a 'pirate', is that *he* was the one who printed that Shakespeare's plays had been 'abused with diverse stolen, and surreptitious copies, maimed, and deformed by the frauds and stealthes of injurious imposters, that exposed them'.⁴⁰

Shakespeare, after all, had always known what it was like to have one's words used by others: the actors of his company each day reappropriated his lines in order to deliver them to the audience. The fact that he was a poet-playwright probably changed his conception of the poetic transaction. Poetry was for him a means to establish privileged links with a specific category of the population, which he could not really do with his plays at the Globe. Indeed, the main consumers of poetry were the aristocrats. 'The exact proportion of English society made up by the nobility and gentry is not known', Peter Hyland observes, 'but it is estimated to have been no more than 2 per cent'. Yet, this small elite constituted 'a very powerful and very privileged group'.⁴¹

But with the advent of print culture, an educated middle class, including women, started reading poems, too. If the enclosed sonnets in *Love's Labour's Lost* seem adapted both to a popular audience eager to mock the manners of the court and to an elite likely to perceive Shakespeare's tongue-in-cheek humour transpiring behind the lords' bad poems, the detached sonnets reproduced in a commonplace book of sorts were designed to please a readership that actually bridged the gap between low and high. This readership asked not only for delightfully familiar commonplaces but also for an exciting courtly flavour, and Jaggard, already a 'successful businessman' by then, simply seized the possibility to combine the two in one and the same book.⁴² It is tempting to imagine that Shakespeare secretly applauded such ingenuity, all the more so as, for him, there was no such thing as bad advertising. Publicity being all that mattered, he could not have been unaware that the reappropriation of his sonnets, even if 'unauthorised', served his reputation more than it damaged it. By the turn of the seventeenth century, he was the fashionable writer to look at, his name was selling, he could not ask for more. If anything, Jaggard's so-called 'piracy' (and a legal one at the time) may simply have showed him the way to 'authorise' the publication of his own sonnets.

Conclusion

In *Love's Labour's Lost*, a witty comedy essentially devoted to the poetic power of language, Shakespeare does not only stage poems-within-the-poem. He shows their power of interaction with the external world. Wendy Wall duly reminds us that '[c]oterie circles […] encouraged a "con-verse-ation" ("verse" from the Latin "vertere," meaning "to turn"), a turning back and forth of scripted messages between writers'[43] and, I would add, readers. This was participatory literature in the broadest sense of the term.

Shakespeare, in this play, also comments on the reception of sonnets and tells us that there is, in fact, no such thing as the 'private' circulation later mentioned by Meres in his *Palladis Tamia*: once written and released, sonnets necessarily became public matters. Shakespeare's *mise en abyme* of poetry in *Love's Labour's Lost* is also strikingly visionary in the sense that, by emphasising the decontextualisation, circulation and misinterpretation of several sonnets or pseudo-sonnets composed by the lords, the play forecasts its own destiny. In other words, the young poet-playwright insists on the fact that poems released for public circulation, whether manuscript or print, always escape from the control of their authors.

Therefore, Shakespeare knew right from the beginning that '[o]thers felt free to transcribe, alter, and arrange [his sonnets] as they saw fit',[44] in other words, the sonnets were part and parcel of what could be called 'collaborative poetics'. Poetic writings, and sonnets in particular, moved from one place to the other, were transcribed, compiled, rewritten and carelessly scattered by their all-powerful readers. Like Armado in *Love's Labour's Lost*, these empowered readers were, in fact, pretty 'sure' that they would 'turn sonnet[s]' (1.2.149–50).

Why not, then, work *with* them rather than *against* them?

Notes

1 I refer here to Francis Meres's 1598 allusion, in his *Palladis Tamia*, to Shakespeare's 'sugared sonnets among his *private* friends'. See F. Meres, *Palladis Tamia: Wit's Treasury*, ed. D.C. Allen (New York: Scholars' Facsimiles and Reprints, 1938), fos 280v–281. However, some early modern poems such as verse libels, for instance, did remain confined to manuscript circulation because they were too openly defamatory to be published.

2 All quotations from the play are taken from W. Shakespeare, *Love's Labour's Lost*, ed. W.C. Carroll (Cambridge: Cambridge University Press, 2009). Unless otherwise indicated, references from other Shakespeare plays are taken from W. Shakespeare, *The Complete Works*, ed. J. Jowett, W. Montgomery, G. Taylor and S. Wells (Oxford: Oxford University Press, 2nd ed., 2005).

3 On this particular aspect, see M. Swann, *Curiosities and Texts: The Culture of Collecting in Early Modern England* (Philadelphia: University of Pennsylvania Press, 2001).

4 C. Shrank, 'Counsel, Succession and the Politics of Shakespeare's *Sonnets*', in D. Armitage, C. Condren and A. Fitzmaurice (eds), *Shakespeare and Early Modern Political Thought* (Cambridge: Cambridge University Press, 2009), p. 109.

5 S. Gubar, '"The Blank Page" and the Issues of Female Creativity', in E. Abel (ed.), *Writing and Sexual Difference* (Chicago: University of Chicago Press, 1982), pp. 73–93.

6 See for instance the sharp dialogue between Rosaline and the Princess in Act 5: '*Rosaline* [...] Nay, I have verses too, I thank Berowne; / The numbers true, and were the numbering too, / I were the fairest goddest on the ground. / I am compared to twenty thousand fairs. / O, he hath drawn my picture in this letter! / *Princess* Anything like? / *Rosaline* Much in the letters, nothing in the praise' (5.2.34–40).
7 T. Tomkis, *Lingua: or The Combat of the Tongue, and the Fiue Senses for Superiority A Pleasant Comoedie* (London: Printed by G. Eld, for Simon Waterson, 1607. STC, 2nd ed., 24104), sig. D3r-v. Tomkis's play was quite successful as it went through several editions throughout the seventeenth century (1617, 1622, 1632, 1657, and one more printing, which is not dated).
8 S. Orgel, 'Introduction', in W. Shakespeare, *The Sonnets*, ed. G. Blakemore Evans (Cambridge: Cambridge University Press, 2006 [1996]), p. 5.
9 On male rhetorical extravagance, see for instance R. Cockcroft, *Rhetorical Affect in Early Modern Writing: Renaissance Passions Reconsidered* (Basingstoke: Palgrave Macmillan, 2003), p. 167.
10 R. Dutton, *Shakespeare, Court Dramatist* (Oxford: Oxford University Press, 2016), p. 129.
11 Ibid. For another take on this issue, see for example J. Kerrigan, '*Love's Labour's Lost* and Shakespearean Revision', *Shakespeare Quarterly*, 33 (1982), 337–9.
12 On the difference between 'metadramatic' and 'metatheatrical', see C. Whitworth, '*Love's Labour's Lost*: Aborted Plays Within, Unconsummated Play Without', in F. Laroque (ed.), *The Show Within: Dramatic and Other Insets. English Renaissance Drama (1550-1642)*, Astraea 4 (1992), 109–26: '"Metadramatic" is, I take it, a more inclusive term which embraces all sorts of images and references, metaphors such as "All the world's a stage", and "Life's but a walking shadow of a poor player", for example. "Metatheatrical" I would want to reserve for events, verbal or physical, which refer specifically to the business of the theatre, technical terms and references – how to bring moonlight into a chamber, how to produce tears by squeezing an onion in a napkin' (p. 112).
13 See Jaques's mention of the 'stanzo' in W. Shakespeare, *As You Like It*, ed. M. Hattaway (Cambridge: Cambridge University Press, 2009), 2.5.14–15: 'Come, more, another stanzo – call you 'em "stanzos"?' See Hattaway's footnote, p. 128. The word 'stanza' or 'stanzo' appears only twice in the Shakespeare canon, while the word 'sonnet' and its derivatives crop up no fewer than fourteen times. The term being new in Shakespeare's England, we may presume that the audience paid particular attention to the poems called as such.
14 See Romeo and Juliet's sonnet in Act 1, scene 5 of the eponymous play, which similarly relies on religious imagery (shrines and atonement) and on the rhetoric of love. See W. Shakespeare, *Romeo and Juliet*, ed. R. Weis (London: Bloomsbury, The Arden Shakespeare, 2012), 1.5.92–105.
15 J. Sterrett, *The Unheard Prayer: Religious Toleration in Shakespeare's Drama* (Leiden: Brill, 2012), p. 51.
16 On the literary refashioning of the sonnets operated by Jaggard's miscellany, see L.A. Reid, '"Certaine Amorous Sonnets, Betweene Venus and Adonis": Fictive Acts of Writing in *The Passionate Pilgrime* of 1612', *Études Épistémè*, 21 (2012), https://journals.openedition.org/episteme/419 (date accessed: 16 August 2016).
17 M. Drayton, *Idea*, 1599, 'To the Reader of these Sonnets'.
18 On sonnets and late codification, see Vuillemin, *Le Recueil pétrarquiste à l'ère du maniérisme*, pp. 31–9.
19 H. Dubrow, 'The Sonnet and the Lyric Mode', in A.D. Cousins and P. Howarth (eds), *The Cambridge Companion to the Sonnet* (Cambridge: Cambridge University Press, 2011), p. 33.
20 J.P. Bednarz, *Shakespeare and the Truth of Love: The Mystery of 'The Phoenix and the Turtle'* (New York: Palgrave, 2012), p. 100.
21 See J. Jowett, *Shakespeare and Text* (Oxford: Oxford University Press, 2007), p. 51.
22 J.P. Bednarz, *Shakespeare and the Poets' War* (New York: Columbia University Press, 2001), p. 125.
23 Ibid.
24 See A.F. Marotti, 'Shakespeare's Sonnets and the Manuscript Circulation of Texts in Early Modern England', in M.C. Schoenfeldt (ed.), *A Companion to Shakespeare's Sonnets* (Oxford: Blackwell, 2010), p. 185.
25 P. Edmondson and S. Wells, *Shakespeare's Sonnets* (Oxford: Oxford University Press, 2004), p. 4.
26 Ibid., p. 7.
27 I am using the term on purpose here. Jaggard was notably portrayed as a 'pirate' by Swinburne who wrote that he was 'the infamous pirate, liar, and thief who published a worthless little volume of stolen and mutilated poetry, patched up and padded out with dirty and dreary doggerel, under the senseless and preposterous title of *The Passionate Pilgrim*'. See A.C. Swinburne, *Studies in Prose and Poetry* (London: Chatto and Windus, 1894), p. 90. This has recently been undermined by critics like P. Cheney (see 'The Passionate Pilgrime' in *Shakespeare, National Poet-Playwright* (Cambridge: Cambridge

University Press, 2004), p. 151–72), but the 'pirate' libel has unfortunately lingered, partly because it provides us with an apparently convenient explanation for the publication of *The Passionate Pilgrim*, and partly because it implies a moral judgement on Jaggard, turning him into a dishonest, yet fascinating figure.

28 I refer here to my previous note. Moreover, Jaggard was far from being the only compiler to ascribe a miscellany to one particular author, regardless of the various poets represented in the volume. A(n) (in)famous example is that of Thomas Newman who, in 1591, published the first edition of *Astrophil and Stella* (STC 22536) as *Syr P.S. His Astrophel and Stella*. This quarto actually included thirty sonnets written by Samuel Daniel as well as texts by Thomas Campion, Fulke Greville and another poet. M.P. Hannay speaks for instance of an 'unauthorized, corrupt edition', in *Philip's Phoenix: Mary Sidney, Countess of Pembroke* (Oxford, New York: Oxford University Press, 1990), p. 69. If, indeed, it was corrupt, it was not completely unauthorised. In fact, as J. Loewenstein explains, 'Newman's *Astrophel and Stella* is a boundary case'. When it appeared, 'Burghley commanded that Newman's edition be confiscated' and, as a consequence, a revised text was published the same year by … Newman himself. See J. Loewenstein, *The Author's Due: Printing and the Prehistory of Copyright* (Chicago: University of Chicago Press, 2002), p. 102. On the perception of Jaggard's enterprise as a 'fraud' or, alternatively, as a 'tribute', see L. Potter, who usefully summarises the debate in *The Life of William Shakespeare: A Critical Biography* (Chichester: Wiley-Blackwell, 2012), pp. 260–1.

29 J. Roe, '"Willobie his Avisa" and "The Passionate Pilgrim": Precedence, Parody, and Development', *The Yearbook of English Studies*, Early Shakespeare Special Number, 23 (1993), 114.

30 J.P. Bednarz, '*The Passionate Pilgrim* and "The Phoenix and Turtle"', in P. Cheney (ed.), *The Cambridge Companion to Shakespeare's Poetry* (Cambridge: Cambridge University Press, 2007), p. 115. See, too, Reid, '"Certaine Amorous Sonnets, Beteweene Venus and Adonis": Fictive Acts of Writing in *The Passionate Pilgrime* of 1612', paragraph 18: 'It seems likely that, from the start, *The Passionate Pilgrime* was envisioned by Jaggard as something of a companion piece to Shakespeare's *Venus and Adonis*. This intention is only confirmed on the title pages of 1612, when Jaggard subtitled the repackaged and expanded contents of the third edition "Certaine Amorous Sonnets, betweene Venus and Adonis".'

31 J. Kerrigan, 'Shakespeare's Poems', in M. De Grazia and S. Wells (eds), *The Cambridge Companion to Shakespeare* (Cambridge: Cambridge University Press, 2003 [2001]), p. 66.

32 J.P. Bednarz, 'Canonizing Shakespeare: *The Passionate Pilgrim*, *England's Helicon* and the Question of Authenticity', *Shakespeare Survey*, 60 (2007), 266.

33 Okes was Heywood's new printer. He had previously reprinted Shakespeare's *The Rape of Lucrece* (1607), first printed by Richard Field in 1594. Interestingly, while Heywood praised his '"care and workmanship" in *An Apology for Actors* (1612)', Ben Jonson 'alluded to him as a "ragged rascal" in *Time Vindicated*'. See M. Straznicky, 'Appendix B: Selected Stationer Profiles', in M. Straznicky (ed.), *Shakespeare's Stationers: Studies in Cultural Bibliography* (Philadelphia: University of Pennsylvania Press, 2013), p. 274.

34 T. Heywood, *An Apology for Actors* (London: N. Okes, 1612), sig. G4rv.

35 The first 1612 title page read: 'THE|PASSIONATE|PILGRIME.|OR|Certaine Amorous Sonnets,| betweene Venus and Adonis,| newly corrected and aug-|mented.|By W. Shakespere.|The third Edition.|Where-unto is newly ad-|ded two Loue-Epistles, the first|from Paris to Hellen, and |Hellens answere backe|againe to Paris.| Printed by W. Iaggard.|1612.' It was then corrected as follows: 'THE |PASSIONATE|PILGRIME.|OR|Certaine Amorous Sonnets,|betweène Venus and Adonis,| newly corrected and aug-|mented.|The third Edition.|Where-unto is newly ad-|ded two Loue-Epistles, the first|from Paris to Hellen, and|Hellens answere backe|againe to Paris.|Printed by W. Iaggard.| 1612.'

36 On this, see P. Cheney, 'The Passionate Pilgrime', p. 153.

37 D. Kathman, 'Heywood, Thomas (c. 1573–1641)', in *Oxford Dictionary of National Biography* (Oxford: Oxford University Press, 2004), www.oxforddnb.com/view/article/13190 (date accessed: 17 August 2016).

38 Well before this incident, Heywood had already fully understood the advantage there was to appear close to the successful Shakespeare. His play *The Rape of Lucrece* (written around 1606–7 and printed in 1608), for instance, followed Shakespeare's narrative poem rather faithfully, and it was a hit.

39 S. Wells, 'Jaggard, William (c. 1568–1623)', in *Oxford Dictionary of National Biography* (Oxford: Oxford University Press, 2004), www.oxforddnb.com/view/article/37592 (date accessed: 7 April 2016).

40 W. Shakespeare, *Mr. William Shakespeares Comedies, Histories, & Tragedies: Published According to the True Originall Copies* (London: 1623), sig. A3.

41 P. Hyland, *An Introduction to Shakespeare's Poems* (New York: Palgrave Macmillan, 2003), p. 10.

42 Wells, 'Jaggard, William (c. 1568–1623)'.

43 W. Wall, *The Imprint of Gender: Authorship and Publication in the English Renaissance* (Ithaca: Cornell University Press, 1993), p. 35.
44 Marotti, 'Shakespeare's Sonnets and the Manuscript Circulation of Texts in Early Modern England', p. 185.

III

Placing the sonnet: sonnets isolated or sequenced

5

'Small parcelles': unsequenced sonnets in the sixteenth century

Chris Stamatakis

> The Spanish proverb informes me, that he is a fool which cannot make one Sonnet, and he is mad which makes two.
> (John Donne, 'To my very true and very good friend Sir Henry Goodere')[1]

The sonnet's fame in the critical history of early modern English literature rests in large part on its appearance in sequences. Even though the classification 'sonnet sequence' is partially anachronistic to the period, only loosely intimated in George Gascoigne's passing reference to 'seuen Sonets in sequence' in his *Poesies*, the tradition of sequenced sonnets in English is a long-standing one, inaugurated by Anne Locke's interlinked sonnet paraphrase of psalm 51 (1560), printed some thirty years before the publication of *Astrophil and Stella* (1591), Sidney's landmark contribution to the genre.[2] However, the *first* English instantiations of the sonnet appeared not in collections or sequences but as isolated fragments – most obviously, in the form of individual poems that translated or paraphrased, in a seemingly haphazard, discontinuous way, random sonnets lifted from Petrarch's *Canzoniere*. The first importers of the sonnet, Sir Thomas Wyatt and Henry Howard, Earl of Surrey, produced sonnets as stand-alone poems that existed in isolation, complete in themselves. These poets deracinated and then further scattered individual poems lifted from out of Petrarch's already self-professedly 'scattered rhymes'. One of the titles by which Petrarch's lyric collection circulated, *Rime sparse*, a phrase borrowed from the opening line of the opening sonnet ('Voi, ch'ascoltate in rime sparse il suono', 'You who hear in scattered rhymes the sound'), implies lyric heterogeneity, ontological aleatoriness and compilatory looseness, bringing under duress any assumptions of a continuous, sequential narrative. Indeed, the Italian tradition, especially in early sonnets before Dante's *Vita nuova*, resists the idea of sequentiality: as William Kennedy remarks, 'most sonnets end with firm periods that obstruct connections with succeeding poems'.[3] Scholars have often attended to the sonnet's accretive nature – its 'propensity for clustering', in Heather Dubrow's words, and its 'predilection for sequences' that attests wider 'processes of gathering' in the period's lyric productions – treating it as a compulsive form that, seeking to fulfil a futile desire for reproduction and self-copying, aims to beget more of itself in extended sequences or collections.[4] Yet this chapter hopes to address the parallel history of the sonnet as a stand-alone form in sixteenth-century English poetry, a form that flourishes in *un*sequenced contexts.

Some critics have doubted whether such a thing as the stand-alone sonnet existed before the Jacobean era. For Richard Strier, the 'stand-alone lyric not meant to be sung and not part of a sequence is an invention of the seventeenth century',[5] although clearly the compositional activities of Wyatt and Surrey in the 1530s, or Arthur Gorges in the 1580s, help to nuance this critical narrative. In one manuscript collection of Gorges's verse (*c*. 1586), entitled 'The Vanytyes of S[i]r Arthur Gorges Youthe' (now British Library, Egerton MS 3165), Gorges cherry-picks individual sonnets for translation, as if at random, from out of Continental sequences, translating them into English denuded of their original contexts. Raided from Joachim Du Bellay's *Les Regrets*, *L'Olive*, and *Les antiquitez de Rome*, Pierre de Ronsard's *Les Amours* and Philippe Desportes' *Diverses amours*, *Diane* and *Hippolyte*, Gorges's sonnets in this manuscript sometimes appear in local clusters, but more often than not are separated by intervening forms of strophic verse that militate against any sense of narrative or formal continuity. This tradition of scattered, unsequenced sonnets – a tradition that has obvious origins in a manuscript culture susceptible to *mouvance*, but which translates readily to the realm of print too, since print was 'not always a more finished or final form than manuscript' – continues to thrive even *after* the sonnet craze of the 1590s when, as Michael Drayton wearily put it in *Idea*, 'every drudge doth dull our satiate eare' with 'Sonnets ... in bundles'.[6] Lamenting this entropic demise of sonneteering into triteness and cliché, the translator and language-tutor John Florio signals a change in aesthetic tastes at the turn of the seventeenth century: Florio's interlingual dictionary of 1611, *Queen Anna's New World of Words*, contains the term 'Sonettúcio', which he Englishes, pityingly, as '*poore sillie Sonnets*', in an addition to his earlier 1598 *Worlde of Wordes* which does not contain the term.[7] This lexicographic addition may suggest that, by the first decades of the seventeenth century, the appetite for extended, self-iterating sequences of sonnets *en bloc* was beginning to wane, just as Donne's Spanish proverb, quoted as the epigraph to this chapter from a letter penned in *c*. 1609, implies that the skill required in fashioning a single sonnet is soon attenuated when the urge to write a connected series overtakes the sonneteer.

This chapter's counter-narrative of the unbundled, unsequenced sonnet's fortunes in English literary culture in part responds to Cathy Shrank's timely *cri de coeur* to consider what she calls the 'companionable, outward-looking potential' of Tudor sonnets. This potential is manifested, for instance, by the use of sonnets as dedicatory or commendatory poems, an area of literary practice that 'has scarcely figured' in critical accounts to date.[8] In these capacities, the stand-alone sonnet (understood in this chapter as any sonnet that is not part of a continuous sequence) typically articulates frustrated desire, or pledges service, or seeks patronage or secures fame. Among several other offices performed in contexts too numerous to survey here, the stand-alone sonnet serves as a medium for personalised elegy, as in George Whetstone's 'Epitaph' for George Gascoigne, the final entry, and sole sonnet, in the short memorial publication *A Remembravnce of ... George Gaskoigne*;[9] it is conscripted for *ad hoc* royal entertainments, or as encomia, not least in celebration of Elizabeth and her entourage of courtly ladies, as in Gascoigne's sonnet 'Beholde (good Quene) A poett with a Speare', a plea for laureation at the front of his illustrated presentation copy of *The Tale of Hemetes the Heremyte*, itself presented as a gift to Elizabeth at New Year, 1576;[10] it appears in the form of 'setpieces in dramas and romances';[11] and it is even exploited for more visually compelling ends, from acrostic verse to inscriptions on portraits, as in the elegy to Sir Thomas Seymour featuring as a kind of sonnetic *impresa* on a portrait of Seymour by an unknown artist.[12] Discussing Gascoigne's verdict, in his short critical treatise 'Certayne notes of Instruction', that 'Sonets serue aswell in matters of loue as of discourse', Shrank helpfully dissects 'that multivalent word *discourse*', the etymology of which encompasses 'both "reasoning" and "conversation"', thereby gesturing to discursive possibilities and perhaps even the self-reflective activities that Marotti calls 'metapoetic and metacommunicative'.[13] So, rather than just a device for voicing frustrated desires – be they amatory, courtly, theological or professional – the sonnet, and particularly the stand-alone sonnet, enjoys a range of discursive properties. Not least among these – and the focus of the rest of this chapter – is its self-consciously canonising function as it exploits the spatial compactness and literary prestige that undergird the sonnet as a poetic form: the stand-alone sonnet co-opts formal self-enclosure in the service of celebrating native eloquence and accommodating foreignness, implicitly or explicitly commenting on the literary authority, cultural status and vernacular identity of the works in which it is found, especially when it serves as a paratext or preface to a volume.

Sonnetic enclosure

Recent critics have noted the tension between the sonnet as an isolated lyric and as a component in continuous narrative sequences – 'the "strain"', as Christopher Warley puts it, 'between lyric and narrative, between sonnet and sequence'.[14] Given this unstable equipoise of the sonnet, as both a self-contained, isolated form and as a constituent of larger sequences, Helen Wilcox has unpacked 'one of the paradoxes of the sonnet': it 'can be cumulatively effective in sequence, establishing a narrative in clusters or over the course of hundreds of individual poems in the same form', but can also 'flourish in isolation or in the context of a variety of other poetic forms'.[15] Alert to these possibilities of individuation, Renaissance commentators tend to characterise the sonnet as a self-contained form rather than (as we are inclined to regard it) a promiscuous, procreative one seeking to regenerate itself in sequences. The sonnet's associations with epigrammatic enclosure have well-established origins. Counterpointing our assumptions about the sonnet's centrifugal movement outwards, its generation of and reaching towards other sonnets, a sonnet by the early fourteenth-century poet Pieraccio Tedaldi instructing novices on how to write sonnets offers a separate conception of the form as a precise, internally coherent, contained verse unit, each line saying what it has to say concisely and 'to the point' ('Dir bene alla proposta').[16] The sonnet is autotelic and self-referential, forgoing any need to replicate itself in a connected series. This idea of what Michael Spiller calls 'foreclosed' or 'pointed'[17] containment particularly applies to the apophthegmatic quality of the *English* sonnet as fashioned by Wyatt, with its distinctive couplet ending, a feature most probably inspired by the epigrammatic couplet that concludes the *strambotti* of Serafino Aquilano, one of Wyatt's principal Italian sources.

In sixteenth-century English practice, there is a formal and conceptual kinship between 'sonnet' and 'epigram'. The two terms are loosely applied to short verse, usually between four and sixteen lines in length, both designating something self-consciously concise. Spiller subtly observes how sonneteers 'try to devise ways of resisting closure while formally retaining it', noting that the sonnet, 'even before it becomes explicitly associated with the epigram' and the epigrammatic, insists upon the concluding, argumentative flourish of its endpoint.[18] One of Sir John Davies's sonnets, 'Fly, merry muse, unto that merry town', describes itself unapologetically as 'an Epigramme'.[19] This enterprise of 'saying much in little' (*multum in parvo*, Dante's ideal in *Paradiso* XIX) is ostentatiously played up in the writings of another John Davies, this time John Davies of Hereford. A prefatory sonnet to his 1603 *Microcosmos*, addressed '*To the iudicious Reader*', one of a series of poetic prefaces to the work, eulogises microcosmic containment and diminutive scale, as if fulfiling the role performed by poetic 'microcosms or miniature heterocosms' envisioned by Anthony D. Cousins and Peter Howarth.[20] In both the sonnet itself and its printed marginal glosses, Davies celebrates a 'Microcosmos' in terms of a bordered, enclosed sovereignty, what he calls 'that *Monarchy* of *Witte*', asserting in the final marginal note that 'Things living though never so small, are better then liveles things, though never so great'.[21] As a poeticised polity, a well-governed verse enclosure, the form is prized as insular and discontinuous, rather than centrifugal and expansive.

One of the earliest Tudor definitions of the sonnet is offered in the prose address 'To the reader' in Richard Tottel's 1557 miscellany of *Songes and sonettes*. Registering the ideal of microcosmic constraint and epigrammatic concision, the opening words of this prefatory address, 'That to haue wel written in verse, yea & in small parcelles, deserueth great praise', liken the sonnet and other short lyric forms to a small piece, particle or package (playing on the Anglo-Norman etymology of 'parcel').[22] To be sure, Tottel's term 'parcelles' additionally recognises how sonnets might be organised into composite configurations, hinting at the short lyric's compilatory versatility: individual sonnets might be arranged into larger gatherings, as *parts and parcels* of a bigger whole.[23] Lyric parcels can be intercalated within, and patterned into, larger connected architectures – sonnet sequences most obviously, or *corone* (interlinked strings of sonnets in which the last line of one is reprised as the opening of the next), or broader narrative frameworks as when a trio of connected sonnets (a self-professed '*Terza sequenza*') is embedded in Gascoigne's 'A Discourse of the Adventures Passed by Master F.J.'.[24] Some critics and editors, notably John Kerrigan, Katherine Duncan-Jones and Thomas P. Roche Jr, have detected in some sonnet sequences a 'Delian' architecture, inaugurated by Samuel Daniel's *Delia* (1592), comprising a sonnet sequence, an Anacreontic interlude, and a long concluding poem in the form of a complaint. Thomas Lodge's *Phillis* and Giles Fletcher's *Licia* (both 1593), Richard Barnfield's *Cynthia* and Edmund Spenser's *Amoretti and Epithalamion* (both 1595), Richard Linche's *Diella* (1596), and Shakespeare's *Sonnets* (1609) all arguably conform to such a superstructure, although Heather Dubrow has questioned the influence, authorial intention and constitutive make-up of this so-called 'Delian' arrangement, identifying in place of a rigid schema only an 'amorphous' and fluid set of inter-sonnet relationships.[25]

Such connective structures, implying a sense of teleological or narrative progress, often come under pressure from the sonnet's inherently particulate status or, in the case of *corone*, from the self-enclosure that sonnet crowns enact, ending where they began. Tottel's editors infamously append titles to Surrey's and Wyatt's sonnets, giving the illusion that the poems formed part of an evolving narrative sequence, yet at the same time their term 'parcel' insistently asserts the sonnet's self-enclosed, partitive identity. Bounded, individuated and discrete, these lyric parcels demand of poets a certain skill in mastering the confinements of form: sonnets, in this conception, resemble what Spiller calls 'momentary' units, 'enclosing the narrated experience in a box that is discontinuous with other boxes'.[26] Moreover, the label 'parcel' also gestures to a spatial enclosure – a portion of land or bounded territory over which a title-holder has a legal claim, pre-empting Davies's terminology of the microcosmos as a commonwealth with its own political or national identity.[27]

Mindful of these formal permutations, Donne offers, in his stanzaic poem 'The Canonization', two conceits for the 'sonnet' (both the specific fourteen-line form and the love lyric more loosely designated by that term), as both a 'pretty roome' and a 'well wrought urne', the latter analogy in particular connoting that kind of poetic self-enclosure especially prized by the New Critics.[28] Of course, as with 'small parcelles', the analogy of a 'pretty roome' implies a flexible definition of the sonnet, as something integral in itself but also as a constituent unit of a larger framework or edifice. Yet both of Donne's conceptions ostensibly privilege the sonnet's self-containment and recognise the skilful artifice required of the sonneteer in negotiating compact form. For Gascoigne, poetic skill lies in mastering enclosure. In his 'Certayne Notes of Instruction', Gascoigne advises novice wordsmiths intent on perfecting 'these sortes of verses' (sonnets, sixains and other short lyric forms) to 'eschue prolixitie and knit vp your sentences as compendiously as you may, since breuitie (so that it be not drowned in obscuritie) is most commendable'.[29] George Puttenham, too, articulates this idea that the sonnet's sense is complete in itself, at least by the concluding couplet, citing as evidence of the rhetorical figure '*Irmus*' one of Wyatt's paraphrases of Petrarch as an example of a sonnet in which 'the whole sence of the dittie is suspended till ye come to the last three words … which finisheth the song with a full and perfit sence'.[30] And at the very end of the century, William Scott, in his 1599 *Modell of Poesye*, presents the sonnet as an inherently self-concluded form of 'Lyricall Epigramme' that always culminates in 'a perfect sense' without needing to refer outside itself for its meaning – it is 'a proportion of fowerteene verses' in which a 'vniforme Conceipt' reaches 'compleatnes in the last verses'.[31]

Elizabethan commentators, then, not to mention practitioners too, routinely theorise the sonnet as, in the first instance, a circumscribed form, in keeping with Tedaldi's strictures. Perhaps the clearest formulation of the sonnet's self-enclosure is offered by Samuel Daniel, for whom the art of writing short lyric forms like the sonnet lies in the 'apt planting' of 'the sentence' (the moral import or *sententia* bound within a single strophic unit) in a place 'where it may best stand to hit'. 'Is it not,' he asks in his 1603 *Defence of Ryme*, invoking the *multum in parvo* motif and the architectural, cameral etymology of the term *stanza*, 'most delightfull to see much excellentlie ordred in a small roome', since Nature itself favours 'these clozes' that encompass potentially unlimited expansiveness, Daniel's term 'close' here happily denoting something both metrical (a 'cadence' at the end of a line of verse) and spatial or structural (an enclosure). For Daniel, the art of enclosing a conceit within an 'Orbe' is to be judged *within* a single sonnet, not across or between sequential sonnets (though in *Delia* he masterfully demonstrates how sonnets can be joined in interconnected runs whereby the opening line of one repeats the closing line of its precursor). Rather, the short lyric, as an 'Orbe', is complete and self-sufficing; sonneteers must 'reduc[e]' a conceit *'in girum* and a iust forme', the first of many etymological puns on the idea of the sonnet as circular. Daniel proffers, in addition to the Latin '*in girum*' (enclosed 'in a circle'), the idea of a 'circuit' (a 'going around', from the Old French), claiming that sonnetic conceits 'would not appeare so beautifull in a larger circuite', and also the idea of syntactic enclosure, what he calls a 'certaine close of delight with the full bodie of a iust period well carried', the Greek term *periodos* here connoting 'a complete sentence' (literally a 'circuit', a 'going around').[32] This theory of the sonnet's circular self-enclosure is commensurate with other European conceptions of the form that militate against principles of collection and sequence: in early seventeenth-century Italian poetics, for instance, Francesco Bracciolini claims, in a sonnet entitled 'Difficoltà, e lode del Sonetto' ('Difficulty, and praise, of the sonnet'), that a sonnet's virtue lies in its self-containment, and that the poet's inspiration ('Calor di Febo') becomes all the more intense when entrammelled within a 'circumscribed space' ('in circoscritto loco', line 3) – enclosed, entire in itself, a strophic room of its own.[33] The sonnet, then, has a special potency when it occurs in isolation, and does not require the encasing framework of other sonnets to have its meaning.

Prefatory thresholds

Unsequenced sonnets are occasionally deployed in the Elizabethan period as a threshold – the vestibule prefacing a work and ushering the well-disposed reader into the rest of the volume. Such prefatory sonnets, sometimes embedded amidst other, non-sonnetic forms and prose addresses, may be conscripted as part of what has been termed the 'paratextual furniture' commending a work to a dedicatee.[34] This kind of unsequenced sonnet fulfils the role of Derrida's *parergon* ('neither work [*ergon*] nor outside the work [*hors d'œuvre*], neither inside nor outside') or Gérard Genette's 'transactional' space – that 'zone between text and off-text, a zone not only of transition but also of *transaction*'.[35] James VI of Scotland specifies this application for the sonnet, in his 1584 *Ane Schort Treatise, conteining some revlis and cautelis to be obseruit and eschewit in Scottis Poesie*, advocating that, for the 'compendious pray-sing of any bukes, or the authouris thairof ... vse *Sonet* verse, of fourtene lynis, and ten fete in euery lyne'.[36] In this context, the prefatory sonnet as *exordium* is endowed with (and endows) some kind of canonicity or literary authority, reflecting the emergent prestige of the sonnet as a sophisticated and fashionable form, revealing what Marotti and Freiman label a 'growing confidence in the sonnet's public status' and what Cathy Shrank terms the sonnet's 'publicly-oriented and morally-serious purposes'.[37] The origins of this tradition by which the sonnet was enlisted for bestowing fame on an addressee lie at least as far back as Petrarch's *Rime* 104 addressed to

Pandolfo Malatesta, Lord of Rimini. And the practice reaches a kind of apotheosis in Hugh Holland's memorial sonnet prefacing Shakespeare's 1623 Folio, a sonnet which announces, and performatively secures, the playwright's *'Fame'*, attesting and perpetuating a literary genealogy and legacy – the 'life yet of his lines'.[38]

As a canonical and canonising form in the European tradition, the sonnet argues for, and even establishes, the literary reputation and cultural authority of the work that it prefaces. Unsequenced English sonnets occasionally serve as critical commentaries: their purpose is often to place the works they preface in an emergent canon or to celebrate the poetic achievement of Englishing Continental verse. This paratextual function is evident in Wyatt's personal volume of manuscript poetry, the Egerton MS (British Library, MS Egerton 2711), which contains verse composed in his own hand. In this volume, John Harington the elder has, at a later date, copied the Earl of Surrey's encomiastic sonnet to Wyatt, beginning 'The great Macedon' (85v), as a critical preface to Wyatt's psalm paraphrases, which follow in Wyatt's own hand immediately after it on the facing page (86r–98v). Surrey's sonnet in part envisages and in part constitutes a memorial constructed 'To Wyates Psalmes', as if Surrey's poem, in this paratextual capacity, represented the 'holly grave' and 'wourthy sepulture' that it claims Wyatt's psalm paraphrases merit (lines 5–6), just as Alexander the Great (the great Macedon) honoured 'Homers rymes' by housing his copy of the *Iliad* in a 'riche arke' (lines 1–3). As a sonnetic introit to and a rudimentary critical commentary on Wyatt's psalm paraphrases, Surrey's eulogy champions Wyatt's enterprise for its cultural monumentality and its literary deftness, its ability to capture the penitent David's 'lyuely faythe' in enargeic terms (line 7).

A similar function is exhibited by what is credited as the first known printed sonnet in English, William Baldwin's commendatory sonnet beginning 'Who so desyreth health got, to preserue', prefixed to Christopher Langton's 1547 *A Uery Brefe Treatise ... of Phisick*, a work of anatomy and pathology steeped in Pliny, Hippocrates, Celsus and Galen.[39] Once again, the sonnet exists by itself as an unsequenced, stand-alone poem reflecting on the art of Englishing and the literary status of the ensuing work. Baldwin's sonnet is the sole paratext between the title page and the table of contents, and it serves as an encomium to and a defence of Langton's book of medical lore. In terms pre-emptive of John Davies's image systems, Baldwin's self-enclosed sonnet voices a celebration of the compactness and microcosmic density of Langton's book, which 'smal though it seme contayneth as much / Of arte ... / As byg myghty bokes' and which is commended for having not only Englished but moreover 'eng-lyshed brefe' a foreign work (lines 5–7, 12). The prefatory sonnet thus celebrates and embodies the virtues of vernacular eloquence and the brevity emblematised by the ideal of *multum in parvo*. From its earliest appearances, then, in both manuscript and print, the sonnet arrogates to itself a commendatory function anchored in the arts of native eloquence, readerly utility and a nascent canon.

Within paratextual spaces, as Arthur Marotti has argued, various, competing authorities converge. Prefaces and dedicatory epistles serve as sites of 'contestation and negotiation among authors, publishers/printers, and readership(s)'.[40] The sonnet, an avowedly foreign import whose Italian origins are built into its very name, acquires particular resonance in these intercultural negotiations. Not surprisingly, the sonnet is frequently adopted for prefatory addresses and commendations to register what Anne Coldiron terms 'tensions between linguistic cultures, and between the national and the transnational'. In particular, those 'paratexts about englishing' reveal 'something like an English inferiority complex' about the status of the vernacular in relation to its European brethren.[41] Accordingly, prefatory sonnets typically serve as a kind of *apologia* for the translator and the practice of translation itself. In this vein, Neil Rhodes has usefully discussed the apologetic function of prefatory paratexts, noting a striking fondness for 'apologies for translation' that try to alleviate anxieties about the cultural status and literary authority of the translator while acting, more forcefully and assuredly, as devices of 'self-accreditation'.[42]

One of the prefatory sonnets in the 1602 edition of Michael Drayton's *Englands Heroicall Epistles* (a sonnet not found in earlier instantiations of his collection) not only offers a defence of translation *tout court* but also invokes an Ovidian conceit of transmigration, tracing a bold line of literary descent from Ovid to Drayton himself. This prefatory sonnet, by William Alexander, argues that

> *Ouids* soule reuiues in *Drayton* now,
> Still learn'd in loue, still rich in rare conceites;
> This pregnant spirit affecting further skill,
> Oft alt'ring forme, from vulgar wits retir'd,
> In diuers Ideoms mightilie admir'd,
> Did prosecute that sacred studie still;
>   While to a full perfection now attain'd,
>   He singes so sweetly ...[43]

Through this Pythagorean analogy, translation becomes an interlingual metempsychosis by which an originary text is revived and reanimated in a new language ('diuers Ideoms'). Alexander's sonnet makes bold claims for Drayton's aesthetic accomplishments, lauding his poetic skill and studiousness and, in an extended gestative metaphor, envisaging a kind of collaborative enterprise between Ovid and Drayton as co-parents of rare poetic conceptions ('conceites') brought to full term ('full perfection') through the agency of Ovid's 'pregnant' anima. The sonnet seems a fitting medium for this celebration of compressed fruition (yet another instance of *multum in parvo* perhaps), and a form well suited to acts of literary canonisation. Comparably, a sonnet by George Gaywood prefacing Josuah Sylvester's epic translation of 1598, *The second weeke*, pits the authority of the French source (Du Bartas's biblical masterpiece, *La seconde sepmaine*, published in 1584) against that of Sylvester's English translation. Once again, the sonnet credits the English poet with the perfection of something latent or borrowed, eulogising not only the French poet's 'world of fame' in 'euerie lyne' but also Sylvester's role as the 'true interpreter' in rendering the original into English (lines 8–9).[44] Whilst the octave (following the abba abba rhyme scheme familiar from Petrarch) acknowledges Du Bartas's literary excellence and deserved canonicity, Gaywood deftly signals, at the *volta*, a shift of tone or momentum: the sestet (rhyming cddcee, the configuration adopted by Wyatt) transfers literary authority to Sylvester, extolling, in Gaywood's coinage, Sylvester's ability to 'vn-french' his source (line 11). Assessing rival literary authorities, this prefatory sonnet actively theorises the arts of literary translation and the skill involved in interlingual transmigration. It becomes a microcosmic testimony to the *translatio studii*.

Authorising vernacularity

In these examples, unsequenced prefatory sonnets exploit the sonnet's cultural prestige to defend and celebrate works in the vernacular, imbuing native literary culture with a kind of authority and even elevating it above its Continental exemplars. Though ostensibly small, light and diminutive, at times playfully dismissed as a 'toy' or trifle, the English stand-alone sonnet is also something surprisingly monumental, canonical and canonising. Cathy Shrank has urged greater attention to what she calls the 'self-consciousness [of Tudor sonnets] regarding their potential contribution in building a native literary heritage'.[45] Thomas Sackville's stand-alone prefatory sonnet (beginning 'These royall kinges') in Thomas Hoby's 1561 translation of Castiglione's *Il Libro del Cortegiano* not only commends the ensuing work, and Hoby as its translator, in conventional fashion but also makes claims for an English appropriation of this Italian *chef d'œuvre* for specific use by 'Brittain folk' (line 14). It seems particularly fitting that Sackville's eulogy, the sole poetic paratext in the work, should take the form of an *English* sonnet, as if the distinctive Surreian rhyme-scheme (abab cdcd efef gg) encoded the claims to Englishness that Sackville makes for Hoby's translation. Sackville's final couplet, 'Whos passing skill lo Hobbies pen displaise / To Brittain folk, a work of worthy praise', counterpoints Hoby's accomplishment with Castiglione's literary portrait, 'richer far in worth' (line 4) than palatial edifices and princely decking.[46] In the cultural and linguistic economy of Sackville's conceit, the 'worth' of Castiglione's work is surpassed or out-valued by the 'worthy praise' that Hoby's translation merits. One of the principal interests of this sort of sonnet lies in this concluding gesture towards a self-congratulatory nativisation, as is indeed confirmed by Hoby's prose address that follows immediately on the facing recto, in which Hoby considers how

> this Courtier hath long straid about this realme, & the fruite of him either little, or vnperfectly receiued … But nowe, though late in deede, yet for al that at length, beside his three principal languages, in the which he hath a long time haunted all the Courtes of Christendome, hee is beecome an Englishman (whiche many a longe tyme haue wyshed, but fewe attempted and none atchieued) and welwilling to dwell in the Court of Englande, and in plight to tel his own cause.[47]

Transformed in its linguistic, national and cultural character, Hoby's *Courtyer* articulates its 'own cause' in its own language as a denizen newly housed in a native, English court. This celebration of domestic literary culture, this rivalry with the humanistic flowers of the Continent (and specifically the 'three principal languages' of Italian, French and Spanish), becomes even more pronounced in later editions, from 1588 onwards, when Sackville's sonnet is printed in italics – as if the typeface most closely associated (not least in name) with Italian humanism had been appropriated for vernacular posturing and pride by distinctly English writers and audiences.[48]

A similar case appears a few years later, in the prefatory sonnet to another translation of a Continental work, this time the 1568 English rendition, by the poet and ambassadorial servant Thomas Jenye, of Pierre Ronsard's *A Discovrs of the Present Troobles in Fravnce*. Jenye's sonnet – dedicated to the English ambassador to France, Sir Henry Norris, whom Jenye served in the 1560s – adopts a defiantly unorthodox rhyme-scheme, if it can be considered a rhyme-scheme at all. None of its lines seems to rhyme consistently with any other, and it resembles instead an audacious example of a blank-verse sonnet. This form also appealed to the precocious Edmund Spenser's sense of prosodic adventurousness the following year, in the fifteen sonnets that he translated from Du Bellay's 'Visions', which appeared, with accompanying woodcuts, in an introductory section under the running-title 'Sonets' (sigs B8r–D5v) in *A theatre wherein be represented as wel the miseries & calamities that follow the voluptuous worldlings*, a collaborative work of translation edited by the Dutch Protestant poet Jan van der Noot. Jenye's sonnet prefacing his translation of Ronsard resists the pressure of more conventional Continental rhyme-schemes and strophic divisions:

> The bale begonne, is when deformed warres,
> Whith civil stroake, embrewes his natiue swoorde.
> For were it not, that rage of rancours roote,
> By growinge evills, had watcht so blacke a tyme,
> I weane envie, by suche owtraginge splene
> Had not brought foorth, this fowle mishapen change
> In maymed state, that RONSARD wayles in ryme,
> And I reduce, whith not resemblinge penne,
> To Englishe grace (though in vnskilful verse)
> By frendes enforst to publish now abroade:
> Whiche I present (SIR) to yowr shrowdinge hande,
> No Trophee, nor masse of mighty myne,
> Nor golden somme, but as à miete of fame,
> Where power failes t'vnlade affections force.[49]

In a curious juxtaposition between France's turbulent, 'maymed state' of internecine conflict and an English republic of letters – a polity in part protected by Norris's 'shrowdinge hande' – Jenye's sonnet self-consciously reflects on the 'reducing' (the rendering or translating) of Ronsard's French 'ryme' into an 'Englishe grace'. This prefatory sonnet brazenly asserts the aesthetic credentials of English vernacular culture, which has achieved the *grazia* – the literary ideal of 'grace' – invoked elsewhere in this period as the poetic apotheosis of 'bonne grâce' in Jacques Peletier's 1555 *Art poëtique*.[50]

The conceit of a *translatio studii*, the transmission of cultural and linguistic authority from one literary milieu to another, recurs later in this publication too. Jenye's coy, parenthetical modesty topos – his claim to have Englished Ronsard's work 'in vnskilful verse' – is offset by another sonnet towards the end of the volume, 'A sonnet to the translatour', a kind of closing paratext, ascribed to Ferdinand Fielding and addressed to Jenye himself.[51] The sonneteer here enumerates the cultural processes that underpin the interlingual transference of cultural authority from Homer to Virgil to Ronsard's 'blowminge grafte' and finally to the translator Jenye, whose 'Englishe pleasant phrase' is grafted on to Ronsard's 'stocke'. In both sonnets, the verse form seems pointedly loaded: Jenye's prefatory blank-verse sonnet may recall the Earl of Surrey's unrhymed epic metrics in his English translation of books II and IV of *The Aeneid*, and Fielding's sonnet, in hexameters, not only pre-empts the first sonnet in Sidney's *Astrophil and Stella* but also embodies the epic credentials that are celebrated in his sonnet's retrospective references to Homer and Virgil. Both sonnets laud native, vernacular poetics by experimenting with metrical schemes that not only recall heroic precursors but also nativise the cultural prestige encoded in anterior epic literature.

Such paratextual sonnets harness praise of native culture with displays of technical innovation. Many more examples of sonnets that gauge the claims of rival vernaculars to aesthetic supremacy could be readily cited. For instance, the apparatus of dedications in the English translation of Giovanni Battista Nenna's *Treatise of Nobility* (1595–1600) contains prefatory sonnets by Samuel Daniel and George Chapman which applaud the translator William Jones's success in making the Italian original an English native. Daniel's sonnet is steeped in the vocabulary of nativisation ('Here dost thou bring [my friend] a stranger borne / To be indenized with vs, and made our owne'), and Chapman's final couplet celebrates the translingual odyssey that the Italian text has undergone, in a lexical *translatio studii* from Italy, via France, to England, culminating in the wish that 'As he hath made one strange an Englishman, / May make our mindes in this, *Italian*'.[52] Daniel seems particularly preoccupied with questions of translatability and cultural interchange. Another of his prefatory sonnets, introducing the English translation (probably by Tailboys Dymoke) of Giovanni Battista Guarini's pastoral tragicomedy *Il Pastor Fido* and addressed to Sir Edward Dymoke (Tailboys's grandfather), celebrates both the Italian work and its English incarnation:

> *Who in thy loue I know tooke great delight*
> *As thou in his, who now in England can*
> *Speake as good English as Italian,*
> *And here enioyes the grace of his owne right.*
> *Though I remember he hath oft imbas'd*
> *Unto vs both, the vertues of the North,*
> *Saying, our costes were with no measures grac'd,*
> *Nor barbarous tongues could any verse bring forth.*
> *I would he sawe his owne, or knew our store,*
> *Whose spirits can yeeld as much, and if not more.*[53]

Daniel's eulogy to the capacious 'store' of the English language, here cast as a vernacular able to accommodate and match or even outmatch the Italian, and his celebration of the processes by which Guarini 'now in England can / Speake as good English as Italian' constitute an audacious act of linguistic nativising – a process once again replicated visually through the bold adoption of italic typeface to fête the English domestication of an Italian work. Daniel stridently nationalises the criteria by which the translated work is to be judged, as he Englishes the aesthetic ideal of 'grazia', the phrases 'grace of his owne right' and 'no measures grac'd' here gesturing to that virtue previously encountered in Jenye's prefatory sonnet to his translation of Ronsard: 'grace' invokes that aesthetic touchstone associated in Italian critical theory of the 1550s with the combined artistic goals of *invenzione*, *disegno* and *varietà*.⁵⁴ Jason Lawrence has argued that this prefatory sonnet voices both a 'sincere expression of Daniel's desire to raise the international status of his native language to counter claims of linguistic barbarity' and an 'endorsement of the translator's achievement', a commonplace feature of commendatory sonnets but laced here with 'added resonance from Daniel's own Tasso translation of the previous year'.⁵⁵ These concerns are reanimated in the unsubscribed 'Sonnet of the Translator' immediately after Daniel's, also dedicated to Sir Edward Dymoke, which reads as a stand-alone piece in itself but also arguably forms a mini-sequence with Daniel's. This sonnet's lexis of nativisation envisages clothing 'Learned *Guarini*' in an English habit to make him an 'English Denizen', acknowledging at the same time both the skill and the difficulties involved in negotiating and adapting extant literature – in 'reform[ing] a frame' that already exists, rather than creating something *ex nihilo*, 'build[ing] from ground worke of ones wit, / A new creation'.⁵⁶

Cultivating lineage

Beyond the insistently architectural, edificial terminology that saturates these poems, a botanical vocabulary, central to this vernacularising and denizening project, is frequently deployed by these sonneteers to theorise the processes by which literary succession is cultivated. In one of five prefatory sonnets celebrating the Ovidian transmigration (a meta-metamorphosis) effected by George Chapman's eruditely obscure epyllion, or even 'anti-epyllion', *Ouids Banquet of Sence* (1595), Thomas Williams marshals a vocabulary of literary cultivation when addressing questions of cultural transference.⁵⁷ Williams reflects on both the practice of nurturing what has been transplanted within a plot and also the subsequent processes of engrafting that help to secure a line of literary descent.

> Vngratefull Farmers of the Muses land
>   That (wanting thrift and iudgment to imploy it)
>   Let it manureles and vnfenced stand,
>   Till barbarous Cattell enter and destroy it:
> Now the true heyre is happily found out
>   Who (framing it t'inritch posterities)
>   Walles it with spright-fild darknes round about,
>   Grafs, plants, and sowes; and makes it Paradise.
> To which without the *Parcæs* golden bow,
>   None can aspire but stick in errors hell;
>   A Garland to engird a Monarchs brow,
>   Then take some paines to ioy so rich a Iewell
> Most prize is graspt in labors hardest hand,
> And idle soules can nothing rich command.⁵⁸

By this analogy, Chapman, dubbed a literary 'heyre', becomes the gardener cultivating 'the Muses land', which stands as a kind of metonymy for the processes of poetic creation that might be nurtured anew. The structural and architectural metaphors of 'framing' a source-text within 'walles' give way to a more organic lexis (elsewhere drawn upon in Samuel Daniel's aforementioned conceit of 'apt planting') of engrafting, planting and sowing, a vocabulary that extends even to the golden bough suggestively alluded to in line 9, the branch instrumental in Aeneas's quest for a new Hesperian homeland. The sonnet revolves around the terminology of enclosure (the etymology of 'paradise' connoting an 'enclosed park, orchard, ... walled vegetable plot') and image systems that foreground the skill and industry ('labors hardest hand') required to achieve this horticultural enclosure.[59] Once again, that a sonnet should be chosen here is not unfitting, given this poet's celebration of microcosmic, circumscribed forms: through its language of 'engird[ing]' and of enclosing something previously 'vnfenced', the sonnet constructs its own *hortus conclusus*.

This horticultural motif is particularly pronounced in the sole sonnet that prefaces *Florios Second Frutes*, John Florio's language-learning handbook structured around a series of parallel Italian–English dialogues. This commendatory sonnet, '*Phaëton to his friend Florio*', addressed by an anonymous friend (the self-styled Phaëton) to the author himself, is rife with botanical analogies, playing on the latent floral possibilities of Florio's name in a slightly wearisome series of puns:

> *Sweete friend whose name agrees with thy increase,*
>   *How fit a riuall art thou of the Spring?*
>   *For when each branche hath left his flourishing,*
>   *And green-lockt Sommers shadie pleasures cease:*
> *She makes the Winters stormes repose in peace,*
>   *And spends her franchise on each liuing thing:*
>   *The dazies sprout, the little birds doo sing,*
>   *Hearbes, gummes, and plants doo vaunt of their release.*
> *So when that all our English witts lay dead,*
>   *(Except the Laurell that is euer greene,)*
>   *Thou with thy Frutes our barrenness o're-spread,*
>   *And set thy flowrie pleasance to be seene.*
> *Sutch frutes, sutch flowrets of moralitie,*
>   *Were nere before brought out of* Italy.[60]

This account – patterned emblematically as a transmigration, as in Gaywood's sonnet celebrating Sylvester's nativisation of foreignness, from a Petrarchan octave (abba abba) to a distinctly English, Wyattian sestet (cddcee) – credits Florio's *Second Frutes* and its appendical collection of some six thousand proverbs (his botanically monikered *Gardine of recreation*) with a blossoming of English vernacular possibilities, and Florio himself with an onomastically fitting flowering of England's linguistic foliage, a cornucopia of verbal 'frutes' not bettered by Italian literary culture. An agent of linguistic renewal, Florio nurtures an otherwise backward, moribund literary plot in a fantasy of perpetual 'increase'. As before, this sonnet depends on a confluence of horticultural and political registers: just as Williams's sonnet above paired its portrait of a literary 'Paradise' with an image of a garland crowning 'a Monarchs brow', and as John Davies of Hereford's prefatory sonnet to *Microcosmos* invoked a verdant polity of 'Things living' in terms of a '*Monarchy of Witte*', so Phaëton's sonnet conjures the idea of a 'franchise' bestowed on 'each liuing thing'. Here, 'franchise' connotes not only a type of legal or political freedom of ownership granted by a sovereign power, the privilege of citizenship and corporate belonging, but also, in a more obviously spatial application, an area of land over which a certain jurisdiction is authorised.[61] As small parcels, poetic heterocosms that are simultaneously spatial plots and self-enclosed polities, stand-alone sonnets like Phaëton's seek to negotiate the contours of national identity and political self-definition, mapping out for their readers and dedicatees a space for a native literary culture to flourish, albeit one seen to have its originary roots in Italy or to be grafted on to a borrowed, Continental stock.

Similar topoi litter Maurice Kyffin's sonnet 'to the Reader' in the front-matter of *The Resolued Gentleman* (1594), a translation by Lewis Lewkenor, a government official newly returned from the Continent, of Olivier de La Marche's fifteenth-century French romance *Le chevalier délibéré*. A *littérateur* from the Spenser, Harvey and Harington circle, Kyffin proffers a sonnet that, first, fulfils the staple paratextual function of commending the translator and, secondly, delineates an interlingual transplanting, a *translatio* of form and genre, most overtly in its final quatrain:

> This Allegorie, shaped first in French,
>   And thence transferd into Castilian verse,
> Conteining Rules our follies to retrench,
>   *Lewknor*, by Metaphrase, doth heere reherse.[62]

Beyond the strikingly early usage of the term 'metaphrase', here designating a prose translation of a verse original in perhaps only the word's second occurrence, after Thomas Cartwright's formative definition of the practice in 1575, these lines are noteworthy for their conceit of denizening foreignness.[63] Kyffin may even be playing on the etymology of 'reherse', from the Old French *rehercier*, denoting the idea of harrowing – of raking or turning over soil to cultivate a new crop.[64] Comparable horticultural motifs underpin the commendatory sonnet ascribed to 'A.B.' in the prefatory material to John Bodenham's 1600 anthology, *The Garden of the Mvses*. Bodenham, the work's inaugural inspiration and dedicatee, was patron of several printed commonplace books for which he compiled material (from his own sedulous reading) that was then arranged under topic headings by editors. This prefatory sonnet opens with an address to the reader:

> *Thou which delight'st to view this goodly plot,*
> *Here take such flowres as best shal serue thy vse,*
> *Where thou maist find in euery curious knot,*
> *Of speciall vertue, and most precious iuyce,*
> *Set by Apollo in their seuerall places,*
> *And nourished with his celestiall Beames,*
> *And watered by the Muses and the Graces,*
> *With the fresh dew of those Castalian streames.*[65]

Peddling the usual metaphors of poetic cultivation, this sonnet now applies the conceit to acts of readerly labour required to cull 'flowres' for personal use from out of 'this goodly plot', the term 'plot' and the related term 'plat', in the sixteenth and early seventeenth centuries, bearing specifically artisanal resonances.[66] Once again, the sonnet's force lies in its interplay of registers, its juxtaposition of competing authorities and interpretative frameworks: the horticultural and the literary overlap in 'knot' both as a flower-bed or garden plot and, in a more figurative sense, as an artwork of baroque complexity;[67] equally, 'place' yokes together the spatial (a fertile area of land to be cultivated under the nourishing watch of Apollo, the Muses and the Graces) and the lectorial (commonplaces to be sifted through by the readerly labourer). Bodenham's compilational industry is, by this analogy, mirrored by the gleaning activities of the anthology's readers. The sonnet's cross-fertilisation of these lexicons gives rise to a functional ambiguity, where 'this goodly plot' may refer immediately to this paratextual sonnet itself as much as to the ensuing work, the edited anthology (this gathering of poetic flowers). As with 'franchise', 'knot' and 'place', Kyffin's keyword 'plot' here encompasses both an enclosed portion of land for gardening and also, in a more self-reflexively literary application, a representational design.[68] Variously defined, unsequenced sonnets, as 'parcelles' in Tottel's terminology, seem systemically to fuse a spatial form (a bounded area of land, a well-governed smallholding, a garden plot) with a representational function (a self-enclosed literary artefact).

A final illustration of these entwined motifs of enclosure, vernacular cultivation and national self-definition can be found in the sonnetic writings of Michael Drayton. One particular sonnet provides an intriguing and late example of that aforementioned strategy practised by Wyatt and Surrey in translating Continental models – namely, the habit of uprooting individual sonnets from a pre-existing sequence and scattering them in new, unsequenced contexts as stand-alone poems in their own right. Drayton's sonnet 'Into these loues' first appears as part of his *Idea* sequence, from 1599 onwards:

> To the Reader of his Poems.
> Sonet. 2.
> Into these loues who but for passion lookes,
> At this first sight, here let him lay them by,
> And seeke elswhere in turning other bookes,
> which better may his labour satisfie.
> No far-fetch'd sigh shall euer wound my brest,
> Loue from mine eye, a teare shall neuer wring,
> Nor in ah-mees my whyning Sonets drest,
> (A Libertine) fantasticklie I sing;
> My verse is the true image of my mind,
> Euer in motion, still desiring change,
> To choyce of all varietie inclin'd,
> And in all humors sportiuely I range;
>   My actiue Muse is of the worlds right straine,
>   That cannot long one fashion entertaine.[69]

In an illustration of the early modern sonnet's mobility and the fragility of poetic sequences, this sonnet is relocated in the final version of Drayton's collection, his 1619 *Poems*. There Drayton cultivates the impression of a sequence straining towards something on the precipice of disorder – a sequence whose poems have been assembled in what Rémi Vuillemin calls an apparently random manner ('façon aléatoire'), a sequence fragmented and broken up ('fragmenté, morcelé') and hiding at every turn any sense of structure ('cacher toute structure'), in an echo of Petrarch's own 'scattered' bricolage. The sonnet above is now relocated from within the sequence to a paratextual place without: it becomes, in Vuillemin's terms, a 'sonnet liminaire' whose liminary or preliminary status is signalled by ornamental woodcut borders at the top of the page.[70] Serving now as a prefatory threshold to the whole sequence, this sonnet 'To the Reader of these SONNETS' not only attests the compilational fluidity of sonnet gatherings (even *printed* sonnets are movable feasts), but also revealingly revises the wording of its sestet, most notably the final couplet:

> *My Verse is the true image of my Mind,*
> *Euer in motion, still desiring change;*
> *And as thus to Varietie inclin'd,*
> *So in all Humors sportiuely I range:*
>   *My Muse is rightly of the* English *straine,*
>   *That cannot long one Fashion intertaine.*[71]

This revised couplet explicitly acknowledges, and grandly lays claim to, the sonnet's vernacular, *English* identity. Drayton's fascinating etymological play on 'straine' introduces the idea of a native literary inheritance, since 'strain' connotes a line of descent and an act of procreation that has now acquired an unambiguous national colour.[72] As Christopher Warley observes, 'strain' means both 'lineage' and 'tension and discontinuity': it means 'both order and absence of order; it suggests a virtually random, isolated poem as well as a more coherent work … a presence and its deconstruction'.[73] For Warley the 'English *straine*' is intrinsically concerned with social manoeuvring, and the sonnet sequence's inherent instability becomes an opportunity for social self-fashioning. Yet Drayton's phrase also points to – and even generates – the very conditions by which foreignness is nativised and the English vernacular imbued with cultural prestige. Beyond the familiar play on the architectural imperatives of poetic compositions – 'strain' shares a root with 'structure' (from the Latin '*struere*', 'to build') – Drayton's 'English *straine*' also announces a literary genealogy. In a myth of autochthonous self-sufficiency, the strain mapped out by Drayton is self-originating, descending from its own stock.[74] Untethered from a larger, encasing narrative sequence, this sonnet now stands apart as a poem that embodies a kind of defiant resistance to the Continental, Italian origins of the form, even though Drayton's paean to 'change', 'Varietie' and 'motion' recalls the terminology of malleability and scattering that undergird the opening sonnet of Petrarch's collection. Drayton's term 'straine' gestures simultaneously to the sonnet's dual identity, or function, in the late sixteenth century, as something inherently foreign whose origins lie elsewhere, but also as something now inalienably native whose origins are (impossibly) English. Made native through successive cultivation, the sonnet – especially one like Drayton's that boasts an English rhyme-scheme – rehabilitates foreignness in an English setting, just as an italic typeface is conscripted for this distinctly English poetics. This fully fledged English sonnet announces and enacts a process of cultural transference and belonging: it performs vernacular eloquence, belligerently domesticating what might seem to be an inimitable, Continental model and establishing the terms by which the native literary canon that it actively helps to fashion might be judged.

Notes

1. J. Donne, *Letters to Severall Persons of Honour* (London: Richard Marriot, 1651), sig. O4rv. I should like to thank Rémi Vuillemin, Anne-Valérie Dulac, Enrica Zanin, Andrew Eastman, Guillaume Coatalen and Hugh Gazzard for advice in preparing this chapter.
2. G. Gascoigne, *The Posies of George Gascoigne Esquire* (London: Richard Smith, 1575), sig. c1r.
3. W.J. Kennedy, 'European Beginnings and Transmissions: Dante, Petrarch and the Sonnet Sequence', in A.D. Cousins and P. Howarth (eds), *The Cambridge Companion to the Sonnet* (Cambridge: Cambridge University Press, 2011), pp. 84–104, esp. p. 86.
4. H. Dubrow, 'The sonnet and the lyric mode', in A.D. Cousins and P. Howarth (eds), *The Cambridge Companion to the Sonnet* (Cambridge: Cambridge University Press, 2011), p. 31; and H. Dubrow, '"You may be wondering why I called you all here today": Patterns of Gathering in the Early Modern Lyric', in Elizabeth Scott-Baumann and Ben Burton (eds), *The Work of Form: Poetics and Materiality in Early Modern Culture* (Oxford: Oxford University Press, 2014), pp. 23–38, esp. p. 24.
5. R. Strier, 'Lyric Poetry from Donne to Philips', in C. Woodring and J. Shapiro (eds), *The Columbia History of British Poetry* (New York: Columbia University Press, 1994), pp. 229–53, esp. p. 229.
6. H.R. Woudhuysen, *Sir Philip Sidney and the Circulation of Manuscripts, 1558–1640* (Oxford: Clarendon Press, 1996), p. 22; M. Drayton, *Englands Heroicall Epistles. Nevvly Enlarged. VVith Idea. By Michaell Drayton* (London: Nicholas Ling, 1599), sig. Q1v (sonnet 31, lines 9–10).
7. J. Florio, *Queen Anna's New World of Words* (London: Edward Blount and William Barret, 1611), sig. Vv3v.
8. C. Shrank, '"Matters of love as of discourse": The English Sonnet, 1560–1580', *Studies in Philology*, 105:1 (2008), 30–49, at 45.
9. G. Whetstone, *A Remembravnce of the Wel Imployed Life, & Godly End, of George Gaskoigne* (London: Edward Aggas, 1577), sig. B4v.
10. G. Gascoigne, 'The Tale of Hemetes the Heremyte' (British Library, Royal 18.A.XLVIII), fol. 2r. See G. Heaton, *Writing and Reading Royal Entertainments: From George Gascoigne to Ben Jonson* (Oxford: Oxford University Press, 2010), pp. 30–43.
11. Marotti, '"Love is not love": Elizabethan Sonnet Sequences and the Social Order', *English Literary History*, 49 (1982), 396–428, esp. pp. 396–7.
12. Anonymous, 'Of person rare, strong limbes & manly shape', in Unknown artist, *Thomas Seymour, Baron Seymour, c.* 1560, oil on panel, London, National Portrait Gallery, 4571.
13. Gascoigne, *The Posies*, sig. U2v; Shrank, '"Matters of love as of discourse"', p. 35; Marotti, '"Love is not love"', p. 406.
14. C. Warley, *Sonnet Sequences and Social Distinction in Renaissance England* (Cambridge: Cambridge University Press, 2005), p. 12.
15. H. Wilcox, 'Sacred Desire, Forms of Belief: The Religious Sonnet in Early Modern Britain', in A.D. Cousins and P. Howarth (eds), *The Cambridge Companion to the Sonnet* (Cambridge: Cambridge University Press, 2011), pp. 145–65, esp. p. 151.
16. P. Tedaldi, 'Qualunque vuol saper fare un Sonetto', line 12, in G. de' Conti, *La Bella Mano di Giusto de' Conti … e una raccolta delle rime antiche di diversi Toscani* (Verona: Giannalberto Tumermani, 1753), p. 229.
17. M.G. Spiller, *The Development of the Sonnet: An Introduction* (London, New York: Routledge, 1992), p. 11.
18. Ibid.
19. J. Davies and C. Marlowe, *Epigrammes and Elegies* (London: s.n., 1599), sig. A3r, l. 12.
20. A.D. Cousins and P. Howarth, 'Introduction', in A.D. Cousins and P. Howarth (eds), *The Cambridge Companion to the Sonnet* (Cambridge: Cambridge University Press, 2011), pp. 1–5, esp. p. 1.
21. J. Davies of Hereford, *Microcosmos, The Discovery of the Little World, with the Government Thereof* (Oxford: Joseph Barnes, 1603), sig. A4r.
22. *Songes and Sonettes* (London: Richard Tottel, 1557), sig. A1v. See 'parcel, *n.*', 2.a, 'part, portion … considered separately', *OED Online*, www.oed.com (date accessed: 15 September 2016).
23. See 'parcel, *n.*', 2.b, 'an integral or component part … Used to emphasise inclusion in the whole', *OED Online*, www.oed.com (date accessed: 15 September 2016).
24. Gascoigne, *The Posies*, sig. N4r.
25. H. Dubrow, '"Dressing old words new"? Re-evaluating the "Delian Structure"', in M.C. Schoenfeldt (ed.), *A Companion to Shakespeare's Sonnets* (Oxford: Blackwell, 2007), pp. 90–103, esp. p. 99.
26. Spiller, *The Development of the Sonnet*, p. 49.

27 See 'parcel, *n*.', 5.a, 'piece of land, freq. one in separate … ownership from those that surround it', *OED Online*, www.oed.com (date accessed: 23 December 2017).
28 J. Donne, 'The Canonization', *Poems, by J.D.* (London: John Marriot, 1633), sig. Dd2r. Cleanth Brooks's iconic embodiment of New Critical reading, *The Well Wrought Urn: Studies in the Structure of Poetry* (New York: Harcourt Brace, 1947), pointedly derives its title from Donne's poem.
29 Gascoigne, *The Posies*, sigs T2r–U2v (sig. U2rv).
30 Puttenham, *The Arte of English Poesie. Contrived into Three Bookes: The First of Poets and Poesie, the Second of Proportion, the Third of Ornament* (London: Richard Field, 1589), sig. V4r.
31 W. Scott, 'The Modell of Poesye', British Library, MS Add. 81083, fols 16v, 48r.
32 S. Daniel, *A Panegyrike Congratulatory … With a Defence of Ryme* (London: Edward Blount, 1603), sig. G8rv.
33 F. Bracciolini, *Delle Poesie Liriche Toscane di Francesco Bracciolini dell'Api, Parte Prima* (Rome: Ludovico Grignani, 1639), p. 189.
34 H. Smith and L. Wilson, 'Introduction', in H. Smith and L. Wilson (eds), *Renaissance Paratexts* (Cambridge: Cambridge University Press, 2011), pp. 1–14, esp. p. 5.
35 J. Derrida, *The Truth in Painting*, trans. G. Bennington and I. McLeod (Chicago: Chicago University Press, 1987), p. 9; G. Genette's 1987 *Seuils*, translated into English as *Paratexts: Thresholds of Interpretation*, trans. J.E. Lewin (Cambridge: Cambridge University Press, 1997), pp. 1–2.
36 James VI of Scotland, *The Essayes of a Prentise, in the Diuine Art of Poesie* (Edinburgh: Thomas Vautrollier, 1584), sig. M4rv.
37 A.F. Marotti and M. Freiman, 'The English Sonnet in Manuscript, Print and Mass Media', in A.D. Cousins and P. Howarth (eds), *The Cambridge Companion to the Sonnet* (Cambridge: Cambridge University Press, 2011), pp. 66–83, esp. p. 70; Shrank, '"Matters of love as of discourse"', p. 45.
38 H. Holland, 'Vpon the Lines and Life of the Famous Scenicke Poet, Master William Shakespeare', in W. Shakespeare, *Mr. William Shakespeares Comedies, Histories, & Tragedies: Published According to the True Originall Copies* (London: Isaac Iaggard and Edward Blount, 1623), sig. A5r, lines 11–14.
39 C. Langton, *A Uery Brefe Treatise, Ordrely Declaring the Pri[n]cipal Partes of Phisick* (London: Edward Whitchurch, 1547), sig. A1v.
40 A. Marotti, *Manuscript, Print and the English Renaissance Lyric* (Ithaca, London: Cornell University Press, 1995), p. 222.
41 A.E.B. Coldiron, *Printers Without Borders: Translation and Textuality in the Renaissance* (Cambridge: Cambridge University Press, 2015), pp. 9–11.
42 N. Rhodes, 'Status Anxiety and English Renaissance Translation', in Helen Smith and Louise Wilson (eds), *Renaissance Paratexts* (Cambridge: Cambridge University Press, 2011), pp. 107–120, esp. pp. 110, 117–18.
43 W. Alexander, 'To M. *Michael Drayton*', in M. Drayton, *Englands Heroicall Epistles Nevvly Corrected. VVith Idea* (London: Nicholas Ling, 1602), sig. A4r, lines 7–14.
44 G. Gaywood, 'To M. *Iosuah Syluester*', in G. Du Bartas, trans. J. Sylvester, *The Second Weeke or Childhood of the World, of the Noble, Learned and Diuine Salustius, Lord of Bartas* (London: P. Short, 1598), sig. A4v.
45 Shrank, '"Matters of love as of discourse"', p. 48.
46 *The Courtyer of Count Baldessar Castilio Diuided into Foure Books*, trans. T. Hoby (London: William Seres, 1561), sig. A2v.
47 Ibid., sig. A3r.
48 Discussing the typographic choices made by printers of polyglot texts, Anne Coldiron notes that 'English poems sometimes appear in italic or roman', suggesting that the decision might visually imply that English poetry, 'finished with its crude, gothic phase' associated with black-letter printing earlier in the century, 'now belongs in this more refined and progressive world of nations' (Coldiron, *Printers without Borders*, pp. 241–2).
49 T. Jenye, *A Discovrs of the Present Troobles in Fravnce, and Miseries of this Tyme* (Antwerp: 1568), sig. A2r.
50 The syntagm recurs frequently in Peletier's work: see 'si bonne grace' in, for instance, *L'Art poëtique de Iaques Peletier du Mans* (Lyon: Guillaume Gazeau, 1555), pp. 37, 39, 67 and 71, and also in his verse itself, as in the 'Opvscvules' appended to *L'Art*, pp. 106 and 107.
51 Jenye, *A Discovrs of the Present Troobles in Fravnce*, sig. D4v (lines 5, 13–14).
52 *Nennio, or A treatise of nobility … Written in Italian by that famous doctor and worthy knight Sir John Baptista Nenna*, trans. W. Jones (London: Paul Linley and John Flasket, 1595), sig. ¶1v (lines 1–2), sig. ¶2r (lines 13–14).

53 S. Daniel, 'To the right worthie and learned Knight, Syr Edward Dymock', in Guarini, *Il Pastor Fido: Or The Faithfull Shepheard. Translated out of Italian into English*, trans. Tailboys Dymoke(?) (London: Simon Waterson, 1602), unmarked verso to the title page, lines 5–14.
54 See, for instance, L. Dolce, *Dialogo della Pittura ... intitolato l'Aretino* (Venice: Giolito, 1557).
55 Jason Lawrence, *'Who the Devil Taught Thee So Much Italian?' Italian Language and Literary Imitation in Early Modern England* (Manchester: Manchester University Press, 2005), p. 95.
56 Dymoke(?), 'A Sonnet of the Translator', in Guarini, *Il Pastor Fido*, unmarked verso to the title page, lines 5, 7, 12–14.
57 For Chapman's poem as an 'anti-epyllion', see W.P. Weaver, 'The Banquet of the Common Sense: George Chapman's Anti-Epyllion', *Studies in Philology*, 111: 4 (2014), 757–85.
58 T. Williams, 'Vngratefull Farmers', in G. Chapman, *Ouids Banquet of Sence, A Coronet for his Mistresse Philosophie* (London: Richard Smith, 1595), sig. A3v.
59 See 'paradise, *n.*', *OED Online*, www.oed.com (date accessed: 23 December 2017).
60 J. Florio, *Florios Second Frutes to be Gathered of Twelue Trees, of Diuers but Delightsome Tastes to the Tongues of Italians and Englishmen. To which is Annexed his Gardine of Recreation Yeelding Six Thousand Italian Prouerbs* (London: Thomas Woodcock, 1591), sig. *2v.
61 See 'franchise, *n.*', 2.a, 'right to own property ... freedom of government'; 2.b, 'special privilege'; 4, 'full membership of a corporation or state'; 3, 'A geographic area ... in which an individual or corporation could ... exercise public jurisdiction', *OED Online* www.oed.com (date accessed: 23 December 2017).
62 M. Kyffin, 'to the Reader', in O. de La Marche, trans. L. Lewkenor, *The Resolued Gentleman. Translated out of Spanishe into Englyshe* (London: Richard Watkins, 1594), sig. A2r, lines 9–12.
63 T. Cartwright, *The Second Replie of Thomas Cartwright: Agaynst Maister Doctor Whitgiftes Second Answer* (Heidelberg: Michael Schirat, 1575), sig. X3r.
64 See 'rehearse, *v.*', 'to harrow again', *OED Online*, www.oed.com (date accessed: 23 December 2017).
65 A.B., 'Of this Garden of the Muses', in J. Bodenham (ed.), *Bel-vedére, or, The Garden of the Mvses* (London: Hugh Astley, 1600), sig. A7v (lines 1–8).
66 On the use of 'plot' to denote 'schematic diagrams or working drawings used by the mason, surveyor, or carpenter', see H.S. Turner, *The English Renaissance Stage: Geometry, Poetics, and the Practical Spatial Arts 1580–1630* (Oxford: Oxford University Press, 2006), p. 21.
67 See 'knot, *n.*', 7, 'A flower-bed laid out in a fanciful ... design'; 10.*fig.*a, 'Something intricate, involved, or difficult to trace out', *OED Online*, www.oed.com (date accessed: 23 December 2017).
68 See 'plot, *n.*', 1, 'A fairly small piece of ground, *esp.* one used for ... building or gardening'; 3.a, 'A plan ... *esp.* a synopsis of a literary work', *OED Online*, www.oed.com (date accessed: 23 December 2017).
69 Drayton, *Englands Heroicall Epistles* (1599), sig. P2v.
70 Rémi Vuillemin, *Le Recueil pétrarquiste à l'ère du maniérisme: Poétique des sonnets de Michael Drayton, 1594–1619* (Paris: Honoré Champion, 2014), pp. 427, 570, 421.
71 M. Drayton, *Poems: by Michael Drayton, Esquire* (London: John Smethwicke, 1619), sig. Kk2v, lines 9–14.
72 See 'strain, *n.1*', 5, 'Pedigree, lineage, ancestry, descent'; 4, 'Offspring, progeny', *OED Online*, www.oed.com (date accessed: 23 December 2017).
73 Warley, *Sonnet Sequences and Social Distinction in Renaissance England*, p. 2.
74 See 'strain, *n.1*', 6.a, 'descendants of a common ancestor; a race, stock', *OED Online*, www.oed.com (date accessed: 23 December 2017).

6

'And sweetly nectarize this bitter gall': Gabriel Harvey's sonnet therapy

Elisabeth Chaghafi

Certaine Sonnets

When we think of Gabriel Harvey, we are unlikely to think of sonnets. Instead, we tend to associate his name either with Edmund Spenser's 'Hobbinol' or with the pedantic academic bore portrayed in the pamphlets of Thomas Nashe. Although the dedicatory epistle of *The Shepheardes Calender* (1579) had specifically urged Harvey to publish 'those so many excellent English poems of his' (which apparently he never did), English poetry was not Harvey's preferred medium.[1] He was – and still is – better known for his Latin verses, such as the poems he contributed to *Lachrymae*, the University of Cambridge's collection of poetic tributes to commemorate Sir Philip Sidney. So it seems surprising at first that, when Gabriel Harvey did try his hand at sonnet-writing, he attempted a whole sonnet sequence.

Harvey's occasion for writing his sonnet sequence, called 'Greenes Memoriall', was rather an odd one. It formed the second part of Harvey's notorious pamphlet *Foure Letters and Certaine Sonnets* (1592), and, despite its title, it was not primarily concerned with commemoration. *Foure Letters and Certaine Sonnets* is mainly known for two reasons: first, it was the pamphlet that sparked off Harvey's prolonged quarrel with Thomas Nashe, who immediately responded to it with *Strange Newes* (1592), and, second, the letters contained some vicious attacks on the poet and playwright Robert Greene, who had died just a few days earlier, apparently in miserable circumstances.[2] Since interest in one (or both) of those two points is generally the reason for turning to the pamphlet, it is hardly surprising that critical attention has been almost exclusively focused on the 'Foure Letters', while the 'Certaine Sonnets' have been all but ignored.[3]

It is also hard to see why Harvey would have wanted to accompany his attacks on Greene with sonnets in the first place, especially considering that it was a form he was unfamiliar with and not particularly skilled at, as the resulting sonnets show. It is unlikely that he was simply trying to bulk out his 'slender Pamflet' by adding the sonnets at the end of the book as an afterthought. There is reason to believe that the sonnets are not just a puzzling and superfluous addition to the letters but actually have a function in the volume. Their inclusion in the title suggests some degree of significance, as does their number. At seventy-five pages' worth of printed text, *Foure Letters and Certaine Sonnets* is a relatively slim quarto, yet it contains not only twenty-two numbered sonnets by Harvey but also a sonnet in rhyming couplets

'And sweetly nectarize this bitter gall'   115

attributed to Christopher Bird and a commendatory sonnet by Edmund Spenser, as well as two Latin epigrams by Harvey, commemorating his brother John Harvey and Robert Greene respectively. Collectively, the poems account for 20 per cent of the volume (fifteen out of seventy-five pages). Additionally, the dedication on the title page 'To all courteous minds, that will voutchsafe the reading' directly echoes that of 'Greenes Memoriall', which reads 'to the foresaid Maister Emmanuell Demetrius, Maister Christopher Bird [the addressees of the first two letters], and all gentle wits, that will voutsafe the reading'. The verbal echo suggests that the sonnets are being presented to readers as an equally significant part of the volume that is equally worthy of their consideration. Consequently, they need to be taken seriously and deserve attention despite their relative lack of poetic merit.

Harvey's occasion for writing the pamphlet – his anger at the fact that Greene, who had insulted the entire Harvey family in his *Quip for an Vpstart Courtier*, had unexpectedly died before Harvey could seek legal satisfaction – hardly called for the pleasant 'sweetness' of style frequently associated with the sonnet form at the time, so his decision to supplement it with a sonnet sequence appears counterintuitive.[4] In this chapter, I propose that Harvey was pursuing three aims in publishing *Foure Letters and Certaine Sonnets*: first, he was of course responding to Greene's insults by vilifying Greene and vindicating his own father and his brothers (especially his youngest brother John, who had died shortly before Greene); second, he was – as ever – seeking to self-advertise and present himself in a favourable light; third, he was allowing his readers to witness his attempts to gradually conquer his anger. Of these three aims, only the first is generally recognised, because it is most closely associated with the letters (as noted above, scholarly interest in the pamphlet overwhelmingly focuses on its role in the Harvey–Nashe quarrel), whereas it is necessary to consider 'Greenes Memoriall' as well as the letters in order to recognise the other two. In the following, I will argue that the sonnets in the volume play a crucial part within Harvey's strategy of portraying himself as a just, fair-minded individual who was able to remain calm even in the face of grave insults by 'tempering' his own anger via the medium of style. Harvey's repeated invocations and evocations of his friend Edmund Spenser are also part of that strategy.

The only sonnet in *Foure Letters and Certaine Sonnets* to have received a moderate amount of critical attention is Spenser's sonnet 'To the right worshipfull, my singular good frend Master Gabriell Haruey, Doctor of the Lawes', which concludes the volume:

Haruey, the happy aboue happiest men
I read: that sitting like a Looker-on
Of this worldes Stage, doest note with critique pen
The sharp dislikes of each condition:
And as one carelesse of suspition,
Ne fawnest for the fauour of the great:
Ne fearest foolish reprehension
Of faulty men, which daunger to thee threat.
But freely doest, of what thee list entreat,
Like a great Lord of peerlesse liberty:

> Lifting the Good vp to high Honours seat,
> And the Euill damning euermore to dy.
> For Life, and Death is in thy doomefull writing:
> So thy renowme liues euer by endighting.
>
> Dublin, this xviij. of Iuly: 1586.
>
> Your deuoted frend during life,
> Edmund Spencer.[5]

The interest of this sonnet lies partly in its odd positioning at the end of the book and partly in the fact that it is by Edmund Spenser, who – unlike Harvey – had, and still has, a reputation as one of the major poets of the 1590s and was more skilled at sonnet-writing. So there is perhaps a sense that the sonnet has attracted more attention because readers felt it was the only *good* sonnet in the volume. A nineteenth-century editor of Spenser's collected works even went as far as to claim it was the only truly great sonnet written by Spenser, because 'it has that quality of strong feeling, of direct expression, which – even in the presence of his other amazing gifts – one must often desiderate in our great Poet'.[6] The dating of the Spenser sonnet suggests it was written for another occasion, perhaps Harvey's obtaining of his doctorate in civil law. In *Foure Letters and Certaine Sonnets*, however, Harvey seems to be producing Spenser's sonnet as a character reference of sorts to vouch for his personal integrity – much like the first letter in the volume, a letter of recommendation from Christopher Bird of Saffron Walden, which commends the bearer as being 'a very excellent general Scholler' as well as 'very honest'.[7] At the same time, Harvey uses it as a way of once again casually reminding readers of his friendship with the celebrated author of *The Faerie Queene*, who would not lavish his 'ouerloouing' sonnets on an undeserving recipient. Technically, of course, the sonnet's early date means that in citing it Harvey was not invoking the authority of Edmund Spenser, author of the first three books of *The Faerie Queene*, but merely quoting the as yet anonymous 'Immerito', author of *The Shepheardes Calender* and another 'slender Pamflet' of printed letters and poetry written in collaboration with Harvey.[8]

The neglecting of Harvey's sonnets by readers of the pamphlet is not a modern phenomenon. Thomas Nashe, no doubt Harvey's harshest critic, mentions the sonnets in *Strange Newes*, his direct response to and 'confutation' of *Foure Letters and Certaine Sonnets*, but overall has very little to say about them.[9] Nashe's reticence on the subject of the sonnets is somewhat surprising, given that he otherwise misses no opportunity to attack Harvey and the sonnets' lack of obvious poetic merit would seem to make them an easy target; yet instead of tearing Harvey for his bad verses, he seems to consider it safer to conduct his character-assassination through attacking Harvey's prose. Towards the beginning of *Strange Newes*, which essentially runs through *Foure Letters and Certaine Sonnets* page by page and line by line, Nashe briefly mocks the clumsiness of Christopher Bird's sonnet – whose first two lines had rhymed 'autor' with 'hauter' – with equally clumsy verses titled 'A Dash through the dudgen Sonnet against *Greene*', which begin: 'Put up thy smiter o gentle

Peter / Author and halter make but ill metre / I scorne to answer thy misshapen rhyme'.[10] Yet despite the fact that Harvey's third letter had mocked the narrator's poem at the beginning of *Pierce Penilesse* at some length (apparently missing the point that Pierce's verses are intended to be bad), *Strange Newes* largely does scorn Harvey's misshapen rhyme and focuses on the letters. After attacking the fourth letter, Nashe merely states:

> His owne regenerate verses of the *iolly Fly*, & *Gibeline and Gwelph* some peraduenture may expect that I should answer. So I would if there were anie thing in them which I had not answerd before, but there is nothing; [...]. Onely I will looke vpon the last Sonnet of M. *Spencers* to the right worshipfull Maister *G.H.* Doctour of the lawes: or it may fall out that I will not looke vpon it too, because (*Gabriell*) though I vehemently suspect it to bee of thy own doing, it is popt foorth vnder M. *Spencers* name, and his name is able to sanctifie any thing though falsely ascribed to it.[11]

This passage suggests that Nashe probably believed the Spenser sonnet to be genuine – his questioning of its authorship seems like little more than a lazy feint.[12] The main purpose of the passage, however, is to subvert the notion of a genuine friendship between Spenser and Harvey: when referring to the Spenser sonnet, Nashe deliberately changes its title, and the part he pointedly omits is the phrase 'my singular good frend'. By Nashe's standards, he is handling the Spenser sonnet with kid gloves and being unusually cautions in only voicing a suspicion. This becomes especially apparent if his dismissive remarks are compared to the passages in which he accuses Harvey of having written the Christopher Bird sonnet himself and of having been the driving force behind the publication of the so-called Spenser–Harvey letters in 1580, in both of which cases Nashe is considerably more aggressive and more confident in his accusation of Harvey.[13]

That Spenser should feature at all in Nashe's response to *Foure Letters and Certaine Sonnets* is less surprising than it may seem at first. The pamphlet war between Harvey and Nashe is generally best known for the increasingly abusive and personal tone in which the two writers addressed each other, yet, in the initial stages of the quarrel at least, there is an element of debate, and the subject of that debate are different models of authorship and authorial careers. Harvey's disapproval of Greene in *Foure Letters and Certaine Sonnets* is partly framed in terms of disapproval of him as a writer, leading him to present Greene as a kind of anti-laureate figure, whom he uses as a foil for Spenser, his model for ideal authorship. This is particularly apparent in the mock-crowning scene, in which Harvey describes Greene's dead body being crowned with a garland of bays by 'his sweet hostisse [...] to shew, that a tenth Muse honoured him more being deade; then all the nine honoured him aliue'.[14] He also uses the example of those two contrasting author figures to warn Nashe not to throw his talents away by writing satire, which Harvey regards as a dead end for literary careers, citing several examples of writers who 'overreached' in experimenting with it: 'euen *Tully*, and *Horace* otherwhiles ouerreched: and I must needs say, Mother Hubbard, in heat of choller, forgetting the pure sanguine of her sweete Feary Queene, wilfully ouer-shott her malcontented selfe'.[15] By contrast, Nashe, in *Strange Newes*, defended the model of commercial, professional authorship practised by Greene, but trod very carefully on the subject of Spenser, preferring instead to question the nature of Harvey's relationship with him and even trying to argue that Spenser may have had a more satirical bent than Harvey gave him credit for, by claiming that all instances of Spenser's praise that Harvey cites are either forgeries or misunderstood satire: 'If euer he praisd thee, it was because he had pickt a fine vaine foole out of thee, and he would keepe thee still a foole by flattring thee'.[16]

In addition to showing Nashe's reluctance to criticise anything 'popt foorth vnder M. *Spencers* name', the passage from *Strange Newes* cited above suggests Nashe was aware that the purpose of Harvey's sonnets was not to introduce any new ideas but to refer back to – and reflect on – key ideas from the letters. Thus he justified his refusal to dignify Harvey's sonnets with a response by claiming they were not worthy of any further comment, because they contained no additional points for him to answer. In a sense, this is a fair assessment. Even the titles of the sonnets recall passages from the letters or provide variations on certain themes that occur at several points. So, for example, 'His Repentance, that meant to call Greene to his aunsweare' (sonnet I) echoes Harvey's – not entirely serious – claim in the second letter that the news that Harvey was going to sue him over the libellous passage in *A Quip for an Vpstart Courtier* literally scared Greene to death, while others, such as 'His admonition to Greenes Companions' (sonnet III) address recurring themes (in this case Harvey's appeal to Nashe to give up satire and put his talent to better use).[17]

Nashe's lack of response to Harvey's sonnets is significant because the reception of *Foure Letters and Certaine Sonnets* has been substantially shaped by scholars' knowledge of its aftermath. Being aware of the pamphlet's role in the Harvey–Nashe quarrel, we are likely to focus on insults to Nashe and Greene and the responses they generated, and to pay particularly close attention to the passages that Nashe chose to attack or contradict. There is nothing wrong with that approach, of course, but it does mean viewing *Foure Letters and Certaine Sonnets* through Nashe's eyes rather than as a text in its own right, which may not have been written and published solely to aggravate him. Effectively, then, Nashe's refusal to dignify Harvey's 'regenerate verses' with a reply is also the reason why the sonnets in the volume have been so little studied.

One point that may need to be stressed in this context is that Harvey's sonnets, whose form is loosely modelled on the one favoured by Edmund Spenser, are not strictly worth reading for their literary qualities. This is the second reason why they have received so little critical attention. Historically, literary studies as an academic discipline was built on value judgements regarding the moral, spiritual or historical worth or the aesthetic 'quality' of literary texts. Harvey's sonnets – or, for that matter, his prose writings – failed to make the literary canon because of their shortcomings on both counts, and he became established as a minor figure, whose interest was limited to his association with better, more important authors, like Nashe, Spenser or Sidney. To an extent it is understandable why Harvey failed to achieve much of a reputation as a sonneteer either in his own time or among modern scholars: even a reader less critically minded than Nashe will have no trouble spotting that, as sonnets go, the twenty-two poems of 'Greenes Memoriall' are mediocre efforts at best. Metrically, they are relatively even, though the defining characteristic of Harvey's sonnet sequence is the unevenness of the sonnets, despite the visual uniformity created by the print layout. This is not necessarily to say that evenness of form is a defining feature of (good) sonnets. Nevertheless, it is a defining feature of Spenser's sonnets, on which Harvey attempted to model his own, so its relative absence in 'Greenes Memoriall' suggests that Harvey's poetic talent was at least not sufficient to achieve everything he set out to achieve. For example, the twenty-two sonnets follow various rhyme-schemes, ranging from a pseudo-Spenserian form (which is very close to that used by Spenser but reverses the rhymes of the second quatrain) to twelve lines of slightly uneven blank verse with a rhyming couplet tagged on.[18] Harvey's rhymes are mostly unremarkable – such as dread/head, meet/sweet, bite/spite or hell/fell – which is arguably something that might be said about the majority of Spenser's rhymes as well. Occasionally, however, Harvey opts for more unusual rhyme words that interrupt the flow of the poem and draw more attention, such as malediction/confusion, peeuishnes/waywardnes or reuiu'd/rehiu'd.[19] One rhyme on an uncommon word that Harvey seems especially fond of is the rhyme selfe/elfe, which he uses three times over the course of the sonnet sequence.[20]

Of course it may be objected that this in itself does not make Harvey a bad poet – Edmund Spenser, for example, also uses the rhyme selfe/elfe several times in *The Faerie Queene*.[21] However, there are still some important differences between the way the rhyme is employed by Spenser and by Harvey. In terms of scale, Spenser uses selfe/elfe three times across all of *The Faerie Queene* (or six times when counting himselfe/elfe), which is equivalent to one selfe/elfe rhyme for every eighty-six pages of verse, so it is not a very common rhyme. Harvey, on the other hand, uses the rhyme three times over the course of just twenty-two sonnets.[22] Also, Spenser's 'elves' all refer to actual residents of 'Faerie londe', so there is some justification for calling them elves, whereas Harvey's 'elves' appear at points when he is clearly not writing about fairies but has merely written himself into a rhyme-corner.[23] When Spenser chooses to describe his elves using adjectives, he chooses fairly standard ones ('hardy', 'cruell' and 'wretched').[24] Harvey's elves, by contrast, are 'ventrous', 'felonious' and 'buried'. The effect of this is comical at best and does little to convince readers that Harvey's verses are not what Nashe termed 'regenerate' – meaning degenerated.[25]

Another sense in which Harvey's sonnets are uneven is, somewhat surprisingly, their length: again, the layout is misleading in this respect, because it suggests that all of the sonnets end after fourteen lines. Yet sonnet VIII calls itself a 'continuation' of sonnet VII and connects seamlessly to it, and in sonnets XIII–XV (whose titles are 'His intercession to Fame', 'A repetition of the former Petition' and 'A continuation of the same Petition') the central idea is even stretched across three sonnets. Arguably this failure to write sonnets that contain distinct ideas expressed in fourteen lines defeats the purpose of choosing the sonnet form in the first place, which raises the question why Harvey might have wanted to write 'Greenes Memoriall' in sonnet form.

At this point it may be objected that dwelling on – or even just acknowledging – the mediocrity of Harvey's sonnets is counterintuitive in the context of an essay that argues they should be studied. This is not the case, however, since the purpose of this chapter is not to argue that the sonnets of 'Greenes Memoriall' should be studied because they are underappreciated poetic masterpieces, but to propose that they should be studied because *Foure Letters and Certaine Sonnets* cannot be fully understood without them. To remove them from the equation (as has been standard practice for the past four centuries, for reasons that are connected to their apparent mediocrity) is to miss the point of the pamphlet as a whole. It is necessary to acknowledge the weaknesses of Harvey's sonnets and his comparative lack of sonnet-writing routine, both because they help to explain the sonnets' (lack of) reception history, and because it leads to a question that is highly relevant in this context: why choose sonnets?

Striving for indifference

As I have mentioned above, the way in which the sonnets are presented in the volume suggests that they are meant to be read as significant for the whole. So to establish why Harvey – who was evidently not one of nature's sonneteers – would attempt to write a sonnet sequence, we need to ask what his purpose in publishing *Foure Letters and Certaine Sonnets* was. To an extent, the answer seems obvious: to vent his anger against the dead Robert Greene and to take a few additional swipes at Nashe, with whom he had crossed swords before. However, whilst that might have been Harvey's occasion for writing *Foure Letters and Certaine Sonnets*, it would be wrong to assume that this is what the pamphlet is all about. In fact, the famous attacks on Greene occur almost exclusively in the second letter, and the swipes at Nashe, while numerous, are never Harvey's main focus of attention. That main focus remains Harvey himself.

A central concept of the volume that Harvey keeps invoking throughout – when referring both to his readers and to himself – is that of indifference (not in the modern sense, but in the sense of impartiality of judgement). *Foure Letters and Certaine Sonnets* contains multiple appeals to the reader to regard both the work and its author with 'indifferency'. Harvey presents his reasons for this request at the end of his preface 'To all courteous mindes, that will voutchsafe the reading', telling the 'courteous mindes' that on this particular occasion courtesy is *not* what he wants:

> Fauour, is a courteous Reader, & a gratious Patron: and no man loueth fauour, wher it is to be honoured, more affectionately then I: yet here I neither desire fauour toward louingest frend: nor wish disfauour toward spitefullest foe: but onely request reason toward both: and so briefly recommend both to your foresaid Indifferency: as to an equall ballance of vpright Iudgement.[26]

In the face of some of Harvey's outbursts against Greene, such as his catalogue of insults in the third letter, this appeal to reason and 'vpright Iudgement' seems strange, because it appears to be at odds with the evident subjectivity of his attitude towards Greene. At the same time, however, one of the themes of *Foure Letters and Certaine Sonnets* is Harvey's own striving for indifference. In this context it is important to note that the concept of 'indifferency' in the sense in which Harvey uses it has strong connotations with balance and justice. In book V of *The Faerie Queene*, it is the quality associated with Mercilla, who is described as 'dealing of iustice with indifferent grace'.[27] Again, this is an image that appears in a similar form in Spenser's character-reference sonnet, which has Harvey sitting aloof from 'this worldes Stage'

'And sweetly nectarize this bitter gall'   121

and passing harsh but fair judgement through his 'doomeful writing'. One way of reading *Foure Letters and Certaine Sonnets*, then, is that it is an attempt on Harvey's part to prove that Spenser's sonnet describes his true character, which had been unjustly maligned by Greene.

From the tone of the second letter – the famous letter in which Harvey openly gloats over Greene's death – it is safe to assume that Harvey's initial reaction to Greene's insults of his family was far from 'indifferent'. Nevertheless, it is important to bear in mind that the letters of the pamphlet are dated and there is actually a sense of progression from the second letter's anger and frustration at the loss of its target (Harvey speaks of being 'depriued of that remedy in Law, that [he] entended against [Greene]') to the more measured and detached tone of the fourth letter.[28] There is also a progression in terms of the letters' readership: Harvey's angriest letter, the second letter in the book, is addressed to a personal acquaintance of Harvey's. It is a response to the first, the letter of recommendation from Christopher Bird containing the angry 'misshapen' sonnet defending Harvey against Greene. The second letter is dated to just a few days after Greene's death and addressed to Christopher Bird, who, as a friend of Harvey's father's, might be expected to be eager to hear of any new developments. The third and fourth letters, however – dated just a few days after the second – are not addressed to Bird but 'To euery Reader, fauourablie, or indifferently affected', that is, to readers of the printed text, which Harvey already imagines in its published form in the fourth letter, which begins 'Honest Gentlemen (for vnto such I especially write) giue me leaue in *this slender Pamflet*, onely to fulfil the importune requestes of a fewe' (emphasis added).[29]

So the letters of *Foure Letters and Certaine Sonnets* show a progression and a growing sense of detachment to Greene and the events preceding and surrounding his death, as well as a conscious effort on Harvey's part to temper his anger and strive towards the 'indifferency' that would allow him to regain his seat as the impartial and even-handed 'looker-on of this worldes Stage'. It is this process that Harvey has in mind when he states in his preface that '[i]t was my intention, so to demeane my selfe in the whole, and so to temper my stile in euery part: that I might neither seme blinded with affection, nor enraged with passion: nor partiall to frend, nor preiudiciall to enemy: nor iniurious to the worst, nor offensive to any: but mildly & calmely shew, how discredite reboundeth vpon the autors'.[30] Harvey's concept of attempting to regain the temper he had previously lost by consciously modifying his writing style – and consequently effecting indifference by first affecting it – is a central idea of the book. It is this idea that also helps to explain the presence of the sonnets.

Sonnets as physic

One function of the sonnets in the volume is to create an even greater sense of distance from the events that Harvey felt provoked by. This becomes especially apparent in sonnet I, whose subject is Harvey's immediate response to the news of Greene's death, which means that the sonnet corresponds to the most notorious passages from the second letter:

> *Alas that I so hastely should come,*
> *To terrifie the man with fatall dread,*
> *That deemed quiet Pennes, or dead, or dum,*
> *And stoutly knock'd poore Silence on the head.*
> *Enough can say: dead is the Dog of spite:*
> *I, that for pitie praised him aliue,*
> *And smiled to see him gnar, and see him bite,*
> *Am not with sory carcasses to striue.*
> *The worst I list of Famous him report:*
> *Powles hath the Onely Pregnant Autor lost:*
> *Aihme, quoth Wit in lamentable sort,*
> *What worthy wight shall now command the rost?*
> *Fame heard the plaint: and pointed at A man,*
> *As greene as Greene, and white as whitest Swanne.*[31]

While those lines of course contain insults to Greene, they are a far cry from the disconcerting mixture of barely concealed glee about Greene's misery and frustration at having lost the object of his wrath that characterises Harvey's tone in the corresponding passages in the second letter. Christopher Bird's 'plain but true sonnet', whose thinly veiled anger clothed in clumsy doggerels only seems comical, is perhaps the best proof that sonnets and spontaneous expressions of anger do not necessarily mix well, but, even so, Harvey's greater sense of detachment in the sonnet is noticeable. If Harvey's objective really had been merely to vilify Greene, to patronise Nashe and to indulge in his own sense of self-importance (which was Nashe's preferred reading of *Foure Letters and Certaine Sonnets*), he could have done so much more easily in prose. Since the type of sonnet on which Harvey is modelling his own efforts is a relatively constrained form in terms of metre and rhyme, it forces the poet to weigh his words carefully and thus actively counters any impulse towards spontaneous angry splurging – especially in someone lacking routine as a sonneteer. That is, writing in sonnet form is what enables Harvey to 'temper his stile'. The word 'temper' is to be taken quite literally here, because the letters, but particularly the sonnets, contain repeated references to the sweetness that is needed to counteract the bitterness of choler in order to restore the correct balance of humours. In the letters, the person in need of temperance is mainly Nashe the satirist – to whom Harvey variously refers as 'Pierce' or 'the Diuels Oratour', so as to distinguish him from 'Nashe', whom he praises for his literary abilities (a distinction that is crucial for Harvey's aim of providing patronising, though perhaps well-intentioned, career advice to Nashe). In the sonnets, however, the choler that needs to be tempered is Harvey's own, most notably in the invocation in the last six lines of sonnet VIII:

> *If euer siluer conduictes were abroche*
> *Of streaming Witt, and flowing Eloquence:*
> *Yee fludds of milke, and hooney reapproche,*
> *And bounteously poure out your Quintessence.*
>   *Gently assemble Delicacies all,*
>   *And sweetely nectarize this bitter gall.*[32]

Just as the two non-Harveyan texts that frame the letters (Bird's letter of recommendation and Spenser's character-reference sonnet) are intended to act as reminders of Harvey's 'true' character both to his reader and to himself, the sonnet form is employed by Harvey as a 'siluer conduict' to guide his writing and thus indirectly temper his choler via tempering his style – a form of literary self-medication, that is. Traditionally, the fact that the results of this self-medication are poetically unconvincing because Harvey visibly struggled with the sonnet form would be treated as yet another example of Harvey's self-importance and exaggerated belief in his own genius. However, in the context of his declared intention to 'temper his stile', which accompanies the poems, it is equally possible that Harvey chose the sonnet form for 'Greenes Memoriall' precisely *because* he found it difficult.[33]

Harvey's attempts in *Foure Letters and Certaine Sonnets* to 'nectarize' the bitterness of his temper and his style are also closely linked with an attempt to associate himself with the author of the 'sweete Feary Queene'. Again, the final sonnet of the volume acts as a point of reference and as an emblem of the Mercilla-like balance and 'indifferency' that Harvey wishes to achieve, or perhaps regain, because they befit an ideal 'Doctor of the Lawes'. This is made clear from the outset through the carefully chosen emblem on the title page, whose Italian motto 'Il vostro malignare non giova nulla' could be loosely translated as 'your spite will get you nowhere', and which depicts a palm tree surrounded by poisonous serpents that can bother the tree but not actually harm it. A very similar image had featured in Geffrey Whitney's *A Choice of Emblemes* (1586), under the heading 'Inuidia integritatis affecta' (Integrity set upon by Envy).[34] The 'moralising' poem underneath the image contains the lines:

> When noble peeres, and men of high estate,
> By iuste deserte, doe liue in honor greate:
> Yet, Enuie still dothe waite on them as mate,
> And does her worste, to vndermine their feate.

There can be little doubt as to whom Harvey was casting in the role of the 'noble' palm tree.[35] The emblem, then, is the pictorial equivalent of lines 7 and 8 of the Spenser sonnet: 'Ne fearest foolish reprehension / Of faulty men, which daunger to thee threat'. At the same time, the palm tree echoes the figure of the Palmer in book II of *The Faerie Queene* ('Of Temperance'), who embodies reason and acts as a corrective to Guyon, the temperate but frail hero of the book.[36]

Yet the figure of Spenser in the volume acts not only as a voice of authority and proper judge of Harvey's true tempered character via the flattering portrait of him as the even-handed Doctor of the Lawes in the character-reference sonnet, but also as a reminder to the favourable or indifferent reader of the book (as well as to Nashe in particular) that even the best may err occasionally. This is exemplified in the 'over-reaching' of *Mother Hubberds Tale*, which is described by Harvey in terms that imply that Spenser's venture into satire was the result of a regrettable imbalance of humours: 'in heat of *choller*', 'forgetting the *pure sanguine*', '*malcontented* selfe' (emphases added).[37] Later, he juxtaposes this description of Spenser's moment of 'choller' with his own situation in sonnet VIII, which in its 'vnfained wish' for a general rebalancing of humours uses some of the same phrases:

> Choler, content thy malcontented selfe:
> And cleerest Humour of right Sanguine pure,
> Neately refin'd from that felonious Elfe,
> With Iouiall graciousnes thy selfe enure.[38]

Harvey's tempering of his style is to a certain extent also an attempt to make it resemble Spenser's. Perhaps the most obvious way in which he does this is by choosing to write in sonnet form and attempting (though generally failing) to follow the rhyme-scheme favoured by Spenser. Although Harvey is not the most skilful of sonneteers and there are indications in the poems that he struggled with the form, it would be wrong to assume his vanity was so great he was entirely unaware of the fact that 'Greenes Memoriall' was perhaps not his finest piece of writing. Similarly, it would be wrong to dismiss them as altogether terrible. If nothing else, Harvey's use of the sonnets and his use of different sonnet forms at least show a serious effort to achieve a certain degree of sophistication, especially in his pointed use of the pseudo-Spenserian form, which he reserves for sonnets XVIII–XXI ('Iohn Harueys Welcome to Robert Greene', 'His Apology of himselfe, and his brothers', 'His Apology of his good Father' and 'His charitable hope: and their eternall repose'). Those sonnets have a particular significance within the sequence (and within the volume) because, as their titles indicate, they are written in the voice of Harvey's dead brother John and contain a vindication of himself and his family, followed by the 'charitable hope' that his surviving brothers Richard and Gabriel should 'Let memory of grosse abuses sleepe'.

Arguably, there might be a Spenserian echo even in the sonnets' theme of tempering the bitterness of gall through the addition of honey or nectar. This is partly because it calls to mind Thomalin's emblem from the March eclogue in *The Shepheardes Calender* ('Of Hony and of Gaule in Loue there is store: / The Honye is much, but the Gaule is more').[39] The connection here is not so much the link of gall and honey in itself, which was not Spenser's invention – the March emblem merely echoes a classical trope – but the fact that Harvey had already cited it before, at an earlier point in his writing career. In the third letter of *Three Proper and Wittie Familiar Letters*, the anonymous letter-writer 'G.H.', who is unambiguously identified as Gabriel Harvey elsewhere in the volume, had expressed his regret at not having written much poetry of late and, by way of a substitute, sent his friend 'Immerito' some writing exercises produced by his precocious young brother John. After setting his brother two translation tasks – a 'Theame out of Ouid' and a few lines of Petrarch quoted in the gloss of the October eclogue of *The Shepheardes Calender* – 'G.H.' writes, he told young John 'Let me see now I pray, what you can doo in your owne Tongue' and set him a composition task based on the two March emblems.[40] While the scene itself may have been a fabrication on Harvey's part (the letters of *Three Proper and Wittie Familiar Letters* were modified, if not written, for publication in print), it is likely that in 1592 he would still have remembered it and associated the two emblems with his recently deceased brother John, who plays a central part in 'Greenes Memoriall', allowing

Harvey to invoke John Harvey and Edmund Spenser simultaneously by alluding to the March emblems of *The Shepheardes Calender*.

By supplementing his 'Foure Letters' with the sonnets of 'Greenes Memoriall', then, Gabriel Harvey was both trying to demonstrate that he was the fair, even-handed Doctor of the Lawes described in Spenser's character-reference sonnet and deliberately setting himself a poetic challenge in order to provide an example to Nashe and temper his choler through a hefty dose of 'sweetness' in sonnet form. This literary self-medication may in itself have been a tribute to his dead brother, who had been a physician – someone professionally trained to administer physic to restore the proper balance of humours in his patients, that is.

The aftermath of *Foure Letters and Certaine Sonnets* is well known and well-documented, of course. As the pamphlet war grew more vicious, the role of poetry understandably diminished. Nashe ventured into sonnet-writing himself only on a single occasion: at the very end of *Strange Newes*, where he theatrically threw down the gauntlet to Harvey in the shape of the first sonnet he published in print:

> Were there no warres, poore men should haue no peace
> Vncessant warres with waspes and droanes I crie:
> Hee that begins, oft knows not how to cease,
> They haue begun, Ile follow till I die.
>   Ile heare no truce, wrong gets no graue in mee,
> Abuse pell mell encounter with abuse:
> Write he againe, Ile write eternally.
> Who feedes reuenge hath found an endlesse Muse.
>   If death ere made his blacke dart of a pen,
> My penne his special Baily shall becum:
> Somewhat Ile be reputed of mongst men,
> By striking of this duns or dead or dum.
>   Awaite the world the Tragedy of wrath,
>   What next I paint shall tread no common path:[41]

Evidently the experience of sonnet-writing did not have much of a purging effect on Nashe. It is similarly doubtful if the self-imposed sonnet regimen had that effect on Harvey, considering the pamphlets he subsequently published. Initially however, he does seem to have been genuine in his efforts to 'temper his stile' through invoking an infusion of sweetness from the author of the 'sweete Feary Queene', and forcing his critique pen to write sugared (or at least sugar-coated) sonnets.

Notes

1 E. Spenser, *The Shepheardes Calender Conteyning Twelue Aeglogues Proportionable to the Twelue Monethes* (London: Hugh Singleton, 1579), sig. ¶iiib.
2 See for example L.H. Newcomb's article on Robert Greene in the *Dictionary of National Biography*. Note however that in this point all biographies of Greene are ultimately derived from Harvey's account of his death in *Foure Letters and Certaine Sonnets* – which appears to have been essentially accurate, because in his biography of Greene Thomas Nashe never substantially challenged it in his thorough 'confutation' of Harvey's pamphlet in *Strange Newes*. Similarly, all existing accounts of Greene's life rely heavily on Greene's own pamphlets, which are of doubtful biographical authority and show signs of deliberate fictionalisation.

3 R.B. McKerrow's overview of the Harvey–Nashe quarrel, which was appended to his 1910 complete edition of Thomas Nashe's works and remains one of the most comprehensive and most balanced accounts of the quarrel, mentions only Harvey's letters. Modern scholars occasionally refer to specific lines from the sonnets to illustrate the viciousness of Harvey's attacks on Greene. Jennifer Richards, for example, selectively quotes the first and fifth line of sonnet XVIII, 'Come fellow *Greene*, come to thy gaping graue: / ... Vermine to Vermine must repaire at last', to support her point that Harvey was being especially 'distasteful' in insulting the dead Robert Greene, in *Rhetoric and Courtliness in Early Modern Literature* (Cambridge: Cambridge University Press, 2003), p. 116. However, to date there are no articles that place a significant focus on the sonnets and their function in the pamphlet.
4 A proximity search of the EEBO-TCP database (phase I) for 'sweet' within 40 characters of 'sonnet' or 'sonnets' (including variant spellings) leads to at least nineteen instances in texts published before 1600 in which sonnets are specifically described as sweet. These include Henry Parker's Petrarch translation *The Tryumphes of Fraunces Petrarcke* (London: John Cawood, 1555), George Gascoigne's 'Master F.J.' in *A Hundreth Sundrie Flowres* (London: Richard Smith, 1573), Thomas Lodge's *Scillaes Metamorphosis* (London: Richard Jones, 1589) and *Rosalynde* (London: T. Gubbin and John Busbie, 1592), Nicholas Breton's *Brittons Bowre of Delights* (London: Richard Jones, 1591), Henry Constable's *Diana* (London: Richard Smith, 1592) and William Ponsonby's preface to Edmund Spenser's *Amoretti* (London: William Ponsonby, 1595). Most examples are clustered around the time when *Foure Letters and Certaine Sonnets* was published, that is the early 1590s. Harvey himself, in *Pierces Supererogation* – his response to *Strange Newes* – associates the form specifically with love poetry, and suggests that sweetness is one of its defining characteristics in claiming that 'Euen amorous Sonnets, in the gallantest and sweetest ciuill veine, are but daintyes of a pleasurable witt' (London: John Wolfe, 1593; p. 46). For the history and significance of 'sweetness' as a stylistic marker especially of poetry see David Wilson-Okamura, *Spenser's International Style* (Cambridge: Cambridge University Press, 2015), pp. 83 ff.
5 G. Harvey, *Foure Letters and Certaine Sonnets: Especially touching* Robert Greene, *and other parties, by him abused: But incidently of diuers excellent persons and some matters of note* (London: John Wolfe, 1592), p. 75.
6 A. Grosart (ed.), *The Complete Works in Verse and Prose of Edmund Spenser* (9 vols), *vol. IV: The Minor Poems* (London: Spenser Society, 1882–84), pp. cvi-cvii. Grosart also found it particularly fitting that the 'strong feeling' in the sonnet should be directed towards Spenser's friend Gabriel Harvey, claiming that this knowledge 'adds to our pleasure' (p. cvii).
7 *Foure Letters and Certaine Sonnets*, p. 3.
8 *Three Proper and Wittie Familiar Letters Lately Passed Between Two Vniversitie Men Touching the Earthquake in Aprill Last, and our English Refourmed Versifying. / Two Other Very Commendable Letters of the Same Mens Writing: Both Touching the Foresaid Artificiall Versifying, and Cartain Other Particulars* (London: Henry Bynneman, 1580). This book, which is sometimes (inaccurately) referred to as the 'Spenser–Harvey letters' was also targeted by Nashe in *Strange Newes*, in which he accused Harvey of having been its sole author.
9 The internal title of *Strange Newes* (continued in the running titles) is 'The Foure Letters Confuted'.
10 T. Nashe, *The Apologie of Pierce Pennilesse: OR Strange Newes, Of the Intercepting Certaine Letters, and a Conuoy of Verses, as They were Going* Priuilie *to Victual the Lowe Countries* (London: John Danter, 1592), sig. Db. On the same page, Nashe also argues, not very convincingly, that, in order to respond to the sonnet in kind, he would have to stoop to equally bad poetry, and that would be of no use to anyone: 'I would trot a false gallop through the rest of his ragged Verses, but that if I should retort his rime dogrell aright, I must make my verses (as he doth his) run hobling like a Brewers Cart vpon the stones, and obserue no length in their feet which were *absurdum per absurdius*, to infect my vaine with his imitation. The Analisis of the whole is this: an olde mechanical meeter-munger would faine raile if he had anie witte.'
11 Nashe, *Strange Newes*, sig. L2b.
12 Though it has clearly been taken out of its original context, there is little reason to doubt Spenser's authorship of the sonnet. In particular, the use of enjambment across more than two lines in the poem is a technique employed frequently (and successfully) by Spenser in his poetry, while Harvey's sonnets in 'Greenes Memoriall' are mostly structured into syntactical units of just one or two lines.
13 On the attribution of the Christopher Bird sonnet, Nashe writes, 'But I cannot be induced to beleue a graue man of his sort shou'd be ere so *rauingly* bent: when all coms to all, *shortest vowels and longest mutes* will bewray it to bee a webbe of your owne loomes M. *Gabriel*'. He then proceeds to claim a similarity between the sonnet's form and the speech of one of the vices in a morality play, and concludes by labelling it 'your *Doctors fart*', in allusion to one of the lines in the sonnet (sigs Db-D2a). Nashe's verdict on the publication of the Spenser–Harvey letters is 'I durst on my credit vndertake, *Spencer*

was in no way priuie to the committing of them to the print. Committing I may well call it, for in my opinion G.H. should not haue reapt so much discredite by beeing committed to Newgate, as by committing that misbeleeuing prose to the Presse' (sigs Ga-Gb).
14 Harvey, *Foure Letters and Certaine Sonnets*, p. 12.
15 Ibid., p. 7.
16 Nashe, *Strange Newes*, sig. La.
17 Harvey, *Foure Letters and Certaine Sonnets*, pp. 61-3.
18 The rhyme-scheme favoured by Spenser is abab bcbc cdcd ee. Harvey's pseudo-Spenserian sonnet form uses the rhyme scheme abab cbcb cdcd ee.
19 Harvey, *Foure Letters and Certaine Sonnets*, pp. 61-5. The rhymes mentioned all occur in sonnets I-VIII.
20 Ibid., pp. 63, 65, 71 (sonnets IIII, VIII, and XVIII respectively). In sonnet XVIII, selfe/elfe is the rhyme of the final couplet. Harvey's lengthy unpublished poem 'The Schollars Looue', included in the manuscript sometimes referred to as his 'Letter-book' (MS Sloane 93 at the British Library), also features several instances of the rhyme selfe/elfe.
21 R. Danson Brown and J.B. Lethbridge, *A Concordance to the Rhymes of* The Faerie Queene (Manchester: Manchester University Press, 2013), pp. 259, 309.
22 This is equivalent to one selfe/elfe rhyme for every 100 lines.
23 The *OED* entry for the noun 'elf' lists a usage 'in a vague depreciatory sense', which may well suit Harvey's intentions in applying it to Greene. Nevertheless, the fact that (unlike Spenser) Harvey uses the word only at the very end of a line to rhyme with another line ending in 'selfe' suggests that rhyme is his main consideration.
24 In his essay on 'The Bondage of Rhyme in *The Faerie Queene*', J.B. Lethbridge notes that Spenser's use of adjectives tends towards the generic, that is, Spenser uses adjectives to make general points about the nature of the things they qualify rather than to evoke specific characteristics (in Brown and Lethbridge, *Concordance*, pp. 128 ff). Consequently, Spenser generally favours somewhat bland, standard adjectives such as the ones he uses to qualify his rhyming elves. Harvey, by contrast, has a clear preference for unusual, evocative adjective such as the ones cited above.
25 See meaning 4 listed in the *OED* for 'regenerate, adj. and *n*.' (*OED Online*, www.oed.com (date accessed: 9 December 2019)).
26 Harvey, *Foure Letters and Certaine Sonnets*, p. 2.
27 E. Spenser, *The Faerie Queene. Disposed into Twelue Bookes, Fashioning XII. Morall Vertues* (London: William Ponsonby, 1596), p. 306 (V.ix.36). Book V had not yet been published in print in 1592, though Harvey may have read it in manuscript form. Such a possibility is substantiated by two letters (one from Immerito to G.H., the other G.H.'s response to Immerito) in *Three Proper and Wittie Familiar Letters* (London: Henry Bynneman, 1580), pp. 7 and 41.
28 Harvey, *Foure Letters and Certaine Sonnets*, p. 9.
29 Ibid., pp. 15, 51.
30 Ibid., p. 2.
31 Ibid., pp. 61-2.
32 Ibid., pp. 65-6.
33 On the inherent appeal of 'hard' poetic forms to early modern writers see Wilson-Okamura, *Spenser's International Style*, pp. 34-7.
34 G. Whitney, *A Choice of Emblemes, and Other Deuises, for the Moste Parte Gathered out of Sundrie Writers, Englished and Moralized. And Diuers Newly Deuised, by Geffrey Whitney* (Leiden: Francis Raphelengius, 1586), p. 118.
35 The same device was used one year later, on the title page of a pamphlet published as a response to *Foure Letters and Certaine Sonnets*, Henry Chettle's *Kind-Harts Dreame* (1593?, also printed by John Wolfe), effectively turning Harvey's own emblem against him and transforming him from a 'gallant palme' into a poisonous serpent. *Pierces Supererogation* (1593), Harvey's response to Nashe's *Strange Newes*, also used the image on its title page.
36 For a detailed account of the Palmer's function in book II, see Maurice Evans, 'Palmer', in A.C. Hamilton (ed.), *The Spenser Encyclopedia* (Toronto: University of Toronto Press, 1997), pp. 526-7.
37 Harvey, *Foure Letters and Certaine Sonnets*, p. 7.
38 Ibid., pp. 65-6, lines 5-8.
39 Spenser, *Shepheardes Calender*, fol. 10a.
40 *Three Proper and Wittie Familiar Letters*, pp. 38-9.
41 Nashe, *Strange Newes*, sig. M2b.

7

Barnabe Barnes's sonnet sequences: moral conversion and prodigal authorship

Rémi Vuillemin

> No more lewde laies of Lighter loves I sing,
> Nor teach my lustfull Muse abus'de to flie,
> With Sparrowes plume and for compassion crie,
> To mortall beauties which no succour bring.
>
> (lines 1–4)[1]

The first quatrain of the very first sonnet of Barnabe Barnes's *A Divine Centurie of Spirituall Sonnets* (1595) explicitly associates love poetry with lust. The terms that are used ('lewd laies', 'lustfull Muse', 'Sparrowes plume') eloquently condemn a type of poetry that the speaker admits to having written in the past.[2] Such a claim to leave behind love poetry to write divine sonnets will undoubtedly remind any reader familiar with Barnes's work of the fact that the poet had published his first (profane) lyric collection, *Parthenophil and Parthenophe, Sonnettes, Madrigals, Elegies and Odes*, in 1593, just two years before *A Divine Centurie of Spirituall Sonnets*. The specificity of Barnes's work as a poet is not so much that he composed both secular and spiritual sonnets: his contemporaries Henry Constable, or of course John Donne, did the same. But he is the only one to have published two volumes including mostly sonnets, one just after the other. No other Elizabethan English poet, as far as I know, published profane and sacred sequences in short sequel. Henry Constable comes closest to Barnes, but he never published his spiritual sonnets.[3] There are of course precedents of associating two works, one secular, one spiritual, in the sixteenth century, but they are to be found in Continental literature.[4]

It is therefore no wonder that criticism on Barnes's poetry has lingered on what looks like a recantation of his previous work, with contrasting conclusions. Anthony Earl, for instance, stated the following:

> [Barnes's] concern is the status of his own soul in the eyes of God, his spiritual worth, and his access to divine favour; in other words, Barnes the love poet of *Parthenophil and Parthenophe* has become the penitent, son of a bishop, the tremulous Calvinist who with some theological naivety but with much literary background was endeavouring to follow the standard Elizabethan theology of the 1590s.[5]

Earl sees Barnes's statements as an attempt to amend his ways, to become a penitent, and to convert his love from an erotic to a spiritual perspective. Thomas P. Roche Jr, however, does not believe in such an interpretation:

[Barnes's] disclaimer in Sonnet 1 that 'No more lewde laies of lighter loves I sing' erroneously suggests that conversion from secular to sacred that has so benighted critical commentary on the sonnets. As I have tried to show, sonnets deal either ironically through a deceived speaker or plainly through an equally grieved lover of the divine.[6]

Should we then believe, along with Earl, that the two sequences stand in sharp opposition one to the other, and convey two essentially separate messages (one profane, the other spiritual), or, along with Roche, that there is strong continuity between them, the only difference being that one is ironic and the other serious?[7] The Petrarchan model lies at the core of this interrogation, as the pattern of recantation and spiritual conversion exposed by Barnes's first sonnet matches the second part of Petrarch's *Canzoniere* particularly well: in the Tuscan poet's collection, Laura's death makes the poet realise that his love has been misdirected by bearing upon a mortal object, and he applies himself to redirecting it towards God.[8] The partition *in vita / in morte di Laura* was undoubtedly known in England, as it was for instance paralleled by the twofold structure of Thomas Watson's influential *The Hekatompathia, or Passionate Centurie of Love*, published in 1582.[9]

Keeping the Petrarchan model in mind, Barnes's spiritual sonnets could easily be construed as the missing second part of *Parthenophil and Parthenophe*, and the two sequences might therefore be understood as a sort of diptych used to insist on Barnes's moral reform. It is therefore surprising that the connections between the two sequences have not been the subject of any in-depth analyses.[10] Considering both internal and external evidence, the present chapter will attempt to determine the relevance of considering the two sequences together rather than separately. But the point will not merely be to find echoes between them. My argument here is that the production and publication of a printed sequence could be seen as a form of social and public act. Examining why and how Barnes was led to express a sense of repentance and a desire for moral conversion – if it was one at all – is also a way of trying to uncover what Barnes was trying to perform by using print. Throughout this chapter, I will understand the term 'conversion' as referring both to moral conversion (the improvement of one's behaviour) and spiritual conversion (the focus on divine rather than on secular matters), in a perspective close to Petrarch's. The term will not be employed in the sense of change from one religious denomination to another or in the rhetorical sense of epistrophe. I will use the term 'conversion' to insist on the represented states of the poetic speaker, both before and after the publication of *A Divine Centurie*. The term 'recantation' will be used to focus on Barnes's gestures of rejection – of his past poetry or of his past sins.[11]

Parthenophil and Parthenophe: pushing the sonnet sequence to the extremes

Parthenophil and Parthenophe was published at the beginning of the 'sonnet craze' of the 1590s, in 1593. In retrospect, looking at the other sequences of the decade, it seems quite peculiar both because of the poetic forms it includes and because of its contents. If the early modern sonnet was, as Leonard Forster argues, 'a training in poetic diction',[12] then Barnes pushed such principle to an extreme. His sonnets are 'innovative in their adaptations of conventional models, coherent in their structural patterns, and kaleidoscopically diverse in both their genres and their structures'.[13] Most of the sonnets at the beginning of the sequence are fifteen-line sonnets with varying structures: the final couplet may be replaced by a tercet, or the final quatrain and couplet might receive one extra line with a rhyme scheme similar to rhyme royal. The rhyme-schemes are diverse and often at odds with the syntactic structures of the sentences – a few sonnets have unrhymed lines.[14] Even the quatorzains are arranged in a variety of ways: the English or 'Shakespearean' structure (three quatrains and one couplet) is often replaced by the Italian and French form (two quatrains followed by two tercets), when one does not find an alternation of quatrains and tercets. The other forms in the sequence allow for even more experimentation. Barnes seems to have relished the very loosely codified madrigal, as it allowed him to try various poem lengths, syllable counts, rhyme-schemes etc. He also tried such difficult forms as the sestina, and especially, at the very end of the sequence, a triple sestina, an extremely difficult poetic form to master.[15] *Parthenophil and Parthenophe* is therefore both Barnes's first published work and the most experimental one – a display of poetic and rhetorical agility through which the poet could seek to establish his reputation.

It could also be argued that the diversity and playfulness of Barnes's poems perfectly suited their topic, love, a subject requiring, in George Puttenham's words, 'a forme of Poesie variable, inconstant, affected and most witty of any others'.[16] The unruly irregularity of Barnes's collection echoes the disorder caused by love – a disorder that is particularly striking in *Parthenophil and Parthenophe*, as the sequence ends with a triple sestina in which Parthenophil has his way with Parthenophe. He first lights a fire and invokes Hecate and the furies (lines 1–6), and starts a strange ritual aimed at stirring desire for him in Parthenophe. The poem ends with the accomplishment of Parthenophil's desire: 'Tis now acquitted: cease your former teares, / For as she once with rage my bodie kindled, / So in hers am I buried this night' (lines 109–11). At the end of Barnes's long sequence (the longest amorous lyric sequence published in the decade), the lover finally consummates the love for which he has been yearning. This consummation is a form of rape, as Parthenophe's consent is obtained through the invocation of the Furies – though there are indications that it might be a dream rather than an actual rape.[17] A further reason why this conclusion to the sequence could only be seen as morally unacceptable at the time is the fact that the final sexual act is brought about by the invocation of Hecate and the practice of witchcraft, a point that has been analysed in detail by Jeffrey N. Nelson. Black magic, as he puts it, 'functions as a metaphor for expressing the dangerous nature of unrequited lust'.[18] *Parthenophil and Parthenophe* is consistent with the moral didacticism that Roche sees in the Elizabethan love sonnet sequences: it teaches by negative example.[19] The notion that the lover might be construed as an anti-model aimed at pointing to the dangers of love, and therefore not to be followed, was convincingly demonstrated by Roche, especially as far as Sidney's *Astrophil and Stella* is concerned.[20] It is therefore particularly interesting to note how Barnes's sequence proclaims its reliance on the Sidneian model by introducing the names of lover and of the beloved in its title – a unique case in the printed lyric sequence of the 1590s. The morally edifying dimension of Barnes's sequence seems to be confirmed by an annotation on the only existing copy of *Parthenophil and Parthenophe*.[21] Barnes's brother John has written on the top of the front page the following motto: 'Principium sapientiae timor Jehovae';[22] in other words, 'the basis of wisdom is the fear of God'.

Roche's contention that *Parthenophil and Parthenophe* delivers the same message as a spiritual sonnet sequence such as *A Divine Centurie of Spirituall Sonnets* by using irony, however, has its limits.[23] The unquestionably edifying ending of the sequence does not prevent the existence of blatantly erotic poems such as madrigals 12, 13 or 26. I believe that such moral ambiguity is fundamental to the sonnet sequences of the 1590s and has too often been overlooked by critics willing to emphasise either their focus on earthly love or their didacticism. Many of the sequences are indeed ambiguous, and do have a moral dimension that can be at odds with their theme.[24] Such ambiguity would have allowed sonneteers to display their wit and make themselves known to an extended readership, while maintaining their moral reputation.[25] Barnes followed this logic to an extreme, experimenting with form, kindling the desires of his readers while presenting them with the disastrous consequences of lust.

Because of its erotic content and striking finale, Barnes's *Parthenophil and Parthenophe* displays these contradictions in a particularly obvious way. In the prefatory material addressed to the reader, the printer explains that the author (whose name does not appear in the book)[26] was unwilling to commit it to the press. Such a claim is conventional; but the printer adds that the author did not want to 'acknowledge' the poems because of their 'levity', a term that could refer to the fact that the poems were mere 'toyes' or 'trifles', as love poets of the period often claim, but that could also allude to something undignified or unbecoming.[27] The printer's note is echoed by a prefatory poem in which the speaker addresses his poems, asking them never to admit who wrote them and where they came from, insisting on their 'baseness' and, again, on their 'levity'. According to the modern editor of *Parthenophil and Parthenophe*, Victor Doyno, it is very probable that Barnes was consulted and that he participated in the production of the book.[28] Not having one's name on the front page was customary for printed poets, all the more so if they were little known.[29] If Doyno is right, Barnes might have been willing to make the most of the situation. By insisting on his wish for anonymity, he might have tried to arouse the curiosity of prospective readers, perhaps as to who the writer might be, but also, more significantly, as to the lewd contents of the book. Looking at the beginning of Barnes's second sequence, his desire to 'manage readers' appears even more clearly.[30]

From *Parthenophil and Parthenophe* to *A Divine Centurie of Spirituall Sonnets*: a staged conversion

It seems that Barnes sought to draw attention to what can be understood as a form of articulation between the two sequences right from the first sonnet of *A Divine Centurie of Spirituall Sonnets*. As the first quatrain of the sonnet has been mentioned at the beginning of this chapter and its contents have been discussed by the critics quoted above, it seems more relevant here to focus on what previous critics have not been much concerned with: the fact that many of the tropes in *A Divine Centurie* are also used in *Parthenophil and Parthenophe*. The list of examples that follows is by no means exhaustive: I have merely chosen the examples that show most clearly the networks of meaning that run in and between the two sequences, focusing on three of those networks.

In *Parthenophil and Parthenophe*, as in many love sonnet sequences, the lover insists on the hardness of his lady's heart: it is, of course, said to be a rock, sometimes walled with or made of adamant, marble or flint, but it is also compared to the steel of an anvil used by Vulcan.[31] Contrary to Parthenophe's hard heart, Parthenophil's is repeatedly said to be pierced not only by Cupid's dart but also by Jove's thunder.[32] Finally, three poems refer to 'melting' that is caused either by the powerful gaze of Parthenophe (sonnets 16 and 46) and of Parthenophil in his past life as a seducer (sonnet 54) or, very significantly, by his final consummation of desire (sestine 5): 'I melt in love, loves marrow-flame is kindled: / Here will I be consum'd in loves sweet furies. / I melt, I melt, watche Cupid my love-teares' (lines 104–6). In *A Divine Centurie*, God and faith are the poetic voice's rocks, but the hard heart that is (or needs to be) pierced, softened or melted is the sinner's heart.[33]

The second network of meaning I will uncover draws together the Fall and the garden of Hesperides. The second spiritual sonnet focuses on Adam's Fall, devoting the second quatrain to the forbidden fruit. By doing so, it is reminiscent of the seventh elegy of *Parthenophil and Parthenophe*, in which Parthenophil alludes to Adam and the 'two forbidden apples', equating the forbidden fruit with the golden apples in the garden of Hesperides. At the end of the poem, Parthenophil concludes: 'Since our forefather for the like offence / With us receiv'd sufficient recompence / For two fayre apples, which procur'd his fall' (lines 29–31). The two apples, Parthenophe's eyes in elegies 12 and 13, are mentioned in a poem about sin and retribution, as they are in *A Divine Centuriall of Spirituall Sonnets*. They are also part of a network of intratextual echoes that activate two structuring myths: the myth of Perseus and the myth of Atalanta.[34]

My last example is the organising conceit of the account book in the seventh spiritual sonnet. The metaphor of money was also used by Barnes in *Parthenophil and Parthenophe* in the somewhat obscure metaphor of pawning, which allowed Barnes to rewrite a string of Petrarchan topoi: Parthenophil's heart, instead of travelling to the beloved, is pawned. Parthenophe, the pawnbroker, steals the heart in so far as she refuses to give it back to Parthenophil. This conceit, along with other references to money, runs through the beginning of Barnes's first sequence.[35] The allusions to money are particularly fitting in a poem asking for retribution, but here the focus on sins as a list of debts consigned in a 'black book' foregrounds another frequent device in Barnes's spiritual sonnets: the reference to books and their contents, and more generally to the writing of poetry itself. Sonnet 23 is a commentary on the love poem, asking poets to turn to God. Sonnet 42 calls for poets to convert to divine fury, asking them to use the skill God has given them in a fitting way, thus echoing the allusion to the parable of the talents found in sonnet 37. Sonnet 45 hints at the question of the spiritual conversion of the muse, and sonnet 71 pictures divine fury as *furor poeticus*. Finally, and most interestingly, sonnet 50 refers to 'the follies of [the speaker's] youth'. The allusions to past indiscretions, the frequent references to poetry and poetics, the mention of a 'black book' keeping count of the poetic voice's sins all point to the same possibility: are not the follies of his youth precisely those that are described in Barnes's previous published book, *Parthenophil and Parthenophe*? In other words, Barnes's spiritual sequence seems fashioned in such a way as to remind readers of his amorous sequence and to lead them to notice the different ways in which the same topoi and intertextual references are treated. To a certain extent, the two sequences could therefore be seen as variations on the same topics, with strikingly different results.

In fact, an element in the paratext of Barnes's first sequence suggests that his recantation might have been planned from the start: the printer states that the author was 'unwilling (as it seemeth) to acknowledge [his love poems], for their levity, till he have redeemed them with some more excellent worke hereafter […] these his over youthfull Poemes' (sig. A2r). It would be tempting to imagine that Barnes might have written all of his sonnets at the same time and decided to issue them separately, but no evidence can be used to prove it. What can be less tentatively asserted is that Barnes might have contemplated writing spiritual sonnets as *Parthenophil and Parthenophe* was in the process of being published, not with the purpose of confessing his wish to make amends for his past sins (or those of his Parthenophil), but rather to make a show of displaying the moral conversion of his verse, of his muse, and to suggest as much as far as his poetic self was concerned. The point is not therefore to determine whether Barnes was really trying to make amends or not – either about his life or about the subject matter of his poetry – but to consider his recantation as a strategic move the purpose of which was to modify his image as a poet.[36] In other words, it is possible, with Roche, to insist on the continuities between Barnes's love sonnet sequence and his spiritual sonnet sequence, but also to acknowledge that the 'conversion' identified by Earl is to be found indeed in *A Divine Centurie*, if one keeps in mind that it is the representation of Barnes's poetic self that has undergone the conversion, not necessarily Barnes himself.[37]

Conversion and bipartition: Elizabethan prodigals

A central point to consider is Barnes's simultaneous insistence on Parthenophil's and his own youth when he wrote *Parthenophil and Parthenophe*. The trope of the folly of youth runs in Elizabethan literature and has been famously analysed by Richard Helgerson in *Elizabethan Prodigals*.[38] Authors such as Gascoigne, Whetstone, Pettie, Saker, Lodge or Harington 'joined in suggesting that they were prodigals and that their prodigality was mixed up with their writing. They had wasted their youthful time on the poetry and fiction of love just as their protagonists waste time on love itself.'[39] As Helgerson reminds us, this pattern can be found, for example, in Petrarch's *Epistle to Posterity*: 'Youth led me astray, young manhood corrupted me, but mature age corrected me and taught me by experience the truth of what I had read long before: that youth and pleasure are vain. This is the lesson of that Author of all times and ages, who permits wretched mortals, puffed up with vain wind, to stray for a time until, though late in life, they become mindful of their sins.'[40] The idea that Barnes was 'overly youthfull' does not correspond to his age when his first sequence was published: twenty-two, by Elizabethan standards, was not particularly young.

Doyno, the editor of *Parthenophil and Parthenophe*, therefore infers that Barnes must have written his poems much earlier.[41] It seems equally possible, however, that this insistence on youth was for Barnes a way to keep at a moral distance from his lewd verse, and that, by the time *A Divine Centurie* was completed, he chose to rely on it to emphasise his moral conversion, be it real or feigned – not an illogical attempt on the part of the son of a suffragan bishop of Nottingham and chancellor of York Minster.[42]

We know that the copy of *A Divine Centurie* now kept in York Minster Library was meant as a gift to Tobie Matthew, Bishop of Durham, from whom Barnes was seeking favour.[43] Anthony Earl's description of Barnes's religious views as expressed in his spiritual sonnets is certainly in line with Matthew's beliefs and Barnes's position:[44] 'Many of his more markedly spiritual phrases derive from the piety common to conforming churchgoers of that time, echo Calvinistic preaching or devotional Puritan literature, and presume the notion of original sin common to all Protestant teaching in the sixteenth century. [...] These sonnets bear the hallmarks of writing intended to conform to, and gratify, an Establishment.'[45] However, the publishing of the sequence necessarily implied a wider readership as well: the buyers of the published book (or, why not, recipients of other presentation copies now lost). Some readers of *A Divine Centurie* must have had some knowledge of *Parthenophil and Parthenophe*. In my last remarks, I would like to contend that Barnes might have worked with his printers to show the connection between the two books while staging the conversion of his muse to a spiritual perspective. The two sequences might therefore be understood as a sort of diptych used to insist on Barnes's moral reform and construct the image of a maturing poet.[46]

Moral conversion in print

Barnes was said by Thomas Nashe to have lodged for some time with the printer John Wolfe, who printed his *Parthenophil and Parthenophe*, and Gabriel Harvey.[47] As Mark Bland has shown, John Wolfe became business partner with Windet, the printer of Barnes's *A Divine Centurie*, merging part of his printing venture with his in the late 1580s and early 1590s. Other confirmations of Barnes's connection with Wolfe appear as elements of the Harvey–Nashe controversy.[48] In his 1596 *Have with You to Saffron Walden*, Thomas Nashe criticised Harvey's role in promoting a poet he described as 'a paltrie *Scrivano*, betwixt a Lawiers Clark & a Poet, or smattering pert Boy whose buttocks were not yet coole since he came for the grammer'. According to Nashe, it was because of Harvey's insistence that the printer John Wolfe ended up publishing 'that Phillistine Poem of *Parthenophil and Parthenophe*, which to compare worse than it selfe, it would plague all the wits of *France*, *Spaine*, or *Italy*'. Nashe then describes Harvey's reaction to the lack of success of Barnabe Barnes's lyric sequence: 'And when hee [Harvey] saw it would not sell, hee cald all the World asses a hundred times over, with the stampingest cursing and tearing he could utter it, for that he having giv'n it his passe or good word, they obstinately contemnd and mislik'd it'.[49]

The harsh judgement passed on Barnes is not just collateral damage resulting from the antagonism between Harvey and Nashe: it is also a response to Barnes's personal contribution to the quarrel. In 1593, Barnes wrote three commendatory sonnets for Harvey's *Pierces Supererogation*, one of which, signed 'Parthenophil', aggressively lampooned Nashe.[50] If Harvey indeed pressured Wolfe to publish *Parthenophil and Parthenophe*, Barnes's commendatory verse might have been a way of returning the favour. It is also quite possible that Wolfe encouraged Barnes to do so: according to Virginia Stern, he had probably played the role of 'urging Harvey to retaliate against Greene and Nashe'.[51] These elements suggest that Barnes might have had a further reason for trying to establish his reputation: to protect himself from the potentially damaging effects of his involvement in the quarrel between Harvey and Nashe. They also mean (along with textual evidence put forward by Doyno)[52] that the conditions would have made it possible for Barnes to have a say in the editorial process of *A Divine Centurie*, which might have helped him carry out his wish to protect himself from slander, building a picture of himself as a morally and spiritually upright poet.

Barnes's second sequence received a particularly ornate title page, which was rather rare in printed sonnet sequences of the 1590s. The use of the motif of the stag, or hart, is particularly interesting. It appears twice, at the top and at the bottom of the page. A medallion at the bottom of the page makes the allusion to the Actaeon myth quite obvious (see Ovid's *Metamorphoses* III, 138–252). It is one of the most usual intertextual references in Renaissance love poetry, but also one that yields itself easily to moralisation and spiritualisation. In the picture, Actaeon is being turned into a stag. This is the moment when his lewd behaviour is exposed, and the moment of danger for him, as his hounds are about to turn against him. In Petrarch's poem 23 ('Nel dolce tempo …'), the lover/Acteon's hunt is explicitly related to his desire ('I' seguì' tanto avanti il mio desire / ch'un dì cacciando sì com'io solea / mi mossi', lines 147–9),[53] and his boldness leads to a deserved punishment. Golding's translation of Ovid's *Metamorphoses* interprets the figure of Acteon in a similar way: he is seen as a wanton man relishing excess, a bawd receiving his due punishment.[54] Such a reading of the myth constructs a narrative that parallels Barnes's narrative of conversion from his sequence of love poetry to his spiritual sonnet sequence. But the myth can equally be interpreted in spiritual terms, as Abraham Fraunce's commentary on the same myth shows: 'We ought not to be over curious and inquisitive in spying and prying into those matter which be above our reache, lest we be rewarded as Actaeon was'.[55] Such a reading of the myth, had Barnes had it in mind, would have helped him introduce his penitent speaker, who repeatedly admits he is an overreacher, as expressing the greatness of God is impossible. The identification of the repentant lover with a stag or a hart could have the further advantage of being reminiscent of psalm 42, in which the soul pants after God like the hart 'brayeth for the rivers of water', an intertextual echo that certainly needs to be taken into account considering the importance of the psalms both in the emergence of the tradition of the sonnet in England and France and in Barnes's religious background.[56] The inclusion of the motif of the stag (a motif I have not been able to find so conspicuously present in any of the title pages of printed English poetic collections of the 1590s) might therefore be a further indication of a form of publishing strategy consistent with the aims of Barnes's poetic writing in *A Divine Centurie of Spirituall Sonnets*.

From conversion to conversation

Barnabe Barnes seems to have followed a deliberate strategy of connecting his two sequences, with the purpose of staging the moral and spiritual conversion of his muse from lewdness to Christian exemplarity – and implying as much for himself, or at least for his public image as a poet. This gesture of recantation surely had to do with Barnes seeking protection and help from Bishop Tobie Matthew. But the printing of his works suggests that Barnes was trying to make this conversion public, or at least more widespread than a manuscript circulation would have allowed. One can only make suppositions here, but there are indications that Barnes desired to construct his reputation and to protect himself from the slander related to the controversy between Harvey and Nashe. What is clear is that, by printing both a secular and a spiritual sonnet sequence, Barnes could advertise both his agility with language and his ability to reform his soul. He modelled his efforts to connect the two sequences on an existing cultural pattern of prodigal authorship.

Several wider conclusions can be drawn from the study of Barnes's two lyric collections. The distinction between the profane and the religious sonnet is quite a clear one, but this does not mean that there are no continuities. It seems therefore justified to regard Barnes's works as two different types of sequence, but not as diametrically opposed endeavours. Admittedly, the love sequence allowed for considerably more moral ambiguity by depicting the very acts it was supposed to condemn. But the two works could also be part of a strategy, if not of self-fashioning, at least of self-representation relying on the printed medium. The example of Barnes suggests that sonneteers, like other poets of the time, had some sense of the potential of the printed page in literary and social terms – and/or that they knew printers who could guide them and advise them in that regard.[57] It also shows that the intra- and intertextuality of the 1590s sonnet sequences is worth investigating. This applies to poets like Daniel and Drayton, who revised their own poems several times, or like Barnes, who published two separate sonnet sequences. In the perspective of the Petrarchan collection, rewriting is a central issue that has not systematically been addressed in the case of Elizabethan sonnet sequences. Thorough studies of intertextual links between the sonnet sequences of the 1590s remain to be done, and would probably yield fruitful and stimulating results which would allow us to understand the extent to which the sequences were responding to, commenting upon or conversing with one another – thereby restoring some sense of the dialogic dynamism of early modern poetic writing.

Notes

1 B. Barnes, *A Divine Centurie of Spirituall Sonnets* (London: John Windet, 1595).
2 That the sparrow was a lustful bird was a commonplace. It is recorded, for instance, in Pietro Valeriano's *Hieroglyphica*: 'Passerum enim mares anno diutius durare non posse compertum est: cuius rei causa salacitas incontinentissima, quae tot hominum etiam ante diem effœtos exhaustosque uiribus tradit senectuti'. See *Hieroglyphica, Sive De Sacris Aegyptiorum Literis Commentarii* (Basel, 1556), p. 150.
3 See J. Grundy, *The Poems of Henry Constable* (Liverpool: Liverpool University Press, 1960), pp. 50–9.
4 This is the case, for instance, of Vittoria Colonna's *Rime*: in 1544, twenty-four spiritual sonnets were added to her love sonnet collection, together with a long poem entitled 'triompho della croce' – a

structure reminiscent of contemporary editions of Petrarch's vernacular poems, which included the *Canzoniere* (with its dual structure *in vita / in morte di Laura*, see below) and the *Trionfi*.
5 A. Earl, 'Late Elizabethan Devotional Poetry and Calvinism: A Re-evaluation of Barnabe Barnes', *Renaissance Studies*, 11:3 (1997), 232.
6 T.P. Roche Jr, *Petrarch and the English Sonnet Sequences* (New York: AMS Press, 1989), pp. 166–7.
7 See also H. Hackett, 'The Art of Blasphemy? Interfusions of the Erotic and the Sacred in the Poetry of Donne, Barnes, and Constable', *Renaissance and Reformation*, 28:3 (2004), pp. 27–54, esp. 40.
8 This shift from secular to sacred love is put forward in sixteenth-century editions of Petrarch's works, whose organisation and editorial features were progressively codified. In print, the 1501 edition of his works, edited by Bembo and published by Manutius, first materialised the division between the first section, *In vita di Laura*, and the second section, *In morte di Laura*. Later editions with or without commentaries, including Vellutello's very influential 1525 edition, tended to retain this division (though they could also have a third section and/or include the *Triumphs* in the same volume).
9 This sequence of love poems of eighteen lines falls into two sections. The second of them, entitled 'My love is past', is made up of poems explaining the speaker's renunciation and rejection of love.
10 Commentators have focused on the use of the Petrarchan language in *A Divine Centurie...*, but without really comparing it to the use of the same language in *Parthenophil and Parthenophe*. See for instance Earl, 'Late Elizabethan Devotional Poetry and Calvinism', pp. 228–30 and 240, or J.G. Scott, *Les Sonnets élisabéthains: les Sources et l'apport personnel* (Paris: Champion, 1929), p. 217: 'Considérons d'abord la *Divine Centurie* de Barnes. Ces poèmes furent publiés en 1595, le poète n'ayant pas tardé à se repentir de ses effusions terrestres'. Few works of literary criticism have devoted more than a passing glance to Barnes's sonnet sequences, but they have been mentioned and included in several major studies of Elizabethan sonnet sequences such as Scott's *Les Sonnets élisabéthains: les Sources et l'apport personnel*, pp. 69–86, Roche's *Petrarch and the English Sonnet Sequences*, pp. 166–84 and 244–71, and Wendy Wall's *The Imprint of Gender: Authorship and Publication in the English Renaissance* (Ithaca, London: Cornell University Press, 1993), pp. 205–7.
11 On recantation and poetry, see P.B. Phillippy, *Love's Remedies: Recantation and Renaissance Lyric Poetry* (Lewisburg, London: Bucknell University Press, Associated University Press, 1995).
12 See 'European Petrarchism as Training in Poetic Diction', pp. 61–83 in L. Forster, *The Icy Fire: Five Studies in European Petrarchism* (Cambridge: Cambridge University Press, 1969).
13 P.E. Blank Jr, *Lyric Forms in the Sonnet Sequences of Barnabe Barnes* (The Hague, Paris: Mouton, 1974), p. 116.
14 They are sonnets 47 and 52 and possibly – but less probably – 84 and 103.
15 Barnes's sestine 5 is a triple sestina in so far as it is made up of eighteen stanzas of six lines, followed by a three-line *envoi*. As in most of Barnes's sestinas, the permutations do not follow any strict rules other than the most fundamental one: the last line of each stanza ends with the same word as the first line of the stanza that follows it.
16 See George Puttenham, *The Arte of English Poesie. Contrived into Three Bookes: The First of Poets and Poesie, the Second of Proportion, the Third of Ornament* (London: Richard Field, 1589), p. 36.
17 'Now I waxe drousie, now cease all my teares, / Whilst I take rest and slumber neare this woode' (ll. 70–1). Barnes has made it impossible to determine whether what ensues is part of Parthenophil's dream or not.
18 J.N. Nelson, 'Lust and Black Magic in Barnabe Barnes's *Parthenophil and Parthenophe*', *The Sixteenth Century Journal: Journal of Early Modern Studies* 25:3 (1994), 595–608, esp. 595.
19 Roche, *Petrarch and the English Sonnet Sequences*.
20 Ibid., pp. 193–242.
21 The only known copy of *Parthenophil and Parthenophe* is kept at the British Library under shelfmark C.132i50.
22 M. Eccles, 'Barnabe Barnes', p. 221 in C.J. Sisson (ed.), *Thomas Lodge and Other Elizabethans* (Cambridge, MA: Harvard University Press, 1933), pp. 165–241.
23 See the introduction to this chapter.
24 For a case study, see Rémi Vuillemin, *Le Recueil pétrarquiste à l'ère du maniérisme: Poétique des sonnets de Michael Drayton, 1594–1619* (Paris: Champion, 2014), esp. pp. 147–58, 165–228 and 391–404.
25 Arguably, this ambiguity was an issue at the time. On a slightly different subject (Barnes's use of Catholic elements in his poems), Helen Hackett notes that '[o]verall, we may sense that Barnes is having it all ways: creating that frisson effect of rubbing up religion – and forbidden religion at that – against sex, while not doing anything that was theologically improper in a Protestant state'. See 'The Art of Blasphemy?', p. 39.

26 That Barnes's name did not appear on the title page is a supposition, as the bottom third of the title page of the only copy we have got left has been torn off. It does appear at the end of the dedicatory sonnets but, according to Doyno, they were probably added after the printing of the rest, and we cannot be sure that they were also to be found in other copies. See *Parthenophil and Parthenophe, A Critical Edition*, ed. V. Doyno (Carbondale: Southern Illinois University Press, 1971), pp. lxxi–lxxii.
27 *OED Online*. 3a and 3c (date accessed: 26 June 2018).
28 Doyno, *Parthenophil and Parthenophe*, p. 138.
29 Even if we consider only sonnet sequences published the year before or the same year as Barnes's *Parthenophil and Parthenophe*, examples abound: it is the case of the two 1592 editions of Samuel Daniel's *Delia*, of Giles Fletcher's *Licia* (1593) and of Thomas Lodge's *Phillis* (1593).
30 I adapt this phrasing from the title of W.E. Slight's *Managing Readers: Printed Marginalia in English Renaissance Books* (Ann Arbor: University of Michigan Press, 2001). It can be argued that the thresholds of the text (be they peritextual elements, paratextual pieces or quite simply the beginning or the end of the text itself), like marginal annotations, can play a major role in framing the text and thereby in shaping the reader's interpretation of it. See also G. Genette, *Paratexts: Thresholds of Interpretation*, trans. Jane E. Lewin (Cambridge: Cambridge University Press, 1997).
31 See respectively sonnets 30, 89, 91 and 92, elegies 12, 15 and 20, ode 11; madrigal 7 and sonnet 82; sonnets 68 and 92; sonnet 87; and the running metaphor of the forge in sonnets 3, 5, 24, 38, 64 and 77, and in ode 15.
32 See sonnets 16, 38, 40, 45, 94, 102 and elegy 20. Presumably, the frequent use of the term 'pierce' is also a pun alluding to Barnes's friend William Percy, the third son of Henry Percy, ninth Earl of Northumberland, to whom *Parthenophil and Parthenophe* is dedicated. See in particular sonnets 45 and 46. Allusions to Jove and/or the association of darts and thunder can be found in madrigal 8 and sonnets 44 and 46.
33 See sonnets 1, 25 and 60. Thunder – now God's thunder (i.e. his wrath) is also mentioned again (see sonnets 33, 46 and 73). Sonnet 12 mentions Christ's 'heart pearc'de with a Launce'. The term 'sting,' on the contrary, refers to temptation (see sonnets 36, 43 and 44).
34 Roche, *Petrarch and the English Sonnet Sequences*, p. 248.
35 See for instance sonnets 6, 11, 18, 20, 35, 36 and, further in the sequence, 'elegie' 6.
36 Apart from Barnes's works themselves and attacks by Nashe (see below), it is the anecdote of Barnes's failed attempt to poison a certain John Browne that has repeatedly been used to insist on his immorality. On the anecdote, and more generally on Barnes's life, see Eccles, 'Barnabe Barnes'; Doyno, *Parthenophil and Parthenophe*, pp. xiii–lxxvi; G. Klawitter, 'Barnabe Barnes (1571–1609)', *Sixteenth-Century British Nondramatic Writers: First Series*, Dictionary of Literary Bibliography (Detroit, Michigan: Dale, 1993), vol. 132, pp. 53–5.
37 I believe some contextualisation is needed here: Roche was writing in the course of the 1980s (his book was published in 1989), arguably before what could be called 'the religious turn' in early modern literary studies happened. To a certain extent, it could even be said that he anticipated it, grounding his analysis in Augustinian morals (keeping in mind that as a whole, Roche's reading is primarily moral, rather than religious). In his desire to show that sonneteers had in mind the moral problems posed by love poems, he might have gone too far, giving a somewhat unqualified vision of the sequences as providers of negative didacticism. His use of the notion of 'irony' is perhaps questionable, since it posits that sonnets can be written either 'seriously' or 'ironically', a dichotomy which tends to downplay their ambiguity. My argument is that there is ground for qualifying Roche's approach (while keeping some of his conclusions) by replacing his concern with irony with a concern for what could be called publishing and authorising strategies. On the 'religious turn', see Ken Jackson and Arthur F. Marotti, 'The Turn to Religion in Early Modern English Studies', *Criticism*, 46:1 (winter 2004), 167–90.
38 R. Helgerson, *The Elizabethan Prodigals* (Berkeley: University of California Press, 1976).
39 Ibid., p. 4.
40 This translation is from Helgerson, *Elizabethan Prodigals*, p. 12. Of course, this also applies to Petrarch's *Canzoniere*, as will be recalled further down.
41 Doyno, *Parthenophil and Parthenophe*, p. 138.
42 See Eccles, 'Barnabe Barnes', p. 167.
43 A. Shell and A. Hunt, 'The Book as Gift in Elizabethan Durham: Barnabe Barnes's *A Divine Centurie of Spirituall Sonnets*', in P. Scott (ed.), *Collaboration and Interdisciplinarity in the Republic of Letters* (Manchester: Manchester University Press, 2010), pp. 117–33.
44 Shell and Hunt describe Matthew as a moderate Calvinist with a high degree of 'evangelical commitment'. See 'The Book as Gift in Elizabethan Durham', p. 124.
45 See Earl, 'Late Elizabethan Devotional Poetry and Calvinism', pp. 226 and 233.

46 There might be several reasons why the two sequences were not printed together. It is quite likely that *Parthenophil and Parthenophe* did not sell very well, so that printing it with the spiritual sonnets was probably not worth the investment. Another, more obvious reason, is that the unsavoury nature of the first volume made that impossible, especially as Barnes was attempting to obtain Bishop Matthew's protection. Still, reading the two sequences together makes the changes even more strongly perceptible. Only one copy is left today, and the work never seems to have been reprinted.
47 See R.B. McKerrow (ed.), F.P. Wilson (rev.), *The Works of Thomas Nashe* (Oxford: Blackwell, 1958), vol. 3, p. 102. As we will see below, it is difficult to give full credit to Nashe's statement. But its mere existence testifies to a form of proximity between Barnes, Harvey and Wolfe.
48 See M. Bland, 'John Windet and the Transformation of the Book Trade, 1584–1610', *Papers of the Biographical Society of America*, 107 (June 2013), 151–92, esp. 171. On the quarrel between Thomas Nashe and the Harvey brothers, see Jennifer Richards, *Rhetoric and Courtliness in Early Modern Literature* (Cambridge: Cambridge University Press, 2003), pp. 115–16; Virgina Stern, *Gabriel Harvey: His Life, Marginalia and Library* (Oxford: Clarendon Press, 1979), pp. 85–124, and McKerrow (ed.), Wilson (rev.), *The Works of Thomas Nashe*, vol. 5, pp. 65–110. See also J.L. Andersen, 'Thomas Nashe and Popular Conformity in Late Elizabethan England', *Renaissance and Reformation*, 25 (2001), 25–43.
49 Doyno, *Parthenophil and Parthenophe*, p. xix. The source is Thomas Nashe's *Haue vvith you to Saffron-VValden. Or, Gabriell Harueys Hunt is vp Containing a Full Answere to the Eldest Sonne of the Haltermaker. Or, Nashe his Confutation of the Sinfull Doctor. The Mott or Posie, in Stead of Omne Tulit Punctum: Pacis Fiducia Nunquam. As Much to Say, as I Sayd I would Speake with Him* (London: John Danter, 1596).
50 Entitled '*Nash*, or the Confuting Gentleman', the sonnet reads: 'The Muses-scorn; the Courtiers laughing-stock; / The Countreys Coxecombe; Printers proper new; / The Cities Leprosie; The Pandars stew; / Vertues disdayne; honesties adverse rock; / Enuies vile champion, slaunders stumbling block. / Graund Orator of Cunny-Catcher's crew; / Base broaching tapster of reports untrue; / Our modern viper, and our Countryes mock; / True Valors Cancer-worme, sweet Learnings rust. / Where shall I finde meete colours, and fit words, / For such a counterfaict, and worthlesse matter? / Him, whom thou raylest on at thy owne lust, / Sith *Bodine*, and sweet *Sidney* did not flatter, / His inuectiue thee too much grace affordes.' See G. Harvey, *Pierces Supererogation, or a New Prayse of the Old Asse, A Preparative to Certaine Larger Discourses, Intituled Nashes S. Fame* (London: John Wolfe, 1593).
51 Stern, *Gabriel Harvey*, p. 102.
52 Doyno, *Parthenophil and Parthenophe*, pp. 137–8.
53 The text is from Marco Santagata's edition of the *Canzoniere*. Other allusions to the myth can of course be found in Petrarch's work, as in the well-known sonnet 190, 'Una candida cerva sopra l'erba', the source of Wyatt's 'Whoso list to hunt'.
54 See the 'Epistle' at the beginning of Golding's translation of the *Metamorphoses*, lines 97–108: 'All such as doo in flattring freaks, and hawks, and howndes delyght, / And dyce, and cards, and for to spend the tyme both day and nyght / In foule excesse of chamberworke, or too much meate and drink: / Uppon the piteous storie of Acteon ought to think. / For theis and theyr adherents usde excessive are in deede / The dogs that dayly doo devour theyr followers on with speede. / Tyresias willes inferior folk in any wyse to shun / Too judge betweene their betters least in perill they doo run. / Narcissus is of scornfulnesse and pryde a myrror cleere, / Where beawties fading vanitie most playnly may appeere. / And Echo in the selfsame tale dooth kyndly represent / The lewd behaviour of a bawd, and his due punishment.' See also Whitney, *A Choice of Emblemes* (1586), emblem 15 ('Voluptas aerumnosa').
55 *The third part of the Countesse of Pembrokes Yuychurch Entituled, Amintas dale. Wherein are the most conceited tales of the pagan gods in English hexameters together with their auncient descriptions and philosophicall explications. By Abraham Fraunce* (London: printed [by Thomas Orwyn], for Thomas Woodcocke, 1592), fol. 43r, quoted in Wall, *The Imprint of Gender*, p. 225.
56 On the centrality of the psalms in early modern culture and literature, see H. Hamlin, *Psalm Culture and Early Modern English Literature* (Cambridge: Cambridge University Press, 2004).
57 A similar point has been made for Samuel Daniel in L.M. Klein, *The Exemplary Sidney and the Elizabethan Sonneteer* (Newark, London: University of Delaware Press, Associated University Press, 1998). On Michael Drayton's publishing strategies, see A. Hadfield's 'Michael Drayton's Brilliant Career', *Proceedings of the British Academy*, 125 (2003), 119–47, and R. Vuillemin's 'From Ideas to Books: The Editorial Writing of Michael Drayton's Sonnet Sequences', in N. Collé-Bak, M. Latham and D. Ten Eyck (eds), *Book Practices and Textual Itineraries 4: From Text(s) to Book(s): Studies in the Production and Editorial Process* (Nancy: Presses Universitaires de Nancy, 2014), pp. 181–95.

IV

Editing the sonnet

8

The Muses Garland (1603): fragment of a printed verse miscellany

Hugh Gazzard

A fragment of printed poems was acquired by the Beinecke Library in 2011, from a verse miscellany called – as its running heads and a title in an ornament on sig. B1a indicate – *The Muses Garland* (hereafter *MG*, see list of sigla on p. 153). It is part of the James Marshall and Marie-Louise Osborn Collection, Beinecke Rare Book and Manuscript Library, Yale University. The work turns out to date probably from 1603, and is a fragment of great intrinsic interest. It includes two otherwise unrecorded sonnets subscribed 'S.P.S.'. It offers new witnesses to known works by Spenser. It presents several poems, some otherwise unrecorded, as being by Robert Devereux, second Earl of Essex, and gives a new text of part of a poem possibly by him. It tells us interesting things about the production and character of printed verse miscellanies. Images of the fragment, shelfmark Osborn pb173, have been digitised and are accessible online at http://brbl-dl.library.yale.edu/vufind/Record/3446174 (date accessed: 26 April 2019). I append reproductions, and offer here an introduction to and diplomatic edition of the fragment. *MG* and a fragment of another, separate printed verse miscellany, also in the Beinecke, have been briefly described by Samuel Fallon and David Scott Kastan.[1]

Publication and printing

The book was most likely published by ('printed for') the bookseller Thomas Archer, to whom it was entered in the Stationers' Register, with no irregularities, on 7 February 1603, as 'A booke called *The Muses garlond*'.[2] It was noted as being licensed by the cleric Zachariah Pasfield, in his capacity as a 'regular, ordinary, or duty supplier of licensing authority'.[3] That day was the eve of the second anniversary of Essex's uprising; in just over six weeks, Queen Elizabeth would be dead. This was only Archer's second Register entry, after one on 4 February 1603. The English Short Title Catalogue yields around 170 records relating to Archer's activities in publishing, from 1603 to 1628, corresponding to perhaps more than 120 extant discrete titles certainly or possibly printed for him; exact numbers for his output are complicated by his involvement in the tangled history of newsbook publication in the 1620s. The earliest items surviving in full, from 1603, typify much of what would become Archer's output: a pamphlet with news from the Netherlands; Henry Timberlake's short travelogue from the Middle East (five times thereafter reprinted for Archer); a translated pamphlet proclamation from the Spanish Netherlands announcing the resumption of trade relations. Before his presentment in January 1603 Archer had been apprenticed to Cuthbert Burby. At least thirteen named printers, and the Eliot's Court press, undertook work for him through his independent career. In dealings with the Stationers' Company, he shows no more than a normal run of infractions: printing without registration, and irregularities in apprentice-keeping. On the other hand, he seems to have got nowhere in the Company hierarchy.[4]

Of literary interest from his output, the following authors were singly or collaboratively published at least once by him: Robert Allyne, Robert Armin, Thomas Dekker, Richard Johnson, Thomas Middleton, Samuel Rowlands, Rachel Speght, Joseph Swetnam and John Webster. He published six plays, the best-known being *The White Devil*. What was, we may surmise, Archer's most lucrative title – he published it seven times, commissioning five printers – was Swetnam's *Arraignment of Lewd, Idle, Froward, and Unconstant Women*. Its 1628 edition was perhaps Archer's final publication. That a publisher might take both sides, and perhaps strive to capitalise on an orchestrated '*querelle*', is surely implied by Archer's publication of Rachel Speght's *A Mouzell for Melastomus* (1617).[5] In the early 1620s Archer pioneered the publication of the *coranto*: the serial newsbook, produced initially in translation from the Dutch, for which his early interest in publishing news from the Netherlands must have prepared him. The format took hold, despite Archer's early difficulties with it (he was briefly imprisoned in September 1621 for his pains), and a *coranto* was printed individually for him and for various publishing syndicates for the rest of his career.[6] All in all, here was a stationer whose foray into courtly verse miscellany right at the start of his independent career looks the more singular given the trend of his later output.

The format of the miscellany was, presumably, octavo: the chain lines are vertical, but due to the very fragile condition of the fragment it has not been possible to detect a watermark, which in any case, for a typical octavo, would be less easily evident, in the upper inner margin.[7] Archer seems to have been responsible for the publication of *MG*, but I have not been able to determine beyond doubt who its printer was. The factotum ornament which heads sig. B1a appears also (with a different medial label, that is, the words within the cartouche) in at least seven items printed by Ralph Blower between 1605 and 1609.[8] There (five of them are printed visitation articles) the wording within the cartouche of course varies, and the letters 'I W' as they appear in *MG* are not present. I find that Blower is known to have printed for Archer only once (STC 21369.5, 1615). On the other hand, the same factotum also appears at the head of the text of *The True Discription of a Royall Masque* (STC 6264, London, 1604), which is, as the later and authorised edition of that work makes clear, the unauthorised edition of Samuel Daniel's court masque, performed at Whitehall in January 1604, and when republished titled *The Vision of the 12. Goddesses*. The imprint of *The True Discription* indicates that it was printed and, it would seem, published by Edward Allde, who as a printer singly or conjointly undertook the most work (counting by title) for Thomas Archer, especially in Archer's early years in business (11 of 27 of Archer's items, 1603–11, on ESTC, for example). The production, proprietorship and deployment of ornaments, including also 'printers' flowers', remain too obscure for very much weight to rest on their evidence, but the 'flowers' surrounding the title of *MG* 10 on sig. B4a, and across the foot of that page, resemble those on sig. E2b of

STC 13703, an octavo sermon printed by Allde in 1603. Those decorating *MG* 7, 8, 9 and 11 (sig. B2b, sig. B3a, sig. B3b, sig. B4b) seem to be the ones used, for example, around the title page and throughout STC 10597.5 (1602), in STC 19803.5 and 19804 (1603), and at the lower border of the Essex ballad STC 6791 (1603; see also below): all of them poetry, all Allde productions.

The printed verse miscellanies

In a way, Elizabethan poetry began the year before the queen's accession. *Songes and Sonettes* (1557, and later editions; generally referred to as *Tottel's Miscellany*, or 'Tottel') had opened a casement into the half-secret courtly chamber of coterie communication for lyric by, especially, Wyatt and Surrey. The steady stream of printed verse miscellanies that followed in, particularly, the 1570s, and towards the turn of the century – even if not exactly a democratisation of elite poetry – at least showed the potential for a degree of popularisation of lyric by a variety of, often, courtly (or would-be-courtly) hands.[9] The miscellanies vary in sophistication, but taken as a whole show a wide range, from balladry to translations from Philippe Desportes, for example. *MG* is a new addition to these. For the sake of both space and relevance, here I relate *MG* to the chief similar miscellanies of the last years of Elizabeth's reign.[10] A more extensive account would pay attention also to augmented collections of poetry by divers hands organised around a central poet.[11] But judging by the fragment, *MG* was probably less like those than like the more diversely composite miscellanies, and especially like *The Phoenix Nest, Englands Helicon* and *A Poetical Rapsody*. I will say something here about the make-up and general character of the books itemised in n.10, by way of comparison with what remains of *MG*.

The social inflection of the miscellanies is of obvious importance. They consistently compliment their readership on its gentility. They glamorise, no less, their constituent poets: the 'most rare and refined workes of Noble *men, worthy Knights, gallant Gentlemen, Masters of Arts, and braue Schollers*', as the title page of *PN* has it. It has been argued that the crossover between elite and popular forms (lyric, and ballad) in the early miscellanies, Tottel's included, has been under-estimated, but also that the elite decisively predominates over the popular by the 1590s, after the hiatus in miscellanies in the previous decade.[12] It has been argued, also, that these later miscellanies boast a boosted confidence in their contents: 'The shift is subtle, yet evident: poetry is not something that simply needs to be dignified by gentlemen, but something that can add dignity to gentlemen'.[13] The contents of *MG* patently confirm this trend – and connected with it might be the phenomenon of associating an anthology with a dead courtly hero. *PN* is prefaced by a prose defence of the Earl of Leicester's posthumous reputation, and opens with three elegies for Sidney. (It is not clear quite how these components and the rest should cohere: *PN*'s contents are very miscellaneous.) Six poems in *BBD* are about or in some way associated with Sidney. What is particularly remarkable about *MG* is the emphasis on so politically a controversial figure as the Earl of Essex, who is made to complain and protest his 'Honour true', and allegiance to his sovereign mistress in the face of disfavour, and to extemporise on his own motto. Very likely the missing subscription of *MG* 11 would have named

Essex its author also, as so many of the manuscript versions of that poem do, and so rehearse it as a very personalised political complaint. The visibility of Sidney and Spenser simply accentuates the impression that material is being assembled here of the highest political and poetic order, and the surviving collection is intensely animated by the twin impulses of magnifying a 'mistress' and deploring the pains of love, courtship and courtiership – more concentratedly and coherently organised so, indeed, even in this remnant, than other miscellanies.

In presentation *MG* is most like *EH* and *PR*, but its text is richer in ornaments, 'printers' flowers', than either. The provision of titles for poems short enough to go into miscellanies was promoted by, though it did not begin with, print, and specifically by Tottel – though titles are rarer in the surviving Elizabethan manuscript miscellanies, and not all poems in printed miscellanies carry titles.[14] Most titles in *BBD* are relatively pared down: simply formal ('A Poem'), thematic ('Of a discontented minde', 'His complaint against Loue and Fortune'), occasionally riddling ('Rare newes'). In *EH* titles are generally briefly formal, and usually make a shepherd or nymph the lover or speaker ('¶ *The Sheepheard* Musidorus *his complaint*'). Titles in *PN*, which do not exactly agree between the list of contents and the text proper, are formal or thematic, as they are in *PR* also. From the 1570s, George Gascoigne and Nicholas Breton especially had developed, often complicatedly, the kind of 'occasional' or 'contextual' title seen here in *MG* 1 to 4, and whose use simply of pronouns ('*He begs a kisse*'; '*Her Answere, in the same Rimes*') is frequent also in *PR*, almost all of whose poems carry some form of title. The often vivid and precise 'occasions' in *PR* might stand as episodes in a romance ('*Vpon his Ladies buying strings for her Lute*'). As for *mise-en-page*: titles in *EH* are in italic preceded by a pilcrow symbol; the default form for titles in *PN* begins with roman font larger than poem-text, and sometimes diminishes to smaller italic font for titles of several lines. Titles in Tottel are in roman type larger than the 'black-letter' poem-text.

Precedents for the mixed contents of *MG* are easy to find in the miscellanies: formal and thematic variety abounds, including sonnets, poems in dialogue with each other, complaints, poems of courtship and courtiership. Miscellany contents were indeed miscellaneous. In setting, speaker and theme the poems of *EH* are pervasively pastoral, even if sometimes they had to be wrested to make them so (e.g. *shepherd* interpolated in Rollins 52). *PR* is formally diverse, but with a central concentration of love-lyric. It offers sonnets and many other stanza forms; palinodes and answer-poems; poems in quantitative metres; a pattern-poem. Exceptions to its amatory content include encomia of the queen, and of (probably) Essex, and of Samuel Daniel, and there is one religious lyric. *MG* begins with linked sonnets seemingly by Essex and certainly in his voice, and these, plus the inclusion of sonnets by Spenser and, possibly, Sidney, would be bound, as I have noted, to advertise the poetic and political prestige of the collection.

A distinction can be drawn between *EH* and the other miscellanies. Poems in *EH* are mostly (116 of 150: 77.3 per cent) taken directly – as Rollins itemised – from printed works: from the Sidney 1598 collected works (15), lyrics in prose romances (47: 25 of those from Bartholomew Yong's *Diana*), individual poetry collections (26), earlier miscellanies (19), songbooks (14), and plays and entertainments (10). They are treated with varying degrees of editorial intervention, some of it quite marked. But (not counting the poems from *BBD* recycled in *AAD*) the great majority of poems in the other four miscellanies derive, so far as is known, directly from manuscript sources, even where they (rarely) might have already appeared or been excerpted in print elsewhere. In other words, *EH* is mostly a record of public taste in print, whereas the others shine a public light on private composition or semi-private circulation. (The poems by Francis and Walter Davison in *PR* might have been designedly written for that miscellany.) What *MG* might have done in total we cannot say, but apparently manuscript sources dominate in the fragment.

Ascriptions of authorship in the miscellanies present some difficulties. Their extent varies: almost all poems in *EH* are signed with names or as anonymous, but fewer than one-fifth in *PR*. Ascriptions include full names, initials, pseudonyms and various notes of anonymity. Copyists and compilers in both print and manuscript miscellanies might from a number of motives manipulate the protocols around attribution and anonymity, authorial conspicuousness, discretion and disavowal, which were features of early modern textuality in general.[15] Copyists and compilers might also err. They might make efforts to correct mistakes, or mis-ascribed poets might protest: either of these might explain the several cases of poems re-ascribed edition to edition. In *EH* there are a few manifest errors. Rollins, and May and Ringler, are non-committal over its ascriptions to Thomas Watson, and doubtful over its ascriptions to Breton, Dyer and De Vere of material reused from other miscellanies. Items signed '*E.B.*' and '*Edmund Bolton*', not known from any other source, are uncertainly assigned to Bolton by Rollins, and by May and Ringler. Perhaps the compiler knew Bolton in person. The great majority of *EH* ascriptions seem to be correct, but, then, its sources were mostly 'open' and printed. In four important cases, '*N. Breton*' or the unidentified '*Ignoto*' are substituted for '*S. Phil. Sidney*', '*S.W.R.*' and '*M.F.G.*', on cancel-slips in several copies (Rollins 33 and 79, drawn from unknown sources; 54 and 71, which derived from *PN*). Why this should be so is not known.[16]

Rollins reckons that ascriptions in *PR* offer 'far more difficulties' than those in other miscellanies, but also (plausibly) that, his disclaimer notwithstanding, Davison himself was most likely responsible for making them.[17] The book's ascription of Rollins 1 and 2 to Sir Philip Sidney is accepted by Ringler (OP 6, 7); the ascription of Rollins 4 to the Countess of Pembroke is accepted by her modern editors.[18] About one-third of *PR A* is advertised as by Francis Davison or his brother Walter. Sir John Davies's modern editors rehearse and accept the arguments for attributing to him the 'Hymne' signed 'I.D.', and the sequence of ten sonnets signed '*Melophilus*' in *PR A* and 'I.D.' in *PR BCD*, and one further poem with initials, and two with his name, in *PR BCD*. They note that copy was 'very likely' not supplied by Davies.[19] Poems subscribed 'Anomos' in *PR A* have not been definitively claimed (the question of 'A.W.' in Davison's manuscript lists of poems is tackled by Rollins in his edition of *PR*). Krueger and Nemser conclude that 'Whoever provided the attributions, in the first two editions [of *PR*] he is never demonstrably wrong'.[20] But it should be noted that almost half of the collection is anonymous.

The trend of attributions in the printed miscellanies, then, is that they are mostly credible. This by itself is of course no reason to credit any given attribution without further argument. But as a whole they are probably more consistently reliable than those in manuscript miscellanies. The ascriptions in *MG* are bold, variably credible and in one case at least very enigmatic.

Compilation

The three poems in *MG* that are found in print elsewhere (3, 6, 10) include distinctive variants, and the other poems are either known from manuscript or not known elsewhere at all. The miscellany's ascribed authors could scarcely be more prestigious, nor its distillation of love-lyric and political complaint more potent. So who edited this miscellany? Already, Richard Tottel (if it was Tottel)[21] had shown that a stationer might be an anthologist of distinction and importance, but nothing in the later career of Thomas Archer suggests that he had the interests, inclination, access to material or initiative to bring *MG* into being – and anyway he was at the beginning of his independent career. It is not certain where primary responsibility for the publication of *BBD* or *AAD* lay (but see n.28 below). The best candidate so far proposed for the 'R.S.' of *PN* remains Rollins's, Richard Stapleton.[22] The stationer Nicholas Ling, who published an important literary list which included *Hamlet* Q1 and Q2, is thought probably – on the strength of putatively transposed initials in its prefatory address, and of likely links with Drayton – to have led the editing of *EH*, but with others' involvement, and under some kind of commission or direction by the little-studied figure John Bodenham, as part of what looks like a project of multiple literary excerption and compilation.[23] Certainly a stationer would be best-placed to access the variety of printed materials that made up *EH*. The case for Anthony Munday's likely involvement in *EH* is strengthened by its inclusion of some of his poems, signed 'Shep. Tonie', and some evidently from manuscript sources.

Francis Davison's preliminary disavowals in *PR* – disavowals of responsibility for print publication, and of 'the mixing … diuerse things by great and learned Personages', alleging them 'as being done by the Printer', so that the printer could fill out a volume, 'and grace the forefront with Sir Ph. Sidneys, and others names' – were probably another example of the disingenuous early modern topos of modesty and authorial inadvertence.[24] Davison manifestly designed the volume. If a single originator of *MG* is to be sought, it was evidently someone with important literary interests and connections, and so probably a writer also. Munday is possible, as is Davison: but then, they had already done this elsewhere. Nicholas Breton is a possibility.[25] He may even be the poet of *MG* 1, 2, 4 and 5, and he seems to have fashioned some verse in the 'voices' of grandees, much as the poems attributed in *MG* to Essex (see notes to *MG* 1–5). He had definite pro-Essex sympathies.[26] The poems attributed here to Sidney may or may not be by Sidney; at any rate, Breton was manifestly a client of the Countess of Pembroke, and in a position to access unpublished Sidneiana.[27] He had a keen sense of the resources of poetry in print, saw some of his work included in manuscript and print miscellanies and in productions of his own made to look like miscellanies, and he probably had an organising role in the compilation and publication of *BBD* and *AAD* which is still not fully understood, and which he and their publisher Richard Jones may have misrepresented.[28] What other late Elizabethan or early

Jacobean poet or man of letters matches all these qualifications? Of plausible candidates who come close, perhaps Gervase Markham, perhaps Robert Pricket, perhaps Richard Barnfield. But guesswork, however educated, remains guesswork, and it is unlikely that we shall ever surely identify the shaping hand here.

Whatever the origins and implications of the fusion in miscellanies of the amatory and the political, the courtly and the lyrical, it is apparent also that they offer an index of taste, a handy *vade mecum*, advertising standards and fashion, for a kind of canon-formation of vernacular poetry. In that context, *MG* looks even more ambitious and impressive than at first appears. And it confirms the elitist trend, in content and contributor, of the 1590s miscellanies generally. Before then, miscellanies had leaned more heavily than is usually recognised on the broadside ballad; then, 'in *England's Helicon* and *A Poetical Rhapsody*, poetry has already been refined, English has already been dignified and poets along with it'.[29] It was probably in part the success of printing the Sidney oeuvre in the 1590s which pointed the way for a revival of miscellany-gathering that decade, mostly dormant since the 1570s. Petrarch, politics, the Sidney paradigm and (in *EH*) pastoral, in varying measures across the 1590s and into the 1600s, secured for these anthologies their special cachet. *MG* offers a concentrated representation of the pleasures and, potently, pains of courtship, courtiership and courtly life.

Manuscript into print

Although none of the surviving manuscript miscellanies, *c.* 1580–1620, can be shown to have been used as copy for anything in print, some of their contents overlap with each other and with print. *C* (see list of sigla below), *Hy*, *Ra*, British Library Add. MS 34064 (the 'Cosens manuscript'), Harley MS 6910: all these preserve courtly lyrics (by *inter alia* Breton, Dyer, Oxford, Peele, Raleigh, Sidney, Spenser and Surrey), and make many credible ascriptions – and three of them preserve versions of *MG* 6.[30] The impact of these manuscript miscellanies is difficult to gauge: how far, for example, did they, rather than print, encourage and extend textual transmission for readers and copyists in, or with contacts in, court circles? And how far did they promote the idea of the 'courtly maker'? They are in a distinct medium, but, albeit in a less forceful and coherent form than that of *MG*, they too attest at least in part to a shaping, courtly vision, and offer 'independent … evidence confirming the homogeneity of tastes'.[31]

Reception

One early reader of *MG*, or owner, is definitely documented: there is a note of *MG* (between *The Rape of Lucrece* and *Paris and Oenone*) among books owned by William Drummond of Hawthornden in 1611.[32] I have not found any trace of *MG* between that note and the book's recovery this century. Its fragmentation might, like the sparse survival of many editions of sixteenth- and early seventeenth-century poetry, be a sign of voracious readership. But it is possible that *MG* was suppressed, 'called in' by the authorities. Its unambiguous projection, at its very beginning, of the plaintive and courtly voice of Essex seems extraordinarily bold; *MG* 10, taken from a poem that had probably been suppressed by the authorities, intensifies the political pressure; and *MG* 11 might be, if the full scope of its veiled *ad hominem* topics and targets could be uncovered, the most combustible of all. It is not easy to imagine the Cecil regime smiling on all this. Censorial sensitivities around the turn of the century were tender, especially in matters relating to Essex, as his career unravelled and then so spectacularly broke up (compare, for example, the controversies surrounding Essex's *Apology*, and Samuel Daniel's *Philotas*). It was also the case that books and authors might be rounded up even after what seems to have been an unproblematic entry into the Stationers' Register, and passage through the not-very-systematic system of pre-publication censorship: Sir John Hayward's *The First Part of the Life and Raigne of King Henry the IIII* (1599) is the obvious, and Essex-related, case; and the second book known to have been licensed by Pasfield was actually suppressed once published.[33]

Notes

1 I owe a very great debt of gratitude to Prof. Tiffany Stern, who generously first drew my attention to *The Muses Garland*, and gave the impetus for this investigation. A number of readers of earlier versions of this piece offered invaluable comments, including Dr Ben Higgins and Dr Katie Murphy of Oriel College, Oxford. Audiences and convenors at the University of Strasbourg ('The Triumph of the Sonnet' conference, May 2016), and Sheffield Hallam University ('Essex: The Cultural Impact of an Elizabethan Courtier' symposium, October 2013), were generous with their time and attention – and my thanks go to Dr Rémi Vuillemin, not least for his patience. See S. Fallon and D. Scott Kastan, 'Signature Verses: Two Previously Unknown Fragments of Early Modern Miscellanies', *Times Literary Supplement*, 5888 (5 February 2016), p. 14.

2 *A Transcript of the Registers of the Company of Stationers of London, 1555–1640 A.D.*, ed. E. Arber, 5 vols (London: priv. publ., 1875–94), vol. 3, p. 226. The year was 1602/3, and not 1603/4: other entries around these months were for books printed with 1603 imprints, and an entry before *MG* from 27 January (*Transcript*, ed. Arber, vol. 3, p. 225: printed as STC 11726) carried news from 'the .xij. of December last in the year 1602'.

3 On Pasfield as press-licenser, see W.P. Williams, '"Vnder the Handes of …": Zachariah Pasfield and the Licensing of Playbooks', in M. Straznicky (ed.), *Shakespeare's Stationers: Studies in Cultural Bibliography* (Philadelphia: University of Pennsylvania Press, 2013), pp. 63–94, at 72.

4 *Records of the Court of the Stationers' Company, 1602 to 1640*, ed. W.A. Jackson (London: Bibliographical Society, 1957), *passim*.

5 For an account of Archer as a specialist publisher for City concerns, whose literary output amounted to 'dialogic publishing', which 'depended', some of the time, on the persistence of the *querelle des femmes*, see Z. Lesser, *Renaissance Drama and the Politics of Publication: Readings in the English Book Trade* (Cambridge: Cambridge University Press, 2004), ch. 4, pp. 115–56. Lesser connects Archer's news and travel books – which he sees as Archer's mercantile speciality – with his shop's location near the Exchange; he analyses Archer's playbooks in the context of the *querelle*.

6 J. Raymond, *The Invention of the Newspaper: English Newsbooks, 1641–1649* (Oxford: Oxford University Press, 1996), pp. 7–8, and refs at n. 34.

7 I am very grateful to Prof. Tiffany Stern, and to Elizabeth Frengel, Research Librarian at the Beinecke Rare Book and Manuscript Library, and to Leland Strang of Yale University, for their physical examination of the fragment. Quarto half-sheet imposition is also a possibility.

8 STC 10158 (sig. A2a), 10159 (sig. A2a), 10225 (sig. A2a), 10289.7 (sig. A2a), 10314.4 (sig. A3a), 10668 (sig. C1a), 23607 (sig. C4a). I am grateful to Dr Ben Higgins for first spotting Blower's use of the factotum.

9 H.E. Rollins's editions of the Elizabethan miscellanies remain invaluable. E.W. Pomeroy, *The Elizabethan Miscellanies: Their Development and Conventions* (Berkeley, Los Angeles, London: University of California Press, 1973) effectively gives a digest of some of Rollins's findings, with additional critical evaluations. One of the richest modern examinations of the miscellanies (both print and manuscript), single-author editions and the dissemination of lyric generally is in A.F. Marotti,

Manuscript, Print, and the English Renaissance Lyric (Ithaca, London: Cornell University Press, 1995). F.W. Baue, *A Bibliographical Catalogue and First-Line Index of Printed Anthologies of English Poetry to 1640* (Lanham, MD, and Oxford: Scarecrow, 2002) remains useful.

10 *Brittons Bowre of Delights* (hereafter *BBD*, 1591 and 1597, STC 3633, 3634); *The Arbor of Amorous Deuises ... by N.B. Gent*. (*AAD*, 1597, STC 3631 – but it was entered in the Stationers' Register 7 January 1594, and there was almost certainly a first edition that year); *The Phoenix Nest* (*PN*, 1593, STC 21516); *Englands Helicon* (*EH*, 1600, 3191); and *A Poetical Rapsody* (*PR*, 1602, STC 6373). The latter two were popular enough for further editions: *EH B* (1614), and *PR B, C, D* (1608, 1611, 1621).

11 For example, T. Newman's first 1591 edition of *Astrophil and Stella* (STC 22536) and the 1595 edition of Henry Constable's *Diana* (STC 5638.3).

12 E. Nebeker, 'Broadside Ballads, Miscellanies, and the Lyric in Print', *English Literary History*, 76:4 (2009), pp. 989–1013.

13 Ibid., p. 996. 'The miscellanies wean themselves from broadside material': p. 1006.

14 See further Marotti, *Manuscript, Print, and the English Renaissance Lyric*, pp. 218–19.

15 For thoughts on aspects of this, see M. North, 'Ignoto in the Age of Print: The Manipulation of Anonymity in Early Modern England', *Studies in Philology*, 91:4 (1994), 390–416: but some of this should be qualified by Rudick, cited below.

16 Michael Rudick doubts that the corrections arose from protests from the courtier-poets and thinks the cancels are 'honest, if futile, efforts at correction': 'The "Ralegh Group" in *The Phoenix Nest*', *Studies in Bibliography*, 24 (1971), 131–7, quotation at 136. This is indeed the simplest explanation, but one that raises more questions about compilation and reception than it can resolve.

17 *A Poetical Rhapsody, 1602–1621*, ed. H.E. Rollins, 2 vols (Cambridge, MA: Harvard University Press, 1931), vol. 2, p. 36.

18 *The Poems of Sir Philip Sidney*, ed. W.A. Ringler (Oxford: Clarendon Press, 1962), p. 498; *The Collected Works of Mary Sidney Herbert, Countess of Pembroke*, ed. M.P. Hannay, Noel J. Kinnamon and Michael G. Brennan, 2 vols (Oxford: Clarendon Press, 1998), vol. 1, pp. 302–3.

19 *The Poems of Sir John Davies*, ed. R. Krueger and R. Nemser (Oxford: Clarendon Press, 1975), pp. 431–4, quotation at 434.

20 Ibid., p. 432.

21 *Tottel's Miscellany*, ed. H.E. Rollins, 2 vols, rev. ed. (Cambridge, MA: Harvard University Press, 1965), vol. 2, pp. 93–101.

22 *The Phoenix Nest 1593*, ed. H.E. Rollins (Cambridge, MA: Harvard University Press, 1931), pp. xxiv–xxxi.

23 See J.W. Hebel, 'Nicholas Ling and *Englands Helicon*', *The Library*, fourth series, 5:2 (1924), 153–60; *Englands Helicon 1600, 1614*, ed. H.E. Rollins, 2 vols (Cambridge, MA: Harvard University Press, 1935), vol 2, pp. 41–63; G.D. Johnson, 'Nicholas Ling, Publisher 1580–1607', *Studies in Bibliography*, 38 (1985), 203–14.

24 *A Poetical Rapsody* (1602), sig. A3a.

25 On Breton's life and work see M.G. Brennan, 'Breton, Nicholas (1554/5–c.1626)', in *Oxford Dictionary of National Biography*, Oxford University Press, 2004, http://ezproxy.ouls.ox.ac.uk:2117/view/article/3341 (date accessed: 6 April 2012), and *Poems by Nicholas Breton Not Hitherto Reprinted*, ed. J. Robertson (Liverpool: Liverpool University Press, 1952), pp. xi–clix.

26 Four years after the Essex uprising Breton dedicated *The Honour of Valour* to Essex's great friend and political ally, Charles Blount, Earl of Devonshire, who was amongst those Essexians rehabilitated under the Jacobean regime. Its publisher, Christoper Purset, also published John Ford's elegy, *Fames Memoriall, or The Earle of Deuonshire Deceased* (STC 11158, 1606), printed by Richard Bradock, who had printed the 1603 edition of Essex's own *Apologie* (STC 6788).

27 In August 1590 the Earl of Pembroke wrote on behalf of 'Brittan a schoolmaster'. In a series of dedications (all of religious works) to the Countess, Breton repeatedly owns a debt of gratitude; in a dedication to a Herbert relation in 1597 he records obliquely some difficulty and default of her patronage; in 1601 he seems to register reintegration into favour (M.P. Hannay, *Philip's Phoenix: Mary Sidney, Countess of Pembroke* (Oxford and New York: Oxford University Press, 1990), pp. 136–9).

28 See H. Gazzard, 'Nicholas Breton, Richard Jones, and Two Printed Verse Miscellanies', *Notes & Queries*, 62:1 (2015), 79–82.

29 Nebeker, 'Ballads, Miscellanies, Lyric', p. 997.

30 L.G. Black, 'Studies in Some Related Manuscript Poetic Miscellanies of the 1580s', 2 vols (D.Phil. thesis, University of Oxford, 1971), remains an important and sustained examination of *C, Ra, Hy*, Archbishop Marsh's Library, Dublin, MS 23.5.21, Folger Shakespeare Library MS V.a.89 and the Arundel Harington MS. On *Ra* and verse miscellanies see further Randall Louis Anderson, '"The

Merit of a Manuscript Poem": The Case for Bodleian MS Rawlinson Poet. 85', in A.F. Marotti and M.D. Bristol (eds), *Print, Manuscript, and Performance: The Changing Relations of the Media in Early Modern England* (Columbus, OH: Ohio State University Press, 2000), pp. 127–71. On Harley MS 6910, see K.K. Gottschalk, 'Discoveries Concerning British Library MS Harley 6910', *Modern Philology*, 77:2 (November 1979), 121–31, summarising her findings in 'British Museum Manuscript Harley 6910: An Edition' (PhD dissertation, University of Chicago, 1974).
31 Anderson, 'The Merit', p. 134.
32 *The Library of Drummond of Hawthornden*, ed. R.H. MacDonald (Edinburgh: Edinburgh University Press, 1971), p. 198.
33 Williams, '"Vnder the Handes of …"', p. 68.

Sigla

AAD *The Arbor of Amorous Deuices* (London: Richard Jones, 1597, STC 3631).
Add British Library Add. MS 5956.
BBD N. Breton, *Brittons Bowre of Delights* (London: Richard Jones, 1591).
C Cambridge University Library MS Dd. 5.75: a verse miscellany, compiled by Henry Stanford (tutor to the household of William, Baron Paget and then Sir George Carey), c. 1585–98. See *Henry Stanford's Anthology: An Edition of Cambridge University Library Manuscript Dd. 5.75*, ed. S.W. May (New York: Garland, 1988); Black, 'Studies', vol. 1, pp. 55–9.
Cutts Michael's College, Tenbury Wells, MS 1018, fol. 10a, as transcribed in J.P. Cutts, '*The Strange Fortunes of Two Excellent Princes* and *The Arbor of Amorous Devices*', *Renaissance News*, 15 (1962), 2–11.
EH *Englands Helicon 1600, 1614*, ed. H.E. Rollins, 2 vols (Cambridge, MA: Harvard University Press, 1935).
F Agreement of the relevant passages from Edmund Spenser, *Prosopopoia. Or Mother Hubberds Tale*, from *Complaints*, in folio editions of Spenser's *Works* of 1617 and 1679 (the *Tale* was omitted from the 1611 folio), as reported in *The Works of Edmund Spenser: A Variorum Edition*, ed. E. Greenlaw, Charles Grosvenor Osgood and Frederick Morgan Pedelford, vol. 2, *The Minor Poems* (Baltimore: The Johns Hopkins Press, 1947).
Hy British Library Harley MS 7392 (2): manuscript, including important Sidney and courtly material, compiled principally by Humfrey Coningsby, probably (at least initially) when he was an undergraduate at Christ Church, Oxford, c. 1580–85. See H.R. Woudhuysen, *Sir Philip Sidney and the Circulation of Manuscripts, 1558–1640* (Oxford: Clarendon Press, 1996), pp. 278–85; Black, 'Studies', vol. 1, pp. 43–54. The compiler's cousin, Thomas Coningsby, had accompanied Philip Sidney on his Continental travels.
JD J. Dowland, *The Third and Last Booke of Songs or Aires* (London: Peter Short for Thomas Adams, 1603, STC 7096).
May S.W. May, 'The Poems of Edward De Vere, Seventeenth Earl of Oxford and of Robert Devereux, Second Earl of Essex', *Studies in Philology*, 77 (1980), 43–64.
MG *The Muses Garland* (London: ?Thomas Archer, 1603).
MR S.W. May and W.A. Ringler (eds), *Elizabethan Poetry: A Bibliography and First-Line Index of English Verse, 1559–1603*, 3 vols (London: Continuum, 2004).
NY Description, transcription and photo facsimiles of New York Public Library MS Arents n.52, fos 1a–2b, in *Tobacco: Its History Illustrated by the Books, Manuscripts, and Engravings in the Library of George Arents Jr*, introduction by J.E. Brooks (New York: The Rosenbach Company, 1937), vol. 1, pp. 352ff.
OP *The Poems of Sir Philip Sidney*, ed. W.A. Ringler (Oxford: Clarendon Press, 1962), Other Poems.
PN *The Phoenix Nest 1593*, ed. H.E. Rollins (Cambridge, MA: Harvard University Press, 1931).

PR A Poetical Rhapsody, 1602–1621, ed. H.E. Rollins, 2 vols (Cambridge, MA: Harvard University Press, 1931).

Q E. Spenser, *Prosopopoia. Or Mother Hubberds Tale*, in *Complaints. Containing Sundrie Small Poemes of the Worlds Vanitie* (London: for William Ponsonby, 1591, STC 23078): Bodleian Library copy (Malone 67), sigs O4b–P1a.

Ra Bodleian Library MS Rawl. poet. 85: a verse miscellany, possibly compiled by courtier and Cambridge graduate John Finet or Finett, in the 1580s. See L. Cummings, 'John Finet's Miscellany' (PhD thesis, Washington University, 1960); Black, 'Studies', vol. 1, pp. 36–42; Anderson, 'The Merit', in Marotti and Bristol, *Print, Manuscript, and Performance*; Marotti, *Manuscript, Print, and the Renaissance Lyric*, pp. 63–5; Woudhuysen, *Sir Philip Sidney and the Circulation of Manuscripts, 1558–1640*, pp. 260–2. But Peter Beal thinks the attribution to Finet 'questionable': www.celm-ms.org.uk/authors/dyersiredward.html, DyE1 (date accessed: 30 April 2018).

S British Library Sloane MS 1446: a miscellaneous collection, compiled 'no earlier than 1633 … and from several different sources'. See M. Hobbs, *Early Seventeenth-Century Verse Miscellany Manuscripts* (Aldershot: Scolar, 1992), pp. 74–8, at 78; Marotti, *Manuscript, Print, and the Renaissance Lyric*, p. 36.

SRO Staffordshire Record Office, Stafford, D5121/3/2/1.

U Union First Line Index of English Verse at http://firstlines.folger.edu/ (date accessed: 26 April 2019).

95 E. Spenser, *Amoretti and Epithalamion* ([London:] Peter Short for William Ponsonby, 1595, STC 23076), British Library copy (G11184) (= copy-text for *Edmund Spenser: The Shorter Poems*, ed. Richard A. McCabe (Harmondsworth: Penguin, 1999), siglum O).

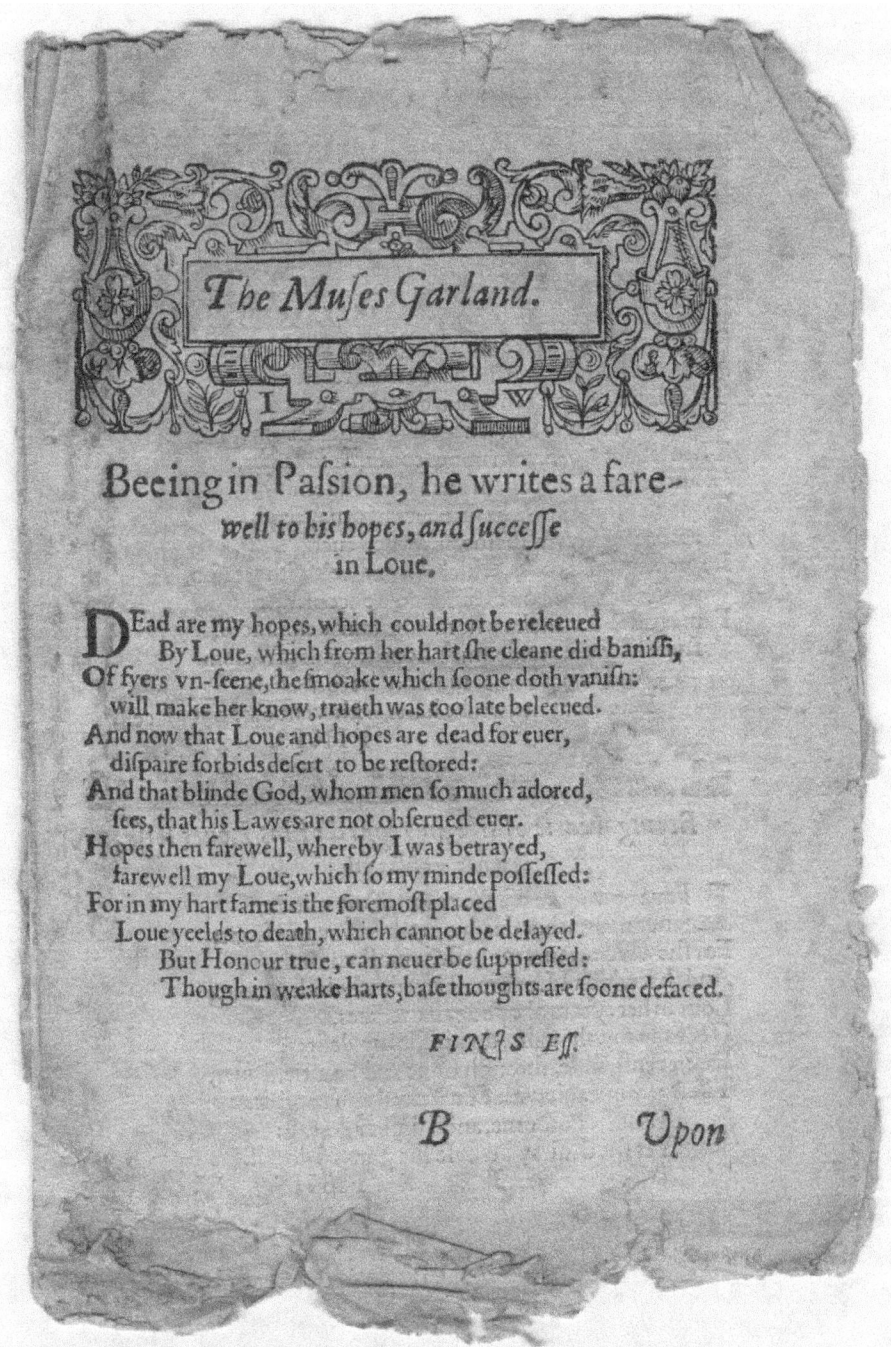

The Muses Garland.

Beeing in Passion, he writes a farewell to his hopes, and successe in Loue.

DEad are my hopes, which could not be releeued
  By Loue, which from her hart she cleane did banish,
Of fyers vn-seene, the smoake which soone doth vanish:
  will make her know, trueth was too late beleeued.
And now that Loue and hopes are dead for euer,
  dispaire forbids desert to be restored:
And that blinde God, whom men so much adored,
  sees, that his Lawes are not obserued euer.
Hopes then farewell, whereby I was betrayed,
  farewell my Loue, which so my minde possessed:
For in my hart fame is the foremost placed
  Loue yeelds to death, which cannot be delayed.
    But Honour true, can neuer be suppressed:
    Though in weake harts, base thoughts are soone defaced.

FINIS E.ss.

B   Vpon

The Muses Garland (?Thomas Archer, 1603). Reproduced with the permission of the curator of the Osborn collection, Beinecke Rare Book and Manuscript Library, Yale University Library.

Vpon better aduise, he writeth an
answere to the same.

Hopes are not dead, but sleepe, by beautie charmed,
  till Loue within her hart be full receiued.
The clearest fiers, of smoke are not bereaued
  time may repayre that which suspect hath harmed,
Then let not Loue, with hopes consume together,
  since that dispayre hath but a cowards end:
Though blinde he be, he such reuenge may send,
  as that his Lawes shalbe preserued euer.
Leaue not those hopes, which neuer dwelt with treason,
  nor Loue, least you of falshood be accused,
Fame hath bene theirs whom constancie embraced,
    Loue may not yeelde, since Loue is voide of reason.
      And honour true, must not be so abased:
      Base thoughts, weake harts, with vertue are not placed.
                    FINIS. *Eſſ.*

Beeing wearie of life, in regard of his Loues loſſe,
he wrote as followeth.

Leaue now deare life the prison of my minde,
  Since naught but death can take away my Loue:
For she which Loues me beste, is most vnkinde,
And that which I Loue most, my death doth prooue.
Loue in her eyes my hope againe reuiues,
Hopes in my thoughts do kindle my desires:
Desires enflamde, through Loue and beautie, striues,
Till she (displeasde with Loue) my death conspires:
    That Loue for me, and I for her do call:
    Yet she denies, because she graunts not all.
                  FINIS. *Eſſ.*

An answere imagined on his Loues behalfe.

LEaue not your life, which libertie may finde,
Nor seeke to change your faith professed long:
Since, if she Loue, her Loue is not vnkinde,
A constant hart subdueth any wrong.
And if that Loue did promise in her eyes,
That hopes within your thoughts should pleasure gaine:
Desire must not presume, that beauties skies
Will be displeasde, or punish Loue with paine.
    For if she graunt what Loue and honour may:
    Loue hath his due, and more you must not pray.
FINIS. Ess.

His conclusion vpon both the former.

IN such a life, no freedome can be found,
Where death must be the change to better hap:
And freeborne Loue, sweares he should not be bound
In chaines, when as he playes in beauties lap.
When to my thoughts, mine eyes had first conuaide,
The causes whence both Loue and wounder grew:
Desire did see no let, or cause of staye,
Till womans will (which reason neuer knewe)
    Her tirannie (by honour) did excuse:
    When she might all (as well) as one refuse.
FINIS. Ess.

To his fairest Mistresse.

MOre then most faire, full of the louely fire,
Builded aboue, the high Creatour neere:
Not eyes, but joyes, with whom all powers conspire,
That to the World, nought else is counted deere.
From your cleare beames does not the blinded guest
Shoote foorth his darts, to blame affections wounde:
But Angels come, to leade fraile mindes to rest,
In chaste desire to heauenly beautie bound.
You mooue my minde, you fashion me within,
You stay my tongue, and force my heart to speake:
You calme the Seas that passion doth begin,
Strong through your lookes, but through your vertues weake,
    Loue is not knowne, where your light shined neuer,
    Well is he borne, that may beholde you euer.

                            FINIS. *H. W. S.*

Of the fauour of the Gods vnto men.

OFt haue I heard of Stories long agoe,
That Gods for fauour they to men did beare:
Did raise them vp, euen from the earth belowe,
To sit aboue (as Gods) in heauens Spheare.
They were but men, whom fauour raisde so hye,
And they were Gods that fauour did rewarde:
In humble sorte contented yet am I,

                            Though

The Muses Garland.

Though in difpaire I dye without regarde,
For, if that Gods, as Gods, will serued be,
Then honour, dutie, feare to them belongs:
And let all earthly men be warnde by me,
How they presume to challenge CVPIDs wrongs.
    For madnes comes by ouer-ruled Looue:
    And madnes doth the Gods to vengeance mooue.

        FINIS.   S. P. S.

He writes a Sonnet vpon his owne poëfie,
vnder his Armes.

Virtutis comes Inuidia.

THe pureft Golde of all will fooneft weare
  With fretting rufte, which doth his vertue eate:
The faireft Trees, that fweeteft Rofes beare,
Of vileft Wormes are clad with plentie great.
The greeneft graffe, whofe blade doth higheft growe,
Is but a place where poyfoned Snakes remaine:
The fineft bodies, fooneft are brought lowe,
By fickneffe force, which doth their beautie ftaine.

Vertue is Golde, whofe woorth no man doth knowe,
Enuie the rufte, which thereon ftill doth feede:
Vertue the Tree, whereon fweet Rofes growe,
Enuie the worme, which doth the Cancker breede.

The Muses Garland.

Vertue the grasse which still doth florish greene,
Enuie the Snake that therein hydes him selfe:
Vertue may well be calde a bodie fine,
Enuie, disease, which would impaire his health.
    Though vertue be a vertue, more then this:
    Yet vnto her, Enuie companion is.

                              FINIS. *Ess.*

As desirous to be his Mystresses Painter.

ALL Things on earth, her fairenes farre excelles,
  All thoughts of men, my Loue as farre doth passe:
My troubled hart exceedes all other helles,
Yet is it to her face a perfect glasse:
Wherein, if she would but vouchsafe to see,
The Painter of her faire and louely hue:
Then should my Loue to her intreate for me,
For such reward as vnto him were due.
And, if she thought (of all men) I did best
Set foorth in collours, and come neere to life:
Then, that she would but trust me with the rest,
And thereby end a long continued strife.
    Then my true faith might ouercome her will:
    And I might wish to be her Painter still.

                    FINIS.   S. P. S.

Concerning his suite and attendance at the Court.

Ost miserable man, whom wretched fate,
Hath brought to Court, to sue for *Had-I-wist*:
That few haue found, and manie one haue mist.
Full little knowest thou, that hast not tryed
What hell it is, in suing long to bide:
To loose good dayes, that might be better spent,
To waste long nights in pensiue discontent.
To speede to day, and be put backe to morrowe,
Now fed with hope, now crost with waile-full sorrow.
To haue thy Princes grace, yet want her Peeres,
To haue thy asking, yet waite many yeeres.
To freat thy soule with crosses, and with cares,
To eate thy hart with comfortlesse despayres.
To fawne, to crouch, to waite, to bide, to run:
To spend, to giue, to want, to be vndone.
    Vnhappie wight, borne to disastrous end:
    That doth his life in so long tendaunce spend.

    FINIS. Edm. Spencer.

The poore labouring Bee.

IT was a time, when sillie Bees could speake,
And (in that time) I was a sillie Bee:
Who fed on time, vntill my heart did breake,
Yet neuer found the time to fauour me.
    Of all the swarme, I onely could not thriue:
    Yet brought I Waxe and Honie to the Hiue.

Thus then I buzde, when time no sappe would giue,
Why is this blessed time to me so drie?
Since (in this time) the lazie Droane doth liue,
The Waspe, the Worme, the Gnatt, the Butterflie.
    Mated with griefe, I kneeled on my knees:
    And thus complained to the King of Bees.

God graunt (my Liedge) thy time may neuer end,
And yet vouchsafe to heare my plainte of time;
While euery fruitlesse Flye hath found a freend,
I am cast downe, yet Atomies do climbe.
    The King replyed: But thou poore peeuish Bee,
    Art borne to serue the time, the time not thee.

The time not thee? this word clipt short my wings,
And made me Worme-like creepe, that once did flye:
A wefull regarde disputeth not with Kings,
Receiues repulse, yet neuer asketh why.
    Then from the time, a time I me with-drewe:
    To feede on Hem-lock, Henbane, Nettles, Rewe.

                                                I fed

B1a   [1]

Beeing in Passion, he writes a fare-
well to his hopes, and successe
in Loue.

Dead are my hopes, which could not be releeued
    By Loue, which from her hart she cleane did banish,
Of fyers vn-seene, the smoake which soone doth vanish:
    will make her know, trueth was too late beleeued.
And now that Loue and hopes are dead for euer,   5
    dispaire forbids desert to be restored:
And that blinde God, whom men so much adored,
    sees, that his Lawes are not obserued euer.
Hopes then farewell, whereby I was betrayed,
    farewell my Loue, which so my minde possessed: 10
For in my hart fame is the foremost placed
    Loue yeelds to death, which cannot be delayed.
        But Honour true, can neuer be suppressed:
        Though in weake harts, base thoughts are soone defaced.

FINIS *Ess.*

Not in *MR, U.*

B1b   [2]

Vpon better aduise, he writeth an
answere to the same.

Hopes are not dead, but sleepe, by beautie charmed,
    till Loue within her hart be full receiued.
The clearest fiers, of smoke are not bereaued
    time may repayre that which suspect hath harmed,
Then let not Loue, with hopes consume together,   5
    since that dispayre hath but a cowards end:
Though blinde he be, he such reuenge may send,
    as that his Lawes shalbe preserued euer.
Leaue not those hopes, which neuer dwelt with treason,
    nor Loue, least you of falshood be accused,   10
Fame hath bene theirs whom constancie embraced,
    Loue may not yeelde, since Loue is voide of reason.
        And honour true, must not be so abased:
        Base thoughts, weake harts, with vertue are not placed.

                FINIS *Ess.*

Not in *MR, U.*

The Muses Garland *(1603)*

[3]

*Beeing wearie of life, in regard of his Loues losse,
he wrote as followeth.*

Leaue now deare life the prison of my minde,
Since naught but death can take away my Loue:
For she which Loues me beste, is most vnkinde,
And that which I Loue most, my death doth prooue.
Loue in her eyes my hope againe reuiues,   5
Hopes in my thoughts do kindle my desires:
Desires enflamde, through Loue and beautie, striues,
Till she (displeasde with Loue) my death conspires:
    That Loue for me, and I for her do call:
    Yet she denies, because she graunts not all.   10

FINIS *Ess.*

MR EV 13272. Texts: *AAD* sig. B3b, *Cutts*.

[**Title**] *Beeing ... followeth.*] The complaint of one being in loue. *AAD; no title in Cutts* **1** now deare life] me O life, *AAD Cutts* **2** Loue:] lotte. *AAD* **3** Loues me best] likes me wel *AAD* loue me best *Cutts* **4** most,] best *AAD* **4–5]** *stanza-break in AAD* **5** hope] hopes *AAD Cutts* reuiues,] reuiue, *AAD Cutts* **6** desires:] desires, *AAD* **7** Desires enflamde,] Desire enflam'd *AAD* beautie, striues,] beauty striue, *AAD Cutts* **9** her] Loue *AAD Cutts* **10** denies,] ~ *AAD*

[**Subscription**] FINIS. *Ess.*] Finis. *AAD; not in Cutts*

B2a   **[4]**

An answere imagined on his Loues behalfe.

Leaue not your life, which libertie may finde,
Nor seeke to change your faith professed long:
Since, if she Loue, her Loue is not vnkinde,
A constant hart subdueth any wrong.
And if that Loue did promise in her eyes,   5
That hopes within your thoughts should pleasure gaine:
Desire must not presume, that beauties skies
Will be displeasde, or punish Loue with paine.
    For if she graunt what Loue and honour may:
    Loue hath his due, and more you must not pray.   10

                 FINIS *Ess.*

Not in *MR, U.*

[5]

His conclusion vpon both the former.

In such a life, no freedome can be found,
Where death must be the change to better hap:
And freeborne Loue, sweares he should not be bound
In chaines, when as he playes in beauties lap.
When to my thoughts, mine eyes had first conuaide,   5
The causes whence both Loue and wounder grew:
Desire did see no let, or cause of staye,
Till womans will (which reason neuer knewe)
    Her tirannie (by honour) did excuse:
    When she might all (as well) as one refuse.   10

FINIS *Ess.*

Not in *MR, U.*

B2b [6]

To his fairest Mistresse.

More then most faire, full of the louely fire,
Builded aboue, the high Creatour neere:
Not eyes, but joys, with whom all powers conspire,
That to the World, nought else is counted deere.
From your cleare beames does not the blinded guest   5
Shoote foorth his darts, to blame affections wounde:
But Angels come, to leade fraile mindes to rest,
In chaste desire to heauenly beautie bounde.
You mooue my minde, you fashion me within,
You stay my tongue, and force my heart to speake: 10
You calme the Seas that passion doth begin,
Strong through your lookes, but through your vertues weake,
    Loue is not knowne, where your light shined neuer,
    Well is he borne, that may beholde you euer.

FINIS. H.W.S.

MR EV 14827. Texts: *95* (sig. A5b), *C* (fol. 37b), *Hy* (fol. 28a), *Ra* (fol. 7b), *S* (fol. 43a).

Title *To … Mistresse*] *not in Ra C S Hy*; SONNET. VIII. *95*

1 More then] O more than *Ra* More fayr then *C*   faire,] ~ *Ra C S Hy*   the] that *S*   louely] living *Ra C S 95 subst.*   fire,] ~ *C S*   **2** Builded] Kindled *Ra C S Hy 95 subst.*   aboue,] ~ *Ra C S Hy 95*   the high Creatour] vnto the maker *Hy 95*   neere:] ~ *Ra C S Hy*   **3** Not] No *Ra S 95 subst.*   eyes, but joys,] ~ ~ ~ *Ra C* ~ ~ ~, *S 95*   with whom] wherew^th *Hy* in which *95*   all powers] the fates *Ra* ye hevvens *Hy* conspire,] ~ *Ra*   **4** to the] to y^e *Hy* in this *S*   World,] ~ *Ra C S Hy 95*   nought] naught *95* not *Hy* may *S*   is] be *Ra C S Hy 95*   deere.] ~ *Ra C*   **5-14** From … euer.] *not in Hy*   **5** From] Through *Ra C S 95 subst.*   your] theire *Ra*   cleare] deer *C* bright *95*   does] doth *Ra C S 95 subst.*   guest] ~, *95*   **6** foorth] out *S 95*   darts,] darte. *Ra* ~ *C S 95*   blame] blase *Ra* bare *C* base *S 95*   affections] affectinge *Ra*   wounde:] woundes. *Ra* ~ *C S*   **7** come,] ~ *Ra C S 95*   rest,] ~. *Ra* ~ *C S 95*   **8** desire] desires *Ra C S 95 subst.*   to] ohe *Ra* on *C S 95*   beautie] beauties *S*   bounde.] ~ *Ra S*   **9** You mooue my minde,] The mor my thoughtes. *Ra* You rule my thoughtes. *C* You hold my thoughtes. *S* You frame my thoughts. *95*   within,] ~. *Ra C S*   **10** stay] tie *S* stop *95*   tongue,] songe. *Ra* ~. *C S*   and] yet *R*   force] moue *C* teach *95*   my] myne *Ra* speake:] ~. *Ra C S* ~, *95*   **11** Seas] storme *Ra 95* stormes *C S* that] when *S*   passion] passions *S* doth] did *Ra 95* doe *S*   begin,] ~. *Ra* ~. *C S*   **12** lookes,] ~. *Ra* looke. *C* power. *S* cause, *95*   through] by *Ra 95*   vertues] vertue *Ra S 95 subst.* bewties *C* weake,] ~. *Ra C S* ~. *95*   **13** Loue is not] Dark is the *95*   knowne,] ~. *Ra C S* world, *95*   light shined] light shineth *S* loue shineth *C*   neuer,] ~. *Ra C* eu^er. *S* ~; *95*   **14** Well is he borne,] Thrise happy he. *Ra* blessed are they *C* ~ ~ ~ ~. *S*   that] w^ch *C*

[Subscription] FINIS. *H.W.S.*] Finis Mr Dier. *Ra* Finis. finis. finis *under horizontal rule H*; *not in C S*

[7]
Of the fauour of the Gods vnto men.

Oft haue I heard of Stories long agoe,
That Gods for fauour they to men did beare:
Did raise them vp, euen from the earth belowe,
To sit aboue (as Gods) in heauens Spheare.
They were but men, whom fauour raisde so hye,   5
And they were Gods that fauour did rewarde:
In humble sorte contented yet am I,
Though in dispaire I dye without regarde,
For, if that Gods, as Gods, will serued be,
Then honour, dutie, feare to them belongs: 10
And let all earthly men be warnde by me,
How they presume to challenge Cvpids wrongs.
    For madnes comes by ouer-ruled Looue:
    And madnes doth the Gods to vengeance mooue.

FINIS. *S.P.S.*

Not in *MR, U.*

[8]

He writes a Sonnet vpon his owne poësie,
vnder his Armes.

Virtutis comes Inuidia.

The purest Golde of all will soonest weare
With fretting ruste, which doth his vertue eate:
The fairest Trees, that sweetest Roses beare,
Of vilest Wormes are clad with plentie great.
The greenest grasse, whose blade doth highest growe,   5
Is but a place where poysoned Snakes remaine:
The finest bodies, soonest are brought lowe,
By sicknesse force, which doth their beautie staine.

Vertue is Golde, whose woorth no man doth knowe,
Enuie the ruste, which thereon still doth feede: 10
Vertue the Tree, whereon sweet Roses growe,
Enuie the worme, which doth the Cancker breede.
Vertue the grasse which still doth florish greene,   B3b
Enuie the Snake that therein hydes him selfe:
Vertue may well be calde a bodie fine,   15
Enuie, disease, which would impaire his health.
  Though vertue be a vertue, more then this:
  Yet vnto her, Enuie companion is.

FINIS. *Ess.*

Not in *MR*; *U* lists *Add* only. Texts: *Add* (fol. 54b), *SRO* (fol. 1a).

Title *He ... Inuidia.*] Virtutis Comes Invidia. | R: Essex:. *SRO* **3** Trees, that] trees which *SRO* **7** finest ... lowe,] Bodyes fine, are soonest brought full low *SRO* **8** beautie] beautyes *SRO* **11** whereon sweet] on which faire *SRO* **12** which] that *SRO* **14** that] which *SRO* **17** be a virtue,] ~, ~ ~ ̫

[Subscription] FINIS. *Ess.*] Rich: Bagott. | 1589. *SRO*

[9]

As desirous to be his Mystresses
Painter.

All Things on earth, her fairenes farre excelles,
All thoughts of men, my Loue as farre doth passe:
My troubled hart exceedes all other helles,
Yet is it to her face a perfect glasse:
Wherein, if she would but vouchsafe to see,   5
The Painter of her faire and louely hue:
Then should my Loue to her intreate for me,
For such reward as vnto him were due.
And, if she thought (of all men) I did best
Set foorth in collours, and come neere to life: 10
Then, that she would but trust me with the rest,
And thereby end a long continued strife.
    Then my true faith might ouercome her will:
    And I might wish to be her Painter still.

FINIS. *S.P.S.*

Not in *MR* or *U*.

B4a   **[10]**

Concerning his suite and attendance at the Court.

Most miserable man, whom wretched fate,
Hath brought to Court, to sue for *Had-I-wist*:
That few haue found, and manie one haue mist.
Full little knowest thou, that hast not tryed
What hell it is, in suing long to bide.   5
To loose good dayes, that might be better spent,
To waste long nights in pensiue discontent.
To speede to day, and be put backe to morrowe,
Now fed with hope, now crost with wailefull sorrow.
To haue thy Princes grace, yet want her Peeres,   10
To haue thy asking, yet waite many yeeres.
To freat thy soule with crosses, and with cares,
To eate thy hart with comfortlesse despayres.
To fawne to crouch, to waite, to bide, to run:
To spend, to giue, to want, to be vndone.   15
    Vnhappie wight, borne to disastrous end:
    That doth his life in so long tendaunce spend.

FINIS. EDM. SPENCER.

Extract from *MR* EV 12867. Texts: *Q, F*.

1 wretched] wicked *Q*   fate,] ~∧ *Q*   **2** *Had-I-wist*:] had ywist, *Q* had-ywist *F*   **3** haue mist.] hath mist; *Q*   **4** thou,] ~∧ *Q*   **5** it is] itis *MG*   bide.] ~: *Q*   **6** spent,] ~; *Q*   **7** discontent.] ~; *Q*   **8** and] to *Q*   morrow,] ~; *Q*   **9** Now ... sorrow.] To feed on hope, to pine with feare and sorrow; *Q*   **10** Peeres,] ~; *Q*   **11** yeeres.] ~; *Q*   **12** crosses,] ~∧ *Q*   cares,] ~; *Q*   **13** with] through *Q* despayres.] ~; *Q*   **14** fawne] ~, *Q*   bide,] ride, *Q*   run:] ~, *Q*   **16** end:] ~, *Q*

[Subscription] FINIS. EDM. SPENCER.] *not in Q, F*

The Muses Garland *(1603)*

B4b **[11]**

The poore labouring Bee.

It was a time, when sillie Bees could speake,
And (in that time) I was a sillie Bee:
Who fed on time, vntill my heart did breake,
Yet neuer found the time to fauour me.
  Of all the swarme, I onely could not thriue: 5
  Yet brought I Waxe and Honie to the Hiue.

Thus then I buzde, when time no sappe would giue,
Why is this blessed time to me so drie?
Since (in this time) the lazie Droane doth liue,
The Waspe, the Worme, the Gnatt, the Butterflie.   10
  Mated with griefe, I kneeled on my knees:
  And thus complained to the King of Bees.

God graunt (my Liedge) thy time may neuer end,
And yet vouchsafe to heare my plainte of time;
While euery fruitlesse Flye hath found a freend,   15
I am cast downe, yet Atomies do climbe.
  The King replyed: But thou poore peeuish Bee,
  Art borne to serue the time, the time not thee.

The time not thee? this word clipt short my wings,
And made me Worme-like creepe, that once did flye: 20
Awefull regarde disputeth not with Kings,
Receiues repulse, yet neuer asketh why.
  Then from the time, a time I me with-drewe:
  To feede on Hem-lock, Henbane, Nettles, Rewe.
      [catch-word] I fed

Fragment of *MR* EV 12846. Texts: *JD* (sig. K4b–sig. L1a: lines 1–18 only), *May*, *NY*.

Title *The … Bee.*] A Poem made on the Earle of Essex (being in disgrace with Queene Eliz): by mr henry Cuffe his Secretary. *May* **1** time,] ~ₐ *May JD* **2** And (… time)] ~ₐ~ ~ ~ₐ *May JD* Bee:] ~. *NY* ~, *May JD* **3** fed] suckt *May* time,] ~ₐ *May JD* did] gan *May JD* breake,] ~. *NY* **4** the] that *May* to] would *May JD* me.] ~; *May* **5** swarme,] ~ₐ *JD* could] did *JD* thriue:] ~, *May JD* **7** Thus then] Then thus *May JD* buzde,] buz'd, *NY* bussedₐ *May* **8** is] should *JD* so] be *JD* **9** Since (… time)] Sithₐ ~ ~ ~ₐ *May JD* liue,] ~. *NY* **10** Butterflie.] ~; *May* ~, *JD* **11** knees:] ~, *May JD NY* **12** to] unto *May JD* Bees.] ~: *May* **13** God … Liedge)] "My leige, god graunte *May* My liege, Gods graunt *JD* **14** vouchsafe] ~, *NY* time;] ~. *NY* ~, *May JD* **15** While] Which *May JD* euery … found] fruitlesse Flies haue found to haue *JD* freend,] ~. *NY* **16** I am] And I *May* downe, yet] ~ₐ while *May* ~ₐ when *JD* climbe.] ~." *May* **17** replyed:] ~, *NY* ~ₐ *May* But thou poore] but thus, "peace *May* but thus, Peace *JD* Bee,] ~. *NY* **18** Art] Th'art *May JD* borne] bound *JD* **19** The] "~ *May* thee?] thee" – *May* **20** creepe,] ~‸ *May* flye:] ~. *NY* ~; *May* **21** regarde] ~, *NY* **22** Receiues] Receaveth a *May* repulse,] ~‸ *NY* yet neuer asketh why.] not askinge whie; *May* **23** time, ... me] tyme I for a tyme *May* with-drewe:] ~, *NY May* **24** Hem-lock, Henbane,] Henbaine, Hemlock, *May* **catch-word** I fed] But from *May (beginning stanza 5)*

Commentary

Title *The Muses Garland*

Floral and arboreal titles for anthologies are of course perennial, or at least became so after Meleager's lost compilation *O Stephanos* ('The Garland'). This title is rich in aureate associations: with the pastoral lyricism of Drayton's *Idea*, whose complementary title is *The Shepheards Garland* (1593); with the modish and commonplace-organised Bodenham-sponsored collection of excerpts, *Belvedére, or, The Garden of the Muses* (1600). The subtitle of the third (1614) edition of *Englands Helicon* is *The Muses Harmony*. There might be a background cluster of associations around Spenser's *The Teares of the Muses* (1591), so on through Breton's 'Amoris Lachrymæ' (a dirge for Sidney), to 'Areteæ Lachrymæ', a subtitle of Gervase Markham's *Devoreux Vertues Teares* (1597), an elegy for Walter Devereux, Essex's brother. A 1610 book of airs set by Robert Jones was titled *The Muses Gardin for Delights*. John Davies of Hereford had devotional and elegiac collections published as *The Muses Sacrifice* (1612) and *The Muses-Teares* (1613).

MG 1–5

In the vein of Elizabethan court poetry, the first speaker's valediction might be taken to be privately amatory, or political, and a matter of courtship in the broadest sense: for the purported poet to be (transparently) the Earl of Essex is positively to enforce the political construction, and so the *she* who is addressed and whose replies are imagined is a very visible sovereign 'mistress'. It is very apt that the sonnet form should be one of those utilised for this. The elements of *MG* 1 and 2 (whose implied occasion is a plea for clemency and favour from the mistress/queen in the aftermath of disavowed 'treason'), and the insistence upon a personal and intact sense of honour in the face of political difficulty and, finally, disgrace, are evident in much of what was reported or written of, and by, Essex, throughout his tortuous life as a royal favourite, about that life.

Were these poems in fact written by Essex? How likely is it that he personally fashioned such a direct and charged suite of poems, but one which left no other trace than the apparently attributable and good texts presented here? The poems would cohere well in theme, if not closely in diction, with most of the eleven poems accepted by Steven May as canonically Essex's (in *May*): a crisis in love and loyalty, often intelligible as political no less than amatory, is their recurrent occasion. Compare, for example, the anguish of *MG* 1–5 with that in 'Change thy minde since she doth change', with its plaintive valediction 'Love farewell more deere to me / Then my life which thou preservest' (*May* no. 4), or 'And my vaine hopes which far to hie aspird / Are dead and buried, and for ever gone', in the sonnet 'To plead my faith where faith hath noe reward' (*May* no. 5). May's suggested reconstructions of specific occasions and uses for some of the poetry he accepts as Essex's – for *May* nos 1 and 3 – are persuasively presented but still, in their finer detail, very speculative. The attribution of *May* nos 4 and 5 looks secure, as does their likely communication to Dowland by Essex's servant musician Daniel Batchelor, but it must be conceded that they are so attributed only in Dowland. *May* nos 7, 8 and 9 might indeed be Essex's, though one witness's specification of an occasion sounds fabricated. Otherwise (and excluding *The Passion of a Discontented Minde*, *May* no. 11), nothing certainly rules out possible attribution to Essex of the rest of those accepted by May as his or possibly his. Perhaps, though, it is the very clarity of theme, and serviceable consistency of style, that makes attribution plausible but insecure: the writing is very imitable, and I have already noted that compilers of manuscript miscellanies might artfully misattribute, or just guess at authorship. Something of the difficulty of attribution under these circumstances is illustrated by John Chamberlain's sending to Dudley Carleton 'some verses that go under the name of my Lord of Essex when he was in disgrace, but I cannot warrant them to be his nor made at that time' (*The Letters of John Chamberlain*, ed. N.E. McClure, 2 vols (Philadelphia: The American Philosophical Association, 1939), vol. 1, p. 50).

It seems to me implausible that these studied poems, 1–5, are productions from Essex's final penitence in the Tower, yet they seem to presuppose just such penitential pleas for favour. May's eleven attributed poems (and a further four 'possibles', one of them the much-witnessed 'It was a time when silly bees could speak' – see *MG* 11 below) include the long penitential poem first printed in 1601 as *The Passion of a Discontented Minde*. I have argued elsewhere that the attribution to Essex of *The Passion* is implausible. It is a poem which, if Essex's, would enhance our sense of the art and scope of Essex's verse, and so lend extra credibility to the attributions in *MG*; but I have further argued, on the basis of internal indications and form, that the poem is probably by Nicholas Breton (Hugh Gazzard, 'Nicholas Breton, the Earl of Essex, and Elizabethan Penitential Poetry', *Studies in English Literature 1500–1900*, 56:1 (winter 2016), 23–42). It is striking that Breton wrote at least twice in prosopopoeia, in the person of his sometime patron, the Countess of Pembroke. Moreover, there is a record of his seeking to pass off a sonnet, most likely his own work, as King James's (see Gazzard, 'Nicholas Breton'). Breton may have sought similarly to present *The Passion* as Essex's, or to exploit some association it might have had with the earl; alternatively, that might have been done by someone else instrumental in the transmission of its text. Are these *MG* poems also by Breton, and similarly dissimulated? My notes below point to at least some suggestive verbal detail in support of what must remain a tentative case for attribution. We cannot know for sure in what context the poems might first have been fashioned, nor how, if they are not Essex's, they came to be attributed to him, save by someone keen to exploit – from factious feeling, from mercenary motives – his famous name.

It is possible that Breton had already also 'personated' Penelope, Lady Rich. A pastoral dream-vision elegy, 'Sitting late with sorrow(s) sleeping', exists in five manuscript versions (including in British Library Add. MS 34064, and *C*). In *Ra* (at fol. 14a) it is subscribed 'Britton'; in Harley MS 6910, 'La: R.' (see Black, 'Studies', vol. 2, pp. 246–7, for text and collation). Nothing else supports the latter attribution, which would present the poem as an elegy for Sir Philip Sidney, and probably the poem is by Breton.

Essex himself had betrayed what proved to be a prescient fear of a self being fashioned by others in a letter to the queen, from house arrest, in May 1600: 'I am gnawed on & torne by ye vilest & basest creatures vpon earth. The prating tavern hanter speaks of me what he list: the frantick libeller writes of me what he list; already they printe me, & make speak to ye world; and shortlye they will play me in what formes they list upon ye stage. The least of these is a thowsand tymes woorse then death' (National Archives, London, State Papers 12/274/138). In texts from the much-reprinted ballad *A Lamentable Dittie* (STC 6791), to

The Muses Garland *(1603)*

political polemic by Thomas Scott, *Robert Earle of Essex His Ghost, Sent from Elizian* ('Paradise', 1624, STC 22084), the earl would indeed be made to speak posthumously. *A Lamentable Dittie* was first printed by Edward Allde in 1603, just at the juncture where it was politic to round off the out-poured grief with 'God saue the King'. These poems add to that posthumous chorus, and seek to exculpate Essex the passionate lover/courtier from the shame of his downfall.

I offer more commentary below, and record a few parallels or similarities in phrasing between, especially, 1 and 2 (for which I think the strongest case for Breton might be made), and works by Breton: some are closer and less common in construction than others. Here and elsewhere information was partly supplied by searches on Literature Online (LION), on authors alive between 1550 and 1630.

1. Title The *he* is at once the subscribed speaker/poet, and, as in Tottel and *PR*, the generalised lover-speaker. This kind of topical and occasional title – seeming to capture the speaker/poet at a particular and vivid moment, creating an illusion of intimacy – is common in the printed miscellanies: compare, among many, '*A Louer finding his loue vnconstant, maketh his last farewell*' (*AAB*, sig. E2b).

1.1 Dead are my hopes The *Dead is / are my* ... collocation is rarer than one might expect: five hits in LION, only two earlier than *MG*, one of them 'Dead is my harte, oh earth receiue my corse', in 'His complaint against Loue and Fortune', in *BBD* (Rollins 25) – a love-complaint attributed to Nicholas Breton with a query in *MR*, and strongly by Rollins.

1.2 Loue, ... banish See Breton, *A Floorish vpon Fancie* (London: [William How for] Richard Jones, 1577, STC 3654, sig. I3b), 'true loue to banish cleane'.

1.9–10 Hopes ... Loue See, amongst its variable valedictions, 'And loue farewell, the Laborinthe of time, ... And hope farewell, the weakest holde of wit', in Breton, 'Sonet. I', 'A farewell to the world and the pleasures thereof' (in *The Passionate Shepheard, or The Shepheardes Loue*, ed. F. Ouvry (London: s.n., 1877), sig. C2a: the original of this, in the Rosenbach Library, is not on Early English Books Online, and I have not been able to check it). But the phrasing here is very conventional, popularised perhaps by the refrain ('*Farewell my hopes, farewell my happy daies*') to '*Menaphons* Song in his bedde' by Robert Greene, *Menaphon* (London: Thomas Orwin for Sampson Clarke, 1589, STC 12272), sig. G4a – adapted, for example, by Michael East, in *Madrigales to 3. 4. and 5. Parts* (London: Thomas Este, 1604, STC 7460), XXIII.

1.14 base ... defaced See Breton, *A Solemne Passion of the Soules Loue* (London: Simon Stafford for William Barley, 1598, STC 3696), sig. B2a: 'Against the power that would my thoughts deface'. *Thoughts* are the object of *defacing* in three other hits on LION.

1. [Subscription] *Ess.* I do not know of any example of Essex signing himself thus, nor being referred to thus elsewhere.

2.4 suspect hath harmed See Breton, *The Passionate Shepheard*, ed. Ouvry, 'Past. 4.' (sig. B3b): 'Where no colde suspect can harme thee': this subject–object construction with this diction is not found elsewhere in LION.

2.10–11 accused ... embraced Half-rhyme; see also *MG* 5.5, 7.

2.13 honour true Essex in effect very nearly went under *honour* as a cognomen; for the contemporary identification of him (in this case posthumously) as the type of the quality, note for example Robert Pricket's elegiac *Honors Fame in Triumph Riding* (London: R. Blower for Roger Jackson, 1604, STC 20339).

2.14 vertue The assertion of virtue's inviolability varies the claim staked in the (well-known) Devereux family motto, *Virtus comes inuidia* (see *MG* 8).

3 Texts A version of this poem had appeared (Rollins 10) in *AAD*, the only extant edition of which is dated 1597. I record its substantive and punctuation variants. The version from manuscript transcribed by Cutts accompanies an 'extraordinarily ornate' musical setting of the lyric; I record Cutts's substantive variants but not punctuation, or near lack of it. Unless its editor or compiler very heavily revised it, the text in *MG* was not derived from either of the versions in *AAD* or *Cutts*. A musical setting is a sign of this lyric's likely popularity. The version and ascription in *MG* render it of a piece with the imploring and plaintive love-weariness which (it is implied) define Essex's demeanour to his (royal) mistress. There has been no confident attribution of this poem, although Ringler implies it might be Breton's (William Ringler, 'Poems Attributed to Sir Philip Sidney', *Studies in Philology*, 47:2 (1950), 126–51, at 129). All that can be said with confidence is that it existed by 1597, and may have been in the lost first edition of *AAD* in 1594 – and that it echoes Sir Philip Sidney.

3.1 Leaue … life The obvious echo – even more obvious in *AAD* – is of the beginning of Sidney's valediction in the last (32) of 'Certaine Sonets' (as they were ordered in 1598 and elsewhere), 'Leave me o Love'. So the voice of Sidney the baffled lover can be heard behind that of Essex, the doomed courtier.

4, 5 Theme and authorship The pattern between 3 and 4 differs from that between 1 and 2, as here the voice of a proxy or advocate is making the '*Loues*' fictive response to 3. The political logic would demand that the speaker is speaking on '*behalfe*' of Essex's '*Loue*' – in part, the queen herself. In 4 and 5 there are some striking parallels apparent, but nothing conclusively to substantiate attribution to Essex, Breton or (tentatively) to somebody with Sidney–Herbert connections.

4.7 beauties skies The phrase migrates from Sidney, *Astrophil and Stella*, 100, 'Oh tears, no tears, but rain from beauty's skies', through five similar uses in Fulke Greville, *Cælica* (sonnets IV, XXXVII, XLI, LIX, LXXI), and on to here, then to John Davies of Hereford in *Wittes Pilgrimage* and to William Drummond (see LION): of those occurrences in sonnets, all are in connection with eyes.

5.3–4 And … chaines Did Samuel Daniel (attentive to all things Essexian) remember and refashion this conceit, in *A Funerall Poem vppon the Death of the Late Noble Earle of Deuonshyre* (London, 1606, STC 6256)? 'And am vntide from any other chaine / Than of my loue, which free-borne draws free breath' (sig. A1b).

5.6 Loue and wounder This coupling occurs first in Sidney's song 8 in *Astrophil and Stella*, line 28; then, *inter alia*, in Greville, *Cælica*, sonnet XLI, and his 'Inquisition vpon Fame and Honour', st. 83, in *Poems and Dramas of Fulke*

Greville, First Lord Brooke, ed. Geoffrey Bullough, vol. 1 (Edinburgh and London: Oliver & Boyd 1938), p. 97; then twice in the sonnet 'Yet, by the accidentall risingfall', in John Davies of Hereford, *Wittes Pilgrimage* (London: Richard Bradock for John Browne, [1605?]), sig. B2b.

5.9 Her tirannie Here, a politically incendiary phrase?

MG 6

This sonnet is a version of one printed in Spenser's *Amoretti*, as 'SONNET. VIII.'. The sonnet is manifestly related to the first three lines of Fulke Greville, *Cælica*, sonnet III: 'More than most faire, full of that heauenly fire, / Kindled aboue to shew the Makers glory, / Beauties first-born, in whom all powers conspire'. Bullough dates Greville's lyric to perhaps no earlier than 1578 (*Poems and Dramas of Fulke Greville*, ed. Bullough, vol. 1, p. 38), and seems to assume that Greville must have been echoing Spenser. But Spenser's precise ties, especially this early, to the Sidney circle remain uncertain. He might have known Greville's poetry in manuscript, and could consciously have emulated this opening. The matter is complicated by *Astrophil and Stella*, sonnet 100, line 3, 'Which ay most faire, now more then most faire show' (*The Poems of Sir Philip Sidney*, ed. W.A. Ringler, p. 231: substantively as 1598; different in Q1): a poem which begins with eyes' tears. It is also striking that, in *Amoretti*, this is the sole exception to the prevailing Spenserian sonnet form. Ponsonby's copy, in *Amoretti* (1595) and elsewhere, was good, and this seems no exception to his series of evidently authorised publications of Spenser through the 1590s; but still the echo and the verse form are awkward features to explain. Probably the priority in composition, across Greville – Sidney – Spenser, will never be established; possibly it does not much matter. The conjoint and new poetic of the Sidney circle – impassioned, Neoplatonist – is manifest here.

As well as these two printed versions of the sonnet, four versions (one incomplete) exist in manuscript, first described and transcribed by Laurence Cummings, 'Spenser's *Amoretti VIII*: New Manuscript Versions', *Studies in English Literature 1500–1900*, 4:1 (winter 1964), 125–35. The version in *MG* was either not derived from print or was so derived but was strongly revised. The variance across these versions is marked and frequent. In the apparatus above I have recorded substantive variants from the manuscripts (I have not yet checked Cummings's transcription of *C* against the original), and I have recorded all variation in punctuation (the manuscript versions are lightly punctuated). I disagree with Cummings on three points of punctuation, and one important substantive: I am sure the *Hy* reading (like all the witnesses) at line 4 is 'world', not the strained 'would', and so also 'y^e' is the definite article and not the second-person pronoun. Except where they might be of possible evidential value for analysing transmission, I have not recorded variant spellings.

Cummings hesitates around authorial revision, scribal licence and scribal error as the chief determinant of the variance on display, but the bulk of his proposed model for the transmission of the poem – a model which appears, by his own admission, 'complex and highly conjectural', and indeed 'flimsy' ('Spenser's *Amoretti VIII*', 132, 133) – is made up of alleged serial scribal error and a succession of authorially revised recensions. He offers explanations for readings which rely on sometimes extremely tenuous speculation about features of hands in hypothesised exemplars. His account is heavy on the errors of hapless copyists: 'mnemonic fault ... confusions ... misreading ... corrupted copy ... an easy mistake' abound (131).

This poem's textual transmission is not my prime concern here, although, for what it is worth, my own reading of the evidence which I have set out in the apparatus above is that *95* and *Hy* belong to one tradition, neither being copied from the other; that *Ra*, *C*, *S* and *MG* belong to another tradition, with *S* (note its late date) probably deriving from a version closely but not immediately anterior to *Ra* and *C* and *MG*; that *Ra* and *MG* may have been copied from the same source; and that there is evident no other immediate anteriority of any one of these texts to any other of them. Given what Cummings observes about the scarcity of Spenser's poems in manuscript it might seem surprising that the texts of this poem imply several more, lost, witnesses. But the poem's relation to the lyric by Greville might have made this in several respects a special case.

This version's origin might lie in a manuscript miscellany like those surviving ones that preserve it. Variants such as those in line 9 may less likely be the product of a complicated series of lapses of legibility than of a process of, perhaps, authorial revision, combined with, certainly, the *social* character of these received texts – some alterations and adaptations made by copyists according to their own tastes in verse, and to the wider conditions of transmission. A model of 'social textuality', most fully developed by Marotti, allows for the results of memorial and oral transmission, and for fairly free conflation of texts, reconstruction, condensation and so on. In one case the copyist in *Ra*, for example, 'either accidentally or deliberately, merged excerpts from two Sidney poems ... to create a new poem' (Marotti, *Manuscript, Print, and Lyric*, ch. 3, esp. pp. 135–47, quotation at p. 143). Copyists – for themselves, for friends, in loose leaves, bifolia and booklets, in commonplace books, on various fugitive occasions, quickly or with care – might feel little inhibition about transmitting texts in a more creative way than models of mere 'corruption' can adequately explain. It might be that 'the time has come ... to move from a genealogy of *texts* to a genealogy of *tastes*' (Anderson, 'The Merit', p. 132).

The sonnet's subscription is a puzzle. I find suggestions around 'Henry Wriothesley Southampton' implausible. There may be some clue in the forms '*G:W. senior*' and '*G.W.I.*' (possibly Geoffrey Whitney, father and son: Andrew Hadfield, *Edmund Spenser: A Life* (Oxford: Oxford University Press, 2012), p. 302) attached to commendatory sonnets in *Amoretti*; is the 'S' here in *MG*, 'Senior'? I still suspect that a possible explanation is a compositorial or scribal misreading of 'EDM. S', where the first element was heavily flourished, to the point of literal ambiguity.

MG 7

I have set out at length elsewhere my analysis of this striking and strong sonnet, and the case which I think can be made for its being indeed the work of the obvious decipherment, Sir Philip Sidney (H. Gazzard, 'Two New Sonnets by Sir Philip Sidney?', *Sidney Journal*, 34:2 (2016), 25–48). This would not be a unique modern addition: Peter Beal's discoveries in the 'Ottley Manuscript' have a little enlarged the Sidney canon (P. Beal, 'Poems by Sir Philip Sidney: The Ottley Manuscript', *The Library*, fifth series, 33:4 (1978), 284–95). I argue that the poem advances a complex caution about the dangers of the favour and disfavour of the gods, and of repining at Cupid's depredations on mortals. (Cupid appears twice elsewhere in *MG*.) I identify analogous contexts in the *Old Arcadia* and *Certain Sonnets*, where it is even possible that this poem originated, and consider the putative attribution in relation to the textual transmission of Sidney's poetry generally, and to relevant aspects of printed and manuscript verse miscellanies. I offer some stylistic analysis pointing to parallel diction and sentiments elsewhere in Sidney's works.

The survival of a Sidney poem not witnessed elsewhere is not so implausible. *Poems*, ed. Ringler, *OP* 6 and 7 each survive in only one substantive early text, and CS 5, 29 and 32 in only two. We know that the Countess of Pembroke did not put into print everything of her brother's work that she might have. The 1613 edition of Sidney's works (whoever was its editor) included a previously unpublished poem. Sidney's work, and poems from *Certain Sonnets* especially, featured prominently in several printed songbooks and verse miscellanies, including those 'Two Pastoralls' (*Poems*, ed. Ringler, *OP* 6 and 7) in the Francis Davison anthology *A Poetical Rapsody* (1602). We can infer that more, perhaps many more, sources for Sidney poems have not come down to us. Whoever wrote *MG* 3 was surely echoing Sidney's *Certain Sonnets* 32 in its first line – or was echoed by it. *MG* 3 had appeared in *AAD* in 1597, and presumably also in the lost edition of that miscellany in 1594. So it seems that the poet of *MG* 3, if echoing, knew *Certain Sonnets* 32 in manuscript (where it now survives only in the Clifford MS), since it did not appear in print until 1598. In other words, at least some Sidney material was being circulated or was accessible in manuscript through the 1590s and even beyond. As for earlier circulation, Woudhuysen notes that *Certain Sonnets* poems might have been 'released piecemeal', and 'it would be rash to suggest anything very certain about the early circulation of the *Old Arcadia* poems. They may have originally been available as a group from which collectors took the ones which caught their fancy, or they may have been released piecemeal: the evidence, such as it is, leans slightly towards the first of these' (Woudhuysen, *Sidney*, pp. 248, 249: and see ch. 9, 'The Miscellanies', generally).

MG 8

The pronoun in the poem's title is, obviously, Essex again. These verses are found in *SRO*, fol. 1a, in a single bifolium, the first item in an unbound bundle of materials apparently detached from some papers of Richard Bagot. The verses, titled as recorded in the collation above, are subscribed by Bagot, dated 1589, and are I think in his hand – and were very possibly composed by him. The Bagots of Blithfield were Staffordshire gentry and later ennobled, and were close allies of the Devereux; at an uncertain date Essex wrote to Richard attesting that 'I must remember my old frendes and best neighbours. amongst whom y^{r}self may challenge one of the first places', signing himself 'y^r very louing neighbour and frend' (SRO D5121/3/1, [fol. 140a]). Substantive variants here are not very significant, and I have not recorded all variant punctuation. The verses were printed, apparently from *SRO*, in *Memorials of the Bagot Family*, ed. William, second Baron Bagot (Blithfield, 1824), p. 46.

The poem is also in *Add*: a miscellaneous collection, mainly Jacobean; Devereux-related material includes copies of some Essex correspondence, and of some documents from the Essex divorce case of the next generation. Other material includes a text of *The First Antimasque of Mountebanks* (performed 1618). There the poem has no title or subscription, but 'ver com: inuid:' is written in the left-hand margin. The stanzas are divided and the concluding couplet indented as in print. The poem – upside-down to the rest of the MS – is lightly scored through with a lattice of penstrokes, as though for deletion. It has no substantive variants from *MG*.

The Devereux family motto, warning that 'envy is the companion of virtue', seems to originate in Cicero, but there is some distance between that and this poem's accumulation of simple saws. The motto's defensiveness became apt for the earl as he saw himself beset by factional enemies and detractors; examples of his and his allies' comments on this are too numerous to itemise, but none of them exactly alludes to the Latin tag as this poem does. The motto is quoted, in the context of a defence of the Earl of Leicester, in 'The dead mans Right', prefixed to *The Phoenix Nest* (sig. A4b). Perhaps, if this poem was composed in 1589, it was occasioned by the very public difficulties and royal disfavour Essex encountered after his insubordinate participation in the Portugal expedition.

Title For this styling, see a poem headed 'The nexte was at request of *Antonie Kynwelmarshe*, who deliuered him this theame, *Satis sufficit*, and therevpon he wrote as followeth', in Gascoigne, *A Hundreth Sundrie Flowres* (London: Henry Bynneman [and Henry Middleton] for Richard Smith, 1573, STC 11635), sig. U3a – for a poem accumulating proverbs occasioned by a Latin tag. This is an 18-line 'Sonnet' as are those in Thomas Watson, *Hekatompathia* (1582).

MG 9

Given my arguments here and in 'Two New Sonnets' about the provenance and transmission of *MG* 7, and the (perhaps slight) likenesses to Sidney work noted in 'Two New Sonnets', the like case can be made for this as for the other 'S.P.S.' poem. *Astrophil and Stella* sonnet 7, a much more complicated poem than this, imagines Nature as having made Stella and her black eyes 'like painter wise', and is about ways of offsetting darkness in pictorial composition. The idea of the sonneteering lover-poet as a painter occurs in several sequences (see Gazzard, 'Two New Sonnets'), beginning with *Astrophil and Stella*.

MG 10

This poem is a version of a passage from Spenser, *Prosopopoia: or Mother Hubberds Tale*, corresponding to lines 892–908 in Richard A. McCabe's edition of Spenser's *Shorter Poems*. With the marked exception of *MG* line 9 / Q line 900, most of the differences (including orthographic differences, not recorded here) are slight, and mainly affect punctuation. But the variant in *MG* line 9 suggests that, unless the line sophisticates something damaged or unclear in printed copy, the copy for *MG* was not the 1591 printed edition – quite possibly difficult to come by – but a manuscript of some authority. The rendering *Had-I-wist* in line 2 seems to me superior to that in print, preserving the probable origin of what was a stock phrase – to sue, only to receive an *If I had only known* brush-off from the powers-that-be; for a long list of instances of the phrase see R. Edwards, *The Paradise of Dainty Devices, 1576–1606*, ed. H.E. Rollins (Cambridge, MA:

Harvard University Press, 1927), pp. 182-3. The whole of the *Tale* survives in manuscript in British Library Harley MS 6910, 'a careful copy of the text according to the Houghton 2 ... copy of Q'. At least two further manuscript fragments of the *Tale* survive but do not preserve these lines (*The Works of Edmund Spenser: A Variorum Edition*, ed. E. Greenlaw, Charles Grosvenor Osgood and Frederick Morgan Pedelford, vol. 2, *The Minor Poems* (Baltimore: The Johns Hopkins Press, 1947), pp. 687-8).

The passage's acrid blast of anti-curial complaint was perhaps very well known to contemporaries. Early commentators singled it out and were ready to construe it as offering, and being understood to offer, a withering glance at Burghley – so Todd in 1805: 'This passage is supposed to have been represented to Lord Burleigh as a censure upon him' (quoted in *Spenser Variorum*, vol. 2, p. 569). It seems likely that the printed *Tale* had been 'called in', as a range of contemporary comment suggests – from Harvey's 'Mother Hubbard in heat of choller ... wilfully ouer-shott her malcontented selfe' (G. Harvey, *Foure Letters, and Certaine Sonnets* (London: John Wolfe, 1592, STC 12900.5), sig. B1a), to Middleton's 'She that was calde in for selling her working Bottle-Ale to Bookebinders, and spurting the Froth vpon Courtiers Noses' (Thomas Middleton, *The Blacke Booke* (London: T.C. for Jeffrey Chorlton, 1604, STC 17875), sig. D4b); see also Nashe's mixed report in *Strange Newes* (1592) (*The Works of Thomas Nashe*, ed. R.B. McKerrow, rev. F.P. Wilson, 5 vols (Oxford: Blackwell, 1958), vol. 1, pp. 281-2). The inclusion of the passage in *MG* strengthens the case for regarding it, and the *Tale*'s satire-fable, as having a specific, as well as general, political application. For further comment on the passage and the whole poem, and on the satire and censorship issues, see *Spenser Variorum*, vol. 2, pp. 568-85, and Spenser, *Shorter Poems*, ed. McCabe, 608-21.

MG 11

This is a version of the first four stanzas of the poem which was perhaps the best-known of those associated with Essex, whether as its understood speaker (the bee himself) or as its author. Steven May's copy-text is British Library Harley MS 6947, fos 230a-231b. At least seventeen of the copies which attribute the poem ascribe it to Essex; indeed, it is *his* 'Bee', his 'Buzze'. Three, including Harley 6947, ascribe it to Essex's secretary, Henry Cuffe. Where they are circumstantial, the most plausible titles date the occasion and composition to the time of Essex's disgrace in the summer of 1598 (see *May*, 111-13). From the number of its manuscript witnesses, this poem probably has the best-attested claim of any of those presented as certainly or possibly by Essex in May's edition – May classes it there as a possible. But, if only on the principle *lectio difficilior potior*, the attribution to Cuffe has some attraction, as a less expected and obscurer name than the earl's (S.W. May, *The Elizabethan Courtier Poets: The Poems and Their Contexts* (Columbia, London: University of Missouri Press, 1991), pp. 250-69, reprints the 'eleven canonical poems' and four possibly by Essex, without commentary or apparatus).

May, 110-11, and 111 n. 64, recorded thirty-five complete or partial, manuscript or printed texts of the poem, and collated twenty-eight of them; *MR* adds one of great interest: *NY*. May notes that seventeen texts 'descend from the author's original through a common ancestor which lacked stanza 5, lines 25-30'

(*May*, 109). *NY* and *MG* agree in all substantives, sometimes against all other witnesses, including in title, and they agree in much punctuation (including, most significantly, in parentheses), the more so if we count some line-terminal periods in *NY* as having the value of a comma's pause. *MG* and *NY* agree so closely, indeed, that either they are each scrupulously accurate in copying a common exemplar or one was copy for the other. The catch-word in *MG* shows that the next stanza, which must have followed on the next leaf, does not begin as it does in any other version save *NY*, which reads 'I fed on weeds when Moone was' instead of 'I worke on weedes when moone is' (*May*, st. 6). *NY*, moreover, lacks stanza 5, so both it and, evidently, *MG* stand in the fourteen-stanza tradition of the poem. But it should be added that May's apparatus shows much agreement between the two 'traditions', and some disagreement within each. *JD* does not show signs of being directly derivative of, or the source for, *MG* or *NY*. *NY* is subscribed 'Finis --- / Essex.'.

Some substantives in *MG* and *NY* lines 15–17 (e.g. 'But thou poore' instead of 'but thus, Peace' or 'but this, Peace') are not found in any other witnesses, and make for a unique construction of the reply of the 'King of Bees'. *MG* and *NY* also agree substantively, sometimes against most or all other witnesses, variously with May's *P* (fourteen-stanza), with May's *S* and with May's *Ta* (both fifteen-stanza), and with combinations of those three; but those three each differ so widely in other, at least as evidential, substantives that no very close relation can be inferred. I think that, rather than hypothesise a whole new stemma which led to those readings, it is more plausible to conclude that the most marked *MG* and *NY* variants might have arisen within either, from freedoms a copyist took in recension of the text.

I record substantive and punctuation variants between *MG*, *May* and *JD*, and in line 7 one orthographic variant. May's edition is diplomatic save that, with punctuation, he 'added apostrophes, quotation, and question marks' (*May*, 22). The textual apparatus for the whole poem in May fills four dense pages. Constraints of space preclude my adding here the remaining eleven stanzas of the poem, as given by May.

This stinging apiarian satirical allegory must have been the best-known, and is in some ways the best, of the poems associated with Essex. Its astringent tone and probably personal scope ensured its wide manuscript circulation, and the only other known appearance in print was of just the first three stanzas in John Dowland's 1603 songbook, an amatory collection not obviously politicising its material (for further comment on the poem, see *May*, 109–14). It is extraordinary that it should have been put into print in the context of this fragment, especially at this time. The poem caps the remarkably rich and important material making up *MG*, and amplifies the plaintive voice of Essex. Bearing the standard for the earl, and making Sidney and Spenser come alive again, it is only to be regretted that this memorable anthology should have been lost for so long, and now should have been found in so fragmentary a condition.

9

The sonnet sequence as speech sound continuum: how we read *Shake-speares Sonnets*

Andrew Eastman

The sonnet's cultural centrality is inseparable, this chapter will argue, from current editing practices and the conceptions which underlie them, as shown in the way Shakespeare's *Sonnets* are usually given us to read. How do we read *Shake-speares Sonnets* – by which I mean the 1609 Quarto, the only edition of the sonnets to be published in Shakespeare's lifetime? Generally, of course, we read them as filtered, revised, rewritten we might even say, in modern, that is to say modernised, editions. What seems to characterise modern editors' approaches generally is a focus on the individual poem, perhaps to the detriment of a generalised poetics of the Quarto. This is borne out by the way the sonnets are given us to read in our modern editions: as isolated texts, two or one to a page, with commentary facing or following. We find this format even when the 1609 Quarto text is presented alongside a modernised version (as in Vendler's *The Art of Shakespeare's Sonnets*); even the recent Oxford 'original-spelling text' edited by Paul Hammond adopts it.[1] Yet, unlike the sonnets of the 1592 *Delia* (by Samuel Daniel) or the 1594 *Ideas Mirrour* (by Michael Drayton), printed one to a page, *Shake-speares Sonnets* unroll in a continuous series, with fragments of sonnets finishing or beginning on every page. Among modern editions – to my knowledge – only Stephen Booth's preserves this pagination. The presentation of the *Sonnets* in the Quarto at least suggests that the basic unit is not the sonnet but the sequence. Reading the sonnets then, would involve tracing recurrences or continuities, linguistic traits or gestures which seem to characterise the writing of the Quarto, or characterise the Quarto as writing, reading the sonnets, then, not as a 'sequence' but as one poem.

What this predominant mode of presentation – one sonnet to a page – implies is that the force of the texts is located in the rhetoric of the individual sonnet, in the way it functions *as* sonnet; while the cumulative force of the 'sequence' as poetic continuum is of less concern, mentioned in passing or in terms of the connections between individual poems. And clearly there is a benefit in this: the sonnet isolated is a boon to ingenious close reading, as great readers like Vendler have shown. But perhaps it also shifts our attention from the poetics of the sequence, as linguistic invention, to the staging of a 'lyric voice' and a speaker's attitudes, to the ways the speaker's language undercuts itself, so that irony becomes the major signifier of literariness. The *Sonnets* is, as MacD.P. Jackson shows, not only a collection of poems but a powerfully connected and cohesive work.[2] If one reads *across* the sonnets, reads the sequence as continuum, a different set of problems is posed: it is a question no longer of the rhetorical means of staging attitudes but rather of what the sonnets are doing to English.[3]

One significant linguistic gesture which is brought into focus when we read *Shakespeare's Sonnets* as a speech sound continuum is Quarto punctuation, especially line-internal, which, I argue, must be attended to. Why punctuation? And what can be said about the erratic, sometimes clearly erroneous pointing of the Quarto? It is precisely when read cross-sequence, and not simply in the context of the individual passage or poem, that punctuation takes on significance and can no longer be dismissed as arbitrary; when we recognise systematicities – 'repeated patterns of usage', notes Carl D. Atkins[4] – which work in significant conjunction with other semantic processes – grammar, position, rhythm, phrasing, phonemic echo. Punctuation thus approached would provide a way of grasping the continuum of subjectivity in the language of the sequence.

Looking at how modern editions treat Quarto punctuation, we come upon a paradox: if what is at stake in the sonnets is, as Vendler writes, creating 'a "real voice" coming from a "real mind" like our own',[5] why is Quarto punctuation so often reduced to the conventions of modern prose? Unsurprisingly, what gets lost when punctuation is modernised is some of the rhythmic gestures of the Quarto. One would think these were essential to the suggestion of emotional nuance, to the representation of a mind thinking. I will attempt to argue that these gestures are simultaneously rhythmic and grammatical – that they are explorations of the limits and implications of English, of how we think the world in English – and, to the extent that they recur systematically in the Quarto characterise a generalised mode of enunciation.

An example of how the problem might be posed can be seen in sonnet 64, shown here first in a transcription from the Quarto (I follow Hammond's edition) and then in the version published by Colin Burrow for the Oxford *Complete Sonnets and Poems*:

> When I haue seene by times fell hand defaced
> The rich proud cost of outworne buried age,
> When sometime loftie towers I see downe rased,
> And brasse eternall slaue to mortall rage.
> When I haue seene the hungry Ocean gaine
> Aduantage on the Kingdome of the shoare,
> And the firme soile win of the watry maine,
> Increasing store with losse, and losse with store.
> When I haue seene such interchange of state,
> Or state it selfe confounded, to decay,
> Ruine hath taught me thus to ruminate
> That Time will come and take my loue away.
>   This thought is as a death which cannot choose
>   But weepe to haue, that which it feares to loose.[6]

> When I have seen by Time's fell hand defacèd
> The rich proud cost of outworn buried age,
> When sometime lofty towers I see down razèd

And brass eternal slave to mortal rage;
When I have seen the hungry ocean gain
Advantage on the kingdom of the shore,
And the firm soil win of the wat'ry main,
Increasing store with loss, and loss with store;
When I have seen such interchange of state,
Or state itself confounded to decay,
Ruin hath taught me thus to ruminate,
That Time will come and take my love away.
 This thought is as a death, which cannot choose
 But weep to have that which it fears to lose.[7]

This poem's reflection on time and loss is organised around the repetition of the verb *have*, which functions, in lines 1, 5, 9 and 11, as the auxiliary verb of the present perfect aspectual form ('I haue seen …', 'Ruin hath taught me'); and, in the closing line, as a 'lexical verb', denoting possession, and this association between 'grammatical' and 'lexical' 'have' is clearly central to a consideration of how possession, or identity, is undone by time. The last line, organised around the opposition between 'to have' and 'to lose', asks *what* having consists in in a world governed by loss; or what may *be* 'had'.

Looking again at the Quarto text, we find that a comma has been introduced after 'haue', marking what for us is an odd, non-logical pause between the verb and its complement, 'that'; but given the fact that Shakespeare's decasyllables often do break, as Puttenham recommends, after the fourth syllable, the pause here is, metrically speaking, natural.[8] However odd its syntactic placement, the comma, as Paul Hammond argues, clearly has the function of emphasising 'haue', in a context where having itself is in question.[9] But it does more: on the one hand it serves to bring together in a speech unit the paradoxically associated 'weepe' and 'haue'; on the other hand, introducing a pause, it also leads us to place some accent or emphasis on the word that follows (partly because a pause requires a new effort or new energy to resume speech), and so on the 'empty' grammatical word 'that', raising the question of just what 'that' is, that we have, love or lose. Most important, here, I think, is the comma's function of grouping: in a poem about losing, it at once links and separates the subject and object of having, marks the problematic connection between haver and had, places a thumb, so to speak, on the sore point of the whole affair.

Looking at Burrow's edition of the sonnets, we see that he has removed the comma; the editions of Ingram and Redpath, Booth, Kerrigan, Vendler, and Duncan-Jones adopt the same punctuation. One problem with Burrow's version, I would argue – but perhaps I am influenced by the Quarto punctuation – is that we do not really know *how* to read it: we are unsure, at first, to what extent the quasi-auxiliary word 'have' should take an accent, and would like to shift the accent to 'that': 'And weep to have thát which it fears to lose'. This comes particularly from the tendency, in English, to subordinate the accent of the verb to that of the object. Probably it is not fair to expect a 'standard' edition of the *Sonnets* to punctuate in ways that are foreign to modern readers. Yet, poetically speaking, the Quarto punctuation must be seen as particularly forcible: it is a rhythmic invention, inseparable from the line's syntax and its rhetorical structure, antithesis, but which, rather than doubling the syntax, introduces a supplementary system of organisation which cuts against syntactic connection; precisely through the separation it effects, it is a grammar, and plays a key role in the sonnet's internal cohesion.

Any attempt at reading the Quarto punctuation is of course caught up in the history of our approaches to this text. The appearance of Paul Hammond's 'Original-spelling edition', published by Oxford in 2012, may mark a shift in attitudes towards the Quarto, a shift which may also be traced in the way editing the sonnets has evolved since the 1960s. Interest in, and justification of, early modern punctuation goes back to the turn of the nineteenth and twentieth centuries; in 1898, George Wyndham published an edition of the poems which, according to Ingram and Redpath, 'argues at length for the authenticity and purposive significance of [the Quarto] punctuation'.[10] Such approaches, however, were brought into question by later twentieth-century bibliographical scepticism. MacD.P. Jackson, in an article from 1970, proposed to show that type for the *Sonnets* was set by two compositors with markedly different approaches to spelling and punctuation;[11] for John Kerrigan, editor of the Penguin Shakespeare *Sonnets* in 1986, Jackson's work 'finally set the textual criticism of these poems on a sound footing'[12] – by which he seems to mean, justified the editor in feeling no compunction about rewriting the poems. Jackson's argument, of course, questioned the 'authenticity' of the punctuation, the extent to which it might be attributed to Shakespeare himself. But, we might note, Jackson made no claims about *line-internal* punctuation, which he took as possible evidence for the poems' date of composition, treating it thus implicitly as 'authorial'.[13]

Hammond's recent 'original-spelling edition' views the 'accidentals' of the Quarto text, even if they are due to a compositor, as having intrinsic interest and value. His approach to punctuation, however, has the effect of reinforcing the focus on the individual sonnet. He cites, for example, two main functions for the comma, first, as metrical pause, second, as emphasis, separating then 'form' and 'content' without showing how they might be related; similarly, he describes early modern punctuation as 'rhetorical', reducing it then to an expressive device, a tool in the staging of speech and the portrayal of psychology – and not then as a rhythmics specifying a way of writing.[14] Hammond draws on the work of Percy Simpson, who, however, in his *Shakespearian Punctuation* of 1911, states the distinction between modern and early modern punctuation in more cogent terms: if the modern system was 'logical', Simpson argues, 'the earlier system was mainly rhythmical'; he notes that this is shown, particularly, in the *Sonnets*.[15] Moreover, Simpson emphasises that the 'earlier system', was, precisely, *not* systematic: he insists on the variety of early modern punctuation, its adaptability to the expression of 'subtle differences of tone'.[16] Even so, Simpson seeks to define the general rules governing Renaissance punctuation, noting at least nineteen different uses for the comma. If we consider, however, that, from the point of view of a poetics, a comma might be doing several things at once, as syntax, metre, rhythm, then what matters is not the period practice it manifests, but the *specific* ways it inflects meaning and grammar. We see this with the Quarto's treatment of the word 'haue'.

Paul Hammond's 'original-spelling edition' includes notes on the 'complex words' of Shakespeare's sonnets, words which are remarkable for what one might call their 'plainness': 'give' and 'love', 'see' and 'self' for example – and notes: 'The *Sonnets* seems to be an extended essay on the meaning of the word "have"'. Hammond alludes to the expression 'to have and to hold' in the marriage service, and looks at the contexts which these verbs ('have' and 'hold') associate throughout the sequence.[17] Clearly, the problematics of having is specific to the narrative in Shakespeare's sequence – given that the situation of which more normative Petrarchan speakers complain is one of *not*-having. Whatever the 'meanings' of 'haue' in Shakespeare, they are inseparable from the ways that the word is positioned in the line and associated, phonemically, with other words, for example 'loue'.

This wish I haue, then ten times happy me. (37.14)

Two loues I haue of comfort and dispaire, (144.1)

Happy to haue thy loue, happy to die! (92.12)

Thus haue I had thee as a dreame doth flatter, (87.13)

So then thou hast but lost the dregs of life, (74.9)

Though thou repent, yet I haue still the losse, (34.10)

Him haue I lost, thou hast both him and me, (134.13)[18]

'Haue', as we have seen, is often placed at the fourth position, where it is marked, or not, by punctuation, and inversion, as in sonnets 37, 144, 92, 87, 74. These constructions appear to suggest that 'having' is inseparable from 'not-having', that possession is an illusion: 'This wish I haue' claims the speaker in sonnet 37. Similarly, having is identified with loss, in constructions like 'Him haue I lost' (134), where the grammatical auxiliary is again punned upon. And 'haue' takes on particular ambiguities when employed in the passive voice, as in sonnet 52: 'Blessed are you whose worthiness gives skope / Being had to triumph, being lacked to hope' (lines 13–14),[19] where it is not entirely clear what is to be had, whether 'worthinesse' or 'you', nor by whom, nor how. In Elizabethan English, Hammond reminds us, 'having' somebody 'often meant to have sexual intercourse with them';[20] with 'have', Shakespeare seems to connect the sexual with the metaphysical.

The problematics of 'having' is central to sonnet 75, which describes sensual pleasure as a state of continual strife and frustration, possession as non-possession, a vicious circle enclosing the speaker in himself. I give the sonnet first as it appears in Hammond's edition:

So are you to my thoughts as food to life,
Or as sweet season'd shewers are to the ground;
And for the peace of you I hold such strife,
As twixt a miser and his wealth is found.
Now proud as an inioyer, and anon
Doubting the filching age will steale his treasure,
Now counting best to be with you alone,
Then betterd that the world may see my pleasure,

> Some-time all ful with feasting on your sight,
> And by and by cleane starued for a looke,
> Possessing or pursuing no delight
> Saue what is had, or must from you be tooke.
>   Thus do I pine and surfet day by day,
>   Or gluttoning on all, or all away.²¹

1. 14 *away.*] Q *away,*

Burrow's version is as follows:

> So are you to my thoughts as food to life,
> Or as sweet seasoned showers are to the ground;
> And for the peace of you I hold such strife,
> As 'twixt a miser and his wealth is found:
> Now proud as an enjoyer, and anon
> Doubting the filching age will steal his treasure,
> Now counting best to be with you alone,
> Then bettered that the world may see my pleasure;
> Sometime all full with feasting on your sight,
> And by and by clean starvèd for a look.
> Possessing or pursuing, no delight,
> Save what is had or must be from you took.
>   Thus do I pine and surfeit day by day,
>   Or gluttoning on all, or all away.²²

The passive participle 'had' appears at the close of the third quatrain: 'Possessing and pursuing no delight/Saue what is had, or must from you be tooke.' The comma following 'had' perhaps suggests that the speaker here corrects himself, and that 'taking delight from you', by force it seems, is much the more usual situation than 'having' it. The line pauses on 'having'; but with the introduction of the passive participle 'had', contrasting here with the active participles 'Possessing' and 'pursuing' of the preceding line, the 'subject' disappears, the passive construction suggesting that the speaker is, finally, turned inwards, not present as a 'person' in a relation with a beloved. Here we see an evolution in the way the comma is treated: whereas Ingram and Redpath, Booth, and Kerrigan, suppressed it, Duncan-Jones and Vendler have maintained it. (Burrow, as we see, erases it anew, and, unfortunately, also miswrites the word order of line 12.) Yet both Vendler and Duncan-Jones suppressed the comma after 'have' in sonnet 64. The syntax, in this case, is different; but one wonders to what extent that justifies altering what the Quarto registers as a rhythmic mark. What is above all noticeable is the incoherence in these editions: the poems are treated one by one, and a purely syntactic logic has been substituted for the poetics of 'have' in the Quarto.

The grammar and context of 'have' in sonnet 75 cannot help but remind a reader of sonnet 129, where the verb 'have' plays an important role in the definition of lust. Here is the sonnet as it appears in Hammond's original-spelling text:

> Th'expence of Spirit in a waste of shame
> Is lust in action, and till action, lust
> Is periurd, murdrous, blouddy full of blame,
> Sauage, extreame, rude, cruell, not to trust,

> Inioyd no sooner but dispised straight,
> Past reason hunted, and no sooner had
> Past reason hated as a swollowed bayt,
> On purpose layd to make the taker mad.
> Made In pursut and in possession so,
> Had, hauing, and in quest, to haue extreame,
> A blisse in proofe and proud and very wo,
> Before a ioy proposd behind a dreame,
>   All this the world well knowes yet none knowes well,
>   To shun the heauen that leads men to this hell.[23]

And here is the version published by Burrow:

> Th'expense of spirit in a waste of shame
> Is lust in action, and, till action, lust
> Is perjured, murd'rous, bloody, full of blame,
> Savage, extreme, rude, cruel, not to trust,
> Enjoyed no sooner but despisèd straight,
> Past reason hunted, and, no sooner had,
> Past reason hated as a swallowed bait
> On purpose laid to make the taker mad,
> Mad in pursuit, and in possession so,
> Had, having, and in quest to have, extreme,
> A bliss in proof and proved a very woe,
> Before, a joy proposed; behind, a dream.
>   All this the world well knows, yet none knows well
>   To shun the heaven that leads men to this hell.[24]

In line 10 of sonnet 129, 'Had, hauing, and in quest, to haue extreame', 'have' is used to define the three successive states which affect the luster, the 'taker' who is made 'mad'. Here the grammar, shifting mid-line between the passive participle 'had' and the active participle 'hauing', makes subject and object interchangeable and indefinite, inscribes 'having' in a logic of reversal; while the comma placed between them introduces a pause or caesura at a particularly unusual and destabilising position in the line, linking the reversible subject positions, agent and patient, in the juxtaposed accents of 'had' and 'having'. Grammar and rhythm function jointly here again to point to the instability of possession.

This dense play on 'having' in line 10 is prepared by another occurrence of 'had' which appears at the end of line 6, within the construction 'Past reason hunted, and no sooner had / Past reason hated'; here, however, in the Quarto text at least, 'had' is not followed by a comma. Looking closely, we note that, aside from the first two lines of the sonnet, in each of which the syntax is clearly incomplete, line 6 is the only one, once the poem's frenetic movement gets going, which does *not* end with a comma or stop of some sort. Yet all of the modern editions I have mentioned place a comma after 'had' in line 6.[25] It may seem far-fetched to argue about a missing comma: perhaps the compositor simply forgot that one; he certainly seems to have made a mess of line 11, where we read, in the Quarto, 'and proud and uery wo'; and, of course, we all know how easy it is to read meaning into anything. Even so, I would argue that here the *lack* of a comma *marks* 'had'. The editors' interpolation of a comma corresponds to the logical separation of clauses, hunted, had, hated; but what is at stake is of course the sudden and paradoxical passage from hunting to hating, and this transition and reversal is marked simply enough by the line end. Paradoxically, the omission of the comma interrupts the furious succession of events and makes possible a suspension, a momentary halt at the fulcrum or point of transition – at the moment of 'having'.

What then are we to do with the third comma in line 10, emended by all the editions so that the line reads 'Had, having, and in quest to have, extreme', rather than 'in quest, to haue extreame'? In a famous article, Robert Graves and Laura Riding defended the original punctuation, seeing in it, as Burrow notes, 'a wish to possess extremity itself'; Burrow himself argues that early modern readers would not have read the Quarto text this way.[26] One can agree, however, with Graves and Riding when they say that the line as emended 'loses point and does not pull its weight';[27] it appears simply as a restatement ('extreme' appears in line 4), and a surprisingly empty one, interesting only as polyptoton. Helen Vendler hangs her entire analysis on the emended version of the line, without once alluding to the fact that it *has* been emended: she makes this 'extreme' a summing up of the speaker's first, condemnatory, approach to his experience, and thus a transition to another, emotional viewpoint.[28] But perhaps this is simply a way of excusing or justifying what finally makes a 'bad' line; for 'extreme' is not necessarily, as Vendler claims, a 'philosophical' term, since it also meant 'violent' in Elizabethan English: the emendation really seems like a way of *stabilising* having. From the point of view of the line's *rhythmic* movement, and the way this rhythmic movement accords with its context, the Quarto reading appears preferable; and through the construction 'to haue extreame' it likewise accords with the way Shakespeare foregrounds, and interrogates, 'having' elsewhere in the sequence.

Punctuation, most particularly early modern punctuation, is, Percy Simpson suggests, an indication for performance.[29] It is thus, implicitly, a form of 'deixis', in the sense that it marks, also, the act of speaking, not only what is said: for Puttenham the comma is also an 'easement to the breath',[30] a 'breather' we might say. In the Quarto, punctuation appears to be linked in various ways to the grammar of enunciation, person and deixis in particular, and deixis is also gestural. As a closing remark, I would like to look briefly at how punctuation determines a grammar of pronominal 'this' in the sequence. The grammar of 'this' in the sonnets seems to do several interesting things. Often, 'this' is closely associated with the second-person forms 'thou' and 'thee', suggesting, perhaps, that the addressee is a creation of the speaker's discourse; and most particularly, of course, pronominal 'this' deictically designates the poem itself that we are reading, as in the following examples:

So long liues this, and this giues life to thee. (18.14)

You liue in this, and dwell in louers eies. (55.14)

The worth of that [my body], is that which it containes,
And that is this, and this with thee remaines. (74.13–14)[31]

In contrast to expressions like 'These plaintive verse' (4.1), 'these lines' (4.13 7.5, 35.2, 10), or 'these my papers' (36.1) found in *Delia* (1592) for example, in Shakespeare the deictic seems to ask implicitly *what this is* that we are reading (or what reading itself is), as though it were something difficult to identify. In order to function deictically, 'this' needs to be marked rhythmically, associated, so to speak, with bodily gesture, and this is done, as we see in all three examples, by the mid-line caesura, by punctuation.

This problematic character of 'thisness' is at work in sonnet 16, which presents a case of rewriting discussed by Carl Atkins.[32] The poem appears – if we follow the Quarto reading – to contain the sequence's first instance of this deictic 'this': the speaker is arguing, here paradoxically, that sexual reproduction is a surer way of preserving the addressee's beauty than is poetry, and proclaims, at lines 9–12: 'So should the lines of life that life repaire / Which this (Times pensel or my pupill pen) / Neither in inward worth nor outward faire / Can make you liue your selfe in eies of men'.[33] Here most modern versions (Booth, Kerrigan, Burrow, Bevington and Evans) erase the deictic pronominal 'this', by making 'this' the determiner of 'Time': 'which this time's pencil or my pupil pen'. Even Vendler, who keeps the Quarto parentheses throughout her edition, erases them here. Yet the editors' reading is also contained in the Quarto text – we can read *through* the parentheses – while the modernised reading completely erases the Quarto. What seems clear is that the Quarto punctuation and the syntax it implies mark 'this' as a deictic form exactly similar to the ones we have seen. The interest of this construction resides perhaps in the fact that what 'this' *is* is left indeterminate, glossed with an alternative, as 'pencil' or 'pen', drawing or writing. This indeterminacy is, apparently, what restrains critics from following the Quarto text: for how can 'this' be 'time's pencil'? By metonymy of course, and simile: the poem draws the addressee, as a pencil would. Sonnet 16 then functions as the first occurrence of a rhythmic marking, and deictic pointing, which runs throughout the sequence, and for this reason alone the Quarto reading, as Katherine Duncan-Jones also seems to think, appears preferable.[34]

Percy Simpson notes the beauty of punctuation, or the rhythm induced by punctuation, in Donne's poetry, and, in discussing Shakespeare, gives numerous examples from Donne.[35] The 1609 Quarto is a beautiful text in its own right, and some of its beauty resides in punctuation. The beauty of the punctuation lies in the fact that we recognise, there, a poetics. We cannot read what the sonnets are doing with the verb 'have' or the deictic pronoun 'this', without reading them in the Quarto punctuation. One is led to note the odd fact that these two poets, Donne and Shakespeare, are treated quite differently from our point of view. We learn the beauty of early modern punctuation from Donne, because his texts, since Grierson's edition, have been given to us *with* their punctuation. *The Complete English Poems* of Donne published by Penguin in 1971 essentially follows the punctuation of the first editions of Donne's poems;[36] the Penguin *Sonnets* edited by John Kerrigan several years later rewrites the Quarto. The aim of this chapter has been to suggest that the beauties of punctuation in the Quarto are inseparable from the speech sound continuum of the sequence, and from its epistemology of English, the way it leads us to reflect on what lies hidden in the words we breathe.

Notes

1 The following editions of Shakespeare's sonnets were consulted for this chapter, in order of publication: M. Seymour Smith (ed.), *Shakespeare's Sonnets* (Oxford: Heinemann Educational, 1963 – reproduces Quarto text with corrections); W.G. Ingram and T. Redpath (eds), *Shakespeare's Sonnets* (London: University of London Press, 1964); S. Booth (ed.), *Shakespeare's Sonnets* (New Haven: Yale University Press, 1977 – facsimile of the 1609 Quarto (Apsley imprint, the Huntington–Bridgewater copy) with an edited text printed in parallel); J. Kerrigan (ed.), *The Sonnets and A Lover's Complaint* (Harmondsworth: Penguin, 1986); K. Duncan-Jones (ed.), *Shakespeare's Sonnets* (London: Arden Shakespeare, Thomas Nelson and Sons, 1997); H. Vendler (ed.), *The Art of Shakespeare's Sonnets* (Cambridge, MA: Harvard University Press, 1997); C. Burrow (ed.), *The Complete Sonnets and Poems* (Oxford: Oxford University Press, 2002); P. Hammond (ed.), *Shakespeare's Sonnets. An Original-Spelling Text* (Oxford: Oxford University Press, 2012 – reproduces Quarto text with corrections). G. Willen and V.B. Reed's *Casebook on Shakespeare's Sonnets* (New York: Thomas Crowell, 1964) also gives the 1609 Quarto text with slight variations of lettering.
2 MacD.P. Jackson, 'Aspects of Organisation in *Shakespeare's Sonnets* (1609)', *Parergon*, 17 (1999), 109–34.
3 In referring to a 'continuum' I am building on the work of Henri Meschonnic, who understands 'the continuous' as 'the interaction language-poem-ethics-politics', in *Langage, histoire, une même théorie* (Paris: Verdier, 2012), p. 719 (my translation). A poetics, according to Meschonnic, must recognise the continuous in discourse, working both with and against the traditionally discontinuous concepts with which we approach language – those of signifier and signified, word and sentence, meaning and form. 'Continuum' and 'continuous' would then be concepts for thinking the systematicity of discourse, the production of associative paradigms based on patterns of phrasing, accent, and phonemic echo, 'rhythmic and prosodic series' of associated words which play a central role both in what we perceive as rhythm and in the enunciation of subjectivity; see G. Dessons and H. Meschonnic, *Traité du rythme: des vers et des proses* (Paris: Dunod, 1998), pp. 41–5, esp. 44. Dessons and Meschonnic view the work of Wilhelm von Humboldt as crucial, historically speaking, for the recognition of the continuous in language; in his study *Über die Verschiedenheit des menschlichen Sprachbaues und ihren Einfluß auf die geistige Entwicklung des Menschengeschlechts* (1836) Humboldt wrote: 'It is impossible to think of the emergence of language as beginning with the designation of objects by words and from there going on to the combination of words in discourse. In reality discourse is not put together out of words which precede it, but on the contrary words rather come forth from the whole of discourse' (Paderborn: Schöningh, 1998, p. 198 (my translation)): discourse, we might say, remakes its words in relation with specific circumstances of utterance. Reading discourse as continuum, Dessons and Meschonnic suggest, involves recognising 'a maximal, and general, subjectivation of discourse, in such a way that the discourse is transformed by the subject and the subject comes into existence by this very transformation' (p. 43, my translation); it follows that 'when there is a poetics of rhythm, it is not sound one hears, but a subject' (p. 44, my translation).
4 C.D. Atkins, 'The Application of Bibliographical Principles to the Editing of Punctuation in Shakespeare's *Sonnets*', *Studies in Philology*, 100:4 (2003), 493–513 (500). Atkins adds, pointedly, that inconsistency 'should not be used as an indication of corruption' (ibid.).
5 Vendler, *The Art of Shakespeare's Sonnets*, p. 18.
6 Hammond (ed.), *Shakespeare's Sonnets: An Original-Spelling Text*, p. 237.
7 Burrow (ed.), *The Complete Sonnets and Poems*, p. 509.
8 G. Puttenham, *The Arte of English Poesie* (Menston: Scolar Press, 1968), p. 62.
9 Hammond (ed.), *Shakespeare's Sonnets: An Original-Spelling Text*, p. 99.
10 Ingram and Redpath (eds), *Shakespeare's Sonnets*, p. xxix.
11 MacD.P. Jackson, 'Punctuation and the Compositors of Shakespeare's *Sonnets*, 1609', *The Library*, fifth series, 30:1 (1975), 1–24. Carl D. Atkins cites evidence questioning Jackson's assumption of two compositors in 'The Application of Bibliographical Principles to the Editing of Punctuation in Shakespeare's *Sonnets*', 500–2. Atkins's excellent discussion concludes: 'it is fair to say that the Quarto's punctuation can be seen to be no less trustworthy than the rest of the text. It follows that alteration of punctuation marks that appear in the Quarto should be undertaken with *as much caution* as any other emendation' (502). Atkins's circumspect approach to Elizabethan pointing is shared but also qualified by Ros King in her article 'Seeing the Rhythm: An Interpretation of Sixteenth-Century Punctuation and Metrical Practice', in J. Bray, M. Handley and A.C. Henry (eds), *Ma(r)king the Text: The Presentation of Meaning on the Literary Page* (Aldershot: Ashgate, 2000), pp. 235–52. Focusing primarily on dramatic texts, King makes rhythm, as opposed to metrical convention, a primary consideration for text editing,

but notes that Elizabethan punctuation practice may also obscure the subtlety of a text's rhythmic movement. The editorial problem is presented in terms of a general opposition between grammatical and oratorical organisation (for example p. 236); my point is that punctuation may not only follow grammar but also determine it. King's argument is sometimes obscured by recourse to the vague and problematic term 'natural rhythm', as used for example, p. 243.

12 Kerrigan (ed.), *The Sonnets and A Lover's Complaint*, p. 66.
13 Jackson, 'Punctuation and the Compositors of Shakespeare's *Sonnets*, 1609', p. 13. He suggests that line-internal commas in the Quarto likely 'derive from the printer's manuscript copy'.
14 Hammond (ed.), *Shakespeare's Sonnets: An Original-Spelling Text*, p. 96.
15 P. Simpson, *Shakespearian Punctuation* (Oxford: Clarendon Press, 1911), p. 8. Simpson notes: 'the printer of the 1609 text was at great pains to indicate the rhythm by the punctuation' (p. 9).
16 Ibid., p. 10.
17 Hammond (ed.), *Shakespeare's Sonnets: An Original-Spelling Text*, pp. 462–3.
18 Ibid., pp. 183, 397, 293, 283, 257, 177, 377.
19 Ibid., p. 213.
20 Ibid., p. 463.
21 Ibid., p. 259.
22 Burrow (ed.), *Complete Sonnets and Poems*, p. 531.
23 Hammond (ed.), *Shakespeare's Sonnets: An Original-Spelling Text*, p. 367.
24 Burrow (ed.), *The Complete Sonnets and Poems*, p. 639.
25 An exception is David Bevington, who places no comma after 'had' in 129.6 in his edition of *The Complete Works of Shakespeare* (sixth edition, New York: Pearson Longman, 2009), p. 1739; otherwise, Bevington punctuates 64.14 and 75.12 as Burrow does. The pointing of these three lines is similar to Burrow's in *The Riverside Shakespeare*, G. Blakemore Evans General editor (Boston: Houghton Mifflin, second ed. 1997).
26 Burrow (ed.), *The Complete Sonnets and Poems*, p. 638.
27 R. Graves and L. Riding, 'A Study in Original Punctuation and Spelling', reprinted in G. Willen and V.B. Reed (eds), *A Casebook on Shakespeare's Sonnets* (New York: Thomas Cromwell, 1964), pp. 161–72 (pp. 166–7).
28 Vendler, *The Art of Shakespeare's Sonnets*, pp. 552–3.
29 Simpson, *Shakespearian Punctuation*, p. 27.
30 Puttenham, *The Arte of English Poesie* (1968), p. 61.
31 Hammond (ed.), *Shakespeare's Sonnets: An Original-Spelling Text*, pp. 145, 219, 257.
32 Atkins, 'The Application of Bibliographical Principles to the Editing of Punctuation in Shakespeare's *Sonnets*', pp. 507ff.
33 Hammond (ed.), *Shakespeare's Sonnets: An Original-Spelling Text*, p. 141.
34 Duncan-Jones (ed.), *Shakespeare's Sonnets*, pp. 142–3.
35 Simpson, *Shakespearian Punctuation*, pp. 26–7, esp. 30.
36 J. Donne, *The Complete English Poems*, ed. by A.J. Smith (Harmondsworth: Penguin, 1971). The editor notes that he has modernised punctuation 'only in a very few instances where the old pointing will confuse a modern reader' (p. 14).

Bibliography

Primary sources

Manuscripts

Bodleian Library MS Rawl. poet. 85
British Library Add. MS 5956 (the 'Cosens manuscript')
British Library Harley MS 7392 (2)
British Library Sloane MS 1446
Gascoigne, George, 'The Tale of Hemetes the Heremyte' (British Library, Royal 18.A.XLVIII).
Scott, William, 'The Modell of Poesye' (British Library, MS Add. 81083).

Printed sources

Alexander, Gavin (ed.), *Sidney's 'The Defence of Poesy' and Selected Renaissance Literary Criticism* (London: Penguin Books, 2004).
Anonymous, *Delectable Demaundes, and Pleasaunt Questions, with their Seuerall Aunswers, in Matters of Loue, Naturall Causes, with Morall and Politique Deuises* (London: In Paules Churchyarde by Iohn Cawood for Nicholas Englande, [1566]).
Anonymous, *A Plaine Pathway to the French Tongue, 1575*, ed. R.C. Alston (Menston: Scolar Press, 1968).
Anonymous, *The Returne from Parnassus* (London: Printed by G. Eld for Iohn Wright, 1606).
[Archer, Thomas (ed.)], *The Muses Garland* ([London]: [Thomas Archer], 1603).
Ascham, Roger, *The Scholemaster* (London: John Daye, 1570).
Baldwin, William, *The Canticles or Balades of Salomon, phraselyke declared in Englysh metres* (London: William Baldwin, 1549).
Barnes, Barnabe, *A Divine Centurie of Spirituall Sonnets* (London: John Windet, 1595).
——, ed. Victor Doyno, *Parthenophil and Parthenophe, A Critical Edition* (Carbondale: Southern Illinois University Press, 1971).
——, *Parthenophil and Parthenophe, Sonnettes, Madrigals, Elegies and Odes* (London: [J. Wolfe, 1593]).
Beaumont, Francis, and John Fletcher, *The Woman-Hater. As it hath beene lately Acted by the Children of Paules* (London: John Hodgets, 1607).
Bembo, Pietro, *Le rime*, ed. Andrea Donnini, 2 vols (Rome: Salerno editrice, 2008).
——, *Prose e rime*, ed. Carlo Dionisotti (Turin: UTET, 1992).

Berry, Lloyd E. (ed.), *The Geneva Bible: A Facsimile of the 1560 Edition* (Madison: University of Wisconsin Press, 1969).

Blount, Edward, *Glossographia Or A Dictionary, Interpreting All Such Hard Words of Whatsoever Language, Now Used in Our Refined English Tongue: With Etymologies, Definitions, and Historical Observations on the Same. Also the Terms of Divinity, Law, Physick, Mathematicks, and Other Arts and Sciences Explicated. Very Useful for All Such as Desire to Understand What They Read. The Second Edition,* [ ] *above Five Hundred Choice* [ ]. *By T.B. of the Inner-*[ ] (London: Printed by Thomas Nevvcomb, 1661).

Bodenham, John (ed.), *Bel-vedére, or, The Garden of the Mvses* (London: Hugh Astley, 1600).

Boissière, Claude de, *Art poeticque reduict et abrégé* (Paris: Annet Briere, 1554).

Bracciolini, Francesco, *Delle Poesie Liriche Toscane di Francesco Bracciolini dell'Api, Parte Prima* (Rome: Ludovico Grignani, 1639).

Breton, Nicholas, *A Floorish vpon Fancie* (London: [William How for] Richard Jones, 1577).

—, *A Solemne Passion of the Soules Loue* (London: Simon Stafford for William Barley, 1598).

—, *Brittons Bowre of Delights* (London: Richard Jones, 1591).

—, *Poems by Nicholas Breton Not Hitherto Reprinted*, ed. Jean Robertson (Liverpool: Liverpool University Press, 1952).

—, *The Arbor of Amorous Deuices* (London: Richard Jones, 1597).

—, *The Passionate Shepheard, or The Shepheardes Loue*, ed. Frederick Ouvry (London: s.n., 1877).

—, '*The Strange Fortunes of Two Excellent Princes* and *The Arbor of Amorous Devices*', ed. John P. Cutts. *Renaissance News*, 15 (1962), 2–11.

Brome, Richard, *The Court Begger* (London: Printed for Richard Marriot and Tho. Dring and are to be sold at their shops, 1653).

Burchiello (Domenico di Giovanni), ed. Michelangelo Zaccarello, *I sonetti del Burchiello* (Turin: Einaudi, 2004).

Burnaby, William, *The Reformed Wife* (London: Printed for Thomas Bennet, 1700).

Campion, Thomas, *Observations in the Art of English Poesie*, in *Elizabethan Critical Essays*, ed. G. Gregory Smith (Oxford: Oxford University Press, 1904), vol. 2, pp. 327–55.

Capell, Edward, *Prolusions; or, Select Pieces of Antient Poetry, II. Edward the Third, a Play, Thought to be Writ by Shakespeare* (London: s.n., 1760).

Cartwright, Thomas, *The Second Replie of Thomas Cartwright: Agaynst Maister Doctor Whitgiftes Second Answer* (Heidelberg: Michael Schirat, 1575).

Castelvetro, Ludovico, *Le rime del Petrarca brevemente sposte per Lodouico Castelvetro* (Basel: Pietro de Sedabonis, 1582).

Castiglione, Baldassarre, trans. Thomas Hoby, *The Courtyer of Count Baldessar Castilio Diuided into Foure Books* (London: William Seres, 1561).

Chamberlain, John, *The Letters of John Chamberlain*, ed. Norman Egbert McClure, 2 vols (Philadelphia: The American Philosophical Association, 1939).

Chapman, George, *Achilles Shield, Translated as the Other Seuen Bookes of Homer Out of his Eighteenth Booke of Illiades*, in *Elizabethan Critical Essays*, ed. G. Gregory Smith (Oxford: Oxford University Press, 1904), vol. 2, pp. 297–307.

—, *All Fools* (London: Printed [by George Eld] for Thomas Thorpe, 1605).

—, *Ouids Banquet of Sence, A Coronet for his Mistresse Philosophie* (London: Richard Smith, 1595).

—, *Sir Gyles Goosecappe* (London: Printed by Iohn Windet for Edward Blount, 1606).

Coles, Elisha, *An English Dictionary* (London: Printed for Peter Parker, 1677).

Constable, Henry, *Diana* (London: Richard Smith, 1592).

Conti, Giusto de', *La Bella Mano di Giusto de' Conti ... e una raccolta delle rime antiche di diversi Toscani* (Verona: Giannalberto Tumermani, 1753).

Corneille, Thomas, *The Extravagant Shepherd*, trans. Thomas Rawlins (London: Printed by J.G. for Tho. Heath, 1654).

Crouch, Humphrey, *An Excellent Sonnet of the Unfortunate Loves, of Hero and Leander Tune of, Gerards Mistris* ([London]: Printed for F. Coles, T. Vere and J. Wright, [c. 1674]).

Crow, Martha F. (ed.), *Elizabethan Sonnet Cycles – Phillis by Thomas Lodge, Licia by Giles Fletcher* (Chicago: A.C. McClurg and Co, 1896).

Daniel, Samuel, *A Defence of Ryme*, in *Elizabethan Critical Essays*, ed. G. Gregory Smith (Oxford: Oxford University Press, 1904), vol. 2, pp. 356–84.

—, *A Funerall Poem vppon the Death of the Late Noble Earle of Deuonshyre* [London: s.n., 1606].

—, *A Panegyrike Congratulatory ... With a Defence of Ryme* (London: Edward Blount, 1603).

—, *Poems*, ed. Arthur Colby Sprague (Cambridge, MA: Harvard University Press, 1930).

Daniello, Bernardino, *Sonetti canzoni e triomphi di M. Francesco Petrarca, con la spositione di Bernardino Daniello da Lucca* (Venice: Pietro e Gionmaria Fratelli de Nicolini da Sabio, 1549).

Davies, John, *The Poems of Sir John Davies*, ed. Robert Krueger and Ruby Nemser (Oxford: Clarendon Press, 1975).

—, and Christopher Marlowe, *Epigrammes and Elegies* (London: s.n., 1599).

Davies of Hereford, John, *Microcosmos, The Discovery of the Little World, with the Government Thereof* (Oxford: Joseph Barnes, 1603).

—, *Wittes Pilgrimage* (London: Richard Bradock for John Browne, [1605?]).

Dekker, Thomas, Henry Chettle, and William Haughton, *Patient Grissil* (London: Imprinted [by E. Allde] for Henry Rocket, 1603).

Dekker, Thomas, and Thomas Middleton, *The Honest Whore* (London: printed by Elizabeth Allde, for Nathaniel Butter, 1630).

Dekker, Thomas, and John Webster, *Northward Hoe* (London: by G. Eld, 1607).

De Robertis, Domenico (ed.), *Sonetti e canzoni di diversi antichi autori toscani*, 2 vols (Florence: Le Lettere, 1977).

Dolce, Lodovico, *Dialogo della Pittura ... intitolato l'Aretino* (Venice: Gabriele Giolito, 1557).

Donne, John, *Letters to Severall Persons of Honour* (London: Richard Marriot, 1651).
—, *Poems, by J.D* (London: John Marriot, 1633).
—, *The Complete English Poems*, ed. A.J. Smith (Harmondsworth: Penguin, 1971).
—, *The Variorum Edition of the Poetry of John Donne Vol. 2 The Elegies*, ed. Gary A. Stringer (Bloomington: Indiana University Press, 2000).
Dowland, John, *The Third and Last Booke of Songs or Aires* (London: Peter Short for Thomas Adams, 1603).
Drayton, Michael, *Englands Heroicall Epistles Nevvly Corrected. VVith Idea* (London: Nicholas Ling, 1602)
—, *Englands Heroicall Epistles. Nevvly Enlarged. VVith Idea. By Michaell Drayton.* (London: Nicholas Ling, 1599).
—, *Poems: by Michael Drayton, Esquire* (London: John Smethwicke, 1619).
—, *Works*, ed. J. William Hebel, Kathleen Tillotson and Bernard Newdigate, 5 vols (Oxford: Clarendon Press, 1931–41).
Du Bartas, Guillaume de Saluste, trans. Josuah Sylvester, *The Second Weeke or Childhood of the World, of the Noble, Learned and Diuine Salustius, Lord of Bartas* (London: P. Short, 1598).
Du Bellay, Joachim, *La Deffence et illustration de la langue françoyse*, ed. Jean-Charles Monferran (Geneva: Droz, 2009 [2001]).
East, Michael, *Madrigales to 3. 4. and 5. Parts* (London: Thomas Este, 1604).
Edwards, Richard, *The Paradise of Dainty Devices, 1576–1606*, ed. Hyder Edward Rollins (Cambridge, MA: Harvard University Press, 1927).
Fausto da Longiano, Sebastiano, *Il Petrarcha col commento di M. Sebastiano Fausto da Longiano* (Venice: Francesco di Alessandro Bindoni e Mapheo Pasini, 1532).
Fletcher, Giles, *Licia, or Poemes of Love, in Honour of the Admirable and Singular Vertues of his Lady, to the Imitation of the Best Latin Poets, and Others* (Cambridge: John Legat, 1593).
Fletcher, John, and Philip Massinger, *The Elder Brother* (London: Imprinted by F[elix] K[ingston] for I. W[aterson] and I. B[enson], 1637).
—, and Francis Beaumont, *The Woman-Hater. As it hath beene lately Acted by the Children of Paules* (London: John Hodgets, 1607).
Florio, John, *A Worlde of Wordes* (London: by Arnold Hatfield for Edw. Blount, 1598).
—, *Florio his firste fruites which yeelde familiar speech, merie prouerbes, wittie sentences, and golden sayings* (London: Imprinted at the three Cranes in the Vintree, by Thomas Dawson, for Thomas Woodcocke, 1578).
—, *Florios Second Frutes to be Gathered of Twelue Trees, of Diuers but Delightsome Tastes to the Tongues of Italians and Englishmen. To which is Annexed his Gardine of Recreation Yeelding Six Thousand Italian Prouerbs* (London: Thomas Woodcock, 1591).
—, *Queen Anna's New World of Words*, introduction by R.C. Alston (Menston: Scolar Press, 1968).
—, *Queen Anna's New World of Words* (London: Edward Blount and William Barret, 1611).

—, *Second Frutes*, introduction by R.C. Simonini Jr (Gainesville: Scholars' Facsimiles and Reprints, 1953).
Gascoigne, George, *A Hundred Sundrie Flowres*, ed. George W. Pigman III (Oxford: Clarendon Press, 2000).
—, *A Hundreth Sundrie Flowres* (London: Henry Bynneman [and Henry Middleton] for Richard Smith, 1573).
—, *The Posies of George Gascoigne Esquire* (London: Richard Smith, 1575).
Gesualdo, Giovanni Andrea, *Il Petrarcha colla spositione di Misser Giovanni Andrea Gesualdo* (Venice: Giovann' Antonio di Nicolini e Fratelli da Sabbio, 1533).
Goyet, Francis (ed.), *Traités de poétique et de rhétorique de la Renaissance* (Paris: Livre de Poche, 1990).
Grazzini, Anton F. (ed.), *Il primo Libro dell'opere burlesche. Di M. Francesco Berni, di M. Gio. della Casa, del Varchi, del Mauro, di M. Bino, del Molza, del Dolce, & del Firenzuola, ricorretto, & con diligenza ristampato* (Florence: [s.n.], 1548).
Greene, Robert, *Gvvydonius The carde of fancie wherein the folly of those carpet knights is decyphered, which guyding their course by the compasse of Cupid, either dash their ship against most daungerous rocks, or els attaine the hauen with paine and perill. Wherein also is described in the person of Gwydonius, a cruell combat betvveene nature and necessitie. By Robert Greene Master of Arte, in Cambridge.* (London: [T. East] for William Ponsonby, 1584).
—, *Menaphon* (London: Thomas Orwin for Sampson Clarke, 1589).
Greville, Fulke, First Baron Brooke, *Poems and Dramas of Fulke Greville, First Lord Brooke*, ed. Geoffrey Bullough, vol. 1 (Edinburgh and London: Oliver & Boyd, 1938).
Guarini, Giovanni Battista, [trans. Tailboys Dymoke], *Il Pastor Fido: Or The Faithfull Shepheard. Translated out of Italian into English* (London: Simon Waterson, 1602).
Guazzo, Stefano, *Dialoghi piacevoli* [...] (Venice: Gio. Antonio Bertano, 1586).
Harvey, Gabriel, *Foure Letters, and Certaine Sonnets: Especially touching Robert Greene, and other parties, by him abused: But incidently of diuers excellent persons and some matters of note* (London: John Wolfe, 1592).
—, *Pierces Supererogation, or a New Prayse of the Old Asse, A Preparative to Certaine Larger Discourses, Intituled Nashes S. Fame* (London: John Wolfe, 1593).
Harvey, Gabriel, and Edmund Spenser, *Three Proper and Wittie Familiar Letters Lately Passed Between Two Vniversitie Men Touching the Earthquake in Aprill Last, and our English Refourmed Versifying. / Two Other Very Commendable Letters of the Same Mens Writing: Both Touching the Foresaid Artificiall Versifying, and Cartain Other Particulars* (London: Henry Bynneman, 1580).
Heywood, Thomas, *Loves Maistresse* (London: Printed by Robert Raworth, for Iohn Crowch, 1636).
—, *The Fayre Mayde of the Exchange* (London: Printed [by Valentine Simmes] for Henry Rockit, 1607).
—, *An Apology for Actors* (London: N. Okes, 1612).
—, *The foure prentises of London VVith the conquest of Ierusalem. As it hath bene diuerse times acted, at the Red Bull, by the Queenes Maiesties Seruants* (London: [by Nicholas Okes] for I. W[right], 1615).

Holyday, Barten, *Technogamia or the Marriages of the Arts* (London: Printed by William Stansby for Iohn Parker, 1618).
Homer, trans. George Chapman, *Achilles Shield, Translated as the Other Seven Bookes of Homer Out of his Eighteenth Booke of Illiades*, in *Elizabethan Critical Essays*, ed. G. Gregory Smith (Oxford: Oxford University Press, 1904), vol. 2, pp. 297–307.
James VI of Scotland, *The Essayes of a Prentise, in the Diuine Art of Poesie* (Edinburgh: Thomas Vautrollier, 1584).
Jonson, Ben, *Euery Man in his Humour* (London: [by S. Stafford] for Walter Burre, 1601).
——, *Poetaster* (London: Printed [by R. Bradock] for M. L[ownes], 1602).
La Marche, Olivier de, trans. Lewis Lewkenor, *The Resolued Gentleman. Translated out of Spanishe into Englyshe* (London: Richard Watkins, 1594).
Langton, Christopher, *A Uery Brefe Treatise, Ordrely Declaring the Pri[n]cipal Partes of Phisick* (London: Edward Whitchurch, 1547).
Laudun d'Aigaliers, Pierre, *Art poëtique françois*, ed. Jean-Charles Monferran (Paris: STFM, 2000).
Lee, Sidney (ed.), *Elizabethan Sonnets: Newly Arranged and Indexed*, vol. 1 (London: Archibald and Co., 1904).
Lodge, Thomas, *Rosalynde* (London: Thomas Gubbin and John Busbie, 1592).
——, *Scillaes Metamorphosis* (London: Richard Jones, 1589).
Lyly, John, *Midas* (London: Printed by Thomas Scarlet for I[ohn] B[roome], 1592).
Markham, Gervase, *The Dumbe Knight* (London: Printed by Nicholas Okes, for Iohn Bache, 1608).
Marston, John, *Parasitaster or the Fawn* (London: Printed by T[homas] P[urfoot] for VV. C[otton], 1606).
——, *The Insatiate Countesse* (London: Printed by T[homas] S[nodham] for Thomas Archer, 1613).
Mayne, Jasper, *The Citye Match* (Oxford: Printed by Leonard Lichfield, printer to the University, 1639).
Mead, Robert, *Combat of Love and Friendship* (London: Printed for M[ercy] M[eighen], G. Bedell, and T. Collins, 1654).
Meninni, Federigo, *Il ritratto del sonetto e della canzone*, ed. Clizia Carminati, 2 vols (Lecce: Argo, 2002).
Meres, Francis, *Palladis Tamia: Wit's Treasury*, ed. D.C. Allen (New York: Scholars' Facsimiles and Reprints, 1938).
Middleton, Thomas, *The Blacke Booke* (London: T.C. for Jeffrey Chorlton, 1604).
Milton, John, *Complete English Poems, Of Education, Aeropagitica*, ed. Gordon Campbell (London: J.M. Dent, 1993).
——, *The Complete Works of John Milton*, vol. III, ed. Barbara Kiefer Lewalski and Estelle Haan (Oxford: Oxford University Press, 2012).
Minturno, Antonio, *L'arte poetica, nella quale si contengono i precetti heroici, tragici, comici, satyrici e d'ogni altra poesia. Con la dottrina de' sonetti, canzoni et ogni sorte di rime thoscane, dove s'insegna il modo che tenne il Petrarca nelle sue rime* […] ([Venice]: G.A. Valvassori, 1563).

Munday, Anthony, *Death of Robert, Earle of Huntington Otherwise called Robin Hood of merrie Sherwodde: with the Lamentable Tragedie of Chaste Matilda, his Faire Maid Marian, Poysoned at Dunmowe by King Iohn. Acted by the Right Honourable, the Earle of Notingham, Lord High Admirall of England, his Seruants* (London: [by R. Bradock] for William Leake, 1601).

Nashe, Thomas, *Haue vvith you to Saffron-VValden. Or, Gabriell Harueys Hunt is vp Containing a Full Answere to the Eldest Sonne of the Halter-maker. Or, Nashe his Confutation of the Sinfull Doctor. The Mott or Posie, in Stead of Omne Tulit Punctum: Pacis Fiducia Nunquam. As Much to Say, as I Sayd I would Speake with Him* (London: John Danter, 1596).

——, *The Anatomie of Absurditie*, in *Elizabethan Critical Essays*, ed. G. Gregory Smith (Oxford: Oxford University Press, 1904), vol. 1, pp. 326–7.

——, *The Apologie of Pierce Pennilesse: OR Strange Newes, Of the Intercepting Certaine Letters, and a Conuoy of Verses, as They were Going Priuilie to Victual the Lowe Countries* (London: John Danter, 1592).

——, *The Works of Thomas Nashe*, ed. R.B. McKerrow, rev. F.P. Wilson, 5 vols (Oxford: Blackwell, 1958).

Nenna, Giovanni Battista, trans. William Jones, *Nennio, or A treatise of nobility ... Written in Italian by that famous doctor and worthy knight Sir John Baptista Nenna* (London: Paul Linley and John Flasket, 1595).

Noot, Jan van der, *A Theatre Wherein be Represented as Wel the Miseries & Calamities that Follow the Voluptuous Worldlings* (London: Henry Bynneman, 1568).

Peletier du Mans, Jacques, *L'Art poëtique de Iaques Peletier du Mans* (Lyon: Guillaume Gazeau, 1555).

——, *Œuvres complètes de J. Peletier du Mans*, ed. Isabelle Pantin (Paris: Champion, 2011).

Petrarca, Francesco, *Canzoniere*, ed. Marco Santagata (Milan: Mondadori, 2008, 2015).

——, *Canzoniere Rerum Vulgarium Fragmenta*, vol. II, ed. R. Bettarini (Turin: Einaudi, 2005).

——, *Petrarch's Lyric Poems*, trans. Robert M. Durling (Cambridge, MA: Harvard University Press, 1976).

——, *The Tryumphes of Fraunces Petrarcke*, trans. Henry Parker (London: John Cawood, 1555).

Phillips, Edward, *The new world of English words, or, A general dictionary containing the interpretations of such hard words as are derived from other languages* (London: E. Tyler for Nath. Brooke, 1658).

Piccolomini, Alessandro, *I cento sonetti*, ed. Franco Tomasi (Geneva: Droz, 2015).

Pricket, Robert, *Honors Fame in Triumph Riding* (London: R. Blower for Roger Jackson, 1604).

Puttenham, George, *The Arte of English Poesie. Contrived into Three Bookes: The First of Poets and Poesie, the Second of Proportion, the Third of Ornament* (London: Richard Field, 1589).

——, *The Arte of English Poesie*, facsimile edition (Menston: Scholar Press, 1968).

Rainolds, John, *Oratio in laudem artis poeticae*, ed. William J. Ringler, trans. Walter Allen (Princeton: Princeton University Press, 1940).

Randolph, Thomas, *Hey for Honesty, Augmented and Published by F.J.* (London: s.n., 1651).

Rollins, Hyder Edward (ed.), *A Poetical Rhapsody, 1602–1621*, 2 vols (Cambridge, MA: Harvard University Press, 1931).

—— (ed.), *Englands Helicon 1600, 1614*, 2 vols (Cambridge, MA: Harvard University Press, 1935).

—— (ed.), *The Phoenix Nest 1593* (Cambridge, MA: Harvard University Press, 1931).

Ronsard, Pierre de, trans. Thomas Jenye, *A Discovrs of the Present Troobles in Fravnce, and Miseries of this Tyme* (Antwerp: s.n., 1568).

Ruscelli, Girolamo, *Del modo di comporre in versi nella lingua italiana* (Venice: Giovanni Battista & Melchior Sessa, [1559]).

S.S., *The Honest Lawyer* (London: printed by George Purslowe for Richard Woodroffe, 1616).

Scott, William, *The Model of Poesy*, ed. G. Alexander (Cambridge: Cambridge University Press, 2013).

Shakespeare, William, *As You Like It*, ed. Alan Brissenden (Oxford: Oxford University Press, 1993).

——, *As You Like It*, ed. Michael Hattaway (Cambridge: Cambridge University Press, 2009).

——, *Complete Sonnets and Poems*, ed. Colin Burrow, The Oxford Shakespeare (Oxford: Oxford University Press, 2002).

——, *Love's Labour's Lost*, ed. William C. Carroll (Cambridge: Cambridge University Press, 2009).

——, *Love's Labour's Lost*, ed. G.R. Hibbard (Oxford: Oxford University Press, 2008).

——, *Mr. William Shakespeares Comedies, Histories, & Tragedies: Published According to the True Originall Copies* (London: Isaac Iaggard and Edward Blount, 1623).

——, *Romeo and Juliet*, ed. René Weis (London: Bloomsbury, The Arden Shakespeare, 2012).

——, *Shakespeare's Sonnets: An Original-Spelling Text*, ed. Paul Hammond (Oxford: Oxford University Press, 2012).

——, *Shakespeare's Sonnets*, ed. Stephen Booth (New Haven: Yale University Press, 1977).

——, *Shakespeare's Sonnets*, ed. Katherine Duncan-Jones (London: Arden Shakespeare, Thomas Nelson and Sons, 1997).

——, *Shakespeare's Sonnets*, ed. W.G. Ingram and Theodore Redpath (London: University of London Press, 1964).

——, *Shakespeare's Sonnets*, ed. Martin Seymour Smith (Oxford: Heinemann Educational, 1963).

——, *The Art of Shakespeare's Sonnets*, ed. Helen Vendler (Cambridge, MA: Harvard University Press, 1997).

——, *The Complete Poems of Shakespeare*, ed. Cathy Shrank and Raphael Lyne (London, New York: Routledge, 2018).

—, *The Complete Sonnets and Poems*, ed. Colin Burrow (Oxford: Oxford University Press, 2002).
—, *The Complete Works*, ed. John Jowett, William Montgomery, Gary Taylor and Stanley Wells (Oxford: Oxford University Press, Second edition, 2005).
—, *The Complete Works of Shakespeare*, ed. David Bevington (New York: Pearson Longman, 2009).
—, *The Riverside Shakespeare*, ed. Colin Burrow and G. Blakemore Evans (Boston: Houghton Mifflin, second ed., 1997).
—, *The Sonnets and A Lover's Complaint*, ed. John Kerrigan (Harmondsworth: Penguin, 1986).
Shirley, James, *Changes* (London: Printed by G[eorge] P[urslowe] for William Cooke, 1632).
—, *The Constant Maid. A Comedy.* (London: Printed by I. Raworth, for R. Whitaker, 1640).
—, *The Example* (London: Printed by Iohn Norton, for Andrew Crooke, and William Cooke, 1637).
—, *The Humorous Courtier* (London: Printed by T[homas] C[otes] for William Cooke, 1640).
Sidney, Philip, *An Apology for Poetry (or The Defence of Poesy)*, ed. Robert W. Maslen (Manchester, New York: Manchester University Press, third edition, 2002).
—, *Astrophil and Stella*, in *The Major Works*, ed. Katherine Duncan-Jones (Oxford: Oxford University Press, 1989).
—, *The Miscellaneous Prose of Sir Philip Sidney*, ed. Jan van Dorsten and Katherine Duncan-Jones (Oxford: Clarendon Press, 1973).
—, *The Poems of Sir Philip Sidney*, ed. William A. Ringler (Oxford: Clarendon Press, 1962).
Sidney Herbert, Mary, *The Collected Works of Mary Sidney Herbert, Countess of Pembroke*, ed. Margaret P. Hannay, Noel J. Kinnamon and Michael G. Brennan, 2 vols (Oxford: Clarendon Press, 1998).
Smith, G. Gregory (ed.), *Elizabethan Critical Essays*, 2 vols (Oxford: Clarendon Press, 1904).
Spenser, Edmund, *Amoretti and Epithalamion* (London: Peter Short for William Ponsonby, 1595).
—, *Complaints. Containing Sundrie Small Poemes of the Worlds Vanitie* (London: for William Ponsonby, 1591).
—, *The Complete Works in Verse and Prose of Edmund Spenser*, ed. Alexander Grosart, 9 vols (London: Spenser Society, 1882–84).
—, *The Faerie Queene. Disposed into Twelue Bookes, Fashioning XII. Morall Vertues* (London: William Ponsonby, 1596).
—, *The Shepheardes Calender Conteyning Twelue Aeglogues Proportionable to the Twelue Monethes* (London: Hugh Singleton, 1579).
—, *The Shorter Poems*, ed. Richard McCabe (London: Penguin, 2006).
—, *The Works of Edmund Spenser: A Variorum Edition*, ed. Edwin Greenlaw, Charles Grosvenor Osgood and Frederick Morgan Pedelford (Baltimore: The Johns Hopkins Press, 1947).

—, *The Yale Edition of the Shorter Poems of Edmund Spenser*, ed. William Oram, Alexander Dunlop et al. (New Haven: Yale University Press, 1989).
Tasso, Torquato, *Opere. V. Dialoghi. Apologia in difesa della 'Gerusalemme liberata'. Lettere*, ed. Bruno Maier (Milan: Rizzoli, 1965).
Thomas, William, *Principal Rules of the Italian Grammar*, ed. R.C. Alston (Menston: Scolar Press, 1968).
Tomasi, Franco, and Paolo Zaja (eds), *Rime diverse di molti eccellentissimi autori. Libro primo* (Torino: RES, 2001).
Tomkis, Thomas, *Albumazar* (London: Printed by Nicholas Okes for Walter Burre, 1615).
—, *Lingua: or The Combat of the Tongue, and the Fiue Senses for Superiority A Pleasant Comoedie* (London: Printed by G. Eld, for Simon Waterson, 1607).
Tottel, Richard (ed.), *Richard Tottel's 'Songes and sonettes': The Elizabethan Version*, ed. Paul A. Marquis (Temple: Arizona Center for Medieval and Renaissance Studies, 2007).
—, *Songes and Sonettes* (London: Richard Tottel, 1557).
—, *Tottel's Miscellany*, ed. Amanda Holton and Tom MacFaul (London: Penguin Books, 2011).
Trissino, Giovan Giorgio, *La pwetica* (Vicenza: per Tolomeo Ianiculo, 1529).
Valeriano, Pietro, *Hieroglyphica, Sive De Sacris Aegyptiorum Literis Commentarii* (Basel: s.n., 1556).
Vaughan, William, *The Golden Grove*, in *Elizabethan Critical Essays*, ed. G. Gregory Smith (Oxford: Oxford University Press, 1904), vol. 2, pp. 325–6.
Vauquelin de La Fresnaye, Jean, *Art poétique françois*, ed. Georges Pellissier (Paris: Garnier, 1885).
Vellutello, Alessandro, *Le volgare opera del Petrarcha con la espositione di Alessandro Vellutello da Lucca* (Venice: Giovanniantonio e Fratelli da Sabio, 1525).
Watson, Thomas, *Hekatompathia or Passionate Centurie of Love* (London: John Wolfe for Gabriell Cawood, 1582).
—, *The Hekatompathia*, ed. and intro. Simeon K. Heninger (Gainesville: Scholars' Facsimiles and Reprints, 1964).
Webbe, William, *A Discourse of English Poesie*, in *Elizabethan Critical Essays*, ed. G. Gregory Smith (Oxford: Oxford University Press, 1904) vol. 1, pp. 226–302.
Webster, John, *The White Devil* (London: Printed by N[icholas] O[kes] for Thomas Archer, 1612).
Weinberg, Bernard (ed.), *Trattati di poetica e retorica del Cinquecento*, 4 vols (Bari: Laterza, 1970–74).
Whetstone, George, *A Remembravnce of the Wel Imployed Life, & Godly End, of George Gaskoigne* (London: Edward Aggas, 1577).
—, *An Heptameron of Civill Discourses* (London: Richard Jones, 1582).
Whitney, Geffrey, *A Choice of Emblemes, and Other Deuises, for the Moste Parte Gathered out of Sundrie Writers, Englished and Moralized. And Diuers Newly Deuised, by Geffrey Whitney* (Leiden: Francis Raphelengius, 1586).
Willet, Laura (ed.), *Poetry and Language in 16th-Century France, Du Bellay, Ronsard, Sébillet* (Toronto: Centre for Reformation and Renaissance Studies, 2003).

Zouch, Richard, *The Sophister* (London: printed by J[ohn] O[kes] for Humphrey Mosley, 1639).

Secondary sources

Afribo, Andrea, *Teoria e prassi della 'gravitas' nel Cinquecento* (Florence: Cesati, 2001).

Albonico, Simone, *Ordine e numero: studi sul libro di poesia e le raccolte poetiche del Cinquecento* (Alessandria: Edizioni dell'Orso, 2006).

Alduy, Cécile, *Politique des «Amours». Poétique et genèse d'un genre français nouveau (1544-1560)* (Geneva: Droz, 2007).

Andersen, Jennifer L., 'Thomas Nashe and Popular Conformity in Late Elizabethan England', *Renaissance and Reformation*, 25 (2001), 25-43.

Anderson, Randall L., '"The Merit of a Manuscript Poem": The Case for Bodleian MS Rawlinson Poet. 85', in *Print, Manuscript, and Performance: The Changing Relations of the Media in Early Modern England*, ed. Arthur F. Marotti and Michael D. Bristol (Columbus: Ohio State University Press, 2000), pp. 127-71.

Antonelli, Roberto, 'L'invenzione del sonetto', in *Miscellanea di studi in onore di Aurelio Roncaglia a cinquant'anni dalla sua laurea*, 4 vols (Modena: Mucchi, 1989).

Aragon, Louis, 'Du Sonnet', *Les Lettres Françaises*, 506 (4 March 1954).

Arber, Edward (ed.), *A Transcript of the Registers of the Company of Stationers of London, 1555-1640 A.D.*, 5 vols (London: priv. publ., 1875-94).

Atkins, Carl D., 'The Application of Bibliographical Principles to the Editing of Punctuation in Shakespeare's *Sonnets*', *Studies in Philology*, 100:4 (2003), 493-513.

Baldassarri, Gabriele, 'Declinazioni del sonetto a Ferrara nel secondo Quattrocento: gli "Amorum libri" e il Canzoniere Costabili', in *Otto studi sul sonetto*, ed. Laura Facini and Arnaldo Soldan (Limena: Libreriauniversitaria.it, 2017), pp. 99-128.

Balsamo, Jean, 'Marot et les origines du pétrarquisme français', in *Clément Marot, 'prince des poëtes françois', 1496-1996*, ed. Gérard Defaux and Michel Simonin (Paris: Champion, 1997), pp. 323-37.

—, '"Nous l'avons tous admiré, et imité, non sans cause". Pétrarque en France à la Renaissance: un livre, un modèle, un mythe', in *Les Poètes français de la Renaissance et Pétrarque*, ed. Jean Balsamo (Geneva: Droz, 2004), pp. 13-34.

Bartolomeo, Beatrice, 'Notizie su sonetto e canzone nelle "Rime diverse di molti eccellentissimi auttori nuovamente raccolte", libro primo (Venezia, Gabriel Giolito de' Ferrari, 1545)', in *'I più vaghi e i più soavi fiori'*, ed. Monica Bianco and Elena Strada (Alessandria: Edizioni dell'Orso, 2001), pp. 43-76.

Bates, Catherine, 'Desire, Discontent, Parody: The Love Sonnet in Early Modern England', in *The Cambridge Companion to the Sonnet*, ed. A.D. Cousins and Peter Howarth (Cambridge: Cambridge University Press, 2011), pp. 105-24.

—, *On Not Defending Poetry: Defence and Indefensibility in Sidney's 'Defence of Poesy'* (Oxford: Oxford University Press, 2017).

—, *The Rhetoric of Courtship in Elizabethan Language and Literature* (Cambridge: Cambridge University Press, 1992).

Baue, Frederic W., *A Bibliographical Catalogue and First-Line Index of Printed Anthologies of English Poetry to 1640* (Lanham, MD, and Oxford: Scarecrow, 2002).

Bawcutt, Priscilla, 'James VI's Castalian Band: A Modern Myth', *Scottish Historical Review*, 80 (2001), 251-9.

Beal, Peter, 'Poems by Sir Philip Sidney: The Ottley Manuscript', *The Library*, fifth series, 33:4 (1978), 284-95.

Bednarz, James P., 'Canonizing Shakespeare: *The Passionate Pilgrim*, *England's Helicon* and the Question of Authenticity', *Shakespeare Survey*, 60 (2007), 252-67.

—, *Shakespeare and the Poets' War* (New York: Columbia University Press, 2001).

—, *Shakespeare and the Truth of Love: The Mystery of 'The Phoenix and the Turtle'* (New York: Palgrave, 2012).

—, '*The Passionate Pilgrim* and "The Phoenix and Turtle"', in *The Cambridge Companion to Shakespeare's Poetry*, ed. Patrick Cheney (Cambridge: Cambridge University Press, 2007), pp. 108-24.

Beltrami, Pietro, *La metrica italiana* (Bologna: Il Mulino, 1991).

Betella, Patrizia, *The Ugly Woman: Transgressive Aesthetic Models in Italian Poetry from the Middle Ages to the Baroque* (Toronto: University of Toronto Press, 2005).

Bianco, Monica, and Elena Strada (eds), *'I più vaghi e i più soavi fiori': studi sulle antologie di lirica del Cinquecento* (Alessandria: Edizioni dell'Orso, 2001).

Black, Joseph L., William R. Bowen and Germaine Warkentin, *The Library of the Sidneys of Penshurst Place, circa 1665* (Toronto: University of Toronto Press, 2013).

Black, L.G., 'Studies in Some Related Manuscript Poetic Miscellanies of the 1580s', 2 vols (D.Phil. thesis, University of Oxford, 1971).

Blanco, Mercedes, *Les Rhétoriques de la pointe: Baltasar Gracián et le conceptisme en Europe* (Paris: Champion, 1992).

Bland, Mark, 'John Windet and the Transformation of the Book Trade, 1584-1610', *Papers of the Biographical Society of America*, 107 (June 2013), 151-92.

Blank, Philip E. Jr, *Lyric Forms in the Sonnet Sequences of Barnabe Barnes* (The Hague, Paris: Mouton, 1974).

Booth, Stephen, *An Essay on Shakespeare's Sonnets* (London, New Haven: Yale University Press, 1969).

Boswell, Jackson Campbell, and Gordon McMurry Braden, *Petrarch's English Laurels, 1475-1700: A Compendium of Printed References and Allusions* (Farnham: Ashgate, 2012).

Boyd, Brian, *Why Lyrics Last: Evolution, Cognition, and Shakespeare's Sonnets* (Cambridge, MA: Harvard University Press, 2012).

Braden, Gordon, 'Shakespeare's Petrarchism', in *Shakespeare's Sonnets: Critical Essays*, ed. James Schiffer (New York: Garland Publishing, 1999), pp. 163-83.

Brennan, Michael G., 'Breton, Nicholas (1554/5-c.1626)' in *Oxford Dictionary of National Biography* (Oxford: Oxford University Press, 2004), http://ezproxy.ouls.ox.ac.uk:2117/view/article/3341 (date accessed: 6 April 2012).

Brigden, Susan, *Thomas Wyatt, The Heart's Forest* (London: Faber & Faber, 2012).

Brooks, Jerome E. (ed.), *Tobacco: Its History Illustrated by the Books, Manuscripts, and Engravings in the Library of George Arents Jr.* (New York: The Rosenbach Company, 1937).

Brown, Richard Danson, and Julian B. Lethbridge, *A Concordance to the Rhymes of The Faerie Queene* (Manchester: Manchester University Press, 2013).

Bruzzi, Zara, '"I find myself unparadis'd": the integrity of Daniel's Delia', *Cahiers Élisabéthains*, 48 (October 1995), 1–15.

Burke, Mary E., 'Queen, Lover, Poet: A Question of Balance in the Sonnets of Mary, Queen of Scots', in *Women, Writing, and the Reproduction of Culture in Tudor and Stuart Britain*, ed. Mary E. Burke and Jane Donawerth (Syracuse: Syracuse University Press, 2000), pp. 101–18.

Burton, Ben and Elizabeth Scott-Baumann, *The Work of Form: Poetics and Materiality in Early Modern Culture* (Oxford: Oxford University Press, 2014).

Cheney, Patrick, 'Halting Sonnets: Poetry and Theater in *Much Ado about Nothing*', in *A Companion to Shakespeare's Sonnets*, ed. Michael C. Schoenfeldt (Oxford: Blackwell, 2007), pp. 363–82.

—, '"O, Let My Books Be ... Dumb Presagers": Poetry and Theater in Shakespeare's Sonnets', *Shakespeare Quarterly*, 52:2 (summer 2001), 222–54.

—, *Shakespeare, National Poet-Playwright* (Cambridge: Cambridge University Press, 2004).

—, *Shakespeare's Literary Authorship* (Cambridge: Cambridge University Press, 2012).

—, ed., *The Cambridge Companion to Shakespeare's Poetry* (Cambridge: Cambridge University Press, 2007).

Clegg, Cyndia S., *Shakespeare's Reading Audiences* (Cambridge: Cambridge University Press, 2017).

Clucas, Stephen S., 'Thomas Watson's *Hekatompathia* and European Petrarchism', in *Petrarch in Britain: Interpreters, Imitators, Translators over 700 years*, ed. Martin McLaughlin, Letizia Panizza and Peter Hainsworth (Oxford: Oxford University Press, 2007), pp. 217–27.

Coatalen, Guillaume, 'Dudley Carleton and "The Libertie of Old Fashioned Poetrie" on 8 November 1596', *Notes & Queries*, 56:4 (2009), 563–6.

—, 'Unpublished Elizabethan Sonnets in a Legal Manuscript from the Cambridge University Library', *Review of English Studies*, 54 (2003), 553–65.

Cockcroft, Robert, *Rhetorical Affect in Early Modern Writing: Renaissance Passions Reconsidered* (Basingstoke: Palgrave Macmillan, 2003).

Cohen, Stephen (ed.), *Shakespeare and Historical Formalism* (Aldershot: Ashgate, 2007).

Coldiron, Anne E.B., *Printers Without Borders: Translation and Textuality in the Renaissance* (Cambridge: Cambridge University Press, 2015).

Coles, Kimberley A., *Religion, Reform, and Women's Writing in Early Modern England* (Cambridge, New York, Melbourne: Cambridge University Press, 2008).

Colie, Rosalie L., *Shakespeare's Living Art* (Princeton: Princeton University Press, 1974).

Cottegnies, Line, *L'Éclipse du regard: la Poésie anglaise du baroque au classicisme* (Geneva: Droz, 2000).

Cousins, Anthony D. and Peter Howarth (eds), *The Cambridge Companion to the Sonnet* (Cambridge: Cambridge University Press, 2011).

Cummings, Laurence, 'John Finet's Miscellany' (PhD thesis, Washington University, 1960).
—, 'Spenser's *Amoretti VIII*: New Manuscript Versions', *Studies in English Literature 1500-1900*, 4:1 (winter 1964), 125-35.
Dasenbrock, Reed Way, *Imitating the Italians: Wyatt, Spenser, Synge, Pound, Joyce* (Baltimore, London: The Johns Hopkins University Press, 1991).
Derrida, Jacques, *The Truth in Painting*, trans. Geoff Bennington and Ian McLeod (Chicago: Chicago University Press, 1987).
Dessons, Gérard and Henri Meschonnic, *Traité du rythme: des vers et des proses* (Paris: Dunod, 1998).
Dionisotti, Carlo, 'Fortuna del Petrarca nel Quattrocento', *Italia medioevale e umanistica*, XVII (1974), 61-113.
Dubrow, Heather, '"Dressing old words new"? Re-evaluating the "Delian Structure"', in Michael C. Schoenfeldt (ed.), *A Companion to Shakespeare's Sonnets* (Oxford: Blackwell, 2007), pp. 90-103.
—, *Echoes of Desire: English Petrarchism and Its Counterdiscourses* (Ithaca, London: Cornell University Press, 1995).
—, '"Incertainties now crown themselves assur'd": The Politics of Plotting Shakespeare's Sonnets', *Shakespeare Quarterly*, 47 (1996), 291-305.
—, 'Neither Here Nor There: Deixis and the Sixteenth-Century Sonnet', in *The Lyric Poem: Formations and Transformations*, ed. Marion Thain and Jonathan Culler (Cambridge: Cambridge University Press, 2013), pp. 30-50.
—, 'The Sonnet and the Lyric Mode', in *The Cambridge Companion to the Sonnet*, ed. A.D. Cousins and Peter Howarth (Cambridge: Cambridge University Press, 2011), pp. 25-45.
—, '"You may be wondering why I called you all here today": Patterns of Gathering in the Early Modern Lyric', in *The Work of Form: Poetics and Materiality in Early Modern Culture*, ed. Elizabeth Scott-Baumann and Ben Burton (Oxford: Oxford University Press, 2014), pp. 23-38.
Duncan-Jones, Katherine, 'Bess Carey's Petrarch: Newly Discovered Elizabethan Sonnets', *Review of English Studies*, 50 (1999), 304-19.
—, *Sir Philip Sidney: Courtier Poet* (New Haven: Yale University Press, 1991).
Duso, Elena Maria, *Il sonetto latino e semilatino in Italia nel Medioevo e nel Rinascimento* (Rome, Padua: Antenore, 2004).
Dutton, Richard, *Shakespeare, Court Dramatist* (Oxford: Oxford University Press, 2016).
Earl, Anthony, 'Late Elizabethan Devotional Poetry and Calvinism: A Re-evaluation of Barnabe Barnes', *Renaissance Studies*, 11:3 (1997), 223-40.
Eccles, Mark, 'Barnabe Barnes', in *Thomas Lodge and Other Elizabethans*, ed. Charles J. Sisson (Cambridge, MA: Harvard University Press, 1933), pp. 165-241.
Eckhardt, Joshua, *Manuscript Verse Collectors and the Politics of Anti-Courtly Love Poetry* (Oxford: Oxford University Press, 2009).
Eckhardt, Joshua, and Daniel Starza Smith (eds), *Manuscript Miscellanies in Early Modern England* (Farnham, Burlington: Routledge, 2014).

Edmondson, Paul, and Stanley Wells, *Shakespeare's Sonnets* (Oxford: Oxford University Press, 2004).
Estrin, Barbara L., *Laura: Uncovering Gender and Genre in Wyatt, Donne and Marvell* (Durham, NC, London: Duke University Press, 1994).
Ettenhuber, Katrin, '"Comparisons are Odious"? Revisiting the Metaphysical Conceit in Donne', *Review of English Studies*, 62:255 (2011), 393–413.
Evan, Robert C., and Jeff Moody, 'The Religious Sonnets of Anne Vaughan Lock: An Overview of Scholarship, 1989–1999', *Ben Jonson Journal: Literary Contexts in the Age of Elizabeth, James and Charles*, 22:2 (November 2015), 269–81.
Evans, Maurice, *Elizabethan Sonnets* (London: Dent, 1977).
Fallon, Samuel and David Scott Kastan, 'Signature Verses: Two Previously Unknown Fragments of Early Modern Miscellanies', *Times Literary Supplement*, 5888 (5 February 2016), 14.
Fedi, Roberto, *La memoria della poesia: canzonieri, lirici e libri di rime nel Rinascimento* (Rome: Salerno editrice, 1990).
Fehrenbach, Robert J., and Elisabeth S. Leedham-Green (eds), *Private Libraries in Renaissance England: A Collection and Catalogue of Tudor and Early Stuart Book Lists*, 5 vols (Tempe: Medieval and Early Renaissance Texts and Studies, 1992–98).
Ferroni, Giovanni, 'Come leggere "I tre libri degli Amori" di Bernardo Tasso (1534–1537)', *Quaderno di italianistica [della Sezione di Italiano dell'Università di Losanna]* (2011), 99–144.
Ferry, Anne, *The 'Inward' Language: Sonnets of Wyatt, Sidney, Shakespeare, Donne* (Chicago: University of Chicago Press, 1983).
Fineman, Joel, *Shakespeare's Perjured Eye: The Invention of Poetic Subjectivity in the Sonnets* (Berkeley: University of California Press, 1986).
Forni, Giorgio, *Forme brevi della poesia: tra Umanesimo e Rinascimento* (Pisa: Pacini editore, 2001).
——, 'Il canone del sonetto nel XVI secolo', *Schede umanistiche*, 2 (1977), 113–22.
Forster, Leonard, *The Icy Fire: Five Studies in European Petrarchism* (London: Cambridge University Press, 1969).
Fowler, Alastair, *Kinds of Literature: An Introduction to the Theory of Genres and Modes* (Oxford: Clarendon Press, 1982).
——, *Spenser and the Numbers of Time* (London: Routledge and Kegan Paul, 1964).
——, *Triumphal Forms: Structural Patterns in Elizabethan Poetry* (Cambridge: Cambridge University Press, 1970).
—— (ed.), *Silent Poetry: Essays in Numerological Analysis* (London: Routledge & Kegan Paul, 1970).
Fowler, Mary, *Cornell University Library Catalogue of the Petrarch Collection Bequeathed by Willard Fiske* (London: Oxford University Press, 1916).
Fox, Alistair, *The English Renaissance: Identity and Representation in Elizabethan England* (Oxford: Blackwell, 1997).
Fraistat, Neil (ed.), *Poems in Their Place: The Intertextuality and Order of Poetic Collections* (Chapel Hill, London: University of North Carolina Press, 1986).
Fumerton, Patricia, *Cultural Aesthetics. Renaissance Literature and the Practice of Social Ornament* (Chicago: University of Chicago Press, 1991).

Gazzard, Hugh, 'Nicholas Breton, Richard Jones, and Two Printed Verse Miscellanies', *Notes & Queries*, 62:1 (2015), 79–82.

——, 'Nicholas Breton, the Earl of Essex, and Elizabethan Penitential Poetry', *Studies in English Literature 1500–1900*, 56:1 (winter 2016), 23–42.

——, 'Two New Sonnets by Sir Philip Sidney?' *Sidney Journal*, 34:2 (2016), 25–48.

Gendre, André, *Evolution du sonnet français* (Paris: Presses Universitaires de France, 1996).

Genette, Gérard, *Paratexts: Thresholds of Interpretation*, trans. Jane E. Lewin (Cambridge: Cambridge University Press, 1997).

Gigante, Claudio, *Tasso* (Rome: Salerno editrice, 2007).

Ginestet, Gaëlle, 'L'Écriture mythologique dans les sonnets amoureux élisabéthains' (PhD dissertation, Université Paul Valéry-Montpellier, 2005).

Going, William T., 'Gascoigne and the Term "Sonnet-Sequence"', *Notes & Queries*, 1 (May 1954), 189–90.

Goldberg, Jonathan, *Sodometries: Renaissance Texts, Modern Sexualities* (Stanford: Stanford University Press, 1992).

Gorni, Guglielmo, 'Il libro di poesia cinquecentesco: principio e fine', in *Il libro di poesia dal copista al tipografo (Ferrara, 29–31 maggio 1987)*, ed. Marco Santaga and Amedeo Quondam (Modena: Panini, 1989), pp. 35–41.

——, 'Le forme primarie del testo poetico', in *Letteratura italiana*, ed. Alberto Asor Rosa (Turin: Einaudi, 1984), vol. 3, pp. 439–518.

Gottschalk, Katherine K, 'British Museum Manuscript Harley 6910: An Edition' (PhD dissertation, University of Chicago, 1974).

——, 'Discoveries Concerning British Library MS Harley 6910', *Modern Philology*, 77:2 (November 1979), 121–31.

Goyet, Francis, 'Le Sonnet français, vrai et faux héritier de la Grande Rhétorique', in *Le Sonnet à la Renaissance, Actes du colloque de Reims*, ed. Yvonne Bellenger (Paris: Aux Amateurs de Livres, 1988), pp. 31–41.

Graves, Robert, and Riding, Laura, 'A Study in Original Punctuation and Spelling', in *A Casebook on Shakespeare's Sonnets*, ed. Gerald Willen and Victor B. Reed (New York: Thomas Cromwell, 1964), pp. 161–72.

Greenblatt, Stephen, *Renaissance Self-Fashioning from More to Shakespeare* (Chicago, London: University of Chicago Press, 1980).

Greene, Roland A., *Post-Petrarchism: Origins and Innovations of the Western Lyric Sequence* (Princeton: Princeton University Press, 1991).

Greene, Thomas M., *The Light in Troy: Imitation and Discovery in Renaissance Poetry* (New Haven: Yale University Press, 1982).

Grundy, Joan, *The Poems of Henry Constable* (Liverpool: Liverpool University Press, 1960).

——, *The Spenserian Poets. A Study in Elizabethan and Jacobean Poetry* (London: Edward Arnold Publishers, 1969).

Gubar, Susan, '"The Blank Page" and the Issues of Female Creativity', in *Writing and Sexual Difference*, ed. Elizabeth Abel (Chicago: University of Chicago Press, 1982), 73–93.

Hackett, Helen, 'The Art of Blasphemy? Interfusions of the Erotic and the Sacred in the Poetry of Donne, Barnes, and Constable', *Renaissance and Reformation*, 28:3 (2004), 27–54.

Hadfield, Andrew, *Edmund Spenser: A Life* (Oxford: Oxford University Press, 2012).

—, 'Michael Drayton's Brilliant Career', *Proceedings of the British Academy*, 125 (2003), 119–47.

Hall, Kim, *Things of Darkness: Economies of Race and Gender in Early Modern England* (Ithaca: Cornell University Press, 1995).

Hamilton, Albert C. (ed.), *The Spenser Encylopedia* (Toronto: University of Toronto Press, 1997).

Hamlin, Hannibal, *Psalm Culture and Early Modern English Literature* (Cambridge: Cambridge University Press, 2004).

Hamrick, Stephen (ed.), *Tottel's* Songs and Sonettes *in Context* (Farnham: Ashgate, 2013).

Hannay, Margaret P., *Philip's Phoenix: Mary Sidney, Countess of Pembroke* (Oxford, New York: Oxford University Press, 1990).

Heale, Elizabeth, 'Songs, Sonnets and Autobiography: Self-Representation in Sixteenth-Century Verse Miscellanies', in *Betraying Our Selves: Forms of Self-Representation in Early Modern English Texts*, ed. Hek Dragstra, Sheila Ottway and Helen Wilcox (Basingstoke: Macmillan-St Martin's, 2000), pp. 59–75.

—, *Wyatt, Surrey, and Early Tudor Poetry* (London, New York: Longman, 1998).

Healy, Thomas, 'Performing the Self: Reformation History and the English Renaissance Lyric', in *Performances of the Sacred in Late Medieval and Early Modern England*, ed. Susanne Rupp and Tobias Döring (Amsterdam, New York: Rodopi, 2005), pp. 65–79.

Heaton, Gabriel, *Writing and Reading Royal Entertainments: From George Gascoigne to Ben Jonson* (Oxford: Oxford University Press, 2010).

Hebel, William, 'Nicholas Ling and *Englands Helicon*', *The Library*, fourth series, 5:2 (1924), 153–60.

Helgerson, Richard, *Self-Crowned Laureates: Spenser, Johnson, Milton and the Literary System* (Berkeley: University of California Press, 1983).

—, *The Elizabethan Prodigals* (Berkeley: University of California Press, 1976).

Herman, Peter, '"Mes subjectz, mon ame assubjectie": The Problematic (of) Subjectivity in Mary Stuart's Sonnets', in *Reading Monarchs Writing: The Poetry of Henry VIII, Mary Stuart, Elizabeth I, and James VI/I*, ed. Peter C. Herman (Tempe: Arizona Center for Medieval and Renaissance Studies, 2002), pp. 51–78.

Herrnstein Smith, Barbara, *Poetic Closure: A Study of How Poems End* (Chicago: Chicago University Press, 1968).

Hieatt, A. Kent, Charles W. Hieatt and Anne Lake Prescott, 'When Did Shakespeare Write *Sonnets* 1609?', *Studies in Philology*, 88 (1991), 69–109.

Hirsch, Edward, and Eavan Boland (eds), *The Making of a Sonnet: A Norton Anthology* (New York, London: Norton & Company, 2008).

Ho, Elaine Y.L., 'Fulke Greville's *Caelica* and the Calvinist Self', *Studies in English Literature*, 32 (1992), 35–57.

Hobbs, Mary, *Early Seventeenth-Century Verse Miscellany Manuscripts* (Aldershot: Scolar, 1992).
Hofmeister, Gerhart, *Petrarkistische Lyrik* (Stuttgart: J.B. Metzler, 1973).
Holton, Amanda, 'An Obscured Tradition: The Sonnet and Its Fourteen-Line Predecessors', *Review of English Studies*, 62:255 (June 2011), 373–92.
Hudson, Hoyt Hopewell, *The Epigram in the English Renaissance* (New York: Octagon Books Inc., 1966).
Humboldt, Wilhelm von, *Über die Verschiedenheit des menschlichen Sprachbaues und ihren Einfluß auf die geistige Entwicklung des Menschengeschlechts* [1836] (Paderborn: Schöningh, 1998).
Hunt, Marvin, 'Be dark but not too dark. Shakespeare's Dark Lady as a Sign of Color', in *Shakespeare's Sonnets: Critical Essays*, ed. James Schiffer (New York, London: Garland Publishing, 2000), pp. 368–98.
Hunter, William B. Jr, *The English Spenserians. The Poetry of Giles Fletcher, George Wither, Michael Drayton, Phineas Fletcher and Henry More* (Salt Lake City: University of Utah Press, 1977).
Hyland, Peter, *An Introduction to Shakespeare's Poems* (New York: Palgrave Macmillan, 2003).
Innes, Paul, *Shakespeare and the English Renaissance Sonnet: Verses of Feigning Love* (London, New York: Macmillan, St Martin's Press, 1997).
Jack, Ronald D.S. 'Petrarch and the Scottish Renaissance Sonnet', *Proceedings of the British Academy*, 146 (2007), 259–73.
Jackson, Ken, and Arthur F. Marotti, 'The Turn to Religion in Early Modern English Studies', *Criticism*, 46:1 (winter 2004), 167–90.
Jackson, MacD.P., 'Aspects of Organisation in *Shakespeare's Sonnets* (1609)', *Parergon*, 17 (1999), 109–34.
—, 'Punctuation and the Compositors of Shakespeare's *Sonnets*, 1609', *The Library*, fifth series, 30:1 (1975), 1–24.
Jackson, Virginia, and Yopie, Prins (eds), *The Lyric Theory Reader: A Critical Anthology* (Baltimore: Johns Hopkins, 2014).
Jackson, William A. (ed.), *Records of the Court of the Stationers' Company, 1602 to 1640* (London: Bibliographical Society, 1957).
John, Lisle C., *The Elizabethan Sonnet Sequences: Studies in Conventional Conceits* (New York: Columbia University Press, 1938).
Johnson, Gerald D., 'Nicholas Ling, Publisher 1580–1607', *Studies in Bibliography*, 38 (1985), 203–14.
Jones, Dorothy, 'An Example of Anti-Petrarchan Satire in Nashe's "The Unfortunate Traveller"', *The Yearbook of English Studies*, 1 (1971), 48–54.
Jones, Richard F., *The Triumph of the English Language: A Survey of Opinions Concerning the Vernacular from the Introduction of Printing to the Restoration* (Stanford: Stanford University Press, 1953).
Jowett, John, *Shakespeare and Text* (Oxford: Oxford University Press, 2007).
Juri, Amelia, 'Sintassi e imitazione nei sonetti di Pietro Bembo', in *Otto studi sul sonetto*, ed. Laura Facini and Arnaldo Soldani (Limena: Libreriauniversitaria.it, 2017), pp. 129–56.

Kalas, Rayna, *Frame, Glass, Verse: The Technology of Poetic Invention in the English Renaissance* (Ithaca, London: Cornell University Press, 2007).

Kambasković-Sawers, Danijela, '"Never was I the golden cloud": Ovidian Myth, Ambiguous Speaker and the Narrative in the Sonnet Sequences by Petrarch, Sidney and Spenser', *Renaissance Studies*, 21:5 (November 2007), 637–61.

Kathman, David, 'Heywood, Thomas (*c.* 1573–1641)', in *Oxford Dictionary of National Biography* (Oxford: Oxford University Press, 2004), www.oxforddnb.com/view/article/13190 (date accessed: 17 August 2016).

Kennedy, William John, *Authorizing Petrarch* (Ithaca, London: Cornell University Press, 1994).

—, 'European Beginnings and Transmissions: Dante, Petrarch and the Sonnet Sequence', in *The Cambridge Companion to the Sonnet*, ed. A.D. Cousins and Peter Howarth (Cambridge: Cambridge University Press, 2011), pp. 84–104.

—, '"Les langues des hommes sont pleines de tromperies": Shakespeare, French Poetry, and Alien Tongues', in *Textual Conversations in the Renaissance*, ed. Zachary Lesser and Benedict S. Robinson (Aldershot: Ashgate, 2006), pp. 91–111.

—, *Petrarchism at Work: Contextual Economies in the Age of Shakespeare* (Ithaca, London: Cornell University Press, 2016).

—, *The Site of Petrarchism: Early Modern National Sentiment in Italy, France, and England* (Baltimore, London: Johns Hopkins University Press, 2003).

Kerrigan, John, '*Love's Labour's Lost* and Shakespearean Revision', *Shakespeare Quarterly*, 33 (1982), 337–9.

—, 'Shakespeare's Poems', in *The Cambridge Companion to Shakespeare*, ed. Margreta de Grazia and Stanley Wells (Cambridge: Cambridge University Press, 2003 [2001]), pp. 65–82.

King, Ros, 'Seeing the Rhythm: An Interpretation of Sixteenth-Century Punctuation and Metrical Practice', in *Ma(r)king the Text: The Presentation of Meaning on the Literary Page*, ed. Joe Bray, Miriam Handley and Anne C. Henry (Aldershot: Ashgate, 2000), pp. 235–52.

Kinney, Claire (ed.), *Ashgate Critical Essays on Women Writers in England, 1550–1700, vol. 4: Mary Wroth* (Farnham, Burlington: Ashgate, 2009).

Klawitter, George, 'Barnabe Barnes (1571–1609)', *Sixteenth-Century British Nondramatic Writers: First Series*, in *Dictionary of Literary Bibliography* (Detroit, MI: Dale, 1993), vol. 132, pp. 53–5.

Klein, Lisa M. *The Exemplary Sidney and the Elizabethan Sonneteer* (Newark, London: University of Delaware Press, Associated University Presses, 1998).

—, 'The Petrarchism of Sir Thomas Wyatt Reconsidered', in *The Work of Dissimilitude. Essay from the Sixth Citadel Conference on Medieval and Renaissance Literature*, ed. Robert A. White (Newark, London, Toronto: University of Delaware Press, Associated University Press, 1992), pp. 131–47.

Knight, Jeffrey Todd, *Bound to Read: Compilations, Collections and the Making of Renaissance Literature* (Philadelphia: University of Pennsylvania Press, 2013).

Lawrence, Jason, '*Who the Devil Taught Thee So Much Italian?' Italian Language and Literary Imitation in Early Modern England* (Manchester: Manchester University Press, 2005).

Lecointe, Jean, 'In cauda venenum: Montaigne et la formation du conceptisme français', *Montaigne Studies*, 18 (2006), 137–52.
Leedham-Greene, Elisabeth S. (ed.), *Books in Cambridge Inventories: Book Lists from the Vice-Chancellor's Court Probate Inventories in the Tudor and Stuart Periods*, 2 vols (Cambridge: Cambridge University Press, 1986).
Lesser, Zachary, *Renaissance Drama and the Politics of Publication: Readings in the English Book Trade* (Cambridge: Cambridge University Press, 2004).
Lesser, Zachary, and Benedict S. Robinson (eds), *Textual Conversations in the Renaissance* (Aldershot: Ashgate Press, 2006).
Lever, Julius W., *The Elizabethan Love Sonnet* (London: Methuen & Co., 1956).
Levin, Phillis (ed.), *The Penguin Book of the Sonnet: 500 Years of a Classic Tradition in English* (London: Penguin Books, 2001).
Levine, Caroline, *Forms: Whole, Rhythm, Hierarchy, Network* (Princeton, Oxford: Princeton University Press, 2015).
Levinson, Marjorie, 'What Is New Formalism?', *PMLA*, 122:2 (March 2007), 558–69.
Lewalski, Barbara, *Protestant Poetics and the Seventeenth-Century Religious Lyric* (Princeton: Princeton University Press, 1979).
Loewenstein, Joseph, *The Author's Due: Printing and the Prehistory of Copyright* (Chicago: Chicago University Press, 2002).
Lyne, Raphael, *Shakespeare, Rhetoric, and Cognition* (Cambridge: Cambridge University Press, 2011).
Maasen, Irmgaard, 'Canonized by Love? Religious Rhetoric and Gender-Fashioning in the Sonnet', in *Performances of the Sacred in Late Medieval and Early Modern England*, ed. Susanne Rupp and Tobias Düring (Amsterdam, New York: Rodopi, 2005), pp. 169–88.
Magro, Fabio and Arnaldo Soldani, *Il sonetto italiano. Dalle origini a oggi* (Rome: Carocci, 2017).
MacDonald, Robert H (ed.), *The Library of Drummond of Hawthornden* (Edinburgh: Edinburgh University Press, 1971).
Marotti, Arthur F., '"Love is not love": Elizabethan Sonnet Sequences and the Social Order', *English Literary History*, 49 (1982), 396–428.
—, *Manuscript, Print, and the English Renaissance Lyric* (Ithaca, London: Cornell University Press, 1995).
—, 'Shakespeare's Sonnets and the Manuscript Circulation of Texts in Early Modern England', in *A Companion to Shakespeare's Sonnets*, ed. Michael C. Schoenfeldt (Oxford: Blackwell, 2007), pp. 185–203.
Marotti, Arthur F. and Marcelle Freiman, 'The English Sonnet in Manuscript, Print and Mass Media', in *The Cambridge Companion to the Sonnet*, ed. A.D. Cousins and Peter Howarth (Cambridge: Cambridge University Press, 2011), pp. 66–83.
Martin, Christopher, 'Retrieving Jonson's Petrarch', *Shakespeare Quarterly*, 45 (1994), 89–92.
Martini, Alessandro, 'Le nuove forme del canzoniere', in *I capricci di Proteo: percorsi e linguaggi del Barocco. Atti del Convegno di Lecce, 23–26 ottobre 2000*, ed. Maria Luisa Doglio (Rome: Salerno, 2002), pp. 199–226.

May, Steven W., *The Elizabethan Courtier Poets: The Poems and Their Contexts* (Columbia, London: University of Missouri Press, 1991).
—, 'The Poems of Edward De Vere, Seventeenth Earl of *Oxford* and of Robert Devereux, Second Earl of *Essex*', *Studies in Philology*, 77 (1980), 43–64.
—, ed., *Henry Stanford's Anthology: An Edition of Cambridge University Library Manuscript Dd. 5.75* (New York: Garland, 1988).
—, and William A. Ringler (eds), *Elizabethan Poetry: A Bibliography and First-Line Index of English Verse, 1559–1603*, 3 vols (London: Continuum, 2004).
Mazzoni, Guido, *Sulla poesia moderna* (Bologna: Il Mulino, 2005).
McCabe, Richard, *Ungainfull Arte: Poetry, Patronage, & Print in the Early Modern Era* (Oxford: Oxford University Press, 2016).
McLaughlin, Martin, Letizia Panizza and Peter Hainsworth (eds), *Petrarch in Britain: Interpreters, Imitators, and Translators over 700 Years* (Oxford, New York: Oxford University Press for the British Academy, 2007).
Meschonnic, Henri, *Langage, histoire, une même théorie* (Paris: Verdier, 2012).
Miller, Naomi J., *Changing the Subject: Mary Wroth and Figurations of Gender in Early Modern England* (Lexington: University Press of Kentucky, 1996).
Minta, Stephen, *Petrarch and Petrarchism: The English and French Traditions* (Manchester, New York: Manchester University Press, Barnes & Noble, 1980).
Monferran, Jean-Charles, 'Le sonnet français: "poème stationnaire" ou "machine à penser"? Étude de l'agencement rimique du sizain autour de 1550', *L'Information Grammaticale*, special issue on the French language in the sixteenth century, 75 (October 1997), 29–32.
Moore, Mary B., *Desiring Voices: Women Sonneteers and Petrarchism* (Carbondale: Southern Illinois University Press, 2011).
Mortimer, Anthony (ed.), *Petrarch's Canzoniere in the English Renaissance* (Bergamo: Minerva italica, 1975).
Moul, Victoria, *Jonson, Horace and the Classical Tradition* (Cambridge: Cambridge University Press, 2006).
Muir, Kenneth, *Life and Letters of Sir Thomas Wyatt* (Liverpool: Liverpool University Press, 1963).
Murrin, Michael, *Trade and Romance* (Chicago: University of Chicago Press, 2014).
Navarrete, Ignacio, *Orphans of Petrarch: Poetry and Theory in the Spanish Renaissance* (Berkeley, Los Angeles, Oxford: University of California Press, 1994).
Nebeker, Eric, 'Broadside Ballads, Miscellanies, and the Lyric in Print', *English Literary History*, 76:4 (2009), 989–1013.
Neely, Carol T., 'The Structure of English Renaissance Sonnet Sequences', *English Literary History*, 45 (1978), 359–89.
Nelson, Jeffrey N., 'Lust and Black Magic in Barnabe Barnes's *Parthenophil and Parthenophe*', *The Sixteenth Century Journal: Journal of Early Modern Studies*, 25:3 (1994), 595–608.
North, Marcy, 'Ignoto in the Age of Print: The Manipulation of Anonymity in Early Modern England', *Studies in Philology*, 91:4 (1994), 390–416.
Orgel, Stephen, 'Introduction', in Shakespeare, William, *The Sonnets*, ed. G. Blakemore Evans (Cambridge: Cambridge University Press, 2006 [1996]).

Parker, Tom W.N., *Proportional Form in the Sonnets of the Sidney Circle: Loving in Truth* (Oxford: Oxford University Press, 1998).
Paulissen, May Nelson, *The Love Sonnet of Lady Mary Wroth: A Critical Introduction* (Salzburg: Institut für Anglistik und Amerikanistik Universität Salzburg, 1982).
Pequigney, Joseph, *Such Is My Love: A Study of Shakespeare's Sonnets* (Chicago: University of Chicago Press, 1985).
Phillippy, Patricia Berrhaou, *Love's Remedies: Recantation and Renaissance Lyric Poetry* (Lewisburg, London: Bucknell University Press, Associated University Press, 1995).
Pomeroy, Elizabeth, *The Elizabethan Miscellanies: Their Development and Conventions* (Berkeley, Los Angeles, London: University of California Press, 1973).
Potter, Lois, *The Life of William Shakespeare: A Critical Biography* (Chichester: Wiley-Blackwell, 2012).
Powell, Jason, 'The Network behind *Tottel's Miscellany*', *English Literary Renaissance*, 46:2 (spring 2016), 193–224.
Praloran, Marco, 'Metrica e tecnica del verso', in *'Prose della volgar lingua' di Pietro Bembo. Atti del convegno di Gargnano sul Garda (4–7 ottobre 2000)*, ed. Silvia Morgagna, Mario Piotti and Massimo Prada (Milan: Cisalpino, 2000), pp. 409–21.
Praz, Mario, *The Flaming Heart: Essays on Crashaw, Machiavelli and Other Studies in the Relations between Italian and English Literature from Chaucer to T.S. Eliot* (Gloucester: Peter Smith, 1966).
Prescott, Anne Lake, 'Du Bellay and Shakespeare's Sonnets', in *The Oxford Handbook of Shakespeare's Poetry*, ed. Jonathan F.S. Post (Oxford: Oxford University Press, 2013), pp. 134–50.
—, *French Poets and the English Renaissance: Studies in Fame and Transformation* (New Haven, London: Yale University Press, 1978).
Prouty, Charles T., *George Gascoigne: Elizabethan Courtier, Soldier, and Poet* (New York: Columbia University Press, 1942).
Rasmussen, Mark David (ed.), *Renaissance Literature and Its Formal Engagements* (Basingstoke: Palgrave, 2002).
Ravelhofer, Barbara (ed.), *James Shirley and Early Modern Theatre: New Critical Perspectives* (London: Routledge, 2016).
Raymond, Joad, *The Invention of the Newspaper: English Newsbooks, 1641–1649* (Oxford: Oxford University Press, 1996).
Reid, Lindsay Ann, '"Certaine Amorous Sonnets, Betweene Venus and Adonis": Fictive Acts of Writing in *The Passionate Pilgrime* of 1612', *Études Épistémè*, 21 (2012). https://journals.openedition.org/episteme/419.
Rhodes, Neil, 'Status Anxiety and English Renaissance Translation', in *Renaissance Paratexts*, ed. Helen Smith and Louise Wilson (Cambridge: Cambridge University Press, 2011), pp. 107–20.
Richards, Jennifer, *Rhetoric and Courtliness in Early Modern Literature* (Cambridge: Cambridge University Press, 2003).
Rigolot, François, 'Qu'est-ce qu'un sonnet? Perspectives sur les origines d'une forme poétique', *Revue d'Histoire Littéraire de la France*, 84 (1984), 3–18.

—, 'When Petrarchan Errors Become Political Crimes: Mary Stuart's French Sonnets to Bothwell', in *Writers in Conflict in Sixteenth-Century France*, ed. Elizabeth Vinestock, David Foster and Neil Kenny (Durham: University of Durham, 2008), 37–50.

Ringler, William J. (ed.), 'Poems Attributed to Sir Philip Sidney', *Studies in Philology*, 47:2 (1950), 126–51.

Roche, Thomas P. Jr, *Petrarch and the English Sonnet Sequences* (New York: AMS Press, 1989).

Roe, John, '"Willobie his Avisa" and "The Passionate Pilgrim": Precedence, Parody, and Development', *The Yearbook of English Studies*, 23, Early Shakespeare Special Number (1993), 111–25.

Roncaglia, Aurelio, 'Note d'aggiornamento critico sui testi del Notaro e invenzione del sonetto', in *In ricordo di Giuseppe Cusimano*, ed. Giovanni Ruffino (Palermo: Centro di Studi filologici e linguistici, 1992), pp. 9–25.

Roubaud, Jacques, 'La Forme du sonnet français de Marot à Malherbe, Recherche de seconde rhétorique' (PhD dissertation, Université Paris IV Sorbonne, 1989).

Royan, Nicola and Sally Mapstone (eds), *Langage Cleir Illumynate: Scottish Poetry from Barbour to Drummond, 1375-1630* (Amsterdam: Rodopi, 2007).

Rudenstine, Neil, *Ideas of Order: A Close Reading of Shakespeare's Sonnets* (New York: Farrar, Straus and Giroux, 2014).

Rudick, Michael, 'The "Ralegh Group" in *The Phoenix Nest*', *Studies in Bibliography*, 24 (1971), 131–7.

Santagata, Marco, *Dal sonetto al canzoniere: ricerche sulla preistoria e la costruzione di un genere* (Padua: Liviana, 1989).

Schaar, Claes, *An Elizabethan Sonnet Problem: Shakespeare's Sonnets, Daniel's Delia and Their Literary Background* (Lund: C.W.K. Gerup, 1960).

Schalkwyk, David, *Speech and Performance in Shakespeare's Sonnets and Plays* (Cambridge: Cambridge University Press, 2002).

Schoenfeldt, Michael C. (ed.), *A Companion to Shakespeare's Sonnets* (Oxford: Blackwell, 2007).

Scott, Janet Girvan, *Les Sonnets élisabéthains: les Sources et l'apport personnel* (Paris: Champion, 1929).

Scott-Warren, Jason, *Sir John Harington and the Book as Gift* (Oxford: Oxford University Press, 2001).

Sessions, William A., *Henry Howard, the Poet Earl of Surrey* (Oxford: Oxford University Press, 1999).

Shell, Alison and Arnold Hunt, 'The Book as Gift in Elisabethan Durham: Barnabe Barnes' *A Divine Centurie of Spirituall Sonnets*', in *Collaboration and Interdisciplinarity in the Republic of Letters*, ed. Paul Scott (Manchester: Manchester University Press, 2010), pp. 117–33.

Shrank, Cathy, 'Counsel, Succession and the Politics of Shakespeare's *Sonnets*', in *Shakespeare and Early Modern Political Thought*, ed. David Armitage, Conal Condren and Andrew Fitzmaurice (Cambridge: Cambridge University Press, 2009), pp. 111–18.

—, '"Matters of love as of discourse": The English Sonnet, 1560-1580', *Studies in Philology*, 105:1 (2008), 30-49.
Simonin, Michel (ed.), *Dictionnaire des lettres françaises: le XVIe siècle* (Paris: Fayard, 2001).
Simpson, Percy, *Shakespearian Punctuation* (Oxford: Clarendon Press, 1911).
Slight, William E., *Managing Readers: Printed Marginalia in English Renaissance Books* (Ann Arbor: University of Michigan Press, 2001).
Smith, Bruce, *Homosexual Desire in Shakespeare's England: A Cultural Poetics* (Chicago: University of Chicago Press, 1991).
Smith, Helen, and Louise Wilson (eds), *Renaissance Paratexts* (Cambridge: Cambridge University Press, 2011).
Smith, Nicholas, 'The Genre and Critical Reception of Jacopo Sannazaro's "Eclogae Piscatoriae" (Naples, 1526)', *Humanistica Lovaniensia*, 50 (2001), 199-219.
Smith, Rosalind, '"Plaintes Full of Dissimulation": The Casket Sonnets, Female Complaint and True Crime', in *Expanding the Canon of Early Modern Women's Writing*, ed. Paul Salzman (Newcastle-upon-Tyne: Cambridge Scholars, 2010), pp. 125-42.
—, *Sonnets and the English Woman Writer, 1560-1621: The Politics of Absence* (Basingstoke: Palgrave Macmillan, 2005).
Sokol, B.J., 'Poets in Shakespeare's Plays', in *Shakespeare's Artists: The Painters, Sculptors, Poets and Musicians in His Plays and Poems* (London: Bloomsbury Arden Shakespeare, 2018), pp. 93-116.
Sokolov, Danila, *Renaissance Texts, Medieval Subjectivities: Rethinking Petrarchan Desire from Wyatt to Shakespeare* (Pittsburgh, PA: Duquesne University Press, 2017).
Spiller, Michael G., *Early Modern Sonneteers from Wyatt to Milton* (Horndon, Tavistock: Northcote House Publishers Ltd, 2001).
—, *The Development of the Sonnet: An Introduction* (London, New York: Routledge, 1992).
Stephens, Dorothy, *The Limits of Eroticism in Post-Petrarchan Narrative: Conditional Pleasure from Spenser to Marvell* (Cambridge: Cambridge University Press, 1998).
Stern, Virginia, *Gabriel Harvey: His Life, Marginalia and Library* (Oxford: Clarendon Press; New York: Oxford University Press, 1979).
Sterrett, Joseph, *The Unheard Prayer: Religious Toleration in Shakespeare's Drama* (Leiden: Brill, 2012).
Straznicky, Marta (ed.), *Shakespeare's Stationers: Studies in Cultural Bibliography* (Philadelphia: University of Pennsylvania Press, 2013).
Strier, Richard, 'Lyric Poetry from Donne to Philips', in *The Columbia History of British Poetry*, ed. Carl Woodring and James Shapiro (New York: Columbia University Press, 1994), pp. 229-53.
Svensson, Lars-Hakan, *Silent Art, Rhetorical and Thematic Patterns in Samuel Daniel's* Delia (Lund: C.W.K. Gleerup, 1980).
Swann, Marjorie, *Curiosities and Texts: The Culture of Collecting in Early Modern England* (Philadelphia: University of Pennsylvania Press, 2001).

Swinburne, Charles, *Studies in Prose and Poetry* (London: Chatto and Windus, 1894).
Tallini, Gennaro, '"Voluptas" e "docere" nel pensiero critico di Antonio Minturno', *Esperienze Letterarie*, 33:3 (2008), 73–100.
Thomas, James, *The First Printed Catalogue of the Bodleian Library, 1605: A Facsimile* (Oxford: Clarendon Press, 1986).
Thomson, Patricia, *Sir Thomas Wyatt and His Background* (London: Routledge and Kegan Paul, 1964).
Tomasi, Franco, *Studi sulla lirica rinascimentale (1540–1570)* (Rome, Padua: Antenore, 2012).
Turner, Henry S., *The English Renaissance Stage: Geometry, Poetics, and the Practical Spatial Arts 1580–1630* (Oxford: Oxford University Press, 2006).
Uman, Deborah, and Sara Morrison (eds), *Staging the Blazon in Early Modern English Theatre*, Studies in Performance and Early Modern Drama (Farnham: Ashgate, 2013).
Vassalli, A., 'Editoria del petrarchismo cinquecentesco: alcune cifre', in Marco Santagata and Amedeo Quondam (eds), *Il libro di poesia dal copista al tipografico* (Ferrara: Panini, 1989), pp. 91–102.
Vendler, Helen, 'Shakespeare's Other Sonnets', in *In the Company of Shakespeare: Essays on English Renaissance Literature in Honor of G. Blakemore Evans*, ed. Thomas Moisan and Douglas Bruster (Madison, NJ; London: Fairleigh Dickinson University Press; Associated University Press, 2002), pp. 161–76.
—, *The Art of Shakespeare's Sonnets* (Cambridge, MA: Belknap Press, 1997).
Verweij, Sebastiaan, 'The Manuscripts of William Fowler: A Revaluation of The Tarantula of Love, A Sonnet Sequence, and Of Death', *Scottish Studies Review*, 8:2 (autumn 2007), 9–23.
Vialleton, Jean-Yves, 'Le Pétrarque des antipétrarquistes français des années 1550', *Cahiers d'Études Italiennes*, 4 (2006), 99–115.
Vickers, Brian, *English Renaissance Literary Criticism* (Oxford: Oxford University Press, 1999).
Vickers, Nancy, 'Diana Described: Scattered Women and Scattered Rhyme', in *Writing and Sexual Difference*, ed. Elizabeth Abel (Chicago, London: University of Chicago Press, 1982), pp. 95–109.
Vignes, Jean, 'Poésie en musique: des *Amours* de Ronsard au "supplément musical"', *Fabula / Les colloques, Relire Les Amours de Ronsard*, www.fabula.org/colloques/document3035.php (date accessed: 2 July 2018).
Vuillemin, Rémi, 'From Ideas to Books: The Editorial Writing of Michael Drayton's Sonnet Sequences', in *Book Practices and Textual Itineraries 4: From Text(s) to Book(s): Studies in the Production and Editorial Process*, ed. Nathalie Collé-Bak, Monica Latham and David Ten Eyck (Nancy: Presses Universitaires de Nancy, 2014), pp. 181–95.
—, *Le Recueil pétrarquiste à l'ère du maniérisme: Poétique des sonnets de Michael Drayton, 1594–1619* (Paris: Champion, 2014).
Wall, Wendy, *The Imprint of Gender: Authorship and Publication in the English Renaissance* (Ithaca, London: Cornell University Press, 1993).

Waller, Gary F., *The Sidney Family Romance: Mary Wroth, William Herbert, and the Early Modern Construction of Gender* (Detroit: Wayne State University Press, 1993).
Waller, Gary F., and Michael D. Moore (eds), *Sir Philip Sidney and the Interpretation of Renaissance Culture: The Poet in His Time and In Ours. A Collection of Critical Scholarly Essays* (London: Croom Helm, 1984).
Warley, Christopher, *Sonnet Sequences and Social Distinction in Renaissance England* (Cambridge: Cambridge University Press, 2005).
Warner, J. Christopher, *The Making and Marketing of Tottel's Miscellany, 1557* (Burlington: Ashgate, 2011).
Watson, George, *The English Petrarchans: A Critical Bibliography of the 'Canzoniere'* (London: Warburg Institute, 1967).
Weaver, William P., 'The Banquet of the Common Sense: George Chapman's Anti-Epyllion', *Studies in Philology*, 111:4 (2014), 757–85.
Wells, Stanley, 'Jaggard, William (c. 1568–1623)', in *Oxford Dictionary of National Biography* (Oxford: Oxford University Press, 2004), www.oxforddnb.com/view/article/37592 (date accessed: 7 April 2016).
Westling, Louise H., *The Evolution of Michael Drayton's Idea* (Salzburg: Institut für Englische Sprache und Literatur, Universität Salzburg, 1974).
White, Micheline (ed.), *Ashgate Critical Essays on Women Writers in England, vol. 3: Anne Locke, Isabella Whitney, Aemilia Lanyer* (Farnham, Burlington: Ashgate, 2009).
White, Robert S., 'Survival and Change: The Sonnet from Milton to the Romantics', in *The Cambridge Companion to the Sonnet*, ed. Anthony D. Cousins and Peter Howarth (Cambridge: Cambridge University Press, 2011).
Whittier, Gayle, 'The Sonnet's Body and the Body Sonnetized in "Romeo and Juliet"', *Shakespeare Quarterly*, 40:1 (1989), 27–41.
Whitworth, Charles, '*Love's Labour's Lost*: Aborted Plays Within, Unconsummated Play Without', in *The Show Within: Dramatic and Other Insets. English Renaissance Drama (1550–1642)*, ed. François Laroque (Montpellier, 1992), 109–26.
Wilcox, Helen, 'Sacred Desire, Forms of Belief: The Religious Sonnet in Early Modern Britain', in *The Cambridge Companion to the Sonnet*, ed. Anthony D. Cousins and Peter Howarth (Cambridge: Cambridge University Press, 2011), pp. 145–65.
Willen, Gerald, and Victor B. Reed (eds), *Casebook on Shakespeare's Sonnets* (New York: Thomas Crowell, 1964).
Williams, Grant, 'Disarticulating Fantasies: Figures of Speech, Vices, and the Blazon in Renaissance English Rhetoric', *Rhetoric Society Quarterly*, 29:3 (1999), 43–54.
Williams, William Proctor, '"Vnder the Handes of … ": Zachariah Pasfield and the Licensing of Playbooks', in *Shakespeare's Stationers: Studies in Cultural Bibliography*, ed. Marta Straznicky (Philadelphia: University of Pennsylvania Press, 2013), pp. 63–94.
Wilson-Okamura, David S., *Spenser's International Style* (Cambridge: Cambridge University Press, 2015).

Woudhuysen, Henry R., *Sir Philip Sidney and the Circulation of Manuscripts, 1558–1640* (Oxford: Clarendon Press, 1996).

Wyatt, Michael, *The Italian Encounter with Tudor England: A Cultural Politics of Translation* (Cambridge: Cambridge University Press, 2005).

Index

Note: 'n.' after a page reference indicates the number of a note on that page

amateur *see* profession
anthology 9n.2, 20, 34–6, 44, 78, 82, 87–8,
    108–9, 145, 148–9, 175, 181, 184
  see also collection; miscellany
artifice 45, 80, 99
authorship 1, 4, 28, 34, 61, 80, 89, 98, 117,
    131, 133, 136, 147–8, 176, 178–80,
    188
  and anonymity 21, 107, 116, 124, 131, 147
  and authority 7, 17, 47–8, 97, 100–4, 116,
    123, 143
  unauthorised publication 23, 42, 85–8,
    144

ballad 6, 38, 41–7, 55n.74, 56n.94, 56n.106,
    56n.107, 66, 69–72, 80, 145, 149, 176
Barnes, Barnabe 1, 5, 8–9, 128–39 *passim*
Beaumont, Francis
  The Woman-Hater 70
beauty 27–8, 57n.112, 67, 69, 71, 81, 164–70,
    178, 179, 193
  physical or spiritual 22–5, 128
  of the poem 38, 41, 100, 193
Bembo, Pietro 2, 17, 31, 33–7, 50n.4, 51n.13,
    51n.17, 76n.50, 137n.8
blazon 5, 67, 70, 73, 76n.49
Bodenham, John 108–9, 148, 175
Bracciolini, Francesco 100
Breton, Nicholas 146–9, 151n.25, 151n.26,
    151n.27, 153, 175–8
  Brittons Bowre of Delights 126n.4
  The Passionate Shepheard 177
Brome, Richard 63
Burnaby, William 62

Campion, Thomas 45, 74n.8, 91n.28
canon 1–5, 8–9, 19, 31, 33–4, 37, 71, 74, 97,
    100–3, 110, 118, 149, 175, 180, 183

canzone 23, 32, 34–7
Cartwright, Thomas 108
Castelvetro, Ludovico 18, 22
Catholicism *see* religion
Chapman, George 105
  Achilles Shield 57n.116
  All Fools 66
  Ouids Banquet of Sence 106, 113n.57
  Sir Gyles Goosecappe 66
class (social) 18, 21–3, 28, 33, 64, 71, 78, 88
  see also nobility
classics 2, 18, 27, 31, 38, 62, 124
  Greek 44, 67, 100
  Latin 18, 35, 47, 51n.8, 56n.104, 114–15,
    182
  see also vernaculars
collection 2–6, 12n.20, 20, 23, 25, 33–42
    passim, 46, 48, 50, 50n.5, 55n.74, 63,
    66, 78, 82, 85–7, 95–6, 100, 102, 107,
    109–10, 114, 128–30, 135–6, 145–7,
    175, 181, 184, 185
  see also anthology; miscellany
comedy 62, 66, 69, 78–81, 83, 89
  see also tragedy; tragicomedy
commentary 6–7, 9, 12n.26, 17–28 *passim*,
    44, 47, 61, 71, 80, 81, 86, 88, 97, 101,
    129, 132, 135–6, 183, 185
commonplace 47, 48, 68, 84, 87–8, 106, 108,
    109, 175, 180
cliché 69, 79, 81, 84, 96
  topos 27, 46, 72, 104, 108, 132, 133, 148
complaint 23, 87, 98, 146, 148, 177
  see also elegy
conceit 44, 45, 50, 55n.80, 63–4, 67–8, 71–2,
    80, 99–100, 102–4, 107–8, 132, 178
  pointe 41, 44, 54n.66, 55n.80
  pointed sonnets 40–1, 97
Constable, Henry 1, 126n.4, 128, 151n.11

Conti, Giusto de' 35
conversion 9, 24, 57n.116, 128, 129, 132–6
coterie 21, 23, 63, 86, 145
court 10n.4 17, 42, 62, 70, 81, 88, 103, 172
    court poetry 1, 6, 20, 28, 33, 43–4,
        56n.106, 86, 144–5, 151n.16, 175
    courtship and courtiership 64, 72–3,
        76n.35, 80, 85, 97, 146, 149, 177–8
    Inns of Court 20–1, 64, 75n.17

Daniel, Samuel 4, 23, 30n.28, 45, 47, 56n.100,
    56n.104, 91n.28, 100, 105–7, 126,
    136, 139n.57, 144, 146
    A Defence of Rhyme 74n.8, 99
    Delia 3, 23, 25–6, 98, 100, 138n.29, 185,
        193
    A Funerall Poem 178
    Philotas 150
Daniello, Bernardino 18, 25–6, 28n.1
Dante (Dante Alighieri) 17, 19, 33–4, 51n.20,
    56n.101, 95, 98
Davies, John 55n.83, 76n.37, 98, 147
Davies of Hereford, John 98–9, 101
    Microcosmos 98–9, 107
    The Muses Sacrifice 175
    The Muses-Teares 175
    Wittes Pilgrimage 178–9
Davison, Francis 147–8, 181
De Vere, Edward, Earl of Oxford 147, 153
Dekker, Thomas 144
    The Honest Whore 68
    Northward Hoe 65
    Patient Grissil 69
Della Casa, Giovanni 35–7
Desportes, Philippe 96, 145
Devereux, Robert, second Earl of Essex 7,
    143, 145–6, 148–50, 151n.26, 153,
    170, 173, 175–8, 181–4
dialogue 17, 24, 33, 35, 36, 107, 146
dizain *see* stanza
Dolce, Lodovico 113n.54
Domenichi, Lodovico 35
Donne, John 1, 11n.7, 62–5, 67, 72, 75n.33,
    95–6, 99, 128, 193
Dowland, John 153, 175, 184
Drayton, Michael 4, 17, 21, 25–6, 28,
    76n.56, 85, 136, 137n.24, 139n.57,
    148
    Englands Heroicall Epistles, 44, 102
    Idea 1, 25–6, 28, 55n.83, 72, 84, 96,
        109–10, 111n.6, 112n.43, 139n.57
    Idea, the Shepheards Garland, 25, 175
    Ideas Mirrour 25, 72, 185

Drummond of Hawthornden, William 2,
    149, 178
Du Bartas, Guillaume de Saluste 102
Du Bellay, Joachim 23, 38–40, 42, 50n.4,
    75n.15, 104
    Les Antiquitez de Rome 23, 27, 96
    La Deffence et illustration de la langue
        françoyse 31, 53n.50, 54n.60
    L'Olive 38, 96
    Regrets 39, 96
Dyer, Edward 147, 149
Dymoke, Sir Edward 105–6
Dymoke, Tailboys 105

economy 6, 8, 64, 103
edition 7, 17–20, 24, 25, 34–5, 72, 78, 85,
    87–8, 91n.28, 102, 104–8, 135,
    137n.8, 144–5, 147, 148, 175, 178,
    181, 185–95 *passim*
    see also print
elegy 2, 36, 38, 44–6, 62–3, 67, 72, 96–7, 128,
    132, 145, 175–6, 178
    see also complaint
eloquence 8, 20, 50n.4, 97, 101, 110, 122
emblem 25, 56n.87, 70, 101, 107, 123–5,
    127n.35, 139n.54
encomium *see* praise
epic 23, 35–6, 55n.81, 102, 105
epigram 2, 6, 13n.27, 35–6, 38, 40–1, 44, 49,
    66, 72, 97–9, 115
epistle 44, 48, 87, 91n.35, 101–2, 114, 133,
    139n.54
epyllion 106, 113n.57
Essex (second Earl of) *see* Devereux,
    Robert

Fausto da Longiano, Sebastiano 18–19, 23,
    28n.1
Fielding, Ferdinand 104–5
Filelfo, Francesco 17–18
Fletcher, Giles 12n.20, 48–9, 98, 138n.29
Fletcher, John 70
    The Elder Brother 72
    The Woman-Hater 70
Florio, John 19, 29n.8
    First Fruites 19
    Queen Anna's New World of Words 96
    Second Fruites 19, 107
    A Worlde of Wordes 76n.50, 96
Fowler, William 2, 11n.8
fragment 6, 9, 41, 95, 109, 143–84 *passim*,
    185
French *see* vernaculars

Gascoigne, George 3, 19, 43, 45–6, 49, 96, 99, 133, 146
   The Adventures of Master F.J. 12n.20, 44, 98, 126n.4
   Certayne Notes of Instruction 43–4, 99
   A Hundreth Sundrie Flowers 29n.10, 42, 126n.4, 182
   The Posies 95
   The Tale of Hemetes the Heremyte 97
Gaywood, George 102, 107
generation 17, 38, 42, 97, 182
Giolito de' Ferrari, Gabriel 35
Greene, Robert 8, 85, 114–25 *passim*, 126n.3, 126n.12, 127n.23, 135
   Gwydonius 64
   Menaphon 177
   A Quip for an Vpstart Courtier 115, 118
Guarini, Giovanni Battista 105–6
Guazzo, Stefano 37

Harington, Sir John 49, 74n.8, 101, 108, 133
Harvey, Gabriel 5, 7–8, 18, 47, 55n.78, 108, 114–25 *passim*, 127n.20, 127n.23, 127n.24, 134, 136, 139n.47, 139n.48
   Foure Letters and Certaine Sonnets 8, 114–25 *passim*, 183
   Pierces Supererogation 126n.4, 127n.35, 135, 139n.50
   Three Proper and Wittie Familiar Letters 124, 126n.8, 127n.27
Herbert, George 1, 11n.7
Heywood, John 20
Heywood, Thomas 8, 69, 78, 87–8, 91n.38
   An Apology for Actors 87, 19n.33–4
   The fayre mayde of the Exchange 66
   The Foure Prentises of London 68
   Loves Maistresse 65
Hoby, Thomas 103
Holyday, Barten 67
Howard, Henry, Earl of Surrey 5, 7, 17, 19–21, 28, 31, 42, 46–7, 55n.70, 56n.98, 95–6, 99, 101, 105, 109, 145, 149
humanism 17, 51n.8, 103
hymn 2, 40, 147
hyperbole *see* trope

identity 4, 187
   national identity 31, 49, 97, 99, 108, 110
imitation 17–30 *passim*, 31–2, 38–41, 47, 64, 74, 75n.15, 79, 126n.10
Italian *see* vernaculars

Jaggard, William 7–8, 78–9, 82–3, 85–9, 90n.16, 90n.27, 91n.28, 91n.30, 91n.36, 91n.42
James VI, King of Scotland 2, 11n.8, 55n.78, 100, 176
Jenye, Thomas 104–5
Johnson, Richard 144
Jones, Richard 148, 151n.28, 153
Jones, William 105
Jonson, Ben 19, 29n.12, 72, 77n.57, 91n.33
   Euery man in his humour 65
   Poetaster 64

Kyffin, Maurice 108–9

La Marche, Olivier de 108
Langton, Christopher 101
Laudun d'Aigaliers, Pierre 39, 54n.59, 54n.62
laureate 77n.66, 96, 117
   see also profession
Lewkenor, Lewis 108
Ling, Nicholas 85, 148, 151n.23
Locke, Anne 1, 10n.6, 42, 95
Locke, Henry 1
Lodge, Thomas 89, 133
   Phillis 98, 138n.29
   Rosalynde 126n.4
   Scillaes Metamorphosis 126n.4
Lyly, John 57n.116, 70
lyric 2–3, 17, 21, 32, 36, 40, 44, 46–7, 62, 78, 95–100, 128, 130, 136, 145–6, 149, 175, 178–9, 185

madrigal 38, 63, 65–6, 128, 130–1, 177
manuscript 7, 26, 42, 44, 51n.10, 63, 78–80, 85–9, 96, 101, 127n.27, 136, 146–9, 176, 178–84
   see also print
Manutius, Aldus 17–18, 137n.8
Marino, Giovan Battista 32, 37, 66
Markham, Gervase 149
   Devoreux Vertues Teares 175
   The Dumbe Knight 72
Marlowe, Christopher 78, 85
Marot, Clément 38–40, 45, 52n.37, 53n.42, 54n.55, 54n.57, 76n.49
Marston, John 69
   The Insatiate Countess 69
   Parasitaster or the Fawn 61
Mary, Queen of Scots 1, 11n.8
Matthew, Tobie (Bishop of Durham) 134, 136, 138n.44, 139n.46
Mead, Robert 69

medieval literature 17–18, 32–3, 43
melancholy 65
Meninni, Federigo 37
Meres, Francis 47, 86, 89
metaphor *see* trope
meter 27, 33–8, 45–6, 50, 53n.38, 54n.60, 67, 100, 105, 118, 187–8, 194n.11
   decasyllable 49, 54n.58, 187
   hendecasyllable 12
   hexameter 25, 105
   pentameter 3, 25, 84
   settenario 32, 51n.13
   tetrameter 84
Middleton, Thomas 144, 183
Milton, John 3, 42, 50n.5, 55n.73, 77n.66
Minturno, Antonio 35–6
miscellany 6, 20, 42, 46, 50, 55n.74, 78, 82–3, 86–7, 91n.28, 98, 143–85 *passim*
   see also anthology; collection
morals 5, 18, 21–4, 35, 48–50, 57n.116, 99–100, 107, 118, 123, 126n.13, 128–39 *passim*
Munday, Anthony 70, 148
music 26, 37, 40, 54n.58, 63, 65, 71, 82, 85, 175, 178
   lute 26, 70, 146
myth 18, 22, 26, 65, 72, 110, 132, 135, 139n.53

narrative 3, 9, 17, 21, 23, 28, 36, 44, 86, 95–9, 110, 117, 135, 189
Nashe, Thomas 7–8, 76n.37, 114–25 *passim*, 126n.3, 134–6, 138n.36, 139n.47–50
   The Anatomie of Absurditie 47, 56n.94
   The Apologie of Pierce Pennilesse or Strange Newes 114, 116–20, 126n.10, 183
   Haue vvith you to Saffron-vvalden 134, 139n.49
nature 22–3, 27, 37, 45, 70, 72, 99, 182
Neoplatonism 22, 48, 179
   see also Plato
nobility 8, 20–1, 23, 36–7, 52n.34, 71, 78, 86, 88, 105, 123, 145, 181
   gentleman 43, 64, 69, 121, 145
   see also class
Noot, Jan van der 42, 104

octave *see* stanza
ode 2–3, 27, 35–6, 38, 40, 46, 53n.48, 54n.60, 128, 138
Ovid 27, 57n.114, 64, 102
   Heroides 44

Metamorphoses 27, 135, 139n.54
Ovidianism 62, 87, 106
Oxford (Earl of) *see* De Vere, Edward

paradox *see* trope
Parker, Henry, Baron Morley 47, 126n.4
parody 4, 26, 39, 55n.83, 67, 75n.15, 76n.50, 81, 83
   see also satire
Pasfield, Zachariah 143, 150, 150n.3
pastoral 65–6, 70, 85, 105, 146, 149, 175–6, 181
patronage 6, 71, 81, 87, 96, 108, 120, 151n.27, 176
Peletier Du Mans, Jacques 39, 44, 49
   L'Amour des Amours 39
   L'Art poétique 40–1, 53n.46, 53n.48, 54n.53, 54n.54, 54n.59, 104, 112n.50
   Œuvres poétiques 38
Petrarch (Petrarca, Francesco) 2–5, 7, 31, 42, 47–8, 51n.14, 53n.42, 53n.44, 55n.73, 56n.91, 56n.100, 57n.114, 61–3, 67–77 *passim*, 81, 84, 99, 102, 107, 110, 124, 132–3, 136, 137n.4, 137n.10, 149, 189
   Canzoniere (*Rerum Vulgarium Fragmenta, Rime sparse*), 17–28 *passim*, 31–9 *passim*, 51n.10, 56n.91, 56n.96, 56n.100, 56n.101, 56n.104, 57n.114, 61, 65, 73–4, 95, 100, 129, 135, 137n.8, 138n.40, 139n.53
   Trionfi 19, 47, 126n.4
Philieul, Vasquin 38
Phillips, Edward 66
Piccolomini, Alessandro 34
Plato 22, 26, 57n.109
   see also Neoplatonism
politics 9, 31, 38, 64, 74, 79, 99, 107–8, 145–6, 148–50, 151n.26, 175, 177–9, 183–4, 194n.3
praise 6, 25, 26, 36, 39, 46–7, 61–2, 65, 67, 69–73, 80, 82, 85, 86, 90n.6, 96, 98, 100, 101, 103, 105, 118, 122, 146
Pricket, Robert 149, 178
print 5, 7, 17–30 *passim*, 34, 42–3, 46–7, 66, 72, 76n.49, 78–89 *passim*, 91n.33, 95, 98, 101, 103, 108, 110, 112n.48, 119, 121, 124–5, 127n.13, 127n.27, 129–31, 134–6, 137n.8, 138n.26, 139n.46, 143–84 *passim*, 185, 195n.13, 195n.15
   see also edition; manuscript
profession 20–1, 23, 62–5, 68, 74, 77n.66, 97, 117, 125
   see also laureate

prose 33, 53n.38, 61, 64, 66, 69, 98, 100, 103, 108, 116, 118, 122, 127n.13, 145, 146, 186
Protestant *see* religion
Provençal *see* vernaculars
proverb 95–6, 107, 182
psalms 44–5, 57n.112, 95, 101, 135
punctuation 24, 178–84 *passim*, 185–95 *passim*
Puritan *see* religion
Puttenham, George 43, 46–7, 56n.91, 56n.101, 99, 130, 187, 192

quatorzain *see* stanza
quatrain *see* stanza

Raleigh (Sir), Walter 78, 85, 149
Randolph, Thomas 66
Rawlins, Thomas 73
religion 49, 82, 90n.14, 129, 134–5, 137n.25, 138n.37, 151n.27
   Catholicism 49, 137n.25
   Protestantism 48, 56n.96, 104, 134, 137n.25
   Puritanism 49–50, 57n.118, 64, 134
   religious poetry 4, 48, 136, 146
rhetoric 6, 12n.26, 17–9, 41, 43, 50n.4, 53n.46, 69, 76n.35, 83, 90n.14, 99, 129, 130, 185–6, 188
rhyme 3, 11n.14, 18, 22, 27, 31–46 *passim*, 53n.38, 54n.53, 54n.56, 54n.58, 54n.60, 56n.107, 61, 65–6, 69, 74, 95, 101–5, 110, 114, 116–17, 119, 122, 124, 126n.10, 127n.18, 127n.19, 127n.20, 127n.23, 130, 177
rhythm 20, 37, 84, 185–93 *passim*, 194n.3, 194–5n.11, 195n.15
romance 23, 97, 108, 146
rondeau 38
Ronsard, Pierre de 28, 32, 38–40, 53n.46, 54n.58, 96, 104–5
Rossetti, Dante Gabriele 3, 12n.20
Rota, Bernardino 35
roundelay 41, 43
Ruscelli, Girolamo 36

Sackville, Thomas 103
Saint-Gelais, Mellin de 38
Sannazaro, Jacopo 31, 66
satire 5–6, 39, 44, 55n.83, 62, 64, 68, 72, 78, 117–18, 122–3, 183–4
   see also parody

Scott, William 44–5, 56n.87, 56n.90, 57n.112, 57n.118, 99
Sébillet, Thomas 7, 38–40, 44, 49, 53n.40, 54n.62
sequence 1, 3–5, 12n.20, 17, 19, 21–4, 41, 47–8, 50, 65, 76n.36, 78, 95–110 *passim*, 114–15, 118–20, 124, 128–36 *passim*, 137n.9, 137n.10, 138n.29, 138n.37, 139n.46, 147, 182, 185–6, 189, 192–3
Serafino Aquilano 97
sestet *see* stanza
sestina *see* stanza
settenario *see* meter
Shakespeare, William 4–5, 9, 11n.7, 17, 21, 25–8, 30n.26, 42, 63, 68–70, 72, 76n.40, 89n.1, 91n.38, 101
   As You Like It 61, 90n.13
   Love's Labour's Lost 8, 78–89 *passim*
   The Passionate Pilgrim 78–89 *passim*
   Romeo and Juliet 61, 84, 90n.14
   Sonnets 1, 6, 9, 25–8, 30n.25, 30n.26, 30n.29, 56n.100, 62–3, 67, 70, 73, 78, 79, 98, 130, 185–93 *passim*
Shirley, James 62–3, 68, 73, 77n.59
Sidney, Sir Philip 1, 5, 9, 17–19, 21–3, 25–8, 45–8, 56n.90, 56n.98, 57n.118, 64, 68, 85, 114, 118, 139n.50, 145–9, 153, 169, 171, 175–6, 178–82, 184
   Arcadia 25
   Astrophil and Stella 21–8 *passim*, 42, 47, 76n.36, 91n.28, 95, 105, 130, 178–9, 182
   Certain Sonnets 181
   The Defence of Poesie 2, 11n.14, 21, 29n.15, 43, 47, 56–7n.108, 57n.109, 57n.112, 74n.8, 75n.13
Sidney Herbert, Mary, Countess of Pembroke 23, 147, 148, 151n.27, 176, 181
sixain *see* stanza
song 3, 6, 21, 26–7, 35, 40, 42, 45–7, 50n.5, 53n.39, 54n.60, 55n.74, 56n.94, 56n.106, 61–6, 69, 72, 75n.13, 75n.23, 85, 96, 99, 107, 109, 128–9, 146, 177, 178, 181, 184
sonnet craze 7, 23, 26, 42, 50, 62–3, 67, 72, 76n.36, 82, 96, 129
Spanish *see* vernaculars
Spenser, Edmund 1, 5, 9, 17, 19, 21, 23–9, 30n.22, 42, 47, 54n.56, 56n.98, 77n.66, 85, 104, 108, 114–25 *passim*, 126n.6, 126n.12, 127n.18, 127n.23, 143, 146, 149, 172, 179–80, 183–4

Spenser, Edmund (*cont.*)
  Amoretti 23–5, 27–8, 98, 126n.4, 154, 168, 179, 180
  Complaints 23
  Epithalamion 23, 98
  The Faerie Queene 23, 116, 119–20, 123, 127n.24
  Foure Letters and Certaine Sonnets 114–125 *passim*, 126–7n.13
  Mother Hubberds Tale 123, 172, 182
  The Ruines of Rome 23, 27
  The Shepheardes Calender 24–5, 114, 116, 124–5
  The Teares of the Muses 175
stanza 32, 36, 38, 41, 81, 90n.13, 99, 137n.15, 146, 165, 174, 182–3
  dizain 11n.14, 38, 43, 53n.41
  quatorzain 31–2, 42, 44–6, 49, 55n.72, 62–3, 66, 130
  quatrain 27–8, 36–7, 39, 41, 43, 108, 119, 128, 130–2, 190
  quartina 32
  octave 102, 107
  sestet 22, 37, 39–40, 54n.53, 102, 107, 110
  sestina 38, 130, 137n.15
  sixain 11n.14, 43, 99
  tercet 36, 41, 73, 130
  terzina 32
strambotto 44, 97
style 17, 28, 33, 35–6, 39, 62–3, 69, 73, 79, 87, 115, 121, 123–4, 126n.4, 176, 182
Surrey (Earl of) *see* Howard, Henry
syllable 11n.14, 35, 37, 43, 53n.38, 54n.58, 66, 130, 187
  see also meter
Sylvester, Josuah 102, 107
synecdoche *see* trope
syntax 27, 36–7, 41, 51n.17, 100, 126n.12, 130, 187–8, 190–1, 193

Tasso, Bernardo 34, 37, 51n.17
Tasso, Torquato 19, 36, 52n.31, 55n.81, 56n.101, 106
Tedaldi, Pieraccio 97, 99
tercet *see* stanza
terzina *see* stanza
tetrameter *see* meter
theatricality 7, 21, 30n.25, 61–74 *passim*, 78–89 *passim*, 90n.12, 97, 115, 120–1, 125, 136, 176, 185–6, 188, 194n.11
theory 2–3, 31–50 *passim*, 99–100, 103, 105–6

Tomkis, Thomas
  Albumazar 63
  Lingua 72, 79–80, 90n.7
Tottel, Richard 11n.7, 13n.28, 20–1, 29n.13, 31, 42, 46–7, 50, 50n.4, 55n.74, 98–9, 109, 145–6, 148, 177
tragedy 66, 80, 125
  see also comedy; tragicomedy
tragicomedy 105
  see also comedy; tragedy
translation 5–6, 18–20, 23, 27–8, 31–2, 38, 42, 47, 49, 50n.4, 56n.91, 62, 64, 73, 76n.36, 95–6, 102–9, 124, 126n.4, 135, 139n.54, 143–5
Trissino, Giovan Giorgio 33–5
trope 22, 28, 66, 74, 81, 87, 124, 131, 133
  hyperbole 26, 62, 68, 69, 81
  metaphor 28, 62–3, 81, 90n.12, 102, 106, 108, 130, 132, 138n.31
  paradox 63, 81–2, 97, 186–7, 192–3
  synecdoche 73
Turberville, George 3, 46
typography 103, 105, 110, 112n.48, 146

Vauquelin De La Fresnaye, Jean 53n.50, 54n.60
Vaux, Thomas (second Baron Vaux of Harrowden) 20
Vellutello, Alessandro 17–20, 22, 137n.8
vernaculars 17–18, 31, 43, 46, 50n.4, 64, 97, 101–10 *passim*, 136–7n.4, 149
  French 1, 3, 6, 11n.14, 18–9, 38, 42, 54n.58, 64, 100, 102–3, 108
  Italian 1, 3, 6, 18–19, 47, 56n.104, 63, 66, 103, 105, 107, 123
  Provençal 33, 63
  Spanish 75n.15, 95–6, 103, 143
  see also classics
virelay 43

Watson, Thomas 19, 47–8, 129, 147, 182
Webbe, William 46, 56n.90
Webster, John 72, 144
Whetstone, George 133
  An Heptameron of Civill Discourses 57n.114
  A Remembravnce of ... George Gaskoigne 96
Whitney, Geffrey 123, 139n.54, 180
Williams, Thomas 106–7
Wills, Richard 43

wit 21–2, 25, 27, 44, 46, 48, 55n.80, 57n.116, 62, 63, 65, 68, 79, 85–7, 98, 102, 106–7, 115, 122, 124, 126n.4, 126n.10, 130–1, 134, 177
Wolfe, John 57n.110, 126n.4, 126n.5, 127n.35, 134–5, 139n.47, 139n.50, 183
Wroth, Lady Mary 1, 10n.6

Wyatt, Sir Thomas 5, 17–21, 28, 29n.13, 42, 44–7, 55n.70, 56n.91, 67, 95–7, 99, 101–2, 107, 109, 139n.53, 145

Zouch, Richard 65

EU authorised representative for GPSR:
Easy Access System Europe, Mustamäe tee 50,
10621 Tallinn, Estonia
gpsr.requests@easproject.com

www.ingramcontent.com/pod-product-compliance
Lightning Source LLC
Chambersburg PA
CBHW070238240426
43673CB00044B/1834